The Erard Grecian Harp in Regency England

The Erard Grecian Harp
in Regency England

Panagiotis Poulopoulos

THE BOYDELL PRESS

The open access version of this publication was funded by the
Volkswagen Foundation ('Research in Museums' Programme)

First published 2023
The Boydell Press, Woodbridge

ISBN 978-1-78327-772-8

The Boydell Press is an imprint of Boydell & Brewer Ltd
PO Box 9, Woodbridge, Suffolk IP12 3DF, UK
and of Boydell & Brewer Inc.
668 Mt Hope Avenue, Rochester, NY 14620–2731, USA
website: www.boydellandbrewer.com

A catalogue record for this book is available
from the British Library

The publisher has no responsibility for the continued existence or accuracy of URLs for
external or third-party internet websites referred to in this book, and does not guarantee
that any content on such websites is, or will remain, accurate or appropriate

This publication is printed on acid-free paper

To my dear parents,
Evgenia and Stavros,
for inspiring me to look into the past,
as well as to my lovely nephews and nieces,
Iasonas, Ariadne, Elli, Aaron, Alcmene and Rita,
for inspiring me to look into the future.

Contents

Illustrations

The author and publisher are grateful to all the institutions and individuals listed for permission to reproduce the materials in which they hold copyright. Every effort has been made to trace the copyright holders; apologies are offered for any omission, and the publisher will be pleased to add any necessary acknowledgement in subsequent editions.

Preface

During the early nineteenth century the harp was transformed into a sophisticated instrument that became as popular as the piano. This was largely the result of the harp's intensive technical, musical and visual upgrading, which gradually led to the transition from the single- to the double-action pedal harp. One of the most important figures in this process was Sébastien Erard (1752–1831), a tireless inventor and prolific manufacturer of harps and pianos operating branches in Paris and London. With the introduction of the so-called 'Grecian' model, the first commercially-built double-action harp, in London in 1811, Erard managed to establish the double-action harp not only as a fashionable, state-of-the-art instrument, but also as a powerful symbol of taste, wealth and status. Erard's new harp was an instant success among professional and amateur musicians and is widely considered to be the predecessor of the modern concert harp.

This book provides a comprehensive overview of the production and consumption of the Erard harp in Regency Britain, drawing upon a wide variety of object-based, archival and iconographical sources, many of which are previously unpublished. Using Erard Nº 2631, a surviving Grecian harp built in London in 1818 and housed at the Deutsches Museum, Munich, as a case study and starting point for further discussion, the book provides a concise account of the evolution of the double-action harp during the late eighteenth and early nineteenth centuries, focusing on the contributions of Erard and his competitors. Furthermore, the book presents and analyses the pioneering design and engineering features as well as the innovative decoration and distinctive branding of Erard Grecian harps, elucidating how they were shaped by the technological, political, economic and sociocultural developments of a turbulent era, ranging from the Industrial Revolution and the Napoleonic Wars to the Enlightenment and Neoclassicism. Moreover, it investigates the manufacture and marketing of these harps within the wider context of the musical instrument-making business and related luxury trades, offering new insights into the organisation, management and operation of the Erard London branch as well as into the promotional strategies, professional networks and customer profile of the firm. Additionally, the book explores the role of the Erard harp in the lifestyle of the Regency period, inspecting the instrument's dominant presence in contemporary education, art, fashion and fiction. Finally, the book examines Erard Grecian harps as artefacts of cultural heritage, concentrating on the current issues and challenges regarding their documentation, preservation, use and display in public and private collections around the world.

Acknowledgments

This book presents the outcome of research that was carried out during the project 'A Creative Triangle of Mechanics, Acoustics and Aesthetics: The Early Pedal Harp (1780–1830) as a Symbol of Innovative Transformation'. The project, which took place between 2016 and 2020, was funded by the VolkswagenStiftung (Volkswagen Foundation) as part of the funding initiative 'Research in Museums'. I am grateful to the VolkswagenStiftung for supporting financially both the above-mentioned project and the publication of this book, and especially to Adelheid Wessler and Annabella Hüfler-Fick for their kind help with administrative issues.

The project was hosted by the Research Institute for the History of Science and Technology at the Deutsches Museum, Munich. I wish to thank Helmuth Trischler, Head of Research at the Deutsches Museum, and Ulf Hashagen, Head of the Research Institute, for facilitating and supporting my work in such an inspiring environment for researchers of all backgrounds and interests. I am also thankful to Silke Berdux, Curator for Musical Instruments, for her constant attention, creative ideas and constructive remarks throughout the project, as well as for her critical reading of early drafts of this book. Furthermore, I am indebted to Wilhelm Füßl and Matthias Röschner from the Deutsches Museum Archiv (archive) for permitting the use of digitised sources in the museum's archives. I am additionally obliged to various colleagues at the diverse departments and workshops of the Deutsches Museum, ranging from the Fotoatelier (photographic atelier), through the Modellbauer (model makers), to the Sammlungsmanagement (collection management), and especially to Andrea Walther, Andrea Lucas and Dorothee Messerschmid at the Research Institute for their untiring assistance with organisational matters.

At various stages of the project I profited much from conversations with the following colleagues at the Deutsches Museum, arranged in alphabetical order: Cristian Breternitz, Leon Chisholm, Alexander Gall, Rüdiger Herrmann, Fabienne Huguenin, Judith Kemp, Anja Kuhlmann, Angela Meincke, Sonja Neumann, Miriam Noa, Marisa Pamplona, Katharina Preller, Stephanie Probst, Johanna Spangenberg, Alexander Steinbeißer, Artemis Yagou, Sandra Walter, Susanne Wittmayer and Rebecca Wolf. My specials thanks go to Luise Richter for assisting me greatly with the object-based investigation of the Erard N° 2631, the harp on which this book focuses, and to Julin Lee, whose help with the systematic classification and interpretation of the Erard correspondence and ledgers enabled the better understanding of the firm's manufacture and sales patterns, particularly during the period that this instrument was built. Many thanks also to Michael Zahnweh and Lisa Berchtold, who helped me with the study and transcription of several written

sources dating from the eighteenth and nineteenth centuries during their intern-
ships at the Deutsches Museum.

The detailed examination of the Erard N° 2631 was further assisted by Peter
Albert and Egon Blumenau (Archäologische Staatssammlung München), Catharina
Blänsdorf (Technische Universität München), Christian Gruber (Bayerisches
Landesamt für Denkmalpflege) and Irmhild Ceynova (Bayerische Staatsbibliothek
München), who provided help and advice with the radiography of the instrument
as well as with the analysis of its decorative coatings. In addition, Volker Haag and
Valentina Zemke (Thünen Institut für Holzforschung, Hamburg) kindly undertook
the wood identification of the harp, while Neeti Phatak examined and identified
the harp's metal parts during her 'Scholar-in Residence' project at the Deutsches
Museum. Niko Plath (Institut für Systematische Musikwissenschaft, Universität
Hamburg) conducted vibroacoustic examination on Erard N° 2631 and similar
instruments and compared his findings with experimental data on harp acoustics
that were kindly offered by Jean-Loïc Le Carrou (Equipe Lutheries-Acoustique-
Musique, Université Pierre et Marie Curie, Paris).

The research material collected for the preparation of this book involved visits
and requests to numerous museums, archives, libraries, universities, conservatoires,
historic houses, etc. I am grateful to the following institutions and their personnel,
listed in alphabetical order according to location, for generously allowing the *in situ*
examination of instruments and archives or for providing information and images
of surviving harps and related material in public and private collections around the
world: Abbotsford, The Home of Sir Walter Scott (Kirsty Archer-Thompson and
Claudia Bolling); Amsterdam: Rijksmuseum (Giovanni Paolo di Stefano and Maria
Smit); Arbroath: Hospitalfield (Lucy Byatt, Laura Simpson and Juliane Foronda);
Baltimore: Hampton National Historic Site (Greg Weidman); Barcelona: Museu
de la Música (Marisa Ruiz Magaldi, Manel Barcons and Esther Fernández);
Basel: Schola Cantorum Basiliensis (Kathrin Menzel and Heidrun Rosenzweig),
Museum für Musik (Martin Kirnbauer); Birmingham: Soho House (Laura Cassidy
and Nadine Lees); Bloomington: The Lilly Library, Indiana University (Anna
Holmes, Erika Dowell and Penny R. Ramon); Boston: Museum of Fine Arts
(Darcy Kuronen and Christine Storti); Brussels: Muziekinstrumentenmuseum
(Pascale Vandervellen, Anne-Emmanuelle Ceulemans, Joris De Valck and Anja
Van Lerberghe); Cambridge: Fitzwilliam Museum (Nik Zolman and Emma
Darbyshire); Pendlebury Library of Music, University of Cambridge (Kate Crane
and James Luff); Copenhagen: Danish Music Museum – Musikhistorisk Museum
& The Carl Claudius Collection (Lisbet Torp, Marie Martens and Ture Bergstrøm);
Edinburgh: Musical Instrument Museums Edinburgh (Jenny Nex, Darryl Martin,
Sarah Deters and Jonathan Santa Maria Bouquet); Fontainebleau: Château
de Fontainebleau (Patricia Kalensky and Fatima Louli); Glasgow: University
of Glasgow Library, Archives & Special Collections (Nikola Russell and Fiona
Neale); Göttingen: Musikinstrumentensammlung der Universität Göttingen
(Klaus-Peter Brenner); Hamamatsu: Hamamatsu Museum of Musical Instruments
(Kazuhiko Shima); Hamburg: Museum für Kunst und Gewerbe (Olaf Kirsch);
Lecce: Casa Museo Spada Antichi Strumenti Musicali (Francesco Spada); Leipzig:
Musikinstrumentenmuseum der Universität Leipzig (Stefan Hindtsche, Joseph

Focht and Sebastian Kirsch); London: British Museum (Lucia Rinolfi), National Portrait Gallery (Jacob Simon), Royal College of Music Museum (Gabriele Rossi Rognoni, Michael Mullen and Susana Caldeira, as well as Mike Markiewicz from ArenaPAL), Science Museum (Ben Russell), Victoria & Albert Museum, Archive of Art and Design (Victoria Platt and Freya Levett); Lawrence: Spencer Museum of Art (Sofía Galarza Liu and Izzy Dino); Mexico City, Coyoacán: Facultad de Música/UNAM, (Miguel Zenker); Milan: Castello Sforzesco (Francesca Tasso), Fernanda Giulini Collection (Fernanda Giulini); Munich: Archäologische Staatssammlung München (Brigitte Haas-Gebhard), Bayerisches Nationalmuseum (Sybe Wartena), Müncher Stadtmuseum (András Varsányi and Sabine Scheibner); New York: Metropolitan Museum of Art (Bradley Strauchen-Scherer, Manu Frederickx and Jennifer Schnitker); Nuremberg: Germanisches Nationalmuseum (Frank Bär and Klaus Martius); Moscow: Glinka National Museum Consortium of Musical Culture (Nataliya Emelina); Paris: Bibliothèque nationale de France (Maria Frausto-Serrano), Musée de la musique (Thierry Maniguet); Philadelphia: Philadelphia Museum of Art (Jonathan Hoppe); Piasco: Museo dell'Arpa Victor Salvi (Roberta Scarzello); Prague: České muzeum hudby – Czech Museum of Music (Daniela Kotašová); Shrewsbury: Shropshire Archives (Sarah Davis, Kerry Evans and Nathaniel Stevenson); Stockholm: Scenkonstmuseet (Dan Johannson), Stiftelsen Musikkulturens Främjande – The Nydahl Collection (Göran Grahn); Trondheim: Ringve Museum (Mats Krouthén, Anne Mette Gottschal and Vera de Bruyn-Ouboter); Urbana-Champaign: University of Illinois, Rare Book and Manuscript Library (Emma Wise and Ana D. Rodriguez); Vienna: Österreichische Nationalbibliothek, Sammlung von Handschriften und alten Drucken (Gertrud Oswald and Hans Peter Zimmer); Vermillion: National Music Museum, University of South Dakota (Margaret Banks and Emanuele Marconi); Worcester: Worcester Museum and Art Gallery (Claire Cheshire and John Jose).

I must also express my deepest gratitude to the harp scholars Robert Adelson, Mike Baldwin, Lewis Jones, Jenny Nex, Hayato Sugimoto and Eve Zaunbrecher; to the harpists Maria Christina Cleary, Masumi Nagasawa, Elisabeth Plank and Nancy Thym; as well as to the harp makers and restorers Klaus Horngacher (Horngacher Harps), John Hoare (Pilgrim Harps), Jon Hunnisett, Michael Parfett and Beat Wolf, all of whom were willing to share their valuable knowledge and expertise on harps by Erard and other makers.

The following individuals, arranged alphabetically, were very helpful in exchanging information about early pedal harps and related instruments: Ingrid Bernous, Cristina Bordas, Franziska Bühl, Audrey Cameron, Stelios Christodoulou, Christopher Clarke, Stephen Dunstone, Tamar Hestrin Grader, Nancy Hurrell, Fanny Guillaume-Castel, Elise Kolle, Laurence Libin, Arnold Myers, Christina Ntaflou, Jean-Michel Renard, Albert Rice, Floraleda Sacchi, David Serra (George Jackson Ltd), Angelos Sotiropoulos, Christine Steinbrecher, Helga Storck, Catalina Vicens, James Westbrook, Ken Yeung and Donna Theresa Youngblood. My apologies to all those who may have helped me in various ways during my research and who I have unintentionally forgotten to mention here.

I have presented much of the material for this book at conferences of the International Committee for Museums and Collections of Instruments and

Music-International Council of Museums (CIMCIM-ICOM), the American Musical Instrument Society (AMIS), the Galpin Society for the Study of Musical Instruments (GS), the Scientific Instrument Commission (SIC), The Society for the History of Technology (SHOT), the Consortium for Guitar Research at Sydney Sussex College University of Cambridge, the COST Action FP1302 WoodMusICK, the research group 'Instrumentenkunde' of the Gesellschaft für Musikforschung (GfM), as well as at various colloquia, symposia, workshops, seminars and lectures organised at the Deutsches Museum. I owe much to the questions and feedback I received from numerous colleagues during my presentations, which helped to shape the structure and content of this book.

I am further thankful to the two anonymous reviewers of the book for their useful comments and suggestions; their criticism proved of immense help in improving the text and in avoiding several misconceptions and errors. I am also grateful to the staff at Boydell & Brewer, particularly to the editor Michael Middeke, for his strong interest in the book from the beginning as well as for his meticulous editorial work, and to Elizabeth Howard for her help with various organisational matters. Finally, I would like to thank my family, and especially my wife Lea, for all their patience, support and encouragement.

Panagiotis Poulopoulos, Munich, 2022

Introduction

'From this short account of the advantages which are derived from the Harp with the Double Movement, one may anticipate that it will become as fashionable as the Piano-Forte.'[1]

A Tale of Two Cities

It all began with a royal signature. In 1785, the instrument maker Sébastien Erard (1752–1831) was granted a privilege by the French king Louis XVI (1754–1793) to build and sell fortepianos in Paris and elsewhere. This privilege essentially allowed Erard to bypass the burdensome restrictions of the fan makers' guild, which controlled the undertakings of Parisian musical instrument makers. Most importantly, this privilege allowed Erard 'to use, either himself or by his workers, the wood, the iron and all the other materials necessary for the improvement and the embellishment' of these instruments.[2] Thus, in contrast to traditional luthiers, who worked almost exclusively with wood, Erard could now use a variety of materials and techniques for the manufacture and decoration of his instruments, as well as employ different specialists all working under the same roof.

Around the same time, Erard started building his first harps in Paris and began experimenting with the harp's design, construction and function. This is no coincidence, since during this period the harp enjoyed great popularity in France. By the early 1760s the single-action pedal harp, an instrument conceived in the early eighteenth century by Jacob Hochbrucker (1673–1763) of Donauwörth, a German town near Augsburg, had already been introduced to the musical circles of Paris as a new, fashionable instrument, especially for female musicians.[3] In the years that followed, the single-action harp became as much a technically advanced sounding device as a highly decorative piece of furniture adorning the homes of the affluent. During the 1770s and 1780s the single-action harp was further developed by makers such as Georges Cousineau (1733–1800) or Jean-Henri Naderman (1734–1799), who were building highly ornamented single-action harps for numerous esteemed customers

---

[1] Robert Nicolas-Charles Bochsa, *A New and Improved Method of Instruction for the Harp* (London: Chappell & Co, c.1819), p. 9.

[2] Cited in Robert Adelson, Alain Roudier, Jenny Nex, Laure Barthel and Michel Foussard (eds), *The History of the Erard Piano and Harp in Letters and Documents, 1785–1959* (Cambridge: Cambridge University Press, 2015), p. 49.

[3] For an overview on the development and use of the single-action harp, also known as the 'harpe organisée', see Maria Christina Cleary, 'The Invention of the 18th Century: the Harpe Organisée and Pedals', *American Harp Journal* 26/2 (2018), pp. 22–38.

within the French beau monde, the most prominent of them being the Queen of France, Marie Antoinette (1755–1793).[4]

Yet, for Erard the single-action harp made by his French contemporaries was apparently an unsatisfactory instrument. The pedal mechanisms on these harps comprised several mechanically connected components, which allowed for the shortening of each string by a semitone typically using L-shaped hooks (*crochets*), or a more complex system of crutch-ended levers (*béquilles*) that was developed in the 1780s by Georges Cousineau. These harps restricted a harpist's options for modulation to a small number of available keys. In addition, due to their construction, these harps were fragile and temperamental. For instance, the mechanisms typically used on single-action harps resulted in frequent string breakage and misalignment, which hindered performance. Moreover, the relatively few metal components of the pedal mechanism that affected the strings were mounted directly on the harp's wooden neck, thus providing limited possibilities for adjusting the intonation or for the repair and regulation of the mechanism without interventions to the wooden structure. Additionally, the tuning of these harps was unstable due to the nature of wood, a material sensitive to fluctuations in humidity and temperature as well as to the tension of the strings. Considering these issues and recognising the harp's potential for improvement, in the late 1780s Erard began to strengthen the harp's wooden frame, changing its shape and construction, and to utilise more metal parts for the pedal mechanism in order to increase its rigidity and functionality. Moreover, he devised a new method for shortening the strings using forked disks (*fourchettes*), which eventually superseded all earlier mechanisms. For the development of the harp, this was a crucial point.

However, the upheaval of the French Revolution in 1789 delayed Erard's plans to launch his new harps in Paris. Determined to protect his invention and profit from it, in 1792 he moved to London, where he established a manufactory solely for the building of pedal harps. The British capital, a thriving metropolis and a centre of commerce and entrepreneurship, proved to be fertile ground, in which Erard was able to present and promote his ideas. Between 1794 and 1810, Erard took five patents for the harp, the last of which proved to be the crowning of his efforts and arguably his most significant contribution to harp design: the double-action harp with forked discs, an instrument which allowed harpists to play in all keys and which has remained in use with relatively minor variations ever since.

With the conception of the double-action harp Erard optimised the statics and mechanics of the pedal harp, efficiently blending several features that had been devised earlier by himself or by others into the new instrument. He also simplified, standardised and accelerated the harp's construction, by adopting industrial practices which enabled the serial production of harps. In parallel, Erard introduced new materials, methods and styles in the decoration and branding of the harp, which were widely imitated by other makers in Britain and abroad. Launched in 1811,

---

4   For more details on the single-action pedal harp in France see Laure Barthel, *Au cœur de la harpe au XVIIIème siècle* (Paris: Garnier-François, 2005), and Eve Zaunbrecher, *An Enlightened Instrument: The Design, Education, and Sociability of the Single Action Pedal Harp in Ancien Régime Paris, 1760–1789* (MA Diss., London: Royal College of Art, 2016).

Erard's 'Grecian' model, so-called because of its neoclassical ornamentation, was the first functionally sound and commercially built double-action pedal harp, becoming the benchmark in the harp trade during the first decades of the nineteenth century.

Due to its increased musical capabilities, superior function and elegant appearance, Erard's double-action harp quickly became a fashionable instrument that rivalled the piano's popularity among amateur and professional musicians. However, as with many innovative endeavours, the road to success was not straightforward. Erard not only had to fight against the harp's inherent deficiencies, but also had to compete with other inventors, musicians and instrument makers who came up with their own ambitious concepts for perfecting the harp. To make matters worse, the political, economic and social turmoil at the end of the eighteenth and the beginning of the nineteenth centuries hindered travel and trade across Europe. Moreover, the resulting uncertainty and insecurity due to revolutionary outbreaks and long military conflicts was harmful for both people and businesses. Erard experienced first-hand the effects of the Napoleonic Wars (1799–1815) and the subsequent financial stagnation: in 1813 his Paris branch was declared bankrupt, while throughout the 1810s the London branch was often in the red.

On the other hand, the new environment in which Erard chose to test his luck offered many advantages. By the end of the eighteenth century Britain's economy had witnessed unprecedented growth. The power of the guilds had already waned, attracting aspiring newcomers, while a capitalist consumer society, which rewarded diversity and novelty, was emerging. London represented the heart of a land rapidly transformed by mechanisation and industrialisation, which in turn promoted innovation and commercial enterprise. At a global level, new territories were being discovered and conquered, new routes and means for the circulation of people, goods and ideas were becoming available, and new, promising markets were being opened in the east and west through expedition and colonialisation.[5] Moreover, the systematic observation and classification of the natural world, based on documentation and experimentation, brought great advances in science, medicine and technology. Furthermore, literature and the fine arts were flourishing, while diffusion through the press and other printed media meant that more people were aware of the latest fashions. Music-making was an important aspect of domestic and public life, reflected in the growing number and variety of musical instruments, published music and concerts that were available especially in London, but also in the British provinces.[6] In this stimulating and competitive environment, Erard had more motivation and more freedom to further develop the design and manufacture of the harp.

In the end, Erard's efforts were fruitful. Introducing novel, progressive methods in harp production and marketing, some of which had already been applied and

---

[5] For an overview of Britain during the late eighteenth and early nineteenth centuries, when Sébastien Erard was active, see Jennifer Mori, *Britain in the Age of the French Revolution: 1785–1820* (Harlow: Longman, 2000); see also John Rule, *Albion's People: English Society 1714–1815* (London: Longman, 1992).

[6] See William Weber, 'London: A City of Unrivalled Riches', in Neal Zaslaw (ed.), *The Classical Era: from the 1740s to the end of the 18th century* (London: Macmillan, 1989), pp. 293–326.

tested in various manufacturing sectors in Britain, Erard managed to revolutionise the way harps were made, consumed and perceived. As the ancestor of the modern concert harp, Erard's Grecian model was at the centre of this transformative process. The Erard Grecian harp gradually established itself as a familiar symbol of status, wealth and taste, leaving its distinctive mark in the lifestyle of contemporary society and having a strong influence in the music, education, art, fashion, and fiction of the early nineteenth century.

Literature Review and Research Aims, Material and Methodology

This book is the first study of Erard Grecian harps, and of the background in which they were developed and thrived, that focuses on the instruments themselves rather than on archives as the primary source of evidence and the starting point for discussion. Despite their great significance in the history of the harp, Erard Grecian harps have been largely neglected by scholars and many details about their production and consumption remain unknown. For instance, the proceedings of the first ever conference on Sébastien Erard in 1994, which celebrated the 200th anniversary of his first patent from 1794, provide new information on the biography and output of Erard, but mention Erard Grecian harps rather marginally.[7] A museum catalogue of historical harps in the Musikinstrumenten-Museum, Berlin, which has become a standard reference work among harp specialists, includes just a short account on the development of the double-action harp, represented by only one specimen of Erard's Gothic harp, which appeared a quarter of a century after the Grecian model.[8] Likewise, recent dictionary articles on Erard[9] or on the double-action harp[10] contain virtually no new material on Grecian harps. In addition, the catalogue of a temporary exhibition in 2011 celebrating 200 years from the introduction of the double-action harp by Erard discusses several important aspects concerning the evolution of Erard harps, although it lacks an in-depth analysis of the Grecian model.[11]

In the last ten years several publications have shed new light on the Erard firm and on the harp trade in the early nineteenth century, but none has so far attempted to describe the development of the Grecian model and its broader impact considering

---

7　Rudolf Frick (ed.), *Sébastien Erard: ein europäischer Pionier des Instrumentenbaus. Internationales Erard-Symposium Michaelstein 13.–14. November 1994, Michaelsteiner Konferenzberichte 48* (Blankenburg: Stiftung Kloster Michaelstein, 1995).

8　Dagmar Droysen-Reber, *Harfen des Berliner Musikinstrumenten-Museums* (Berlin: Staatliches Institut für Musikforschung Preußischer Kulturbesitz, 1999), pp. 252–260.

9　See, for example, Ann Griffiths, Robert Adelson and Jenny Nex, 'Erard', in Laurence Libin (ed.), *The Grove Dictionary of Musical Instruments* (2nd edn, New York: Oxford University Press 2014), vol. 2, pp. 234–237.

10　See, for instance, Sue Carol Devale, 'Harp: V7.III: The double-action pedal harp', in Laurence Libin (ed.), *The Grove Dictionary of Musical Instruments* (2nd edn, New York: Oxford University Press, 2014), vol. 2, pp. 574–576.

11　For more details see Robert Adelson, Laure Barthel, Michel Foussard, Jenny Nex and Alain Roudier (eds), *Erard and the Invention of the Modern Harp, 1811–2011* (Nice: Musée du Palais Lascaris, 2011). The exhibition took place at the Musée du Palais Lascaris, Nice, from 13 May to 17 October 2011.

the numerous surviving specimens worldwide. For example, the systematic examination of the Erard firm within the context of the musical instrument-making business in Georgian London contains only limited information on surviving Erard harps.[12] Similarly, the publication of meticulously edited archival material relating to Erard as harp and piano manufacturer by a team of acknowledged scholars includes brief details of Erard instruments in introductory texts and footnotes.[13] A thorough overview of the harp industry in London during the early nineteenth century built upon the case of the Erat firm, one of Erard's main competitors, is based on the quantitative analysis of the firm's archives, with sporadic references to extant instruments of the Grecian model by Erat, Erard or other makers.[14] A recent economic study of Erard's Paris and London branches involved the systematic examination of Erard's manufacture and sales patterns before the introduction of the double-action harp as documented in the Erard ledgers, considering to a lesser extent surviving Erard harps.[15] Similarly, an article that illuminates the operation of Erard's Paris workshop by looking into the firm's rich correspondence with business associates, agents, suppliers and customers, offers only minor evidence relating to extant Erard instruments.[16] A new book on the Erard family relies mainly on the examination of documentary sources pertaining to the later years of the Erard firm, particularly after 1855.[17] Finally, in the latest and most comprehensive publication on the history of Erard harps, the discussion of extant instruments plays a rather secondary role compared to the study of the firm's business and family archives.[18]

Arguably, the main issue with such a task is that extant Erard harps are scattered all over the world, with the majority being held in private collections, thus making their accessibility and examination difficult. Even detailed studies of surviving Erard harps have usually focused on instruments in one particular collection or place. For example, the scientific investigation of two Erard Grecian harps in private and public ownership in Munich provides new valuable insights on the construction and decoration of Erard harps, although due to the restricted scope of these works, there

---

[12] Jenny Nex, *The Business of Musical-Instrument Making in Early Industrial London* (PhD Diss., London: Goldsmiths College, 2013).

[13] Adelson et al, *The History of the Erard Piano and Harp*.

[14] Mike Baldwin, *The Harp in Early Nineteenth-century Britain: Innovation, Business, and Making in Jacob Erat's Manufactory* (PhD Diss., London: London Metropolitan University, 2017). Baldwin's PhD dissertation has been recently published as a book; see Mike Baldwin, *Harp Making in Late-Georgian London* (London: Baldwin & Bright Light, 2020).

[15] Fanny Guillaume-Castel, *Erard: study of a firm based in Paris and London between the 1790s and 1810s through the manufacturing and sales of the harps* (Masters Diss., Paris: Université Paris 1 Panthéon-Sorbonne, 2017).

[16] Robert Adelson, 'Inside an Eighteenth-Century Instrument Builder's Workshop: Erard's Letter Copy Book (1791–1797)', *Journal of the American Musical Instrument Society* 47 (2017), pp. 5–57.

[17] Giuliano Marco Mattioli, *La famiglia Érard: Un percorso storico fra documenti e strumenti musicali* (Varese: Zechini Editore, 2022).

[18] Robert Adelson, *Erard: Empire of the Harp* (Ancenis: Les Harpes Camac, 2022).

are few mentions of similar instruments, which could enable further comparisons.[19] Technical descriptions of Erard Grecian harps in public[20] and private[21] collections offer useful summaries of the features of these particular instruments, without, however, taking into account the numerous harps dispersed internationally.

Focusing on surviving specimens, this book aims to present the Erard Grecian harp not only as a musical instrument, but also as a multidimensional symbol of transformation within the context of the musical, technological, aesthetic, economic, political, social, intellectual and cultural developments that occurred during the late eighteenth and early nineteenth centuries. The rather unconventional scope and narrative of this book result firstly from the thorough interdisciplinary study of a single artefact, a surviving Erard Grecian harp in the Deutsches Museum; secondly from the widening of the research framework with the inclusion of similar harps in other collections; and thirdly from an investigation of the historical environment in which these harps were produced and consumed, helping to identify links between actors and networks that were previously unknown. This will consequently lead to new questions and will open new possibilities regarding our understanding of harps and other musical instruments as multifaceted objects of material culture.[22]

Despite their powerful symbolism and use in different sociocultural contexts, musical instruments have been surprisingly absent from material culture studies as well as from broader historical research. This fact has been remarked on in a recent article about the sociocultural influences reflected on the development of musical instruments, whose author has pointed out that 'the shape, construction, decoration, and other physical details, whether revealed by extant instruments or iconography in artworks, provide critical clues to an instrument's relationship to

[19] Franziska Bühl, *Untersuchung einer Erard-Doppelpedalharfe von 1820–1825* (BA Diss., Studiengang Restaurierung, Kunsttechnologie und Konservierungswissenschaft, Munich: Technische Universität München, 2014); Luise Eva-Maria Richter, *Fassungsuntersuchung der Doppelpedalharfe No. 2631 von Sébastien Erard aus dem Deutschen Museum München: Ein Beitrag zur Harfenforschung* (BA Diss., Studiengang Restaurierung, Kunsttechnologie und Konservierungswissenschaft, Munich: Technische Universität München, 2016); and Luise Eva-Maria Richter, *Ergänzende Untersuchung an der Doppelpedalharfe No. 2631 von Sébastien Erard aus dem Deutschen Museum München* (Project Diss., Studiengang Restaurierung, Kunsttechnologie und Konservierungswissenschaft, Technische Universität München, Munich, 2017).

[20] Daniela Kotašová, 'Erard Harps in the Collection of the Czech Museum of Music', *Musicalia: Journal of the Czech Museum of Music* 10/1–2 (2018), pp. 85–114, at pp. 94–95.

[21] See Dagmar Droysen-Reber, 'Schedules of the harps from no. 42 to no. 52', in John Henry van der Meer (ed.), *In Search of Lost Sounds: Art and Music in the Instruments Collection of Fernanda Giulini* (Milan and Briosco: Villa Medici Giulini, 2006), pp. 432–501, at pp. 486–491 and 492–497; see also Roslyn Rensch, *Three Centuries of Harp Making* (Chicago: Western Central, 2002).

[22] Considering its concept, this book shares many similarities with the study of a Naderman harp built in Paris in 1774, now in the Musikinstrumentensammlung der Universität Göttingen, Göttingen (Inv. No. 383). For more details see Klaus-Peter Brenner, *Die Naderman-Harfe in der Musikinstrumentensammlung der Universität Göttingen. Ein französisches Instrument des 18. Jahrhunderts als Maschine, Skulptur, Möbel, Prestigefetisch, Ware und Klangwerkzeug. Orbis Musicarum 14* (Göttingen: Edition Re, 1998).

instruments of other times and places, and thus to cultural exchange', further adding that 'Instruments, like any other art motif or transferred technology, embody in themselves evidence of connections between societies across space and over time. In this and other ways, then, music, and musical instruments in iconography are subject to the gamut of material culture analysis.'[23] The author has also noted that:

> …it helps us bring music into history if we think about music and musical instruments in a certain way: as enmeshed in physical and social networks (of materials, instrument dealers, performers, consumers, divine and human patrons) and semantic and cultural webs. Every instrument is linked to other instruments before it and in other places through its mode of construction, technical features, stylistic details, and the like. Every performer learned from other players, as every composer borrows from the work of others. Instruments and musical genres are coded by class, gender, ethnicity, and social venue, and these codings link them to discourses about music in society, about spirituality, pleasure, propriety, solidarity, and other concerns.[24]

Following this paradigm, which considers musical instruments less as sound-producing devices and more as carriers of multilayered historical information, this book uses the Erard Grecian harp to provide a vivid snapshot of the past. In addition, the book intends to redress the balance between theoretical and practical approaches in harp studies by merging empirical knowledge with scientific analysis and scholarly research, thus contributing to the establishment of reference data and guidelines for similar initiatives. The research material and methodology employed for this book comprises a combination of diverse sources presented below.

Surviving Erard Grecian Harps in Public and Private Collections

The first source of information on the development of the Erard Grecian harp, and the Erard firm during the time this model was developed, is the large number of surviving Erard harps housed in public and private collections around the world. In comparison to Erard archives, which as already described have been extensively researched by scholars, extant Erard harps constitute a far less explored source. Using surviving artefacts as primary evidence, which is a traditional methodological concept of organology, also corresponds to the latest shift among various academic disciplines towards material culture. As has been suggested by authors working in different fields, the study of an object's biography can significantly enhance our understanding about its manufacture, usage and appreciation in different locations, cultures and historical periods.[25] The object-based investigation of Erard harps greatly helped to corroborate the results of archival research with the aim of pro-

---

[23] James A. Millward, 'The Silk Road and the Sitar: Finding Centuries of Sociocultural Exchange in the History of an Instrument', *Journal of Social History* 52/2 (2018), pp. 206–233, at pp. 208–209.

[24] Millward, 'The Silk Road and the Sitar', p. 209.

[25] For a thorough discussion about the concept of object biography relating particularly to musical instruments see Geerten Verberkmoes, *Boussu Inside Out: A multifaceted*

viding a comprehensive account of the Erard Grecian harp, and the Erard London branch in particular, during the formative years before and after the introduction of the double-action harp by Erard in 1811.

This investigation built upon and expanded the concise synopsis of Erard's Grecian model that was presented by the author in an article on the manufacturing aspects of Erard harps.[26] The main object of study was Erard N° 2631, a typical example of the Grecian model built in 1818 (see Figure 5), housed in the Deutsches Museum, Munich (Inv. No. 16147).[27] Since it survives in relatively good condition and in its original state, this harp was used as a point of reference for comparisons to other Erard harps. Apart from macroscopic observation, which included various measurements and technical descriptions using a prototype template, the documentation of this harp involved several lab-based analytical methods that were applied for the first time for the examination of an Erard Grecian harp. Special techniques were used for specific materials, such as X-Ray Fluorescence (XRF) for the identification of metal elements and 3D-reflected-light microscopy for the identification of wood species.[28] Moreover, vibroacoustic examination was conducted based on measurements of the mechanical mobilities of the soundboard and soundbox and the calculation of mean values of mobility, as proposed in a recent study of historical harps,[29] which allowed for comparisons of Erard N° 2631 to similar Erard harps in public and private collections.[30] In addition, non-destructive imaging methods, such as digital endoscopy and

---

organological study of the life, instruments and methods of the violin maker Benoit Joseph Boussu (1703–1773) (PhD Diss., Ghent: Ghent University, 2020), pp. 39–42.

[26] Panagiotis Poulopoulos and Julin Lee, 'A Synergy of Form, Function and Fashion in the Manufacture of the Erard Harp', in Marco A. Pérez and Emanuele Marconi (eds), *Wooden Musical Instruments: Different Forms of Knowledge* (Paris: Cité de la Musique – Philharmonie de Paris, 2018), pp. 367–398, at pp. 377–384.

[27] For a brief description of this harp see Bettina Wackernagel, *Europäische Zupf- und Streichinstrumente, Hackbretter und Äolsharfen. Deutsches Museum München. Musikinstrumentensammlung Katalog* (Frankfurt am Main: Bochinsky, 1997), pp. 184–185.

[28] See 'Sonic, Visual and Exhibition Cultures' in *Deutsches Museum Jahresbericht 2018* (Munich: Deutsches Museum, 2019), p. 74. The results of these identifications have been summarised in two unpublished reports: Neeti Phatak, 'Analysis of Erard Harp N° 2631 with XRF' (Munich: Deutsches Museum, 2018), and Volker Haag, 'KO/1385/18: Holzartenbestimmung Erard Harfe (London 1818, Inventarnummer DM 16147), Deutsches Museum München' (Hamburg: Thünen-Institut für Holzforschung, 2019). The wood identification of the Erard harp was also briefly described in Volker Haag, Valentina Zemke, Swati Tamantini and Panagiotis Poulopoulos, 'Das Barberini-Harfen-Projekt: Untersuchungen an einem Meisterwerk aus dem Jahr 1630', *Holz-Zentralblatt* 147/49 (2021), pp. 881–882.

[29] Jean-Loic Le Carrou, Sandie Le Conte and Joel Dugot, '18th and 19th [century] French Harp classification using vibration analysis', *Journal of Cultural Heritage* 27 (2017), pp. 112–119.

[30] See 'Sonic, Visual and Exhibition Cultures' in *Deutsches Museum Jahresbericht 2017* (Munich: Deutsches Museum, 2018), pp. 76–77. The results of this examination have been summarised in an unpublished report: Niko Plath, 'Vibroacoustic Examination of Erard Harp N° 2631' (Hamburg: Institut für Systematische Musikwissenschaft, Universität Hamburg, 2017); they have also been presented in Panagiotis Poulopoulos, Marisa Pamplona, Luise Richter and Niko Plath, 'Conservation Issues on Historical

radiography, helped to detect the internal structure of the instrument, particularly the profile and outline of the various surfaces and joins, enhancing and confirming the results of visual observation. For instance, the X-Ray images revealed previously undocumented manufacturing techniques relating to the use of screws to join the soundboard on the soundbox of the harp or the mounting of large composition ornaments on the harp's capital with metal pins. Advanced microscopy and spectroscopy techniques, including Scanning Electron Microscopy - Energy Dispersive X-Ray Spectroscopy (SEM-EDX), Fourier Transform Infrared Microspectroscopy (FTIR) and Pyrolysis-Gas Chromatography-Mass Spectrometry (Py-GC-MS) assisted the analysis of cross sections of samples for the identification of the harp's diverse decorative coatings.[31]

Apart from Erard N° 2631, a corpus of 20 Erard Grecian harps was examined for the purposes of this book. These harps were made in London from the early 1810s to the late 1830s, covering the years in which the Grecian model was in production. Selected primarily due to their accessibility, condition of preservation, originality or rarity, these harps were inspected, documented and photographed *in situ* during research visits to various public and private collections. Other harps that were examined during the preparation of this book include six single-action Erard harps, the earliest three built in Paris c.1790 and the latest three built in London in the 1800s, as well as several single- and double-action Erard harps built in Paris in the first decades of the nineteenth century. The object-based survey of surviving instruments additionally included numerous single- and double-action harps by makers such as Cousineau, Naderman, Challiot, Erat, Stumpff, Dodd or Delveaux, that were produced during the late eighteenth and early nineteenth centuries. The examination of the instruments depended on the available time, facilities and circumstances in each collection. Therefore, some harps were examined in detail in designated spaces, often with the kind assistance of museum staff or of private owners, while others were viewed only briefly in dark museum storerooms or in crowded exhibition galleries, usually behind glass. It is important to note that several of these harps have been extensively repaired, restored or modified in the past, and may thus not retain their original features, a fact which, if overlooked, can lead to wrong conclusions. The documentation of representative surviving instruments enabled further illumination

Pedal Harps: Preserving Tangible and Intangible Properties', in Pascale Vandervellen (ed.), *Preservation of Wooden Musical Instruments: Ethics, Practice and Assessment. Proceedings of 4th Annual Conference of the COST Action FP1302 WoodMusICK* (Brussels: Muziekinstrumentenmuseum, 2017), pp. 69–72, at pp. 70–71.

31   See 'Sonic, Visual and Exhibition Cultures' in *Deutsches Museum Jahresbericht 2016* (Munich: Deutsches Museum, 2017), pp. 54, 63 and 65. The results of this research have been extensively discussed in Panagiotis Poulopoulos, Marisa Pamplona and Luise Richter, 'The Industrialisation of the Early Pedal Harp: Detecting Evidence on Wood and Metal', in Marco A. Pérez and Sandie Le Conte (eds), *Making Wooden Musical Instruments: An Integration of Different Forms of Knowledge. Proceedings of the 3rd Annual Conference of the COST Action FP1302 WoodMusICK* (Barcelona: Museu de la Música, 2016), pp. 185–190, and in Panagiotis Poulopoulos, Marisa Pamplona, Luise Richter and Elke Cwiertnia, 'Technological Study of the Decoration on an Erard Harp from 1818', *Studies in Conservation* 65/2 (2020), pp. 86–102.

of the chronological and typological evolution of pedal harps and identification of similarities or differences between diverse harp models, as well as between various makers working in different times and places.

The material collected from the *in situ* investigation and 'hands-on' interaction with these harps was compared to and complemented with data from harps by Erard and other makers that have been described and depicted in various sources. These include scholarly articles and books, academic dissertations, exhibition and auction catalogues, conference proceedings, dictionaries, museum checklists, conservation and restoration reports and websites and discussion forums on the internet. Regardless of the varying levels of accuracy and depth, these secondary sources are valuable research tools for studying Erard harps. However, it is important to point out that in some cases the provided information may be limited, outdated, incomplete or even incorrect, and therefore many of these sources need to be treated with caution. The collected data were processed in a database that was created for their further interpretation and dissemination, e.g. in the form of a virtual collection.[32] A checklist of Erard Grecian harps is presented in the Appendix, which the reader should refer to for details of individual instruments mentioned in the text.[33] Due to various limitations, a study of the repertoire or performance practice relating to Erard Grecian harps was beyond the scope of this book, although several details on the musical aspects and sound characteristics of these harps are occasionally provided.

Surviving Erard harps as a primary source of information are employed in the first three chapters of this book. Chapter One describes the transition from the single- to the double-action harp from the 1780s to the 1810s, providing an overview of the evolution of the Erard harp during this time, leading to the arrival of the Grecian model in 1811. Chapter Two examines the pioneering design and engineering aspects of Erard Grecian harps, investigating the various influences that industry and business had on the manufacture of these instruments. Chapter Three presents and analyses the decoration and branding of Erard Grecian harps, especially from the perspectives of innovation, adaptation and substitution in materials, techniques and styles during the late eighteenth and early nineteenth centuries.

---

[32] The author is currently preparing a virtual collection of surviving Erard Grecian harps built in London between 1811 and c.1845. For more details see Panagiotis Poulopoulos, 'Serial Numbers as Information Source and Tool for Building Virtual Instrument Collections', in *Proceedings of the CIMCIM Conference 'Global Crises and Music Museums: representing music after the pandemic', London (Royal College of Music-Horniman Museum and Gardens), 6 to 8 September 2021* (forthcoming). An early version of this article was presented by the author in his paper 'Serial Numbers as Information Source and Tool for Building Virtual Instrument Collections', presented at the Annual Conference of CIMCIM 'Global Crises and Music Museums: representing music after the pandemic', Royal College of Music and Horniman Museum and Gardens, London, 6 to 8 September 2021.

[33] In order to enable the easy identification of Erard Grecian harps mentioned in the text, and to avoid unnecessary repetitions, the harps in the Appendix and in the text have been labelled according to their serial number as 'Erard N° XXXX'; for example Erard N° 2631 refers to the harp built in 1818 and housed at the Deutsches Museum. Details of all other harps by Erard that are referred to in the text are typically mentioned in footnotes.

Erard Archives: Administrative, Communication and Promotional Documents

The second source of information on Erard Grecian harps and the Erard London branch comprises archival material, including sales ledgers, letters, bills, catalogues, patents, advertisements, trade directories, harp tutors and treatises, which were used by the firm for administrative, communication and promotional purposes. Although some of these documents have been extensively investigated, others remain less known, and therefore this material has benefited from new study and interpretation within the purposes of this book.

The Erard firm utilised a meticulous system of administration, which is revealed in the Erard London Harp Ledgers, held at the Royal College of Music, London.[34] Comprising three volumes, the Erard Ledgers encompass important information on the manufacture and sale of Erard harps made in London from c.1798 to 1917. Most relevant for the aims of this book is the second volume of these ledgers, listing the Erard harps N° 1375 to N° 4214 and spanning the years from 1811, when the first double-action harp by Erard was sold in London, to 1829, when the double-action harp had been firmly established in Britain. However, equally significant is the first volume, which contains the workshop accounts of Erard between 1807 and 1809, listing expenses for raw materials, tools and supplies, as well as payments for work carried out in the firm's premises or by subcontractors. Similar ledgers concerning the manufacture and sale of both pianos and harps survive for the firm's Paris branch.[35]

The regular communication between Sébastien Erard, the founder of the firm, and his nephew, Pierre-Orphée Erard (1794–1855), as well as their contacts to other persons, are vividly illustrated in the surviving correspondence of the firm. The numerous extant letters, owned by the AXA insurance group and deposited with other Erard archival material at the Centre Sébastien Erard – Association Ad Libitum in Etobon, France, have now been digitised, transcribed and translated, facilitating their diffusion and study.[36] The letters were written chiefly by Pierre and span the years from 1814, when he was put in charge of the London branch after his uncle Sébastien had moved to Paris, to 1831, when Sébastien died. Many of these letters disclose interesting details about the workshop organisation and workforce of the Erard firm, thus providing the opportunity to discover the personalities and daily activities not only of those at the head of the firm, but also of those involved in the actual production of instruments or those undertaking managerial tasks and

---

34 Erard London Harp Ledgers, Royal College of Music, London, Special Collections (RCM 497), hereafter referred to as Erard ledgers. The ledgers have been recently digitised and are available at archive.org.

35 Archives Érard (1788–1983), Musée de la Musique, Paris (E.2009.5.40–E.2009.5.177). The archives have been digitised and are available at http://archivesmusee.citedelamusique. fr/pleyel/archives.html, accessed 3 June 2022.

36 Adelson et al, *The History of the Erard Piano and Harp*. Each letter is hereafter referred to as L followed by the corresponding number as presented in this publication. For the original letters see the section 'Correspondence' in 'Centre Sébastien Erard', https:// www.sebastienerard.org/en/, accessed 3 June 2022.

other duties in Erard's workshop. Moreover, these letters contain a wealth of information on Erard's clientele, on the family's friends and associates, as well as on their critics and competitors. The correspondence exposes the close personal and professional relationships of Sébastien and Pierre Erard with various renowned music teachers, publishers, composers, performers and musical instrument makers, but also their acquaintance with prominent craftsmen and entrepreneurs occupied in various manufacturing sectors outside of the music business. The correspondence additionally illustrates Erard's strong connections to the British and European royalty and nobility, to which many of the firm's customers belonged.

The customer profile and financial transactions of the Erard firm are further unveiled in surviving bills, two of which, regarding the purchases of Erard N° 2524 and Erard N° 2372 respectively, are discussed in detail in this book.[37] The gender, financial standing, social class and rank of the purchasers provide useful clues to the monetary as well as social value of Erard harps. Apart from listing the descriptions and prices of the various items, the bills also demonstrate the firm's marketing and advertising practices, thus illuminating the associations between producer and consumer in the harp market of Regency Britain.[38]

Erard's promotional tactics are also evidenced in an extant Erard harp catalogue dating from c.1819–1821.[39] This catalogue lists harps offered for sale by Erard, with details on the different models, decorative elements and prices of double- and single-action harps, as well as on a large variety of harp-related accessories, such as music stools and stands, sounding boards, strings and packing cases sold by the firm. The Erard catalogue is a valuable reference source for decoding and classifying the features of Erard harps built in the late 1810s, particularly concerning their sizes and decoration. Furthermore, the catalogue elucidates the range of services provided by the firm, including, for instance, the exchange, conversion and hire of harps, or the application of additional ornamentation upon request, shedding new light on the trade of harps as fashionable objects during the early nineteenth century.

---

37 Attingham Park Collection, Shropshire Archives, Shrewsbury (112/6/54/381), and Ridgely Family Papers, Maryland Historical Society, MS 692, respectively.

38 The Regency era in Britain spans the years from 1811, when George, Prince of Wales, the eldest son of King George III, was appointed Prince Regent due to his father's mental illness, until 1820 when he became King George IV after his father's death. However, the term 'Regency' commonly refers to the longer period between c.1795 and 1837, which is also the historical period discussed in this book. During this period, the English currency was divided into pounds (£), shillings (s) and pence (d), with one pound comprising 20 shillings and one shilling 12 pence. Another currency unit that was often used was the guinea, equalling 21 shillings (or £1 1s). For more details see 'Currency, Coinage and the Cost of Living' (available at https://www.oldbaileyonline.org/static/Coinage.jsp, accessed 3 June 2022).

39 Erard Harp Catalogue (London: Erard, c.1819–1821), University of Glasgow Archives & Special Collections, A.x.24. I am grateful to Robert Adelson for bringing this catalogue to my attention.

The public face of the Erard firm is additionally represented by other printed sources, including patent texts and drawings,[40] promotional essays and treatises,[41] published harp music,[42] as well as by references to Erard in newspaper advertisements,[43] trade directories,[44] music dictionaries,[45] conduct manuals[46] and music magazines,[47] which served to boost the firm's reputation and to discourage its rivals. The digitisation, indexing and availability of many of these sources, some of which are non-English, in online repositories has made them easily accessible to scholars, enabling their further identification and investigation.[48]

Most of this archival material is discussed in the fourth and fifth chapters of this book. Chapter Four focuses on the internal processes of the Erard London branch, where the Grecian model was produced, analysing various aspects of business organisation, management and operation. In contrast, Chapter Five will concentrate on the external activities of the firm, investigating Erard's marketing strategies as well as

[40] See, for instance, Sébastien Erard's patent entitled 'Pianofortes and Harps', British Patent N° 3332 (London, 1810). This patent describes and depicts Erard's specifications for the double-action harp with fourchettes upon which the Grecian model was based. A summary of this patent is included in Bennett Woodcroft, *Patents for Inventions, Abridgements of Specifications relating to Music and Musical Instruments, AD. 1694–1866* (facsimile edn of the original 1871 edn; London: Bingham, 1984), p. 60.

[41] See Pierre Erard, *The Harp: In its present improved State Compared with The Original Pedal Harp* (London: Erard, 1821).

[42] See Robert Nicholas-Charles Bochsa, *Forty Studies Expressly Composed for Sebastian Erard's Double Movement Harp* (London: Chappell & Co, 1818). A copy of this tutor survives in a bound volume containing harp music entitled '48 Exercises or Fantasias / Dizi', held in the Pendlebury Library of Music, University of Cambridge, XRa.850.18A.X22.

[43] See the advertisement entitled 'Mr Sébastien Erard,' *The Morning Chronicle*, 30 October 1811. This advertisement, in which Erard announced his new patent double-action harp in London, has been discussed in Baldwin, *The Harp in Early Nineteenth-century Britain*, pp. 195–197.

[44] See, for instance, the listing of Erard as 'Erard, Seb. *Patent harp manufacturer*' in Andrew Johnstone, *Johnstone's London Commercial Guide and Street Directory* (London: Barnard & Farley, 1818), p. 325. A copy of this directory survives in the Sammlung von Handschriften und alten Drucken of the Österreichische Nationalbibliothek, Vienna, 213798-B.Alt-Mag.

[45] A remark on the public reception of Erard's double-action harp is included in John Sainsbury, *A Dictionary of Musicians, from the Earliest Ages to the Present Time, Vol.1* (2nd edn; London: Sainsbury, 1827), p. 376.

[46] See, for example, the comment on Erard's role in the improvement of the harp in Elizabeth Appleton, *Private Education; or a Practical Plan for the Studies of Young Ladies. With an Address to Parents, Private Governesses, and Young Ladies* (London: Henry Colburn, 1815), pp. 165–166.

[47] See, for instance, the discussion of Erard's contribution to harp design in 'A Second Series of Twelve Fantasias, or Exercises for the Harp', *The Quarterly Musical Magazine and Review* 5 (1823), pp. 101–104, at pp. 101–103.

[48] Unless otherwise stated, for the reader's convenience any non-English quotations have been translated by the author in the main text, with the original texts in German, French, etc. provided in the footnotes. The spelling and punctuation of original texts cited in the book has been retained.

the firm's customer profile. Both chapters will be based on a survey of instruments and archives for the year 1818, in which Erard N° 2631 was built, and enriched with references to the firm's manufacture and sales methods in earlier or later periods. This choice is not arbitrary: 1818 was the first year in the production of the Grecian model during which the date of registration in the Erard ledgers, corresponding approximately with the date of completion of a harp, was noted along with the date of first transaction (e.g. sale, hire or shipment) of the instrument, thus enabling reliable statistical analysis and elucidation.

Contemporary Iconography and Fiction Related to Erard Harps

Two other sources which can offer important clues about the reception and cultural impact of Erard Grecian harps are iconography and fiction. The integration of Erard harps or their imitations in contemporary lifestyle is shown in numerous portraits, fashion plates and caricatures, in which harps like Erard N° 2631 are depicted as artistic props. Similarly, the powerful symbolism and allure of the harp is demonstrated in countless references to harps in novels and poems from the early nineteenth century, some of which may have been inspired by Erard harps, like Erard N° 2631. Focusing on the interpretation of diverse iconographic and written sources, Chapter Six will explore the role of the Erard harp in contemporary education, art and fashion, whereas Chapter Seven will discuss the presence of Erard harps, and harps in general, in the literature of the Romantic era, analysing the works of several eminent authors ranging from Jane Austen to Leo Tolstoy.

Erard Harp Records in Museums and Private Collections

Another valuable source concerning Erard Grecian harps, particularly as collectible objects, are various records which are held by museums or private collectors, and which include interesting details about the acquisition, preservation and exhibition of Erard harps. These records are significant, since in combination with the study of extant instruments and archives, they reveal how these harps were used, repaired, modified or disposed according to changing tastes and demands, and also how they were valued, treated and repurposed by their different owners through the years. This material will be mentioned in Chapter Eight, which will investigate the transformation of Erard harps from functional instruments to artefacts of cultural heritage within the contexts of obsolescence, recycling and musealisation.

CHAPTER ONE

The Shift from the Single- to the Double-Action Harp: The Emergence of the Erard Grecian Model

'At length, in 1810, Erard's genius triumphed over all obstacles, and he was able to employ the double-action fully – the instrument being generally known as the "Grecian" harp.'[1]

As mentioned in the introductory section, the starting point and focus of this book is Erard Nº 2631, a double-action harp of the so-called Grecian model built by Erard in London in 1818. Although the harp, an instrument known since antiquity, has appeared in countless variations and has been used in different locations, cultures and historical periods, arguably the most crucial phase in the development of the instrument, at least within a Western European context, was during the late eighteenth and early nineteenth centuries. In the decades before and after 1800 the single-action pedal harp or 'harp organisée', a technically advanced type of harp that had been developed at the start of the eighteenth century, became firmly established in European art music.

The same era witnessed the gradual transition from the single- to the double-action harp, an instrument that would occupy a permanent place in symphonic orchestras around the world. This procedure was characterised by intense experimentation, collaboration and competition, evidenced in the considerable number of inventions and patents registered for the harp.[2] By referring to the main protagonists and events, this chapter will describe the transformation of the pedal harp from the 1780s to the 1810s, with particular emphasis on the evolution of the Erard harp from the early single-action instruments built by Erard in Paris to the emergence of Erard's double-action Grecian model in London.

<hr>

[1] William Henry Grattan Flood, *The Story of the Harp* (London: Scott & New York: Scribner, 1905), p. 158.

[2] For a detailed overview of the patents registered for the harp in Britain between 1794 and 1845 see Mike Baldwin, *The Harp in Early Nineteenth-century Britain: Innovation, Business, and Making in Jacob Erat's Manufactory* (PhD Diss., London: London Metropolitan University, 2017), pp. 175–241.

The Single-action Harp from Hochbrucker to Erard

The concept of a harp equipped with a pedal mechanism to shorten the strings, thus raising their pitch and producing notes unavailable by the open strings, was developed in south Germany at the beginning of the eighteenth century. The invention of the pedal harp is usually credited to Jacob Hochbrucker (1673–1763), a harp maker working in Donauwörth, a small town in Bavaria, although other persons may have played a decisive role in the early development of the instrument.[3] The single-action pedal harp devised by Hochbrucker, and later improved by other makers, could produce two different notes per string: that of the open string and, when a pedal was pressed by the player's foot, a semitone higher, with this motion simultaneously raising the pitch of all the strings of the same note. On earlier harps built without pedal mechanisms, such as hook harps, harpists could shorten the string length by turning small J-shaped hooks, thus limiting or interrupting the action of their hands. Contrary to hook harps, single-action pedal harps freed harpists' hands and fingers entirely, providing them with maximum flexibility during performance.

Although it cannot be confirmed, the concept of introducing pedals to the harp may have been inspired by the application of pedals in keyboard instruments, such as organs, harpsichords and, later, pianos, as well as of foot-powered mechanisms on various devices, such as lathes or weaving looms, whose functionality was greatly enhanced by the effective use and coordination of both hands and feet. In this context, it is also worth noting that the first mechanisms for the fast tuning of timpani using hand levers and screw threads were invented in the early nineteenth century, when the pedal harp was at the peak of its popularity. Around 1840 August Heinrich Daniel Knocke (1793–1863), a mechanic from Hannover who worked in Munich, developed the earliest timpani with a foot-operated tuning system that for the first time left the hands of the player completely free for performing while tuning the drums. Knocke must have had an interest in mechanised musical instruments, as evidenced by a surviving single-action pedal harp bearing his signature.[4] Knocke's foot-operated mechanism may have inspired later timpani designs that employed pedals to raise or lower the pitch of the drum head, culminating with the so-called 'Dresden model' patented by Carl Gottlieb Pittrich (1831–1908) in 1881, which became widely adopted among percussionists.[5]

---

[3] See Panagiotis Poulopoulos, '"So wenig kultivirt, so ganz vernachlässigt": Die Pedalharfe in Deutschland um 1800', *Phoibos: Zeitschrift für Zupfmusik* 19 (2021), pp. 131–158, at pp. 147–148.

[4] The harp is housed in the Schlossmuseum Beromünster. According to a restoration report by Beat Wolf this harp is signed 'Aug Knocke / Mechanicus / in München' on the left side of the two brass plates housing the mechanism. Wolf states that the harp is a big, heavy instrument decorated in the so-called 'Empire' style and equipped with a pedal mechanism that is built in the old manner, but perfected. Since Knocke was a mechanic and not an instrument maker, it is not clear whether he manufactured (or improved) only the pedal mechanism of this harp or the entire instrument. For more details see report for harp BW 33/047/200, dated 17 February 1998, in Beat Wolf, *Harp Archives* (Schaffhausen: Wolf, 2016).

[5] Edmund A. Bowles, 'Nineteenth-century innovations in the use and construction of the timpani', *Journal of the American Musical Instrument Society* 5–6 (1980), pp. 74–143, at pp.

Paradoxically, as frequently happens with new ideas, the pedal harp, a product of German origin, was not destined to become a great success in the German-speaking regions, but in France and Britain, as will be described later.[6] Neither Vienna, the capital of the Austro-Hungarian empire and one of the greatest centres of European music, nor any of the large German cities, such as Berlin, Hamburg, Leipzig, Munich or Nuremberg, where stringed instruments had been produced for centuries, developed a strong tradition in the making and playing of the pedal harp during the eighteenth and early nineteenth centuries.[7] Even as late as 1823, more than a decade after the introduction of the double-action harp by Sébastien Erard in London, his nephew Pierre claimed that 'in Germany one is not very familiar with the harp', adding that the new harp, 'should make a great sensation in Germany, a musical country'.[8]

In contrast, when the pedal harp was introduced to Paris around the mid-eighteenth century, mainly by German harpists and harp makers that had moved to France, it instantly became a favourite instrument of the aristocracy and polite society, particularly among young ladies. This was due to the pedal harp's majestic sound and extended range, which made it suitable for solo or ensemble performances and for song accompaniment, like other keyboard and plucked stringed instruments. Equally important was the harp's conversion from a relatively small, portable instrument into a larger freestanding object, with the addition of a pedalbox and supporting feet,[9] as well as its opulent decoration with carved, painted and gilded ornaments in the so-called 'Louis XVI' style, which gave the instrument an air of fashion and taste. Moreover, as will be described in Chapter Six, the graceful posture that the harp required for its playing allowed female harpists to display not only their talent, but also their elegance and beauty. From the late 1760s onwards, several Parisian makers, such as Georges Cousineau (1733–1800) or Jean-Henri Naderman (1734–1799), were producing pedal harps of various designs (Figure 1), while numerous music teachers offered lessons and wrote tutors for the instrument.[10]

103–131. Only one pair of kettledrums equipped with Knocke's foot-operated mechanism, built by the firm of J. L. Kaltenecker & Sohn in Munich, is known to have survived. The two instruments are housed in two different collections in Munich, the first in the Deutsches Museum (Inv. No. 79220) while the second is in the Münchner Stadtmuseum (Inv. No. MUS-83-9).

6   For a concise account of the evolution of the pedal harp in Western Europe and North America see Roslyn Rensch, *Harps and Harpists* (Bloomington and Indianapolis: Indiana University Press, 1989), pp. 153–245.

7   For more details on the pedal harp in Germany around 1800 see Poulopoulos, '"So wenig kultivirt, so ganz vernachlässigt": Die Pedalharfe in Deutschland um 1800', pp. 131–158.

8   See L 344, 25 July 1823, in Robert Adelson, Alain Roudier, Jenny Nex, Laure Barthel and Michel Foussard (eds), *The History of the Erard Piano and Harp in Letters and Documents, 1785–1959* (Cambridge: Cambridge University Press, 2015), pp. 808–810, at p. 809.

9   See Eve Zaunbrecher, *An Enlightened Instrument: The Design, Education, and Sociability of the Single Action Pedal Harp in Ancien Régime Paris, 1760–1789* (MA Diss., London: Royal College of Art, 2016), p. 23.

10   For more details on the performance aspects, teaching methods and repertoire of the single-action harp see Maria Christina Cleary, *The 'harpe organisée', 1720–1840:*

Figure 1. Single-action harp by Cousineau père et fils, built in Paris c.1780.
Rijksmuseum, Amsterdam (Inv. No. BK-2016-98-5).

Much in vogue, the pedal harp appeared frequently in Parisian salons and wealthy houses, with the French queen, Marie Antoinette, being one of the most esteemed devotees and exponents of the instrument; in 1784 harp instruction occupied no less than 58 harp teachers in the French capital.[11] Descriptions and drawings of the single-action pedal harp, referred to as 'Harp organisée', were included in the eighth volume of Diderot's groundbreaking *Encyclopédie ou Dictionnnaire raisonné des sciences, des arts et des métiers*, published in 1765, as well as in the related fifth volume of the *Recueil de Planches, sur les sciences, les arts libéraux, et les arts méchaniques, avec leur explication*, published in 1767.[12] The inclusion of the harp in this emblematic publication of the European Enlightenment underlines the instrument's strong presence in French culture and lifestyle.

Despite their popularity, single-action harps were often criticised for their fragile construction, lack of volume, poor intonation and limited versatility in modulation, especially when compared to keyboard instruments. Initially built with five and later with seven pedals, early single-action harps were typically equipped with metal L-shaped hooks (*crochets*) for shortening the strings by a semitone. Such mechanisms were problematic and unreliable, as the crochets pushed the strings out of vertical alignment and caused their frequent breakage due to friction, therefore hampering tuning and playing. Furthermore, any adjustments to the intonation or any essential regulations and repairs without affecting the harp's wooden frame were difficult, since the numerous mechanical parts were fixed directly on the harp's wooden neck rather than on a separate, detachable platform. In the 1780s Georges Cousineau designed a new mechanism that included a system of two small crutch-ended levers (*béquilles*) that shortened each string, aiming to improve the deficiencies of earlier crochet mechanisms. The béquilles mechanism also included movable nuts with vertical screw threads for correcting the intonation of the semitones. The screw threads could be adjusted using a small watch-key, similarly to the tuning machines often found on various plucked and bowed instruments from the late eighteenth and early nineteenth centuries, such as guittars (English guitars), French cistres, Portuguese guitars, lyre guitars, trumpet marines and psalteries.[13] Cousineau's béquilles mechanism was an ambitious but complex concept that was not adopted widely by other makers. Regardless of several mechanical improvements introduced to the single-action harp

---

Rediscovering the lost pedal techniques on harps with a single-action pedal mechanism (PhD Diss., Leiden: Leiden University, 2016).

[11]   Sue Carol Devale and Nancy Thym-Hochrein, 'Harp: V7.I. Hook harps and single-action pedal harps', in Laurence Libin (ed.), *The Grove Dictionary of Musical Instruments* (2nd edn, New York: Oxford University Press, 2014), vol. 2, pp. 572–573, at p. 572.

[12]   Dagmar Droysen-Reber, *Harfen des Berliner Musikinstrumenten-Museums* (Berlin: Staatliches Institut für Musikforschung Preußischer Kulturbesitz, 1999), pp. 54–59.

[13]   For more details on the origins and use of the watch-key tuning machine see Panagiotis Poulopoulos, *The Guittar in the British Isles, 1750–1810* (PhD Diss., Edinburgh: The University of Edinburgh, 2011), pp. 383–417, and also Panagiotis Poulopoulos and Rachael Durkin, '"A very mistaken identification": The "Sultana" or "Cither viol", and its Links to the Bowed Psaltery, Viola d'Amore and Guittar', *Early Music* 44/2 (2016), pp. 307–333, at pp. 317–319.

by Cousineau or other makers, and despite the instrument's growing appeal in France and elsewhere, the main disadvantage remained its inability to play in all keys.[14]

The above-mentioned issues were most likely known to Sébastien Erard, an instrument maker from Strasbourg who would become one the most influential figures in the history of the harp and piano. Erard, who had started his career as a maker of keyboard instruments, began building his first harps in Paris in the late 1780s, probably inspired by his contacts and collaborations with eminent Parisian harp makers and harpists.[15] The earliest surviving Erard harps, produced in Paris from the late 1780s to the early 1790s (Figure 2), resemble in many aspects the French harps of the late eighteenth century, indicating Erard's direct influences from established harp makers, such as Cousineau and Naderman. For example, the soundbox is made with an odd number of maple staves (typically seven), reminiscent of the body of a lute. Furthermore, the thin fluted column is ornamented with gilded wood carvings on its top and bottom, while the neck housing the mechanism that shortens the strings forms a shallow S-shaped curve from capital to shoulder. Moreover, the short pedalbox enclosing the seven pedals is attached to the soundbox with three large screws and has a small round hole at its bottom, allowing access for slight adjustments to the pedal mechanism. Each of the seven pedals comprises two interlinked levers and is attached on a metal frame screwed to the bottom of the soundbox. Some early Erard harps are also equipped with a swell mechanism, which can be activated with an additional eighth pedal that opens five rectangular shutters on the back of the soundbox. Devised by the harpist Jean-Baptiste Krumpholz (1742–1790) and the harp maker Naderman around 1785, this mechanism allowed for subtle changes in dynamics and was commonly used on French single-action harps.[16]

However, early Erard harps also have some notable differences when compared to older French single-action harps, showing that Erard was already experimenting with the harp's design and construction during this time. For example, the top of the column on early Erard harps has the form of a capital instead of a scroll, a shape widely used on French harps and typically associated with the Baroque style. Additionally, there are no soundholes on the soundboard, as on older French harps,

---

[14] For a concise overview of the technical and musical features of the single-action harp see Beat Wolf, 'Timeline: The development of the single action harp' (available at http://beatwolf.ch/Portals/14/pdf/Timeline_pedalharps_2012.pdf?ver=2014-09-12-140457-193, published 2014, accessed 3 June 2022).

[15] For more information on Erard's first harps see Adelson et al, *The History of the Erard Piano and Harp*, pp. 26–30. Technical details of these harps are provided in Panagiotis Poulopoulos and Julin Lee, 'A Synergy of Form, Function and Fashion in the Manufacture of the Erard Harp', in Marco A. Pérez and Emanuele Marconi (eds), *Wooden Musical Instruments: Different Forms of Knowledge* (Paris: Cité de la Musique – Philharmonie de Paris, 2018), pp. 367–398, at pp. 370–372.

[16] The development of this mechanism has been discussed in Droysen-Reber, *Harfen des Berliner Musikinstrumenten-Museums*, pp. 64–65, and in Joël Dugot, 'Sonorités inouïes: la nouvelle harpe de Messieurs Krumpholtz et Naderman', *Music, Images, Instruments* 7 (2005), pp. 86–109. For an analysis of the swell mechanism from a performer's perspective see Mike Parker, 'The Eighth Pedal, Fact or Fiction?' (published 2008; available at http://www.harpspectrum.org/historical/the_eighth_pedal.shtml, accessed 3 June 2022).

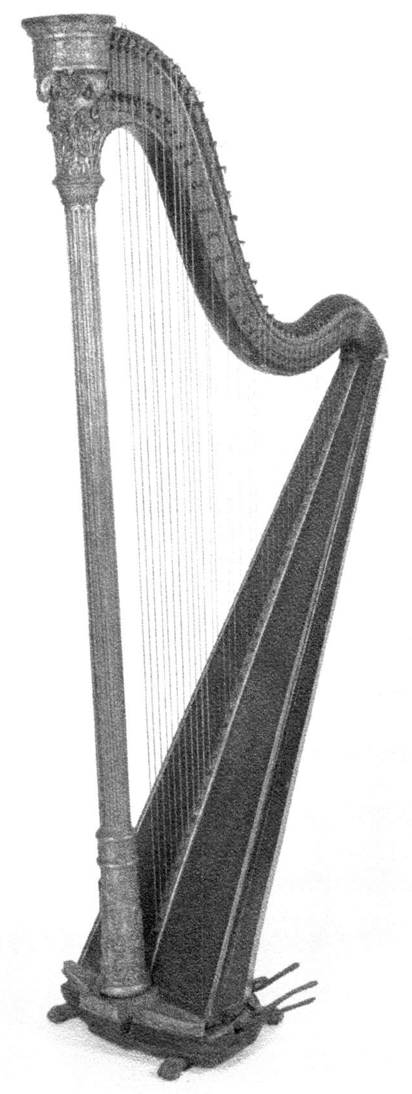

Figure 2. Early single-action harp by Erard, built in Paris c.1790 and bearing no serial number. Muziekinstrumentenmuseum, Brussels (Inv. No. JT0005).

perhaps to avoid weakening the thin soundboard wood. Furthermore, apart from the gilded carved ornaments on the column and pedalbox, early Erard harps are generally plain, without the elaborate painted embellishments often found on earlier French harps.

The most important difference, though, lies in the pedal mechanism. Instead of the usual crochets or béquilles, the pedal mechanism of early Erard harps operates with small forked discs (*fourchettes*), an advanced feature which eliminated the problems of string misalignment and breakage frequently observed on older French harps. Erard had probably already developed the idea of a pedal mechanism with fourchettes in the mid-1780s, but would officially present it in his first patent registered in London in 1794, as will be mentioned later. Early Erard harps have 39 or 40 strings that are secured with wooden pins on the bridge and also tied on metal tuning pins on the top of the neck. The strings are further stretched on an intermediate row of immovable nuts fixed on a brass plate covering the fourchettes. These nuts determine the vibrating string length of the open strings, while their distance from the fourchettes provides the length required to achieve the higher semitone per string when a pedal is pressed.

From the late 1790s Erard's fourchettes mechanism became a standard feature on pedal harps and was widely imitated by other harp makers.[17] It is worth noting that on the earliest surviving Paris-made Erard harps the fourchettes are hidden inside the brass plate, with only their protruding pins being visible, while on later specimens built in the early 1790s the fourchettes are fully exposed. In both cases the back of the mechanism is covered with a wooden panel screwed on the neck that can be opened for repairs and adjustments. Interestingly, although the name and address of Erard ('Erard frères à Paris // Rue du Maille N° 37') is usually engraved on the brass plate covering the fourchettes mechanism, none of the early harps signed by or attributed to Erard, of which about ten are presently known, bear a visible serial number.[18] Considering that in the late 1780s Erard had already started using serial numbers on his pianos, the absence of numbers on his earliest harps suggests that they were probably experimental instruments produced in relatively small numbers. However, it is notable that several wooden and metal parts on these instruments are stamped, engraved or inscribed with Latin or Arabic numerals, similar to those found on Erard pianos produced in Paris around the same time, presumably to assist the assembly of the various instrument parts.

---

[17] An interesting variation of Erard's fourchettes mechanism includes a disc with an attached ring, through which the strings pass, a system that was used by Erard's rival Jacob Erat. For more details see Cleary, *The 'harpe organisée'*, p. 29.

[18] Details of these harps are included in Wolf, *Harp Archives*, 450 Erard London EP, Harps BW 36 – 250 – 001 to – 009. Another early harp by Erard not listed by Wolf was acquired in 2016 by the Musée de la musique, Paris (Inv. No. E.2016.1.1). I am thankful to Thierry Maniguet for helping me to examine this instrument.

Erard's Further Upgrading of the Single-Action Harp: The Empire Model

Throughout the 1790s Erard concentrated on the further improvement of the single-action harp. In 1792 he opened a harp manufactory in London, where in 1794 he registered his first patent concerning his new mechanism with fourchettes, which permanently replaced older systems with crochets or béquilles. From around 1798 the Erard London branch began producing single-action harps based on Sébastien Erard's 1794 patent. The single-action harp with fourchettes became known as Erard's 'Empire' model, a term that referred to its decoration in the Empire style that was prevalent in Europe during the Napoleonic Wars from about 1800 to 1815 (Figure 3).[19]

Erard's upgraded single-action harp signalled a clear departure from the older French harps, as well as from the harps Erard had built in Paris in the late 1780s and early 1790s. With the Empire model Erard introduced several novel features and established the pedal harp as a fashionable instrument in Britain, paving the way for the arrival of the double-action harp. To begin with, the overall size of the Empire harp, as well as the dimensions of its various individual structural components, increased considerably compared to earlier harps. Moreover, on the Empire model, Erard abandoned forever the staved soundbox of earlier French harps and introduced a new soundbox design in a semi-conical shape constructed from laminated wood, usually maple, with additional horizontal and vertical internal bracing. Furthermore, Erard's Empire harps were fitted with a significantly thicker soundboard than that on earlier French harps, especially on the bass register. Empire harps were also built with a thicker column compared to earlier harps produced by Erard and other makers, with the increase of the column's diameter aiming to improve the rigidity of the wooden frame and to allow for sufficient room for the seven long metal rods that connect the pedals with the action of the mechanism on the neck. Additionally, the slender neck was made from several pieces of wood glued together rather than from a single piece carved to shape, as on older harps.

These new construction features provided additional strength and support which was necessary to withstand not only the extended range of 41 to 43 strings with which Erard's Empire harps were usually equipped, but also the extra string tension due to changes in the string materials and gauges used from the end of the eighteenth century onwards. These changes had a strong impact on the vibroacoustic behaviour of Erard harps. As proven by vibroacoustic analysis, the resonating corpus with a round soundbox and thick soundboard of Erard Empire and Grecian harps has less flexibility and consequently less mobility when compared, for instance, with earlier harps by Cousineau, which were typically built with staved soundboxes and thinner soundboards.[20] The particular construction of Erard harps, which was intended to adapt them to cope with greater mechanical stress, resulted to some extent in the

---

[19] For a concise overview of Erard's Empire model see Poulopoulos and Lee, 'A Synergy of Form, Function and Fashion in the Manufacture of the Erard Harp', pp. 372–377.

[20] Jean-Loic Le Carrou, Sandie Le Conte and Joel Dugot, '18th and 19th [century] French Harp classification using vibration analysis', *Journal of Cultural Heritage* 27 (2017), pp. 112–119.

Figure 3. Erard N° 333, a typical single-action harp of Erard's Empire model, built in London in 1800. Royal College of Music Museum, London (Inv. No. RCM 298).

loss of responsiveness and brightness, but could provide a fuller sound with more sustain and power, particularly on the bass.

Another development that affected the silhouette of Erard's Empire harps can be observed on the neck profile, which is made with a deeper, more pronounced curve in the middle towards the treble strings. This feature, which is easily noticeable when Empire harps are viewed side-by-side with earlier harps by Erard or other makers, corresponded to the gradual rise of pitch during the late eighteenth and early nineteenth centuries. A further difference concerns the pedalbox, which is slightly higher than on earlier harps to allow more room for the new type of single-arm pedals that were introduced by Erard around 1803.[21]

Empire harps also demonstrate Erard's measures to improve the tuning stability, intonation and functionality of the single-action harp. For example, the entire fourchettes mechanism on Erard's Empire harps is enclosed between two brass plates and is mounted on the bottom of the neck with screws. With this inventive feature, which will be analysed in the next chapter, the mechanism was separated from the wooden neck, facilitating adjustments, repairs or replacements without risk of damage to the wooden frame. Moreover, a row of sliding adjustable nuts close to the tuning pins securing the stings enabled the fine regulation of intonation. As already mentioned, this feature had already been employed from the mid-1780s on Cousineau's harps equipped with a béquilles mechanism and it should be remarked that movable nuts with long vertical screws very similar to those of Cousineau were included in Erard's 1794 patent. However, on Erard's surviving Empire harps, these nuts are attached more robustly on the left brass plate with two horizontal screws, and their position can be adjusted using a screwdriver with a slotted head rather than using a watch-key. There are usually no fourchettes or adjustable nuts on the top two or three treble strings near the harp's shoulder.

As innovative as the technical improvement was the decorative updating of Erard's Empire harps, which was driven as much by stylistic as by financial reasons. The decoration of these harps was strongly influenced by Neoclassicism, a prevailing cultural movement during the early nineteenth century, as well as by the application of new materials and techniques that allowed the cheap, fast and reliable decoration of various manufactured goods, as will be mentioned in detail in Chapter Three. Although various colours, such as red, violet or purple, were occasionally used on Empire harps, the most common finish was a glossy black coating, evoking the black japanned furniture that was quite popular in contemporary households. That black was Erard's standard finish is confirmed by the inspection of the finish on several extant Erard harps, by the listing of numerous harps in the Erard London ledgers as 'Noire' (black), as well as by the fact that no other pigment except for ivory black is mentioned in Erard's London workshop accounts between 1807 and 1809.

Empire harps were additionally embellished with thin gilt lines on the soundbox, soundboard, neck and top of the capital, while the column and pedalbox were usually decorated with alternating stripes of black coating and gilding on the fluted areas. The soundboard of some early Empire harps by Erard was adorned with colourful floral and geometrical paintings, not unlike those found on French harps from the eighteenth century. However, from about 1800, Erard introduced decoupage, a technique involving printed and gilded paper which could be cut and pasted on wooden surfaces, to decorate harp soundboards and shutters. The black coating in combination with gilding and decoupage prints with gilt red 'Etruscan' borders and

---

[21] Michael Parker, *Child of Pure Harmony: A Source Book for the Single-Action Harp* (London: Parker, 2005), p. 13.

figures gave Erard's Empire harps a classical appearance reminiscent of the black-red pottery produced in ancient Greece.

Equally inspired by the neoclassical style was the sculptural decoration of Erard's Empire harps. On the capital it typically included three gilded ram's heads linked with garlands, above which swags or floral motifs were located, although on some harps Egyptian elements, such as mummies, which were popularised after Napoleon's campaign in Egypt (1798–1801), were occasionally used. Likewise, the top of the pedalbox and the base of the column were adorned with gilded acanthus leaves and repetitive ornamental patterns, such as pearls or beads. On Erard's Empire harps these three-dimensional ornaments, which on earlier harps were carved solely out of wood, consisted of a mix of wood carvings and ornaments made out of composition, a thermoplastic material that could be cast in moulds in large numbers and could be glued with minor preparation on wooden surfaces, as will be described in Chapter Three.

A study of the harps recorded in the Erard ledgers shows that about 1,500 single-action harps of the Empire model were produced in London by Erard from c.1798 to the late 1830s, although after 1821 only 25 of them were apparently built, with the last specimen, Erard N° 4013, registered in June 1837.[22] Apart from Erard's name and London address at 18 Great Marlborough Street, these harps also bear a serial number typically engraved on the right brass plate of the mechanism, which can help to identify and date them, as will be discussed in Chapter Three. From c.1799 Erard's Paris branch also started building Empire harps like those produced in London, using a similar serial numbering system. For instance, Erard N° 7, dated 1799, which is Erard's earliest numbered harp built in Paris to have survived,[23] is almost identical to Erard N° 333, made in London in 1800 (shown in Figure 3).

Nevertheless, Erard's Paris branch made much fewer harps than London, since it was focusing on the production of pianos. This is evidenced by the fact that from the late 1790s to the early 1810s Erard built only about 375 harps in Paris, but more than 1,300 harps in London. It is, however, important to note that despite the lower production rate compared to the London branch, Erard's Paris branch was equally essential for sustaining Erard's international harp market. Primarily building instruments of the single-action Empire model up until the 1830s, Erard's Paris branch sold numerous harps outside of France, particularly to European courts and noble homes, as verified in Erard's surviving Paris ledgers.[24]

---

[22] Erard London Harp Ledgers, vol. 2, p. 264. A handwritten note on an unnumbered page before page 1 of this volume states that 'very few single-action harps were made after 1821. Indeed apparently there were but 25 made after that year', followed by a list of these harps.

[23] Musée de la musique, Paris (Inv. No. E.981.6.1).

[24] Musée de la musique, Paris (Inv. No. E.2009.5.40–E.2009.5.177 and E.2009.5.98–E.2009.5.173).

Experimentation, Collaboration, Competition:
The Invention of the Double-action Harp

As mentioned earlier, one of the main issues with the single-action harp was its limited capability for modulation, a fact that was commonly recognised by musicians and makers alike. The earliest recorded attempt to overcome this problem was in 1782, when Georges Cousineau was granted a patent for a harp with 14 pedals. Cousineau's patent harp, the first ever version of a double-action harp, was equipped with two rows of béquilles that were operated by two rows of seven pedals respectively, resulting in a fully chromatic harp that could produce three notes per string: flat, natural and sharp. Despite its technically advanced and novel features – or perhaps because of them – this harp did not become widespread, most likely due to its complicated function; there is only one known surviving specimen of Cousineau's harp in a private collection, which had reportedly belonged to Erard's own collection since the late 1790s.[25]

In the following years the concept of a pedal harp able to play in all keys continued to be a stimulus for experimentation among harp makers. In 1799 George Cousineau and his son Jacques-Georges (1760–1836), in cooperation with the Belgian engineer Michel-Joseph Ruelle, presented a new double-action harp equipped with rotating tuning pins (*chevilles tournantes*), a novel idea which greatly simplified the mechanics of the harp, but which changed the string tension of the instrument.[26] Although Erard had already introduced a mechanism with fourchettes for the single-action harp in his first patent from 1794, in 1801 he took his own patent for a double-action harp with rotating tuning pins, apparently influenced by the instrument devised by the Cousineaus and Ruelle. However, this harp never went into production because of its unsatisfactory functionality. Erard was granted two more patents in London in 1802 and 1808, both of which illustrate his further trials concerning a fully chromatic pedal harp, before taking his 1810 patent for a double-action harp with two rows of interlinked fourchettes (Figure 4).[27]

In 1811, Erard announced the advantages of his new double-action harp, also known as the double-movement harp, in a newspaper advertisement:

> MR. SEBASTIAN ERARD, N⁰· 18, Great Marlborough-street, respectfully informs the Nobility, Gentry and the Public in general, who have so long and liberally patronized his IMPROVED HARP, that after much expence and three years exertions he has at length obviated all the defects which hitherto circum-

---

²⁵ The features of this harp have been analysed in Robert Adelson, Alain Roudier and Francis Duvernay, 'Rediscovering Cousineau's fourteen-pedal harp', *The Galpin Society Journal* 63 (2010), pp. 159–178.

²⁶ For more details see Dagmar Droysen-Reber, 'Die Cousineau-Harfe mit den "chevilles tournantes"', *Musica instrumentalis* 3 (2001), pp. 129–137.

²⁷ The five patents registered by Sébastien Erard from 1794 to 1810 are British Patents N° 2016, N° 2502, N° 2595, N° 3170 and N° 3332, respectively. Summaries of these patents are provided in Woodcroft, *Patents for Inventions*, pp. 28, 40, 46, 55 and 60 respectively. For a discussion of Erard's five patents see also Baldwin, *The Harp in Early Nineteenth-century Britain*, pp. 175–198.

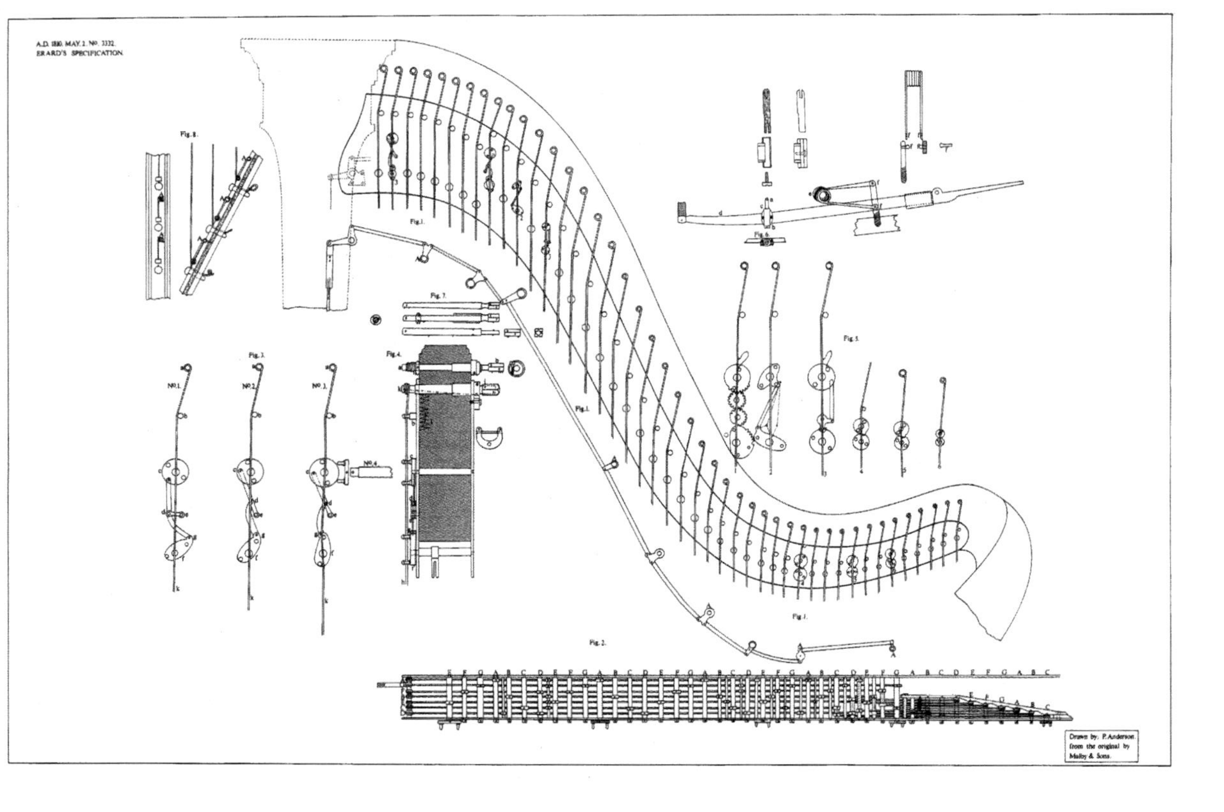

Figure 4. The drawings accompanying Erard's 1810 patent for a double-action harp with fourchettes. Drawn by P. Anderson after the original by Malby & Sons.

scribed the talents of the composer and performer, by giving as great a variety of note and facility of execution as is possessed by any instruments whatever. This is effected by means of each of the strings producing three distinct tones instead of two, as on the old Harp; in consequence of which the performer, instead of being confined as heretofore to a very limited number of keys, can now play in every known key, and perform the most extensive and abstruse modulation with perfect facility. The hand is also allowed more and sufficient room in the top of the instrument. These improvements have the advantage of conferring on this noble instrument every possible degree of solidity and elegance.[28]

Despite Erard's long-standing attribution as the inventor of the double-action harp because of his 1810 patent, recent research has shown that Erard built upon a patent which had been registered in 1807 by the Polish inventor Charles Gröll (1770–1857), and which Erard purchased shortly after.[29] The 'much expence and three years exertions' mentioned in the above advertisement most likely correspond to the costs and time Erard invested firstly to obtain Gröll's patent, so that no other maker could use it, and secondly to develop it further, take his own patent and set up his workshop for the production of the new model. According to Pierre Erard, his uncle started working intensively on the double-action harp around 1808, pursuing 'a series of laborious experiments' based on the fourchettes mechanism that he had introduced for the single-action harp in 1794, further stating that 'it was not until 1811, after having spent no less than twenty thousand pounds in establishing in his manufactory the different machines upon which the nicety of the execution of a mechanical work so essentially depends, that he brought out his present double action harp'.[30] Notwithstanding any debates regarding the facts and figures surrounding the origins of the double-action harp, Erard's introduction of the double-action mechanism with fourchettes was a major contribution to the development of the harp, leading to the permanent shift from the single- to the double-action harp in the first half of the nineteenth century.[31]

Commonly known as the 'Grecian' model (Figure 5) because of its distinctive decoration inspired by Greek antiquity, as will be discussed in detail in Chapter Three, Erard's new double-action harp with fourchettes was as much an entirely new instrument as a creative synthesis of older concepts.

---

[28]　*The Morning Chronicle* (London), 30 October 1811.

[29]　For a comprehensive account of Gröll's input in the development of the double-action harp see Robert Adelson, 'Originality and Influence: Charles Gröll's Role in the Invention of the Double-action Harp', *Muzyka* 64/1 (2019), pp. 3–21 at pp. 8–20. Gröll and Ruelle, who had worked with the Cousineaus, may have been related, as argued in Baldwin, *The Harp in Early Nineteenth-century Britain*, p. 191.

[30]　Pierre Erard, *The Harp: In its present improved State Compared with The Original Pedal Harp* (London: Erard, 1821), p. 9.

[31]　The evolution of the pedal harp from the single- to the double-action harp has been discussed in Panagiotis Poulopoulos, 'The Pedal Harp in Europe between 1780 and 1830', unpublished paper presented at the Forschungskolloquium of the Institut für Musikwissenschaft, Ludwig-Maximilians-Universität, Munich, 15 June 2016.

Figure 5. Erard Nº 2631, a typical double-action harp of Erard's Grecian model, built in London in 1818. Deutsches Museum, Munich (Inv. No. 16147).

Interestingly, the use of the term 'Grecian' to describe Erard's first double-action harps was never officially adopted by the firm, as in the case of the subsequent 'Gothic' model introduced in 1836, although references to Grecian harps were sparingly used during the second half of the nineteenth century.[32] By the beginning of the twentieth century the term had been firmly established in harp literature, as evidenced by explicit references to Erard's Grecian harp in publications from the late 1900s onwards.[33]

Erard's double-action harp, hereafter referred to as the Grecian harp, followed in many ways the design established with Erard's earlier single-action Empire model, but also had several distinct differences. Regarding the size and dimensions, as well as the overall proportions and geometry, Erard Grecian harps are very similar to Erard's Empire harps. Both models have a semi-conical soundbox made of laminated wood, usually with a swell mechanism with five shutters, while the neck is made of several wooden layers glued together rather than from a single piece of wood, as was common on earlier harps. Regarding the efficiency of the neck construction on Erard Grecian harps, Pierre commented in 1822: 'We glued as many as six veneers on the necks of your harps and we sold a good number'.[34] On the other hand, the column of Erard Grecian harps is slightly thicker than on Empire harps, apparently to add extra support to the frame, and is carved in the middle section with 20 rather than 12 flutes.

The most noticeable alteration to the outline of the Grecian harp is the enlargement of the pedalbox, which is rendered necessary because of the two 'zigzag'-shaped notches per pedal (as opposed to the single 'L'-shaped notch for pedals used on single-action harps), a feature retained from Erard's 1801 patent for a double-action harp with rotating pins. Moreover, apparently due to the use of more metal parts for the pedal mechanism, there was a significant increase in the weight, from about 18 kg on Empire harps to about 20 kg on Grecian harps.

The standardised finish with a glossy black coating, gilt lines, decoupage and gilt composition ornaments, which had started with the Empire model, continued on the Grecian model, although more elaborate finishes with additional colours and painted embellishments were also available at extra cost. However, on Grecian harps, composition ornaments entirely replaced the painstaking and time-consuming wooden carvings on the column and pedalbox, as will be described in Chapter Three.

Other novel features of the Grecian model can be observed in the design and function of the pedal mechanism. Although based on the fourchettes mechanism of the Empire model, the mechanism of the Grecian model presented new challenges relating to mechanical connections and the transfer of motion. A key aspect of Erard's double-action harp was the employment of the 'dead centre' engineering principle for the linkage of the two fourchettes. The 'dead centre' allowed the

---

[32]　Baldwin, *The Harp in Early Nineteenth-century Britain*, p. 95.

[33]　See, for instance, Grattan Flood, *The Story of the Harp*, pp. 158–160, and Alfred Kastner, 'The Harp', in *Proceedings of the Musical Association* 35/1 (1908), pp. 1–14, at p. 4.

[34]　L 337, 15 October 1822. Adelson et al, *The History of the Erard Piano and Harp*, pp. 800–802, at pp. 801–802.

fourchettes on the top and bottom rows to rotate independently from one another, while eliminating friction between the mechanical parts. Therefore, when pressing the pedal to the second notch to activate the bottom fourchette, the top fourchette did not rotate simultaneously, but remained fixed to the position it had held after the pressing of the pedal to the first notch.[35] This feature is visible in Erard's 1810 patent, marking an important difference to Gröll's 1807 patent, which does not depict a 'dead centre' linkage.

The mechanisms on Grecian harps also demonstrate augmented possibilities for intonation and noise damping, as well as for fine tuning and repair, when compared to earlier harps. For example, the mechanism of the Grecian model is fitted with sliding adjustable brass nuts fixed with horizontal screws on the brass plates for regulating the intonation, a feature already introduced on Empire harps. These nuts allow for small amendments of the first higher semitone, the second being defined by the fixed distance between the two fourchettes.[36] On Empire harps these nuts face towards the capital, whereas on Grecian harps they are reversed, facing towards the shoulder, presumably because of space limitations due to the presence of the second fourchette and also to prevent buzzing due to the vibrations of the nut on the brass plate when a string is plucked.

It is worth noting that, although on early Empire harps by Erard the bass strings are equipped with adjustable nuts, on Grecian harps the first 12 bass strings do not have this feature. This may be due to the increased tension of the bass strings, which would render the function of movable nuts ineffective; besides, the overwound bass strings may have had less intonation issues than the gut strings used on the rest of the harp's compass.[37] Probably due to limited space, the last treble string on the Grecian model has neither a fourchette nor an adjustable nut. Another remarkable feature concerns several small screws with wide heads on the right brass plate, which secure the ends of the rotating axles on which the fourchettes on the left brass plate are mounted, in order to prevent any unwanted vibration noises.

According to a review published in 1823 in a music magazine, Erard's double-action mechanism was characterised by 'great simplicity, considering its mechanical operation and effects', since it was pointed out that 'Five pieces only are employed, of which the flat plate or disk, and prongs, are two, and the motion distributed form one axis only.'[38] The author further noted that 'MR. ERARD made some other arrangements respecting the base strings, which by abating the tension upon

---

[35] See Rainer Thurau, 'Die Harfenmechanik Erards – ihre Funktion und Restaurierung', in Rudolf Frick (ed.), *Sébastien Erard: ein europäischer Pionier des Instrumentenbaus. Internationales Erard-Symposium Michaelstein 13.–14. November 1994, Michaelsteiner Konferenzberichte 48* (Blankenburg: Stiftung Kloster Michaelstein, 1995), pp. 28–29, at p. 28; see also Bühl, *Untersuchung einer Erard-Doppelpedalharfe*, pp. 50–51.

[36] Patrizio Barbieri, 'Harps Versus Pianos: Parisian *querelles* on Tuning 1770–1830', *The Galpin Society Journal* 77 (2017), pp. 45–63, at pp. 54–55.

[37] I am thankful to the harp maker Klaus Horngacher (Horngacher Harps, Starnberg), for this observation.

[38] 'A Second Series of Twelve Fantasias, or Exercises for the Harp', *The Quarterly Musical Magazine and Review* 5 (1823), pp. 101–104, at p. 102.

parts rendered the whole more perfect, more free from the danger of distorting the frame, and consequently more likely to preserve its intonation. He also improved the mechanism of the pedal by a contrivance which directed it to the notches when required, facilitating the action to the performer.'[39]

This last sentence may refer to Erard's novel design of the harp pedals, which constitutes a further example of mechanical improvement. Whereas Empire harps are equipped with two-arm pedals operated by springs fixed inside the neck for controlling the motion of the pedals, Grecian harps have single-arm pedals with springs placed next to each pedal, thus facilitating repairs or replacements. In March 1821 Pierre noted that 'in case of that spring breaking in the country or in a distant climate, another may be introduced with the greatest facility, whilst in other harps, where the springs are placed within the mechanism itself, the harp must be taken entirely to pieces to be repaired.'[40] Furthermore, contrary to earlier Erard harps, the pedalbox of the Grecian model has a large opening at its bottom to allow easier access to the pedals for adjustments and repairs, and probably also to provide more sound volume.

The Grecian model typically had 43 strings, made of gut for the treble and of silk overwound with a metal alloy, such as brass, for the bass strings. Contrary to Erard's Empire harps, which had 41 to 43 strings, the string number on Grecian harps did not fluctuate, but remained constant throughout its production, further confirming the standardisation of the Grecian model. According to Erard's advertisement presented earlier, the string arrangement of the double-action harp also provided more room for the fingers on the treble strings. From a musical viewpoint, the main advantage of Erard's Grecian harp when compared to earlier single-action harps was that it possessed increased range and potential for modulation and virtuosity, since it permitted two additional semitones per string to be produced using the mechanism with fourchettes. The Grecian harp was capable of playing in all keys, raising the standards of both harp manufacture and harp performance.

In terms of ergonomics, the Grecian model was a larger and heavier instrument with increased string tension compared to earlier harps, demanding more physical effort from the player. This became a point of criticism by Erard's competitors, such as the son of Jean-Henri Naderman, Henri Naderman (1783–1842), who maintained that the double-action harp was 'heavier and so tiring to play that with twice the physical strength it is still impossible to obtain the special tone quality that makes the normal harp superior to other instruments', adding that 'The size and the weight of the instrument are much too great for it to feel comfortable in the hands of ladies'.[41] This is why contrary to London, in Paris the acceptance of the double-action harp was quite slow, with the vogue of the single-action harp continuing well into the 1830s largely because of Naderman's influence and his propaganda against Erard's harp. This may have additionally been due to a prevailing traditionalism and

---

[39] 'A Second Series of Twelve Fantasias, or Exercises for the Harp', pp. 102–103.

[40] L 297, 16 March 1821. Adelson et al, *The History of the Erard Piano and Harp*, pp. 763–767, at p. 766.

[41] Quoted in Adelson et al, *The History of the Erard Piano and Harp*, p. 534.

conservatism among the Parisian music public, which is reflected in the rejection of new, innovative musical instruments, including experimental types of violins and guitars, which appeared at the same time as Erard's double-action harp.[42]

Apart from more physical strength, the double-action harp also required adaptation to new pedalling techniques, since the pedals on Grecian harps were positioned at a higher level, and were shorter and harder to press down and hold than on earlier harps. In addition, the three levels of movement – from flat to natural and from natural to sharp – rendered the fixing of the pedals necessary, also meaning that in order to produce certain notes several pedals were not on the same horizontal plane, but placed higher or lower. These facts affected the movements of the harpist's feet and to some extent prevented the simultaneous use of two or more pedals, which was an essential performance element of single-action harps.[43] Nevertheless, Grecian harps had a louder, fuller and more dramatic sound, with a darker timbre, which better suited the Classical and Romantic repertoires of the early nineteenth century.

The first double-action harp of the Grecian model, Erard N⁰ 1377, was sold on 24 October 1811. Erard's new harp became instantly popular and the Erard ledgers show that about 3,500 Grecian harps were produced by Erard in London between 1811 and 1836. That year they began to be slowly superseded by the 'Gothic' model, a larger double-action harp with 46 strings decorated in Gothic style that was patented by Pierre Erard in 1835,[44] with Erard N° 5011, built in May 1836, being the first commercially-built recorded example.[45] Apart from an updated mechanism with fourchettes, the Gothic model had several easily noticeable differences compared to the Grecian model. For instance, the column was made thicker to withstand the increased stringed tension and had a hexagonal form, while the notches for the pedals were cut into the lower part of the soundbox, rather than in a separate pedalbox, as on the Grecian harp. In addition, the decorative elements were inspired by religious themes and motives found on Gothic buildings and churches that were quite popular in Britain during the early Victorian era because of the Gothic revival. These features can be observed on a relatively early example of the Gothic model, Erard N° 5409, shown below (Figure 6).

Like Erard's Grecian model, Erard's new Gothic harp became instantly successful and was soon imitated by other makers. However, Grecian harps remained in production and were purchased by Erard's customers up to the early 1840s, as confirmed by surviving specimens, such as Erard N⁰ 5485, which was made in 1841 and sold in 1845. Although after 1836 it is rather difficult to distinguish between Gothic and

---

[42] For more details see Panagiotis Poulopoulos, 'The Impact of François Chanot's Experimental Violins on the Development of the Earliest Guitar with an Arched Soundboard by Francesco Molino in the 1820s', *Early Music* 46/1 (2018), pp. 67–86, at pp. 79–81.

[43] Cleary, *The 'harpe organisée'*, pp. 215–224.

[44] British Patent N° 6962. For more details of this patent see Woodcroft, *Patents for Inventions*, pp. 118–119, and Baldwin, *The Harp in Early Nineteenth-century Britain*, pp. 224–225.

[45] A prototype of Erard's Gothic model built in Paris in 1829 has been presented in Adelson, *Erard: Empire of the Harp*, pp. 130–131.

Figure 6. Erard Nº 5409, a typical double-action harp of Erard's Gothic model, built in London in 1840. Deutsches Museum, Munich (Inv. No. 2002-589).

Grecian harps in the Erard ledgers, it seems that Erard N° 5633, built in September 1844, is probably the last example of the Grecian model made by Erard.

Conclusions

The single-action pedal harp, which had been introduced by Hochbrucker in the early eighteenth century and was further developed by Parisian makers such as Cousineau and Naderman from the late 1760s onwards, was a highly popular instrument, albeit with many defects. Following an experimental phase, which started in Paris during the 1780s, Erard initially improved upon and rationalised the design of the single-action harp. Especially with the Empire model, Erard presented several novel features that would characterise the design and manufacture of Erard harps in the years to come. From around 1800 Erard joined the race for the double-action harp, a process that was marked by intense collaboration and competition among several inventors and makers. Erard may have played an important role in the development and establishment of the double-action harp, but was not its originator. Erard's Grecian model was an effective fusion of several earlier inventions that aimed to overcome the limitations of the single-action harp, starting with Cousineau's 1782 patent for a 14-pedal harp with béquilles and culminating in Erard's 1810 patent for a double-action harp with fourchettes. The Grecian harp encompassed many previous innovative ideas applied for the first time on a musically advanced, functionally reliable, visually attractive and thus highly marketable instrument, which can be considered the original predecessor of the modern concert harp. The next chapter will analyse how industrial and commercial practices influenced the design and engineering of Erard Grecian harps, allowing the Erard firm to produce fine, uniform instruments in large numbers.

CHAPTER TWO

The Design and Engineering of the Erard Grecian Harp: Influences from Industry and Business

'To Mr. Sebastian Erard, whose talents in architecture and mechanism have been so appreciated in his own country, the improvement of the harp is solely due.'[1]

Erard N⁰ 2631, the Grecian harp housed at the Deutsches Museum, is not a unique, experimental or prototype instrument. This harp is similar to most Grecian harps built by Erard in London from the early 1810s to the mid-1840s. Although some of these harps may differ from others in terms of their decoration and branding, as will be described in the next chapter, they are almost identical in terms of form and size, all sharing more or less the same outline and dimensions. The uniformity of the Grecian model was the result of novel design and engineering approaches that were introduced by Erard in the manufacture of harps and that allowed for the serial production of these instruments. Many of these approaches, which had already been used with success in other trades since the late eighteenth century, answered the challenges for faster, cheaper, more flexible and more controllable production of goods. Heavily influenced by changes brought by industrialising processes usually referred to as the 'Industrial Revolution', and the subsequent rearrangement of various manufacturing sectors in Britain and elsewhere, Erard gradually established new structural and mechanical principles that radically transformed the harp from a technical viewpoint.

Improvement of Stability and Reliability: The Transition from Wood to Metal

The first noteworthy aspect in the design and engineering of Erard Grecian harps, and of Erard harps in general, concerns the transition from wood to metal in the construction and mounting of the pedal mechanism. On earlier harps, such as those built in France by Cousineau or Naderman during the late eighteenth century, the relatively few metal components of the mechanism were mounted directly on the

---

[1] Elizabeth Appleton, *Private Education; or a Practical Plan for the Studies of Young Ladies. With an Address to Parents, Private Governesses, and Young Ladies* (London: Henry Colburn, 1815), p. 165.

harp's wooden neck. Due to the nature of wood, a material sensitive to fluctuations in humidity and temperature, as well as to the tension of the strings, the tuning of these harps was unstable. Additionally, mechanisms of this kind provided limited possibilities for adjusting the intonation or for the repair and regulation of the mechanical parts without interventions to the wooden structure.

One of Erard's major contributions to harp design was the enclosing of the mechanism between two brass plates that were fixed on the harp's neck with screws. This feature was described in Erard's first patent for the harp from 1794 which included 'two plates of copper fixed to the sides of the arm between which the mechanism which forms the semitones is placed [...] the whole mechanism is placed under the arm of the harp, and shut up by a thin plate of copper.'[2] This not only rendered the mechanism's function independent of the temperamental wood, but also enabled its manufacture and assembly separately from the harp's triangular wooden frame, while allowing for the easier repair or replacement of parts.[3] This innovative feature became standard on all Erard harps built after 1794, although on surviving instruments the plates are not made of copper, as stated in the patent, but of brass, as confirmed by the examination of the plates and other metal parts on Erard N° 2631 (Figure 7) with X-Ray Fluorescence (XRF).[4]

As a flexible and versatile material, brass had several advantages over wood and was widely used in the making of functional objects, such as musical and scientific instruments, on which precision and strength were important. Formed in flat sheets, brass could be 'bent, hammered, cut with shears and filed to shape'; moreover, it could be 'cast in moulds to make into individual components or even single-piece instrument frames'.[5] Brass also allowed for a superior finish because it could be 'highly polished, engraved and stamped, and given a coat of lacquer to protect the surface'.[6] In the course of the eighteenth century brass was progressively used on a variety of consumer goods 'ranging from buckles to bedsteads' as well as 'in the manufacture of clocks, instruments, guns, tools and aspects of some machinery'.[7]

---

[2] Patent N° 2016, 17 October 1794. A summary of this patent is included in Bennett Woodcroft, *Patents for Inventions, Abridgements of Specifications relating to Music and Musical Instruments, AD. 1694–1866* (facsimile edn of the original 1871 edn; London: Bingham, 1984), p. 28.

[3] The replacement of wood by metal in the construction and mounting of the pedal mechanism has been discussed in Panagiotis Poulopoulos, 'Das neue Holz: Bruch mit der Tradition am Beispiel der Pedalharfe', unpublished paper presented at the conference 'Knock on Wood: Holz, Handwerk und Wissen im Instrumentenbau', organised by the research group 'Materiality of Musical Instruments: New Approaches to a Cultural History of Organology', Deutsches Museum, Munich, 17 and 18 January 2019.

[4] I am thankful to Neeti Phatak, who in 2018 as 'Scholar-in-Residence' at the Deutsches Museum, carried out an examination of the metal parts of the harp with XRF and helped with the interpretation of the results.

[5] Ben Russell, *James Watt: Making the World Anew* (London: Reaktion Books, 2014), p. 55.

[6] Russell, *James Watt: Making the World Anew*, p. 55.

[7] Alison D. Morrison-Low, *Making Scientific Instruments in the Industrial Revolution* (Aldershot: Ashgate, 2007), p. 177. For the advantages of copper and brass in the manufacture of scientific instruments see especially pp. 175–183.

Figure 7. Detail of the right brass plate of the mechanism on Erard Nº 2631.
Deutsches Museum, Munich (Inv. No. 16147).

The extensive use of brass, iron and other metal components on Erard harps also transformed the design of the firm's pianos, strongly influencing the work of other piano makers. As has been argued, 'Whereas other piano-makers tended to elaborate mechanical designs based principally on the use of wood, using metal only sparingly, Érard drew largely on his harp-making expertise – and his workshop facilities – to integrate metallic elements into the heart of the piano.'[8] From the 1830s onwards metal bracing, and later a complete metal frame, was applied to pianos to strengthen their construction and to cope with the added string tension. The introduction of metal framing, which coincided with the widespread adoption of Erard's so-called double-escapement action, patented in 1821, gradually changed the standards of piano building and playing.[9]

---

[8]   Christopher Clarke, 'The Locksmith's Tale: How Harp-making Practice Shaped the Érard Firm's Pianos', available at https://earlypedalharp.wordpress.com/abstracts/#clarkeabs, accessed 3 June 2022.

[9]   Michael Cole, *The Pianoforte in the Classical Era* (Oxford: Clarendon Press, 1998), pp. 275–280.

Erard's concept was presumably influenced by contemporary advances in the manufacturing sector, where by the early nineteenth century wood was gradually being replaced by metal. This is evident, for instance, in the manufacture of mechanical devices requiring precision and durability. Although the demand for high-quality machines and tools was increasing, accuracy and firmness were lacking because 'nearly all machinery in the last quarter of the eighteenth century was made of wood with iron, brass and leather fittings'.[10] During this time machines were typically 'framed in wood, to which a minimum number of metal parts, usually blacksmith-forged, were fixed with nuts and bolts'; these machines required 'constant attention to make them work well, since the wood raked with humidity and temperature, causing the metal parts to lose adjustment very easily'.[11]

The solution was the shift from a partly-metal to an all-metal construction, wherever this was possible. The use of metal particularly in the frames and movable parts of machine tools, scientific instruments and mechanical contraptions considerably improved their stability and accuracy. One representative example is the industrial lathe. Until the end of the eighteenth century the lathe was typically built with iron components fixed on a wooden frame, a construction which was not rigid enough to allow for precision work. From around 1797 Henry Maudslay (1771–1831) introduced screw-cutting lathes that were entirely of metal construction, enabling the production of uniform precision screws that were suitable for industrial applications. In addition, by intentionally avoiding sharp interior angles, Maudslay's lathes were both functional and elegant.[12] Thus, the lathe 'went from being largely constructed of timber, and used to work wood, horn or ivory, to being a more robust iron-framed machine capable of standing up to the rigours of working metal'.[13] Utilising metal and making the parts of a device independent and replaceable became integral for industrial purposes. For example, Maudslay's 1807 patent for a table engine specified 'every part being fixed to, and supported by, a strong frame of cast-iron, perfectly detached from the building in which it stands' prevented it from being 'put out of order by the sinking of the foundations'.[14]

Metal was adopted in devices designed for the textile industry, which previously relied on wood. In 1788 Joseph Eve (1769–1835) devised a gin for cleaning cotton, which had 'the singular advantage of the rollers not being liable to be broken' due to their metal construction.[15] Likewise, the cotton gin invented in 1794 by Eli Whitney

---

[10]   Anthony P. Woolrich, 'The London Engineering Industry at the time of Henry Maudslay', in John Cantrell and Gillian Cookson (eds), *Henry Maudslay and the Pioneers of the Machine Age* (Stroud: Tempus, 2002), pp. 39–53, at p. 41.

[11]   Anthony P. Woolrich, 'Joseph Clement', in John Cantrell and Gillian Cookson (eds), *Henry Maudslay and the Pioneers of the Machine Age* (Stroud: Tempus, 2002), pp. 94–108, at p. 97.

[12]   John Cantrell, 'Henry Maudslay', in John Cantrell and Gillian Cookson (eds), *Henry Maudslay and the Pioneers of the Machine Age* (Stroud: Tempus, 2002), pp. 18–38, at p. 31.

[13]   Russell, *James Watt: Making the World Anew*, p. 56.

[14]   Quoted in John Cantrell, 'Henry Maudslay', pp. 25–26.

[15]   Angela Lakwete, *Inventing the Cotton Gin: Machine and Myth in Antebellum America* (Baltimore and London: Johns Hopkins University Press, 2003), pp. 40–44.

(1765–1825), which increased efficiency and productivity in cotton processing, consisted of numerous metal parts for the separation of the cotton fibre from the seed.[16]

Another field in which metal substituted wood was architecture, as observed in the design of windows. In the course of the eighteenth century, first iron and then also finer metals or alloys, such as copper, bronze and brass, were commonly used for the window frames of private and public buildings in Britain. This was due to the introduction and refinement of industrial processes that increased the availability and quality of metals for building purposes, while reducing their cost.[17] Unlike wooden windows, which were susceptible to warping, swelling or cracking under extreme weather conditions, metal windows were durable and functional, as well as fire-resistant. In addition, they met the contemporary needs for more light, air, comfort and luxury, since they could be made in thinner sections than timber and could be shaped in a variety of sizes and forms. In 1793 a contemporary writer pointed out that

> the change now taking place in the materials for sashes, skylights, fanlights, staircases etc from Wood to Metal, has besides the elegance of appearance, the advantages of strength and extensive durability. The difference of expense in the former and latter is so inconsiderable, as not to be worthy of notice; nay, in many cases, such as curved-lineal and Gothic work, the expense is less in Metal than in wood.[18]

The rise of the metal window trade toward the end of the eighteenth and the beginning of the nineteenth centuries was a direct result of the industrialisation and mechanisation of the building sector. However, it was also accelerated by other factors such as 'shortages of timber during the Napoleonic Wars, the campaign for non-combustible construction and the emergent functionalist doctrine', which led to the transformation of this trade 'from an individualistic craft-based system of production and distribution to an essentially factory-based one'.[19]

Arguably the most prominent case where the implementation of metal parts led to significant improvements was in the development of the steam engine, the symbol of industrialisation in Britain. Particularly with the introduction of the cast-iron working beam by the firm of Boulton & Watt, which replaced the earlier wooden beam on rotative steam engines from around 1800, as well as with the gradual adoption of metal for the supporting frame and moving parts, the steam engine became more efficient and reliable.[20] This innovative transition from wood to cast iron has been attributed to 'a combination of factors, including the scarcity, and possibly the cost, of timber for large beams during the Napoleonic Wars, the need to design durable steam engines for the tropical climate of the West Indies, and the needs of

---

[16] Lakwete, *Inventing the Cotton Gin*, pp. 47–57.

[17] Hentie L. Louw, 'The Rise of the Metal Window during the Early Industrial Period in Britain, c.1750–1830', *Construction History* 3 (1987), pp. 31–54.

[18] Quoted in Louw, 'The Rise of the Metal Window', pp. 43–44.

[19] Louw, 'The Rise of the Metal Window', pp. 50–51.

[20] James Andrew, Jeremy Stein, Jennifer Tann and Christine MacLeod, 'The Transition from Timber to Cast Iron Working Beams for Steam Engines: A Technological Innovation', *Transactions of the Newcomen Society* 70/1 (1998), pp. 197–220.

textile mills to be effectively fireproofed'.[21] This and the other examples discussed above highlight the increasing importance of the metalworking crafts in the creation of new designs and new products at a time when the pedal harp was becoming popular in Europe.

Standardisation, Rationalisation and Interchangeability: Model-based Harp Building

The second noteworthy aspect of Erard Grecian harps, which largely resulted from the technological developments discussed earlier, was the standardisation and rationalisation of manufacture. This process, which had began with Erard's Empire harps, was epitomised by the arrival of Erard's double-action harp. The organological inspection of surviving Grecian harps by Erard built in London between the early 1810s and the late 1830s has shown that they are uniform in terms of their design and construction; for example, all examined Grecian harps have almost identical overall dimensions, with a maximum height of 1,700 mm, a maximum width of 360 mm at the bottom of the soundboard and a maximum depth of 830 mm from capital to shoulder, with smaller components also being proportionally similar.[22] The main distinguishing trait of these instruments is their decoration, which to a certain extent is also standardised. In addition, most parts of Erard's Grecian harps were interchangeable, which meant that they could be built in batches and kept in stock, a process that Erard had started with the Empire model. Since the Grecian model remained consistent throughout its production, these parts could be fitted on demand on any instrument of this model produced by the firm, enabling the easier and faster assembly of new harps as well as the repair of old ones.

Keeping the model consistent also meant that the materials, moulds and templates required for the construction of the metal or wooden parts for Erard's double-action harp could be easily exchanged between the London and Paris branches. For example, in November 1814 Pierre informed Sébastien that 'the wood that we bought here recently is not dry enough. There is a good batch of wood set aside for the harps in our Paris branch. It would be very helpful if you could send us a small amount of it. They have the model for your new harp and they could cut it up in Paris. It is dry enough to use right away and you know, my dearest uncle, that it is

---

[21] Andrew et al, 'The Transition from Timber to Cast Iron Working Beams for Steam Engines', p. 212.

[22] Panagiotis Poulopoulos, Marisa Pamplona, Luise Richter and Niko Plath, 'Conservation Issues on Historical Pedal Harps: Preserving Tangible and Intangible Properties', in Pascale Vandervellen (ed.), *Preservation of Wooden Musical Instruments: Ethics, Practice and Assessment. Proceedings of 4th Annual Conference of the COST Action FP1302 WoodMusICK* (Brussels: Muziekinstrumentenmuseum, 2017), pp. 69–72, at p. 71. An early version of this article had been presented by the authors at the 4th annual conference of the COST Action FP1302 WoodMusICK (Wooden Musical Instrument Conservation and Knowledge), 'Preservation of Wooden Musical Instruments: Ethics, Practice and Assessment', Muziekinstrumentenmuseum, Brussels, 5 to 7 October 2017.

really difficult now to find wood on the market.'[23] Moreover, working from a model could help in saving raw materials and staff expenses. In April 1818, Pierre argued that he could drastically reduce the firm's labour costs, but that this 'would only be with your new model'.[24] Likewise, in July 1819 Pierre suggested that 'by giving 2 or 2/6 per harp to one of the good workers in order to ensure that the models are closely followed, the wood well used, the repairs done with care all will be fine'.[25] He also noted that 'a change in the machines is desirable in order to reduce the manpower that can only be diminished with new models ready made. Perhaps with new workers, without stopping the old harps, until one has got ahead by a certain number of new ones.'[26]

Sébastien Erard apparently anticipated high sales from his new double-action harp, investing in it and organising its production accordingly. This is reflected in the size of Erard's personnel in the years before and after the arrival of the double-action harp. A comparison of the expenses for wages has shown that between the late 1800s and the mid-1810s the Erard London branch doubled in size in terms of its inhouse workforce.[27] Thus, whereas in the years between 1807 and 1809 Erard's personnel comprised 30 to 35 workers of various specialisations, around 1815 the firm reportedly employed about 60 to 70 workers, presumably to cope with the more complex manufacture of the new harp as well as to meet an increase in orders.

Erard must have been quite confident about the commercial success of his new double-action harp and had envisioned its manufacture in large numbers. This is evident in the construction of the double-action pedal mechanism, which was arguably the most technically demanding component of Erard's Grecian model, requiring skilled precision work. In June 1817, Pierre wrote to his uncle Sébastien that 'all the parts that you had prepared for a thousand harps are used up, so that the workers in charge of mechanisms must prepare everything before assemblage, which always puts them behind. It would be extremely helpful if we could have new parts prepared, but if you make changes for next season, any work done ahead of time based on old models would become a pure loss.'[28] The preparation of parts for the mechanisms of 1,000 harps at a time when the firm produced less than 200 harps annually clearly demonstrates Erard's foresight and business acumen.

<hr>

23   See L 111, 11 November 1814, in Robert Adelson, Alain Roudier, Jenny Nex, Laure Barthel and Michel Foussard (eds), *The History of the Erard Piano and Harp in Letters and Documents, 1785–1959* (Cambridge: Cambridge University Press, 2015), pp. 562–564.

24   L 220, 10 April 1818. Adelson et al, *The History of the Erard Piano and Harp*, pp. 677–678, at p. 677.

25   L 263, 4 July 1819. Adelson et al, *The History of the Erard Piano and Harp*, pp. 722–723, at p. 722.

26   L 264, 9 July 1819. Adelson et al, *The History of the Erard Piano and Harp*, pp. 723–724, at p. 724.

27   Jenny Nex, *The Business of Musical-Instrument Making in Early Industrial London* (PhD Diss., London: Goldsmiths College, 2013), pp. 221–223.

28   L 197, 26 June 1817. Adelson et al, *The History of the Erard Piano and Harp*, pp. 652–654, at p. 653.

Standardisation and interchangeability had already been implemented in other industries during the late eighteenth century; for instance, they were key factors in the design of firearms. Military technology provided a strong impetus for industrialisation and large-scale production, since the army 'offered a unique mass market for relatively cheap and undifferentiated products'.[29] In France the military sector coexisted with large civilian markets, with guns being exported to 'Europe, the Levant, and the African slave trade'.[30] In order to effectively supervise and control the expanding firearms trade, French military engineers imposed standards that helped to build uniform and interchangeable parts. Interchangeability indicated that 'the parts of an artifact have been made so precisely that they can be assembled without a final "fitting"'.[31] This improved the quality and reliability of guns, while lowering the costs for their manufacture and repair, since semi-skilled workers could undertake tasks usually carried out by trained craftsmen.

Moreover, the introduction of novel techniques of mechanical drawing as well as the implementation of gauges, jigs and machinery enabled both armourers and military inspectors to verify that the finished components corresponded to the required manufacturing and operational tolerances. In this way, 'the production process itself acted as an intrinsic check on the proper conduct and workmanship of the artisan'.[32] This in turn allowed for a more objective comparison and evaluation of the final product, limiting the influence that armourers, arm merchants and examiners had on the production process.

Analogous procedures can be observed in furniture-making, where by the late eighteenth century standardisation and interchangeability were common. Especially in large firms, 'components were serially produced in batches' and 'fairly repetitive and routine items', such as table legs and feet, 'may have been made in quantity and stored ready-made for use when needed'.[33] Such work exemplified 'a rational use of time', since even when a firm was not producing complete pieces, its personnel, especially apprentices, could build components that could be used at a later stage for various products.[34]

Similar measures to increase the speed of production and consequently to correspond to potential demand were applied to the manufacture of machines for industrial applications. For example, the steam engines built by James Watt (1736–1819) and his partner Matthew Boulton (1728–1809) utilised standardised parts, which allowed for 'quicker initial construction and easier provision of spares in the event of

---

[29] Ken Alder, 'Innovation and Amnesia: Engineering Rationality and the Fate of Interchangeable Parts Manufacturing in France', *Technology and Culture* 38/2 (1997), pp. 273–311, at p. 276.

[30] Alder, 'Innovation and Amnesia', p. 285.

[31] Alder, 'Innovation and Amnesia', p. 275.

[32] Alder, 'Innovation and Amnesia', p. 275.

[33] Pat Kirkham, 'The London Furniture Trade, 1700–1870', *Furniture History* 24 (1988), pp. 1–219, at p. 13.

[34] Kirkham, 'The London Furniture Trade', p. 13.

a breakdown'.[35] Although comparing harps with steam engines, and Erard with Watt, may seem rather unusual, it is important to mention here one technological connection that until now has remained overlooked: in the early 1770s Watt conceived a 'double-acting' steam engine in which both the downwards and upwards strokes in the working cylinder developed power, thus increasing efficiency.[36] Introduced in 1775, Watt's 'double-acting' engine gradually replaced the earlier 'single-acting' engines, in the same manner that Erard's new double-action harp would supersede earlier single-action harps from the 1810s onwards. The concept of double motion to optimise function was further incorporated by Erard in his already mentioned 'double-escapement' action for pianos. Another unnoticed similarity is that, as on Watt's rotative steam engines, on which the linear, reciprocal motion of the piston was transformed by a system of a parallelogram and 'sun and planet' gear into the rotary motion of the flywheel, the pedal mechanism on harps essentially transmitted the vertical movement of the pedal rods inside the column of the harp to the levers on the neck, which in turn turned it into the circular movement of the forked discs.

Improving uniformity and efficiency, saving on materials and resources, and minimising waste seems to have been a major concern for inventors and manufacturers alike, regardless of whether they built machines, engines or musical instruments. In 1824 the prominent engineer Richard Roberts (1789–1864), who had been an employee of Henry Maudslay between 1814 and 1816, developed his most famous invention, a self-acting spinning mule for the textile industry, taking a patent for it in 1825. Roberts expected to receive many orders for his mule, since from the beginning of its production he utilised a system of templates and gauges which enabled the construction of identical standardised parts.[37]

Focusing on a single product, the double-action harp, and building it using a standardised, consistent model was an important ingredient for the financial survival of the Erard London branch. Although Sébastien Erard was a tireless inventor, he had probably also realised that continuous innovation could hinder business. This is evidenced by the fate of many talented engineers, who did not enjoy the financial rewards of their inventions because they were more interested in experimentation and novelty than in business planning and management. For instance, despite his mechanical ingenuity, the above-mentioned Roberts died impoverished due to his constant craving for invention. In contrast, the work of James Nasmyth (1808–1890), who is mainly known as the inventor of the steam hammer, was characterised by a brief and focused period of innovation. Once the steam hammer was in commercial production, Nasmyth stopped experimenting, offering essentially the same assortment of products for many years, a practice that enabled him to earn great profits.[38]

35　Russell, *James Watt: Making the World Anew*, p. 136.

36　Ben Marsden, *Watt's Perfect Engine: Steam and the Age of Invention* (New York: Columbia University Press, 2002), pp. 115–117.

37　Richard L. Hills, 'Richard Roberts', in John Cantrell and Gillian Cookson (eds), *Henry Maudslay and the Pioneers of the Machine Age* (Stroud: Tempus, 2002), pp. 54–73, at pp. 61–62.

38　Gillian Cookson, 'Introduction', in John Cantrell and Gillian Cookson (eds), *Henry Maudslay and the Pioneers of the Machine Age* (Stroud: Tempus, 2002), pp. 12–17, at pp. 15–16.

Simplification and Acceleration of Assembly: The Application of Screws

The standardisation, rationalisation and interchangeability of Erard Grecian harps are further reflected in the extensive use of screws on the wooden and metal parts. The examination of surviving specimens of the Grecian model has shown that each of these harps contains several hundred screws of different sizes, including both binding and adjusting screws. Binding screws 'are intended to mechanically hold two or more components rigidly together and thus must be able to withstand the stress from mechanical loading';[39] such screws were typically used to join the harp's wooden and/ or metal parts. On the other hand, adjusting screws 'are intended to permit controlled motion and adjustment of the relation between components',[40] in which case the critical factor is smoothness of operation rather than mechanical strength. Adjusting screws were mainly used on parts of the pedal mechanism, such as, for instance, on the small movable brass nuts that enable the regulation of intonation.

Additional evidence for the use of screws comes from the Erard workshop accounts between 1807 and 1809.[41] During this period the firm purchased screws regularly by the gross (an amount equal to twelve dozen) from various suppliers. For instance, in 1807 Erard bought screws from 'Mr Bond', while in 1808 from 'Elvans' and from 'Dockree'; in the same year the firm purchased a screwdriver. Prices varied depending on the size of the screws; for instance, on one occasion two-inch screws cost 4s 6d per gross.[42] Interestingly, Jacob Dockree was a 'Brass Turner, Galway St, Bath St, City Road' who also supplied Erat, one of Erard's competitors, with screws and metal components for harps between 1819 and 1822.[43]

Although the entries for screws in the Erard accounts do not include specific information about their size or design, it is most likely that the screws that Erard used were machine-made. Early machine-made screws are easily recognisable because they 'had blunt ends and were not self-starting', so 'it was necessary first to drill a lead hole'.[44] Such screws and metal pins, usually connecting wooden parts, are commonly found on Erard's Grecian harps: for example, on the shoulder at the back of the neck or on the round top of the capital, as revealed during the examination of

---

[39] Randall Chapman Brooks, *The Precision Screw in Scientific Instruments of the 17th–19th Centuries: with Particular Reference to Astronomical, Nautical and Surveying Instruments* (PhD Diss., Leicester: University of Leicester, 1989), p. 1.

[40] Brooks, *The Precision Screw in Scientific Instruments*, p. 1.

[41] Erard London Harp Ledgers, vol. 1, 'Expenses' section, pp. 1–62. A transcription of these accounts is included in Nex, *The Business of Musical-Instrument Making in Early Industrial London*, pp. 393–434.

[42] Nex, *The Business of Musical-Instrument Making in Early Industrial London*, p. 228. As a comparison, the price for 1,000 nails was only 3s.

[43] Mike Baldwin, *The Harp in Early Nineteenth-century Britain: Innovation, Business, and Making in Jacob Erat's Manufactory* (PhD Diss., London: London Metropolitan University, 2017), pp. 395, 436 and 450.

[44] Witold Rybczynski, *One Good Turn: A Natural History of the Screwdriver and the Screw* (New York: Scribner, 2000), p. 77.

Erard Nº 2631 with radiography. This feature was also detected by radiography on Erard Nº 8, a single-action harp built in Paris and dated 1805. This instrument has a broken drill part inside the shoulder, which indicates the use of a screw similar to that on Erard Nº 2631.[45]

It is worth noting that between 1810 and 1812, the first years in the production of double-action harps, Erard purchased various tools and accessories from Holtzapffel & Co, as will be discussed in detail in the next section. The relevant entries in the Holtzapffel & Co ledgers include several 'Screw Tools', which may refer to screwdrivers; a 'Screw Plate', presumably for the cutting of screws; and related items, such as 'Round headed Screw Bolts', 'Washers' and 'Nutts' of brass and iron in different sizes. The listed items also include measuring and marking tools such as 'Gouges', 'Callipers' and 'Compasses', as well as 'Pliers', 'Chissels', 'Gravers' and 'Files', which would have been used for metalworking.[46]

On Grecian harps, even the soundboard, the most sound-sensitive component, is fixed with several screws on its outer edges, where it meets the soundbox. These screws, usually covered by long strips of wood, were also visible in radiographs of Erard Nº 2631, an instrument that retains its original soundboard (Figure 8). In contrast, on Erard's earliest extant harps, which were made in Paris during the 1790s, the soundboard was typically glued to the soundbox and no screws were used, as confirmed by the investigation of an Erard harp bearing no serial number that dates from this period, housed at the Musikinstrumentenmuseum der Universität Leipzig, Leipzig (Inv. No. 402). Another change of design due to the use of screws concerns a removable Γ-shaped wooden block at the bottom junction of the capital and the neck, which allows access to the pedal mechanism. On Erard's Grecian harps, this block is firmly secured with a small screw on the brass plate housing the mechanism, whereas on Erard's earlier harps the same part is usually attached to the capital rather loosely with one or two wooden dowels.

The adoption of screws in the manufacture of harps demonstrates Erard's awareness of contemporary developments in industrial engineering, where high-quality screws were indispensable 'for accuracy of construction, accuracy of measurement and the promotion of interchangeability and mass production'.[47] Although the concept of the screw thread had been known in various civilisations since antiquity, for centuries screws were laboriously made by hand and sparingly used; it was only at the end of the eighteenth century that quality screws began to be produced in large numbers using machine tools.[48] Previously, as claimed in a German source on the history of screws, a smith specialising in tools ('Kleinschmied') who worked alone,

---

45 For more details see Beat Wolf, *Harp Archives* (Schaffhausen: Wolf, 2016), BW 33/250/008.

46 Records of Charles Holtzapffel and Company, University of Edinburgh Centre for Research Collections, Gen. 879F–882F (4 vols; F H and K between 1811 and 1822 and customers' journal 1892–1897). I am grateful to Jenny Nex for providing me with a transcription of these archives.

47 John Cantrell, 'Henry Maudslay', p. 29.

48 For more details on the historical development and importance of screws see Rudolf Kellermann and Wilhelm Treue, *Die Kulturgeschichte der Schraube* (Munich: Bruckmann,

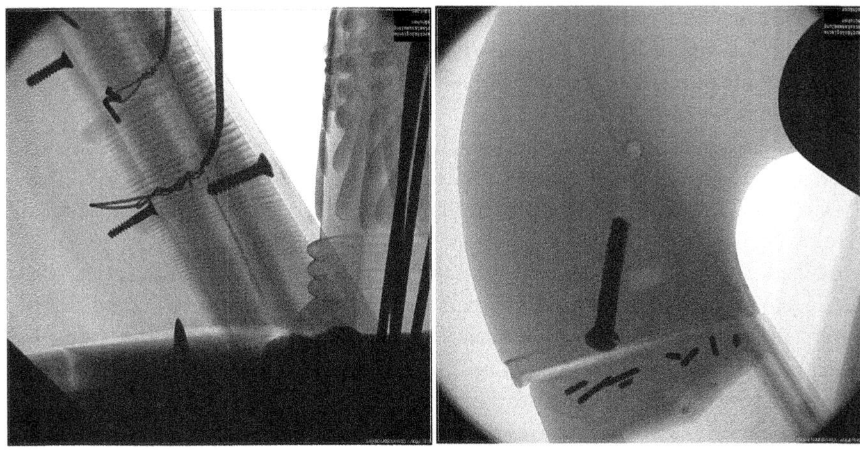

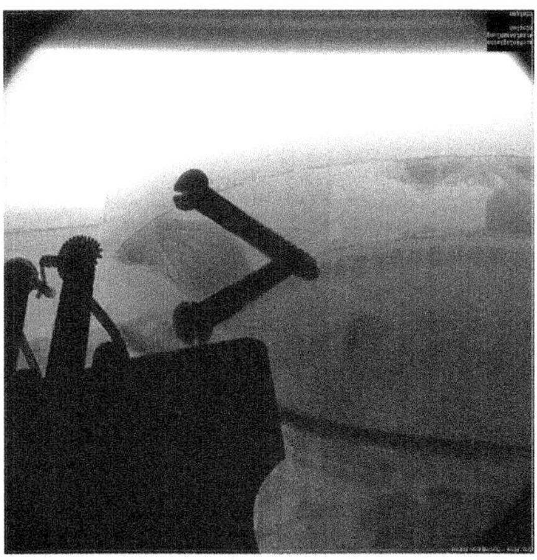

Figure 8. Screws of various sizes on the soundboard, shoulder and capital of Erard N°
2631, housed at the Deutsches Museum, Munich (Inv. No. 16147), revealed during its
examination with radiography.

usually as a subcontractor for a dealer, could make about 400 screws per day, the
length of which could not exceed 130 mm ('1/2 Zoll').[49]

Machine-made screws, on the other hand, could be produced faster, and
were better and cheaper in comparison to hand-made screws: around 1800 the
annual production of screws in Britain harp about 100,000 gross (about 15 million
screws), with a dozen screws costing less than twopence.[50] By the beginning of

---

1962) and Randall Chapman Brooks, 'Origins, Usage and Production of Screws: An
Historical Perspective', *History and Technology* 8/1 (1990), pp. 51–76.

49 Kellermann and Treue, *Die Kulturgeschichte der Schraube*, p. 186.

50 Rybczynski, *One Good Turn*, p. 76.

the nineteenth century, machine-made precision screws, which originated in the clock-making industry, had become irreplaceable devices, especially in the tool- and machine-making trades.[51] The musical instrument trade responded accordingly: although the building methods for some instruments, like lutes or violins, remained conventional, avoiding the use of screws or other metal parts, for new, highly mechanised instruments with numerous metal parts, such as pedal harps or pianos, screws eventually became obligatory.

The application of screws offered various advantages in comparison to earlier methods employed in wood- or metalworking trades, reducing production costs and minimising both the manufacture and repair time required. To begin with, utilising screws enabled a precise, uniform and stable construction, allowing for standardisation and serial production. Furthermore, screws were a less expensive, less time-consuming and more reliable alternative to traditional techniques that had been employed in several crafts. For example, the drying or removal of animal glue on wooden objects or the soldering of parts on metal objects were relatively slow and sometimes irreversible processes that usually demanded designated workshop spaces, facilities and resources.

In contrast, the application of screws allowed the development and use of interchangeable and adjustable components, which facilitated later repairs, replacements and modifications. Compared, for instance, to nails, which once fixed to surfaces remained static, screws could be easily removed or adjusted, enabling the mechanical regulation of structural or functional components. Screws also greatly assisted the manufacture of folding, portable objects, including musical instruments, which became quite popular in the course of the eighteenth century.[52] Additionally, the assembly of multiple parts with screws, in combination with jigs, moulds and templates, could often be carried out even by unskilled workers or apprentices, simplifying significantly the manufacturing procedures and permitting trained, experienced employees to focus on more demanding or complex tasks.

Most importantly, the increased use of high-quality precision screws played a major role in the design and development of new machines, which strongly affected production efficiency. This is evidenced, for example, by the machinery installed at the Portsmouth blockmaking manufactory, which in 1805 began building pulley blocks for ships under commission by the British Royal Navy. The advanced blockmaking machines at Portsmouth had been designed between 1802 and 1805 by Marc Isambard Brunel (1769–1849) in cooperation with Samuel Bentham (1757–1831) and Henry Maudslay.[53]

Recognised as the first application of mass-production practices that incorporated the use of machine tools in Britain, the Portsmouth block mill demonstrated the advantages of the new machine-based production system. Contrary to earlier and more traditional production methods employing manual skills and artisanal

---

[51]　Brooks, *The Precision Screw in Scientific Instruments*, p. 41.

[52]　For an overview of fashionable portable objects developed in the eighteenth century see Gianenrico Bernasconi, *Objets portatifs au Siècle des lumières* (Paris: CTHS, 2015).

[53]　Carolyn C. Cooper, 'The Portsmouth System of Manufacture', *Technology and Culture* 25/2 (1984), pp. 182–225, at pp. 192–198.

expertise, the various manufacturing tasks now relied on machines whose operation required 'the skill of a machine operator but not of a craftsman'.[54] Once these machines had been set up, 'no longer needed were the steady and dexterous hand, judgment, and timing that a turner, a joiner, or a carpenter, as well as a traditional blockmaker, took years of practice to acquire.' Instead 'that skill was, for most operations, "built into" the machines'.[55]

Thus, the use of screws enabled the construction of new machines that were not just 'replacements for traditional craft methods', but 'tools that were capable of previously unimagined accuracy'.[56] Precision screws were the catalyst that eventually transferred the control of production from human hands (and minds) to increasingly sophisticated, automated machines. These 'self-acting machines that could replace hand-work' were characterised by 'the 'degree of accuracy embodied in their construction, and which they were capable of reproducing', bringing 'large-scale standardised and interchangeable manufacture into prospect'.[57] Allowing 'structures to be held together, and to be dismantled again', the screw can be considered 'a building block of the modern industrial world, and one that is easy to take for granted'.[58]

The extended usage of machinery at the Portsmouth block mill was combined with new production strategies, such as division of labour, whereby manufacturing tasks were arranged by skill rather than by craft, as well as recycling odd-sized, discarded materials, thus increasing efficiency and decreasing costs.[59] Because of these measures, 'relatively few, less skilled workers were able to turn out large numbers of uniform wooden and metal parts for assembly in low-cost products of standardised design'.[60] A comparable production scheme had been implemented a few decades earlier by the famous potter Josiah Wedgwood (1730–1795). In order to mass produce pottery for middle-class customers, Wedgwood had devised moulds which enabled 'semi-skilled workers rather than master potters' to 'turn out saleable articles', thus aiming 'to make such machines of men as cannot err'.[61] Based on the Portsmouth model, the army boot and shoe factory established in 1810 by Brunel at Battersea utilised machinery that was 'operated not by skilled cobblers but by

---

54 Cooper, 'The Portsmouth System of Manufacture', p. 207.

55 Cooper, 'The Portsmouth System of Manufacture', p. 207.

56 Rybczynski, *One Good Turn*, p. 109.

57 Ben Russell, 'The British Machine Tool Industry (1790–1825)', *Ferrum: Nachrichten aus der Eisenbibliothek der Stiftung der Georg Fischer AG* 81 (2009), pp. 37–44, at p. 41.

58 David Waller, *Iron Men: How One London Factory Powered the Industrial Revolution and Shaped the Modern World* (London and New York: Anthem Press, 2016), p. 28.

59 Cooper, 'The Portsmouth System of Manufacture', pp. 194–195.

60 Cooper, 'The Portsmouth System of Manufacture', p. 225.

61 Richard Tames, *Josiah Wedgwood: An illustrated life of Josiah Wedgwood, 1730–1795* (2nd edn; Aylesbury: Shire Publications Ltd, 1984), p. 25. See also Neil McKendrick, 'Josiah Wedgwood: An Eighteenth-Century Entrepreneur in Salesmanship and Marketing Techniques', *The Economic History Review* 12/3 (1960), pp. 408–433, at pp. 408–409.

some 25 unskilled disabled army veterans, who could be trained in a matter of hours'
resulting in 'greater precision, uniformity and economy'.[62]

The intense organisation, mechanisation and specialisation of manufacture
exemplified at Portsmouth revolutionised industrial production, paving the way for
future developments in other manufacturing sectors and setting the standards for
the years to come. It is tempting to assume that a person with the engineering curiosity of Sébastien Erard would have been informed about the latest advances in industrial manufacturing in Britain either personally or through his nephew. For example,
in April 1818 Pierre Erard visited a London sawmill producing the veneer wood for
harps. He was surprised to see large circular saws able to cut very thin veneers;
reportedly, one of the saws had a diameter of 19 feet (about 5.8m). Pierre informed
his uncle that these saws were operating on a machine driven by a 16-horsepower
engine made 'by someone named Brunel, a Frenchman who has established the
famous Black House in Plymouth, which you have heard so much about!'[63]

Judging from Pierre's descriptions, it is most likely that the sawmill he observed
was the steam-powered veneer-cutting sawmill that Brunel had built in 1806–1807
at Battersea. The site had been severely damaged by a fire in 1814, but was rebuilt
and fully operating again in 1816, two years before Pierre's 1818 visit.[64] The fact that
Sébastien had 'heard so much about' the achievements of his compatriot suggests
that he was aware of Brunel's novel production methods.[65] Besides, Pierre was occasionally going to the docks to buy wood at low prices,[66] so he might have witnessed
first-hand the new manufacturing systems adopted by the British Navy.

Serial Numbers and Manufacturing Marks on Erard Harps

The novel design and manufacturing strategies described above allowed Erard to
produce harps in series. This is confirmed by the firm's adoption of a characteristic
serial numbering system, which can permit the identification and chronological
classification of Erard harps and which is worth analysing in depth. The serial numbers of Erard harps are typically found in the inscriptions engraved on one of the

---

[62]　Colin Thom, 'Fine Veneers, Army Boots and Tinfoil: New Light on Marc Isambard
　　　Brunel's Activities in Battersea', *Construction History* 25 (2010), pp. 53–67, at p. 60.

[63]　L 220, 10 April 1818. Adelson et al, *The History of the Erard Piano and Harp*, pp. 677–678.

[64]　Thom, 'Fine Veneers, Army Boots and Tinfoil', pp. 57–63.

[65]　The connections and influences between Erard and other leading manufacturers and
　　　entrepreneurs of his time have been discussed in Panagiotis Poulopoulos, 'Engineering
　　　the Harp: The Erard London Firm 1800–1830', unpublished paper presented at the 37th
　　　Symposium of the Scientific Instrument Society (SIC), 'Instruments and the "Empire of
　　　Man over Things"', Session 'Sound', Leiden and Haarlem, 3 to 7 September 2018.

[66]　'The beautiful wood in the shops is very expensive. I learned that the best way to buy is to
　　　buy at the docks and to export it directly'. L 204, 25 July 1817. Adelson et al, *The History of
　　　the Erard Piano and Harp*, pp. 661–662, at p. 661; 'by buying in bulk and in the *Docks* one
　　　would have the best price'. L 263, 4 July 1819. Adelson et al, *The History of the Erard Piano
　　　and Harp*, pp. 722–723, at p. 723; 'since we would buy in the docks for export, there would
　　　be 21/2d in duties to deduct from the above prices'. L 266, 5 August 1819. Adelson et al, *The
　　　History of the Erard Piano and Harp*, pp. 725–726, at p. 726.

two brass plates housing the mechanism, which will be discussed later. Due to the fact that in these inscriptions the number is usually placed next to the word 'Patent', the serial number has been often been mistaken for a patent number. The number on the brass plate of an Erard harp, which will hereafter be referred to as the official or primary serial number, is also listed in the surviving ledgers of Erard's London and Paris branches. Since this number is often supplemented in the ledgers with brief details of the instrument as well as with the dates of entry and sale, it can help to identify and accurately date surviving Erard harps.[67]

The earliest Erard harps, which were built in Paris during the late 1780s or early 1790s, did not bear any serial numbers. As already mentioned, the features of these harps were not uniform, suggesting that they were rather experimental instruments produced on a small scale. However, when the London branch started manufacturing harps of a more standardised design based on Erard's 1794 patent with the fourchettes mechanism, the firm began to number these instruments systematically and consistently, with the official number engraved on the brass plate. On some Grecian harps, the official number has been additionally engraved on smaller parts of the pedal mechanism, such as on rectangular bars connecting the two brass pates.

Each of the two Erard branches in London and Paris employed a single numbering sequence for harps throughout the firm's production. This sequence, which started on Erard's single-action Empire model in the late 1790s, continued on the double-action Grecian model that was launched in 1811. Therefore, Erard N° 1377, the first double-action harp sold by Erard in London on 24 October 1811, was not given the number 1, but simply continued the numbering from Erard N° 1376, a single-action harp. The serial number of Erard harps thus indicated the entire production of the branch rather than the production of a particular harp model. This was in contrast to Erard pianos, on which different sequences were used for different models (square piano, grand piano, etc.).

However, apart from the visible official serial number on the brass plate, Erard harps also bear secondary numbers and other marks, which are usually stamped on hidden or inaccessible areas of wooden parts. On Erard's Grecian model, the secondary serial numbers are typically stamped on a removable Γ-shaped block at the bottom junction of the capital and the neck, which allows access to the pedal mechanism. However, they may also be located on the underside of the neck near the shoulder or inside the pedalbox. On some harps the secondary number can even be found engraved on parts of the mechanism.

The examination of several Erard Grecian harps has not revealed any correlation between the official serial numbers and the secondary numbers. On some harps, the secondary number stamped on the wooden parts is higher than the official number engraved on the brass plate, while on others it is lower. Only exceptionally has the same number been used on both metal and wooden parts. Moreover, whereas there

---

[67] For more details see Panagiotis Poulopoulos, 'Serial Numbers as Information Source and Tool for Building Virtual Instrument Collections', in *Proceedings of the CIMCIM Conference 'Global Crises and Music Museums: representing music after the pandemic'*, *London (Royal College of Music-Horniman Museum and Gardens), 6 to 8 September 2021* (forthcoming).

are harps that have been stamped several times with the same secondary number, there are also harps that bear up to four different secondary numbers. Although archival sources offer little information on the meaning and role of secondary numbers in Erard's workshop operation, they most likely aimed to facilitate the assembly of various harp parts.

Apart from secondary numbers, the wooden parts of Erard Grecian harps often bear initials that are stamped close to these numbers, particularly on the underside of the neck near the shoulder. The most common initials are 'RB', found on harps built between 1817 and 1821, although there are harps made before, during or after these dates bearing other initials, such as 'R', 'K', 'S', 'H', 'C', 'JC' and 'WH'. These initials and other inscriptions presumably referred to certain workers or workshop sections in Erard's London manufactory or to subcontractors who may have supplied finished or roughly worked wooden harp parts to Erard.

Erard harps are also occasionally marked with additional symbols and inscriptions, such as names and dates, which can be found on the metal or wooden parts. Although some of these marks obviously point to later restoration work, most have been applied during the manufacture of the instruments. For example, on several Grecian harps the levers of the eight pedals inside the pedalbox have been engraved with Roman (I, II, III, etc.) or Arabic numerals (1, 2, 3, etc.). Additionally, small holes corresponding to each pedal's number are punched onto a rectangular wooden plank above the pedal levers, apparently to facilitate the correct positioning and fixing of the pedals inside the pedalbox. Considering the size and output of Erard's workshop, these manufacturing marks must have been indispensable for organising and controlling the various stages of production. Although initials of workers and manufacturing marks can be occasionally found on keyboard instruments from earlier dates, it seems that this practice became widespread with the gradual industrialisation and expansion of instrument-making.

The addition of hidden manufacturing marks was common in contemporary workshops arranged for serial production of standardised items. For instance, a similar marking system was used by Gillow, an important furniture manufacturer in Lancaster during the early nineteenth century. Although the firm's name would be prominently displayed on a piece of furniture, hidden inscriptions and stamps were also added on various parts. Such marks enabled the internal communication and quality control among numerous craftsmen that were occupied in different departments. For example, the application of 'signatures and dates would have enabled a journeyman to identify his work for payment purposes', while simultaneously enabling 'his employer to monitor and check the quality of his employee's workmanship'.[68]

In the trade of scientific instruments, concealed numbers often indicate production in batches. This is evidenced, for instance, in surveying instruments built in the early industrial era, which 'were assembled in small groups or batches, but because the parts were only approximately interchangeable, each was identified by a number within the batch, so that all components with a particular number could be finely-adjusted to fit that individual instrument'; interestingly, 'only by dismantling such

---

[68] Susan Stuart, 'A Survey of Marks, Labels, and Stamps used on Gillow and Waring & Gillow Furniture 1770–1960', *Regional Furniture* 12 (1998), pp. 58–93, at p. 59.

instruments do these numbers come to light, but they give an idea of the size of batches produced in an individual workshop'.[69] In other cases, concealed signatures point to a system of subcontracting: for example, an extant Bohnenberger gyroscope is conspicuously inscribed with the retailers' details 'W. & S. JONES, // 30 Holborn // LONDON', but also bears the hidden signature of the actual maker, William Stiles, who built the instrument in June 1831.[70]

The use of official serial numbers and secondary numbers, initials and other manufacturing marks on Erard harps can be demonstrated on Erard Nº 2631. Although the official serial number '2631' is engraved on the brass plate, the harp is additionally stamped '2634 RB' on the underside of the neck, while the number '2634' is also stamped on several wooden parts inside the pedalbox (Figure 9). Additionally, the pedal levers are engraved with Roman numerals and the wooden plank above them is punched with holes compliant with the pedal number.

The application of official and secondary numbers on Erard harps may have served several purposes. To begin with, numbers helped to identify parts of the same instruments while they were being worked on in different areas within a workshop. Furthermore, they enabled quality control, since once a defect was found in the manufacture of a particular product batch, the numbers could help in finding further items which may also be affected. In addition, they assisted the control of instruments in stock and the organisation of sales records. Numbers also facilitated the identification of instruments for after-sales service and repairs as well as for the supply of replacement parts. Moreover, in combination with signatures and inscriptions, they were essential in preventing counterfeits and in tracing stolen items. Finally, Erard's adoption and continuation of a single numbering sequence representing the firm's total output, which reached quite high numbers after the introduction of the double-action harp, certainly raised Erard's profile as a harp manufacturer.[71]

The serial numbering and marking of Erard harps can be better understood when examined within the broader context of the musical instrument-making business, where standardisation and large-scale manufacture became widespread in the course of the nineteenth century. From the perspective of serial production, the Erard harp shared similarities with the harp lute, a hybrid plucked instrument that

---

[69] Morrison-Low, *Making Scientific Instruments in the Industrial Revolution*, p. 29.

[70] Alison D. Morrison-Low, 'The Gentle Art of Persuasion: Advertising Instruments during Britain's Industrial Revolution', in Alison D. Morrison-Low, Sara J. Schechner and Paolo Brenni (eds), *How Scientific Instruments Have Changed Hands. History of Science and Medicine Library 56: Scientific Instruments and Collections* (Leiden and Boston: Brill, 2017), pp. 43–56, at pp. 44–46.

[71] For more details on the role of serial numbers on Erard harps see Panagiotis Poulopoulos and Julin Lee, 'A Synergy of Form, Function and Fashion in the Manufacture of the Erard Harp', in Marco A. Pérez and Emanuele Marconi (eds), *Wooden Musical Instruments: Different Forms of Knowledge* (Paris: Cité de la Musique – Philharmonie de Paris, 2018), pp. 367–398, at pp. 389–390. On the interpretation of serial numbers on musical instruments see also Arnold Myers, 'Use of Serial Numbers in Dating Musical Instruments', in Stéphane Vaiedelich and Anne Houssay (eds), *'Dater l'instrument de musique': Actes de la journée d'étude du 6 juin 2009* (Paris: Cité de la musique, 2009), pp. 36–47, at pp. 36–41.

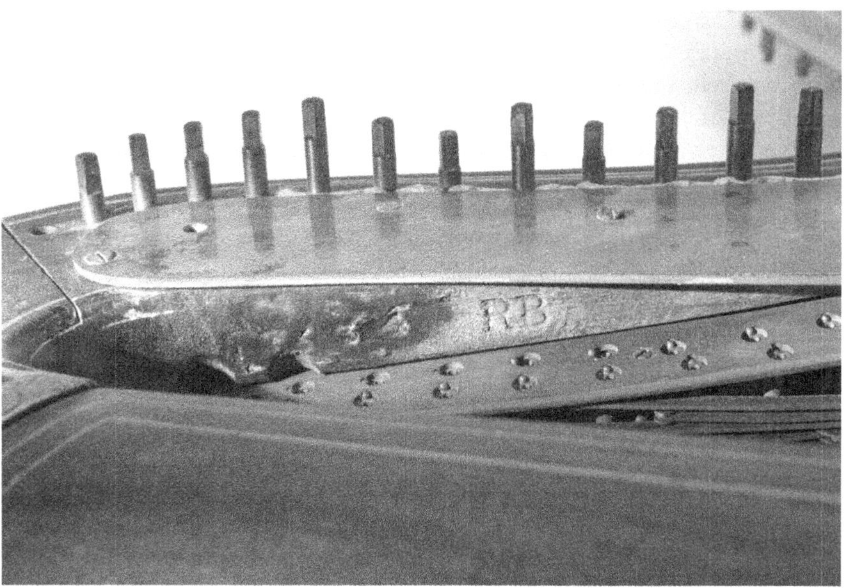

Figure 9. Detail of the stamp '2634 RB' on the underside of the neck on Erard N° 2631. Deutsches Museum, Munich (Inv. No. 16147).

combined features of the harp, lute, cittern and guitar.[72] The harp lute was introduced in London around 1807 by Edward Light (c.1747/8–c.1832), being advertised as a portable substitute for the harp. The popularity of Erard's harps may have influenced the development of harp lutes, and advocates of harp lutes must have been familiar with the firm's instruments and production methods. For instance, a 'Mr. Levien', who in 1819 purchased Erard N° 2613,[73] was probably Mordaunt Levien (c.1784–1854), the inventor of the *guitare harpe*, a variation of the harp guitar devised by Light .[74]

[72] The interaction between the harp and other plucked stringed instruments has been discussed in Panagiotis Poulopoulos, 'The Harp, Lyre, Lute, Cittern, and Guitar around 1800', unpublished paper presented at the 4th Colloquium of the Consortium for Guitar Research, Sidney Sussex College, Univeristy of Cambridge, 9 to 12 April 2016.

[73] Erard London Harp Ledgers, vol. 2, p. 124.

[74] For more details on Levien see Hayato Sugimoto, 'Mordaunt Levien and his Instruments', *The Galpin Society Journal* 71 (2018), pp. 57–72. According to Sugimoto, between 1817 and 1819 Levien may have lived in different (or dual) addresses. Although the address at 83 Baker Street listed in the Erard ledgers is not corroborated by other documents, Levien may have resided there temporarily or used it as an alternative business address, since it was located at the same London area as his other reported addresses.

Like the earliest harps made by Erard, the earliest harp lutes built between 1807 and 1813 were characterised by a diversity of features and were not numbered.[75] However, from around 1813, when the harp lute 'had reached the stage of virtual completion and standardisation',[76] Light began using serial numbers on his instruments, starting from around 450, presumably to take into account the unnumbered instruments produced in previous years. As in the case of Erard's harps, the numbered harp lutes are more uniform when compared to earlier specimens, having a consistent design and identical dimensions. For Light, the application of serial numbers was an additional measure against forgery, since in his *New and Compleat Instructions for playing on the Harp-Lute* he warned customers that only those instruments that are numbered and bear his name and address have been produced under his authorisation and are thus 'the real Harp-Lutes':

> As many imperfect imitations of this admired little Instrument have crept abroad, & are imposed upon Ladies as E.L's real Harp-Lute. The Inventor thinks it here a duty incumbent on him to declare, that all Instrument manufactor'd for him, & by his order, are numbered, & have also his name & address upon them, & that no others are the real Harp-Lutes.[77]

Another contemporary example of serial numbering on plucked stringed instruments concerns the work of Louis Panormo (1784–1862), the leading maker of guitars in nineteenth-century London. Panormo started numbering his guitars around 1823, when he began to use fully printed labels on his instruments. These labels included serial numbers that, contrary to Erard, did not show the firm's total production, since Panormo seems to have started with the number 401. As has been pointed out about Panormo's numbering system, 'with a couple of exceptions, each year the first digit changed by one, for example 1823 was in the 400 range, 1824 in the 500s and so on, until sometime in 1828 when another system was introduced'.[78] The change in Panormo's numbering is confirmed by the existence of an enharmonic guitar from 1829 bearing the number 1766.[79]

The serial production of Erard harps also resembled in many aspects the production of pianos in Britain. In the early nineteenth century the piano industry witnessed rapid development and growth, during which diversity and individuality gave place to standardisation and serial production.[80] One of the leading firms behind the establishment of the piano was Clementi & Co, the firm directed by Muzio Clementi

---

75 Hayato Sugimoto, *Harp Lutes in Britain, 1800–1830: A Study of the Inventor, Edward Light and His Instruments* (PhD Diss., Edinburgh: University of Edinburgh, 2015), pp. 231–232.

76 Sugimoto, *Harp Lutes in Britain*, p. 232.

77 Edward Light, *New and Compleat Instructions for playing on the Harp-Lute* (London: Light, c.1813), p. 1. I am grateful to Hayato Sugimoto for bringing this source to my attention.

78 James Westbrook, 'Louis Panormo: "The only Maker of Guitars in the Spanish style"', *Early Music* 41/4 (2013), pp. 571–584, at p. 574.

79 James Westbrook, 'General Thompson's Enharmonic Guitar', *Soundboard, Quarterly Magazine of the Guitar Foundation of America* 38/4 (2012), pp. 45–52, at p. 48.

80 Cole, *The Pianoforte in the Classical Era*, pp. 272–291.

(1752–1832), a renowned musician, composer and music publisher. Largely due to Clementi's broad international network and great reputation within European musical circles, Clementi & Co became the largest exporter of musical instruments from England during the early nineteenth century.

Travelling extensively and taking advantage of his multilingual abilities as well as his management skills, Clementi attracted many customers and business partners across Europe. Even the trade embargos that were enforced during the Napoleonic Wars did not stop the firm from making and selling thousands of instruments, which were praised in contemporary reviews for their fine quality and sound. Despite facing strong competition from other piano manufacturers, and surviving a devastating fire in 1807, Clementi & Co managed to produce 1,100 to 1,200 pianos per year around 1810–1811 at the zenith of his output, being second in the London piano trade only to the Broadwood firm.[81]

There are several connections between Clementi and Erard, which enable a comparison of their profiles as musical instrument manufacturers, especially from the perspective of serial production.[82] Firstly, Muzio Clementi was a lifetime contemporary of Sébastien Erard: both were born in 1752, with Clementi outliving Erard only by one year, since he died in 1832. Therefore, the two men lived in the same historical and sociocultural background and must have similarly experienced the changes in the music business in the decades either side of 1800.

Secondly, both Clementi and Erard were talented immigrants who established successful musical instrument firms in London during the early nineteenth century. This suggests that they were equally aware of the potentials and challenges of a global market that was expanding in the east and west. Thirdly, Erard and Clementi were acquainted on a professional, perhaps also a personal, level. In 1803 Clementi was already reporting that one of his Russian customers, a 'Mr. Davidoff', wanted, apart from a grand pianoforte, 'a harp elegant and good; I told him he may rely on me: that is, if ours without the least partiality be not as good now as *Erard's*, we shall send him one if his: but remember well – *elegant* and *good*. He is in no hurry. Direct both instruments to Baron de Rall Banker in Petersburg. Remember once for all that the Russians in general possess good ears for *sound* tho' they have none for *sense* and *style*.'[83]

---

[81] Leif Sahlqvist, 'Clementi & Co 1798–1830: Pianoforte Manufacture in London' (available at http://www.friendsofsquarepianos.co.uk/the-clementi-page/, published 26 May 2013, updated 4 February 2014, accessed 3 June 2022), pp. 1–34, at pp. 4–17.

[82] It should be mentioned that although Clementi was undoubtedly at the head of Clementi & Co and played a significant role in the development of the pianos produced by the firm, the piano-making staff were led by Frederick William Collard (baptised 1772–1860), later together with his brother William Frederick Collard (baptised 1776–1866). It is also worth noting that the piano patents used by the firm were either bought in, as in the case of the 1798 patent by William Southwell (c.1736/7–1825), or were registered in the name of William Frederick Collard (1811 and 1821), rather than by Clementi. I am thankful to the second anonymous reviewer for this information.

[83] Letter dated 17 August 1803, quoted in Leon Plantinga, *Clementi: His Life and Music* (London and New York: Oxford University Press, 1977), pp. 192–193.

A study of the Erard ledgers shows that during the 1810s the firm sold numerous harps to Clementi & Co, while Clementi is often mentioned in the correspondence between Pierre and Sébastien Erard. For instance, in January 1815 Pierre wrote, 'one of Clementi's colleagues came to ask what discounts we would give them on harps, as they wish to send double actions to India'.[84] Fourthly, although in London Erard focused on the manufacture of harps, he was simultaneously involved in the manufacture of pianos, which took place mainly in his Paris branch, and he may have thus been well-informed about Clementi's production and marketing strategies.

In contrast to Erard and other makers, who used a single sequence for all the instruments they produced, regardless of the different instrument types or models, Clementi & Co applied multiple numbering and marking which reflected the firm's manufacturing procedures. The analysis of more than 300 surviving instruments has shown that pianos by Clementi & Co were numbered with 'a rather sophisticated system, apparently more elaborated than for other instrument manufacturers'.[85] This system included as many as four different serial numbers as well as various manufacturing marks, labels, inscriptions and stamps applied on a single instrument.

Regarding the Clementi & Co numbering, a stamped number in the outer left-hand corner (A number) denoted the production of a particular piano model (square, grand, upright, etc.), while a number written in ink usually on the wrest plank in the inner right-hand corner (B number) indicated the total production of the firm since 1798. For example, a square piano by Clementi & Co, built in London in 1805 and housed in the Deutsches Museum (Inv. No. 1991–735), bears the stamped number 4095 (A number) and the inked number 4447 (B number).[86] This indicates that from 1798 until 1805 the firm had produced 4,095 square pianos out of a total of 4,447 different pianos and other keyboard instruments.

A third number (C number) was usually stamped on the spine of the piano case, which was constructed in the cabinet-making department of the firm. Finally, a fourth handwritten or stamped number (D Number), often accompanied with a name, referred to individual Clementi & Co employees. These numbers were added during the different stages of production: the C number was stamped on the piano case, which was the first component that had to be completed, whereas the D number was usually applied to smaller parts, such as the nameboard, the action or the keys, that were built separately from the case in batches. The A number would be stamped on a piano once the internal parts (action, wrest plank, tuning pins, etc.) had been installed. The B number was most likely written after the instrument was finished and was ready for transport and sale.[87]

A study of the numbers and marks on Erard's Grecian harps suggests that the Erard London branch operated with a comparable pattern of batch production. The wooden parts used to construct the soundbox, neck, column and pedalbox of the

---

84   L 129, 17 January 1815. Adelson et al, *The History of the Erard Piano and Harp*, pp. 581–582, at p. 581.

85   Sahlqvist, 'Clementi & Co', p. 8.

86   For more details of this instrument see Hubert Henkel, *Besaitete Tasteninstrumente. Deutsches Museum. Kataloge der Sammlungen. Musikinstrumenten-Sammlung* (Frankfurt am Main: Bochinsky, 1994), pp. 229–230.

87   Sahlqvist, 'Clementi & Co', pp. 8–15.

Figure 10. Detail of the stamped and inked numbers on the removable Γ-shaped blocks of two Erard Grecian harps. Left: Erard Nº 1945. Hospitalfield, Arbroath. Note the secondary number '1989' and the letter 'K' stamped below the inked official number '1945'. Right: Erard Nº 4568. Musical Instrument Museums Edinburgh (MIMEd), Edinburgh (Inv. No. 176). Note the secondary number '4622' stamped above the inked official number '4568'.

harp were presumably built in batches by Erard's cabinet makers, and after being stamped with the secondary number discussed earlier, would be prepared for decoration. Since Erard harps varied considerably in the type and complexity of their decoration, as will be described in the next chapter, the parts used for the plainer instruments within a batch would be ready for assembly and finishing sooner than those demanding more time for a finer or customised embellishment. In the meantime, Erard's machinists would construct the pedal mechanism, on which the official serial number would be engraved. During the final stage of production, the mechanism would be mounted on the completed and decorated wooden frame and the instrument would be ready for a last inspection, stringing and tuning.[88]

It is important to point out that the removable Γ-shaped block mentioned earlier, a piece that was most likely added at the very end, bears both the official and secondary numbers. It is also worth noting that the official serial number on this block is written in ink rather than stamped, suggesting that it was added at the last minute, thus providing flexibility in case the mechanisms needed to be swapped between harps (Figure 10). This is quite similar to Clementi & Co, where stamped

---

[88] Erard's serial numbering and marking system has been discussed in Panagiotis Poulopoulos, 'Serial Production and Trademarking on Historic Musical Instruments from Ruckers to Erard', unpublished paper presented at the Oberseminar, Deutsches Museum, Munich, 3 July 2017. I am grateful to musical instrument conservator Susanne Wittmayer for her useful comments on piano manufacture and her suggestions on Erard's production and numbering methods during this presentation.

numbers were added during production, but an inked number was applied upon completion of a piano.

The details described above show that the wooden and metal parts were built in groups in separate departments of Erard's manufactory and were not numbered simultaneously. A further fact confirming the production in batches is the minor discrepancy observed between the official and secondary numbers. In most cases, only the final one or two digits of the number engraved on the brass plate are different (higher or lower) to the number stamped on the wooden parts.

Analysing Erard within the Context of Mechanical Engineers in London

Although it is legitimate to examine Erard's profile against other eminent musical instrument manufacturers, such as Broadwood or Clementi, it is also interesting to compare him to some leading mechanical engineers in London. One of them is the already-mentioned Henry Maudslay, who has been credited with important improvements in the tool- and machine-making industry. Although almost a generation younger than Sébastien Erard, Maudslay represents the inventiveness and entrepreneurship that also characterised Erard. A comparison between the two men is therefore feasible both in terms of their professional activities as well as in terms of their biography, especially since both Erard and Maudslay died in 1831.

To begin with, both men were familiar with the patent system, which to some extent promoted and rewarded experimentation and innovation. Between 1805 and 1824, Maudslay took six patents,[89] almost as many as Erard, who was granted seven patents for the harp and piano between 1794 and 1822.[90] In addition, they both used publicity to boost their image as inventors: Maudslay was registered in Johnstone's trade directory of 1818 as 'Maudsley, H. *Patent machine manufac.*', similarly to Erard who was listed as 'Erard, Seb. *Patent harp manufacturer*'.[91] Moreover, Maudslay's workshop attracted several talented young engineers, allowing them to gain valuable training and experience that they used in their future careers.[92] Likewise, Erard's London manufactory was a hotspot for aspiring harp makers, such as Stumpff, Delveaux or Schwieso, who later opened their own businesses, as will be described in Chapter Four.

---

[89] Christine MacLeod, *Inventing the Industrial Revolution: The English Patent System, 1660–1800* (Cambridge: Cambridge University Press, 1988), pp. 105–106. For more details of Maudslay's patents see Cantrell, 'Henry Maudslay', pp. 24–25.

[90] For more details of Erard's seven patents see Woodcroft, *Patents for Inventions*, pp. 28, 40, 46, 55, 60, 88–89 and 90. Although developed by Sébastien, the 1821 and 1822 patents (Nº 4631 and Nº 4670 respectively) were actually registered in Britain by Erard's nephew Pierre.

[91] Andrew Johnstone, *Johnstone's London Commercial Guide and Street Directory* (London: Barnard & Farley, 1818), pp. 118 and 325, respectively.

[92] Cookson, 'Introduction', pp. 13–15.

A further element connecting Erard and contemporary engineers in Maudslay's circle is a skill in draughtsmanship. Before becoming an instrument maker, Erard had reportedly studied mechanics, geometry and drawing;[93] his drawing abilities are evidenced by numerous detailed sketches found in his letters. Similarly, despite their diverse backgrounds, many of the engineers employed by Maudslay were competent draughtsmen.[94] This probably resulted from the prevailing notion in Britain that in order to improve design there was a 'need to promote drawing and other artistic skills among skilled workmen'.[95] In the course of the eighteenth century, 'Arts based on technical drawing – that is dependent upon drawing instruments such as compasses, protractors and rulers – developed to standards of excellence which suppressed foreign competition far more effectively than arts dependent upon freehand drawing skills.'[96] It is likely that 'the tendency in British culture to concentrate on technical drawing and planning was associated with the realization of the difficulty in competing in freehand "taste based" fields of design. In the advanced development of such skills lay the roots of later eighteenth-century economic triumphs in the field of mechanized production.'[97]

For large firms producing standardised objects based on specific models with precise and consistent sizes and dimensions, technical drawing became important as it 'promised to organize the workshop on both procedural and social levels'.[98] This was related to the growth of the manufacturing sectors during the eighteenth century: 'Businesses which expanded rapidly, taking on a far greater number of commissions than could be serviced by a workshop master and a group of assistants, needed numerous employees who could handle work from conception onward. The premium, therefore, was upon training individuals to model, draw and master core business skills such as mensuration.'[99] For British manufacturers the notion of design, exemplified by the intensive application of technical drawings, templates and models, 'was conceived of as a process of ordering and placing shape upon disorder'.[100]

In the early industrial era, drawings and three-dimensional models were important means through which artisans, engineers and mechanics could describe, rationalise, improve and communicate their work.[101] As portable media that often

---

93 Adelson et al, *The History of the Erard Piano and Harp*, p. 5.

94 Cookson, 'Introduction', pp. 13–14.

95 John Styles, 'Design for Large-Scale Production in Eighteenth-Century Britain', *Oxford Art Journal* 11 (1988), pp. 10–16, at p. 15.

96 Matthew Craske, 'Plan and Control: Design and the Competitive Spirit in Early and Mid-Eighteenth Century England', *Journal of Design History* 12/3 (1999), pp. 187–216, at p. 201.

97 Craske, 'Plan and Control', p. 201.

98 Alder, 'Innovation and Amnesia', p. 282.

99 Craske, 'Plan and Control', p. 206.

100 Craske, 'Plan and Control', p. 198.

101 The significance of drawing and model-making during the late eighteenth and early nineteenth centuries has been discussed in Celina Fox, *The Arts of Industry in the Age of Enlightenment* (New Haven, Conn.: Yale University Press for The Paul Mellon Centre for Studies in British Art, 2009), pp. 45–177.

combined utility with ornament, drawings and models allowed the visualisation, evaluation and transfer of new ideas and concepts, and could thus be used for both production and publicity purposes. Moreover, their production required precision skills, as well as the ability to observe, measure and calculate, which helped to bring together theory and practice.[102] As has been pointed out, drawings and models 'bridged the gap between the mind and the hand, the idea and form, memory and muscle'.[103] This is why draughtsmanship and model-making became indispensable in the training of craftsmen, scientists and engineers in the course of the eighteenth century.

Apart from Maudslay, another case worth discussing in this context is that of Jean-Jacques Holtzapffel (1768–1835), an engineer whose biography and output are closely connected to Erard. Like Erard, Holtzapffel was from Strasbourg and in the early 1790s he moved to London, where he established a business as a maker of machines and tools. Holtzapffel's company is listed in the same trade directory from 1818 as Maudslay and Erard.[104] Between 1798 and 1928 the firm of Holtzapffel & Co produced over 2,500 lathes of various types.[105] Like Erard harps, these lathes were typically numbered and recorded in a register, demonstrating that the practice of serial numbering was also common in the manufacture of machines and tools. Holtzapffel's lathes were marked with a single sequence number usually engraved on a visible area of the headstock below the firm's name and address. Similarly to Erard harps, Holtzapffel lathes were quite expensive state-of-the-art devices; in 1816 a rose engine lathe was sold for £150, almost as much as a richly decorated Erard double-action harp. Apart from their use for industrial purposes, many of these lathes were purchased by wealthy amateurs, both gentlemen and ladies, with an interest in ornamental turning.[106]

By the time of Holtzapffel's death in 1835, the firm had reportedly sold about 1,600 lathes. Two of them, one number 4 and one number 5, were bought by Erard in 1810, the year Erard registered his patent for the double-action harp.[107] Two more Holtzapffel lathes, Nº 793 and Nº 794, each described as 'a 5 Inch Centre Lathe',

---

[102] The role of technical drawings and models has been analysed in Panagiotis Poulopoulos, 'The Role of Technical Drawings and Models in the Promotion of the Steam Engine', unpublished paper presented at the 41st Symposium of the Scientific Instrument Society (SIC), 'The Past, Present, and Future of Scientific Instrument Studies', Session '18th and 19th Century Instruments', National Hellenic Research Foundation, Athens, 19 to 23 September 2022.

[103] Fox, *The Arts of Industry in the Age of Enlightenment*, p. 137.

[104] 'Holtzapffell & Deyerlien, Tool manufac.' Johnstone, *Johnstone's London Commercial Guide and Street Directory*, p. 131.

[105] The lathes are listed in the ledgers of Holtzapffel and Company, London Metropolitan Archives, CLC/B/121/MS09475.

[106] Stephen O'Keeffe, 'The Art of Ornamental Turning', *Studies in Design Education Craft & Technology* 12/1 (1979), pp. 46–52, at pp. 46–50. Turning with lathes was a favourite pastime of European royals and aristocrats; for more details see Klaus Maurice, *Der drechselnde Souverän: Materialien zu einer fürstlichen Maschinenkunst* (Zurich: Ineichen, 1985). I am thankful to Silke Berdux for bringing this source to my attention.

[107] Baldwin, *The Harp in Early Nineteenth-century Britain*, p. 411.

were bought by Erard in March and April 1811 for £27 18s and £36 10s respectively.[108] Along with the two lathes, Erard also purchased from Holtzapffel various tools and accessories mostly relating to metalworking. As this was only a few months before Erard launched his patented double-action harp in London, it may be assumed that the lathes and tools would have been acquired to assist the manufacture of Erard's new harps, particularly the double-action mechanism.

These lathes may have been used, for instance, to turn the wood for the harp's column and capital or to turn various metal components of the pedal mechanism, such as screws, rods, nuts or tuning pins. Given their common origins and age, as well as their prominence as leading manufacturers in their respective fields, it is not surprising that Erard and Holtzapffel were acquainted on a professional, and possibly personal, level. Holtzapffel may have supplied lathes to Erard earlier than 1810, because the use of lathes is mentioned in three occasions in Erard's 1807–1809 workshop accounts, without, however, any references to their features or their manufacturer.[109] Moreover, Holtzapffel again sold a large number of tools and accessories to Erard in 1812.[110]

Apart from Erard, Holtzapffel supplied lathes to other harp makers, such as Stumpff and possibly Erat, with whom he was related through the marriage of his daughter Ann Caroline to Erat's son Jacob.[111] Holtzapffel's involvement in the harp trade is further indicated by the fact that his son Charles (1806–1847), who continued his father's business, included several references to the manufacture of harps in his influential treatise on turning.[112]

Conclusions

The example of the Grecian model illustrates the pioneering design and engineering features that were conceived and incorporated by Erard in the manufacture of harps. Firstly, the transition from wood to metal for the construction and mounting of the complex pedal mechanism considerably improved the stability and reliability of pedal harps. Secondly, the introduction of standardised, interchangeable and adjustable components not only resulted in higher consistency and efficiency of manufacture, but also enabled later repairs, amendments and modifications, which on earlier harps had been difficult to execute. Thirdly, the extensive use of screws for joining or regulating various parts greatly simplified and accelerated the assembly

---

[108] See *Records of Charles Holtzapffel and Company*.

[109] The use of lathes is mentioned in February and April 1807 as well as in December 1808. See Nex, *The Business of Musical-Instrument Making in Early Industrial London*, pp. 393, 395 and 426.

[110] See *Records of Charles Holtzapffel and Company*.

[111] Baldwin, *The Harp in Early Nineteenth-century Britain*, pp. 404 and 411.

[112] Charles Holtzapffel, *Turning and mechanical manipulation intended as a work of general reference and practical instruction on the lathe, and the various mechanical pursuits followed by amateurs* (3 vols; London: Holtzapffel & Co; vol. 1 1843; vol. 2 1846; vol. 3 published posthumously 1850). Brief references to the manufacture of harps are included in vol. 1, pp. 62, 86–87, 90–91, 107; in vol. 2, pp. 563–564, 596, 793, 891, 930; and in vol. 3, p. 1039.

and maintenance of harps, while adding strength and precision. These measures significantly reduced production costs and time, simultaneously lowering Erard's need for skilled personnel. In addition, the application of serial numbers and other manufacturing marks, which became integral for Erard harps, demonstrate the implementation of industrial practices involving rationalisation of construction, division of labour and 'assembly-line' systems at Erard's London workshop. The effective production strategies described so far helped the Erard firm to build instruments of fine, uniform quality, while coping with the rapidly growing demand for harps in Britain and abroad. Equally inventive as their design and construction was the decoration and branding of Erard Grecian harps, as will be discussed in the next chapter.

CHAPTER THREE

The Decoration and Branding of the Erard Grecian Harp: Innovation, Adaptation and Substitution

'I should also warn you that all of the makers are now copying your capital with three faces'[1]

Erard Nº 2631, the Grecian harp preserved at the Deutsches Museum that was discussed in Chapters One and Two, is a highly adorned instrument. When compared to other wooden stringed instruments built in the early nineteenth century, such as violins or guitars, this harp instantly stands out, firstly because of its impressive appearance in black and gold, incorporating elaborate sculptural as well as pictorial decorative elements, and secondly because of its conspicuous labelling with engravings that provide several details about its manufacturer. The decoration and branding of Erard Grecian harps, which will be the focus of this chapter, epitomised the transformation of the harp from an aesthetic viewpoint. As will be described below, the Grecian model was shaped by the application of new decorative materials and techniques which originated in various crafts relevant to instrument-making and which complemented or entirely replaced those traditionally used by harp makers until the end of the eighteenth century. Moreover, as revealed by its name, the Grecian model was fashioned by the introduction of a new decorative style that had its roots in Neoclassicism, a movement that prevailed in the lifestyle of many European countries at the dawn of the nineteenth century. Furthermore, it was greatly affected by new methods of trademarking, which coincided with the establishment of brand identity within the rapidly changing consumer society of Regency Britain.

Composition Ornaments: A Substitute for Woodcarvings

One of the most distinctive features of Erard Grecian harps concerns their decoration with composition ornaments on the column, pedalbox and neck. Composition, often referred to as compo, is essentially a thermoplastic moulding compound,

---

[1]   L 251, 2 March 1819, in Robert Adelson, Alain Roudier, Jenny Nex, Laure Barthel and Michel Foussard (eds), *The History of the Erard Piano and Harp in Letters and Documents, 1785–1959* (Cambridge: Cambridge University Press, 2015), pp. 708–710, at p. 710.

which comprises several organic and inorganic ingredients divided into three types: fillers (e.g. chalk, gypsum, starch and lead white), binding media (e.g. drying oils, animal glue and resins) and evaporating solvents (e.g. water). Composition is a quite flexible material: while in a warm and moist state, it is soft and malleable, and can be pressed in rigid wooden or metal moulds. However, as it cools and dries, it becomes quite hard and durable, taking a precise shape. By using hot water steam, it can be softened repeatedly and shaped again in new forms.[2]

Composition became widespread in Great Britain and other European countries from the third quarter of the eighteenth century. Typically formed in reverse-carved moulds made of boxwood or brass, composition ornaments were considerably cheaper as well as faster and easier to make in comparison to traditional woodcarving. Although they were more fragile than wood, they were also more practical to handle, repair or replace. The adhesion of ornaments to different surfaces was often aided by applying glue or fresh composition, or by using nails and pins. Large ornaments were usually supported by adding threads or wires in the composition.

From an economic perspective, composition's main advantage was its low cost compared to woodwork. It is worth noting, for instance, that 'in the second half of the eighteenth century, composition ornaments were claimed to be at least fifty per cent cheaper than wooden ones'.[3] From an artistic and commercial perspective, composition allowed the manufacture of numerous identical ornaments with complex, delicate patterns that were difficult to carry out in wood, which made it ideal especially for standardised objects produced in series.

Regarding the widespread adoption of composition and similar casting materials in the furniture trade, it has been argued that apart from cost-cutting factors, 'aesthetic considerations were also important because designs which would have defied the skills of a plasterer or wood carver could be executed in the new materials'.[4] Moreover, composition ornaments could be applied with minor preparation (usually with a grounding such as gesso) directly on flat or curved wooden surfaces, and could then be gilded or painted, making them almost indistinguishable from wooden ornaments. Thus, during the late eighteenth and early nineteenth centuries, composition gradually became a relatively inexpensive and reliable substitute for the painstaking and time-consuming woodcarvings, finding many applications in architectural components, picture frames, furniture and musical instruments.

Erard was one of the first, if not the first, harp manufacturers to use composition ornaments on harps. Until the end of the eighteenth century, pedal harps produced

---

[2]　For an overview of composition see Judith Wetherall, 'History and Techniques of Composition', in Sophie Budden (ed.), *Gilding and Surface Decoration* (London: United Kingdom Institute for Conservation, 1991), pp. 26–29, as well as Jonathan Thornton and William Adair, 'Applied Decoration for Historic Interiors: Preserving Composition Ornament', *Preservation Briefs* 34 (1994), pp. 1–16.

[3]　Pat Kirkham, 'The London Furniture Trade, 1700–1870', *Furniture History* 24 (1988), pp. 1–219, at p. 117.

[4]　Kirkham, 'The London Furniture Trade', p. 117. It should, however, be considered that the wooden moulds for the production of composition ornaments would have to be reversely carved, so carving skills were still required in this process, albeit for a different purpose. I am thankful to the second anonymous reviewer for this observation.

in France and elsewhere were typically adorned with elaborate woodcarvings. Erard initially followed this trend, judging from the woodcarvings found on the first harps that were built by the firm in Paris during the 1780s and 1790s; one representative example is a single-action Erard harp bearing no serial number and dating from this period, housed in the Musikinstrumentenmuseum der Universität Leipzig, Leipzig (Inv. No. 402). From around 1800 Erard begun to supplement woodcarvings with composition ornaments to decorate the single-action Empire harps. These ornaments were usually supplied by specialists, such as 'Mr Thorpe', a composition maker, who was paid the considerable amount of around £100 per year between 1807 and 1809.[5] This was most likely James Thorp(e) (fl.1788–1818), who worked as 'Ornament and Composition maker' at 24 Princess Street, Soho.[6]

However, with the launching of his double-action harp in 1811 Erard completely abandoned woodcarvings, exclusively using composition for the three-dimensional ornaments of harps, as confirmed by the examination of Erard N° 2631 and similar instruments (Figure 11).[7]

For the newly introduced Grecian model, which required a complete set of new ornaments, Erard turned to George Jackson (1779–1850), a composition manufacturer whose workshop at 50 Rathbone Place was located in close proximity to Erard's London manufactory. A leading manufacturer in his field, Jackson was listed in the same London directory from 1818 as Erard.[8] His clientele included esteemed customers who were attracted by composition's low cost and flexibility. It is worth noting that when Arthur Wellesley, 1st Duke of Wellington (1769–1852) decided to redecorate his property at Apsley House in 1828, the renowned architect Benjamin Dean Wyatt (1775–1852) recommended the Jackson firm 'for their paste composition ornaments which only cost £400 in total whereas woodcarving would have amounted to £2,000'.[9] On another occasion, Wyatt claimed that Jackson's work would be 'better and cheaper' than other plasterers, his secret lying in the use of Jackson's 'paste composition than real woodcarving', simply because 'once it was gilded, nobody could tell the difference'.[10] Interestingly, Pierre Erard was acquainted with Wyatt, since in 1815 he had sought the architect's advice on the situation of the

---

5   Jenny Nex, *The Business of Musical-Instrument Making in Early Industrial London* (PhD Diss., London: Goldsmiths College, 2013), p. 224.

6   Timothy Clifford, 'The Plaster Shops of the Rococo and Neo-Classical Era in Britain', *Journal of the History of Collections* 4/1 (1992), pp. 39–65, at p. 64. The will of James Thorp, 'Plasterer of St James Westminster' is dated 13 April 1812 (PROB 11/1532). I am grateful to Jacob Simon for this information.

7   For more details see Panagiotis Poulopoulos, Marisa Pamplona, Luise Richter and Elke Cwiertnia, 'Technological Study of the Decoration on an Erard Harp from 1818', *Studies in Conservation* 65/2 (2020), pp. 86–102, at pp. 88–98.

8   'Jackson, G. *Composition ornam. manuf.*' Andrew Johnstone, *Johnstone's London Commercial Guide and Street Directory* (London: Barnard & Farley, 1818), p. 407.

9   Marion R. May, *The ornamental Jacksons: a brief history of George Jackson & Sons Limited, ornamental composition manufacturers* (London: May, 2001), p. 13.

10 May, *The ornamental Jacksons*, p. 17.

Figure 11. Left: Gilded woodcarvings on the capital of an Erard harp built in Paris in the 1790s bearing no serial number. Musikinstrumentenmuseum der Universität Leipzig, Leipzig (Inv. No. 402). Right: Gilded composition ornaments on the capital of Erard Nº 2631, built in 1818. Deutsches Museum, Munich (Inv. No. 16147).

firm's premises at Marlborough Street, mentioning that 'I took this opportunity to point out to M. Wyatt the bad condition of the house (Marlboro St.)'.[11]

The surviving ledgers of the Jackson firm reveal that between October 1811 and June 1812 Jackson charged Erard for ornamenting harps and harp-related accessories, as well as for cutting boxwood moulds (Figure 12).[12]

Taking into account that Erard's first double-action harp, Erard Nº 1377, was sold on 24 October 1811, the sum of £66 dated 3 October 1811 corresponding 'To 55 harps ornamentd compleat' most likely refers to the first 55 double-action harps Erard ever made. Erard's payment to Jackson for harp ornamentation confirms that the Erard firm occasionally relied on subcontractors for specialist work. On the other hand, the commission of new moulds suggests that some of the composition ornaments for the Grecian model may have been produced in Erard's premises.

This is further confirmed in the firm's correspondence and financial documents from later years. For example, in March 1819 Pierre asked Sébastien to send to him from Paris new moulds for the decoration of the harp capital, since the original design

---

[11]		L 166, 27 December 1815. Adelson et al, *The History of the Erard Piano and Harp*, pp. 621–622, at p. 621.

[12]		George Jackson and Sons Ledger, V&A Archive of Art and Design, London, AD/2012/1/2/1, pp. 1–2.

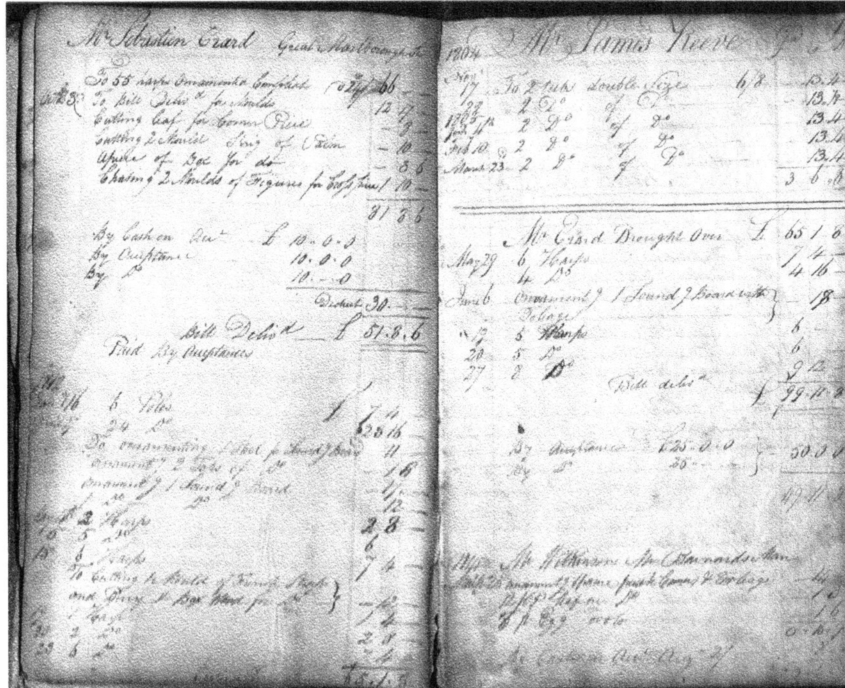

Figure 12. List of costs for ornamenting harps and harp-related accessories, as well as for cutting moulds for Erard in 1811–1812 in the account books of George Jackson, a composition manufacturer in London working in close proximity to Erard. George Jackson and Sons Ledger, V&A Archive of Art and Design, London, AD/2012/1/2/1.

with the three caryatids, which was a trademark of the Grecian model, was being copied by Erard's competitors in London. Pierre stated characteristically that 'all of the makers are now copying your capital with three faces'.[13] Likewise, a few months later Pierre asked his uncle to commission and send him a brass mould 'for the little rim or moulding which is stuck above the neck plates [...] because our moulding is very poor', adding that 'it would be better to have a new one made in Paris rather than here where those things are expensive and poorly made'.[14] Moreover, payments to 'The composition maker' are listed among other expenses for Erard's staff in a financial statement of 1822, indicating that some composition ornaments for Grecian harps were presumably made in-house at the Erard London branch during that time.[15]

Nevertheless, despite its low cost and flexibility in application, composition also had disadvantages. The ageing and deterioration of composition due to

---

[13] L 251, 2 March 1819. Adelson et al, *The History of the Erard Piano and Harp*, pp. 708–710, at p. 710.

[14] L 264, 9 July 1819. Adelson et al, *The History of the Erard Piano and Harp*, pp. 723–724, at p. 724.

[15] Robert Adelson, *Erard: Empire of the Harp* (Ancenis: Les Harpes Camac, 2022), p. 205.

environmental conditions often resulted in its 'shrinking, warping and loss of adhesion with the substrate'.[16] These problems are commonly observed on surviving historical harps, on which the ornaments have cracks or missing sections.[17] Apart from visual issues, harps decorated with composition ornaments were also thought to have inferior acoustic properties in comparison to those with woodcarvings. For example, in 1844 the harp maker Alexander Richard Blazdell (1775–?), a former apprentice of Erard from Germany who had set up his own business at 42 Wigmore Street, London, announced that he made harps 'carved in the Elizabethan order, without composition ornaments, thereby producing a very powerful tone, and capable of withstanding the effects of every climate'.[18]

Decoupage Prints: An Alternative to Painted Decoration

Another characteristic feature of Erard Grecian harps regards their decoration with decoupage prints. Also known as *découpure*, *lacca contrafatta* or *lacca povera*, decoupage is a decorative technique that involves 'cutting out and coloring prints, later to be pasted onto a specially prepared surface and then varnished'.[19] The cut-out prints were usually adhered to surfaces with starch, animal glue, fine gesso or chalk primer, and once they had dried, several layers of transparent varnish were applied to them. The number of varnish layers determined the smoothness and lustre of the surfaces as well as the overall quality of decoupage: while insufficient layers resulted in visible level differences between the print and the surface, by adding adequate layers, it was quite difficult to distinguish the pasted prints from real painting.[20]

In the course of the eighteenth century, decoupage became increasingly popular in Italy, France and other European countries, especially as a substitute for japanning, a technique which aimed at imitating the black, glossy lacquer of Asian furniture.[21] Ornaments made with printed gold leaf adhered to a layer of paper and applied on a contrasting dark ground could create a highly attractive visual effect. Decoupage was a favourite pastime for male and female amateurs, who employed this technique to decorate small household objects, such as boxes, trays or stands. Misses Bertram, two of the heroines in *Mansfield Park* by Jane Austen (1775–1817)

---

[16] Wetherall, 'History and Techniques of Composition', p. 27.

[17] This issue has been described in Panagiotis Poulopoulos, 'Composition Ornaments on Historic Harps: From Research to Exhibition', unpublished paper presented at the annual conference of CIMCIM 'Presentation, Preservation, Interpretation – The Challenges of Musical Instrument Collections in the 21st Century', Basel and Bern, 22 to 25 February 2017.

[18] *The Musical World* 19 (London: G. Purkess, 1844), p. 274. Such announcements should be read with caution, as they were often used for marketing purposes.

[19] Daniëlle O. Kisluk-Grosheide, '"Cutting up Berchems, Watteaus, and Audrans": A *Lacca Povera* Secretary at The Metropolitan Museum of Art', *Metropolitan Museum Journal* 31 (1996), pp. 81–97, at p. 81.

[20] For a brief historical overview on decoupage see Hiram Manning, *Manning on Decoupage* (2nd edn; New York: Dover Publications, 1980), pp. 21–27.

[21] Clive Edwards, *Encyclopedia of Furniture Materials, Trades and Techniques* (Aldershot: Ashgate, 2000), p. 72.

may have been practising decoupage when they were 'making artificial flowers or wasting gold paper'.[22] However, on larger objects, such as pieces of furniture, coaches or musical instruments, decoupage was usually carried out by skilled professionals. Although it was mostly applied on three-dimensional objects, decoupage was occasionally used to decorate interior spaces; even 'entire rooms are also known to have been embellished with decoupage'.[23]

Concerning its professional usages, the main advantage of decoupage was that it was significantly cheaper and less difficult to execute compared to painting, thus reducing manufacturing costs and time considerably. Furthermore, it was a technique that combined quality and consistency with artistic freedom and flexibility, since the different selection and arrangement of the same prints permitted the creation of customised designs according to the special wishes and tastes of the manufacturers or their clients. Drawings and paintings by master artists as well as popular motives and engravings could be 'printed up by the thousands, and the printed designs could then be hand-colored by the humble apprentices, cut out, and glued onto furniture and panels in an infinite variety of decoupage designs'.[24] In this way, decoupage enabled the easy reproduction and circulation of fine art on a wide range of manufactured goods produced in series.

Decoupage benefited significantly from the development of the printing industry towards the end of the eighteenth century. This resulted from the refinement of existing printing techniques, such as copperplate engraving or etching, or from the introduction of new ones, such as lithography. Invented in the late 1790s in Munich by Aloys Senefelder (1771–1834) for printing theatrical plays and music sheets, lithography enabled the production of large numbers of identical, high-quality prints, particularly those combining texts and images.[25] Although it has not been verified that the decoupage prints on Erard harps were produced with lithography, Erard was presumably acquainted with this technique due to the firm's activities as a music publisher from around 1800.[26]

This printing technique would have suited Erard's serial production of harps as it was:

> a quicker and less costly method of printing, and, in the end, speed and low cost were among the reasons for the success of lithography. An artist drawing on stone could see a completed work in hours or days whereas another medium might take weeks. Furthermore, much larger editions were possible.[27]

[22] Jane Austen, *Mansfield Park: A Novel* (3 vols; London: Egerton, 1814), vol. 1, p. 25.

[23] Kisluk-Grosheide, '"Cutting up Berchems, Watteaus, and Audrans"', p. 81.

[24] Manning, *Manning on Decoupage*, p. 26.

[25] Dennis Bryans, 'The Double Invention of Printing', *Journal of Design History* 13/4 (2000), pp. 287–300, at pp. 288–290. On lithography see also Walter Koschatzky, *Die Kunst der Graphik. Technik, Geschichte, Meisterwerke* (11th edn; Munich: Deutscher Taschenbuch Verlag, 1993), p. 185.

[26] Florence Gétreau, 'Erard', in Ludwig Finscher (ed.) *Die Musik in Geschichte und Gegenwart. Personenteil 6 E-Frau* (2nd edn; Stuttgart: Bärenreiter/Metzler, 2001), p. 394.

[27] Karen F. Beall, 'The Interdependence of Printer & Printmaker in Early 19th-Century Lithography', *Art Journal* 39/3 (1980), pp. 195–201, at p. 201.

One of the hypothetical advantages of lithography was that 'a very large number of impressions – many more than could be taken from an engraved plate – could be obtained from a single stone without degradation of the resulting image, although the process was subject to its own hazards such as stones breaking'.[28] Decoupage prints with lithography or other techniques could thus offer Erard the opportunity to produce standardised, exclusive and instantly recognisable decorative designs, which helped the firm's instruments to stand out among competitors.

During the late eighteenth century, decoupage prints were occasionally used for the decoration of keyboard instruments. However, as in the case of composition ornaments discussed above, Erard was probably the first harp manufacturer to employ decoupage for the decoration of harps.[29] Pedal harps built in the eighteenth century were often adorned with lavish paintings on the soundboard. Although Erard's early harps were also decorated with paintings, from around 1800 these were progressively replaced by decoupage prints. Referred to as 'vignettes', decoupage adornments were commonly applied to the harp's largest, flattest and most visible areas, namely the soundboard and the five shutters on the back of the soundbox (Figure 13). As revealed by the examination of Erard N° 2631 and similar harps, the vignettes were usually printed on high-karat gold leaf pasted on thin paper.[30]

An Erard catalogue from the late 1810s, which will be analysed in Chapter Five, shows that decoupage was the standard decoration particularly on the firm's low-priced harps, while painting was reserved for the more expensive ones. For example, double-action harps listed as 'Black, with single gold vignettes (generally called plain ones)' and 'Black, with double gold vignettes, burnished gilding' were the cheapest at £110 5s and £126 respectively;[31] the terms 'double' and 'single' in the above descriptions probably refer to the thickness of gold leaf in the decoupage.[32]

This information, combined with the burnished gilding observed on Erard N° 2631, suggests that this instrument was most likely the 'Black, with double gold vignettes, burnished gilding', the second-cheapest double-action harp, costing £126.[33] In contrast, blue, green or red harps that were 'painted with Raphael's Arabesks' were the

---

28 Michael Kassler, 'Vollweiler's Introduction of Music Lithography to England', in Michael Kassler (ed.), *The Music Trade in Georgian England* (Farnham and Burlington: Ashgate, 2011), pp. 451–506, at pp. 476–477.

29 The innovative techniques employed in the decoration of Erard harps have been discussed in Panagiotis Poulopoulos, 'Technological substitution and innovation in the production of musical instruments at the turn of the 19th century', unpublished paper presented at the Annual Conference of the Society of the History of Technology (SHOT) 'Exploring the Interface between Technology, Art, and Design', Session 'Technology and Luxury', Museo Nazionale della Scienza e della Tecnologia 'Leonardo Da Vinci', Milan, 24 to 27 October 2019.

30 For more details see Poulopoulos et al, 'Technological Study of the Decoration on an Erard Harp from 1818', pp. 88–98.

31 Erard Harp Catalogue (London: Erard, c.1819–1821), University of Glasgow Archives & Special Collections, A.x.24, p. 1.

32 Mike Baldwin, 'The Erat Harp Manufactory: Painted and Gilded Decoration 1821–1826', *The Galpin Society Journal* 66 (2013), pp. 149–164, at p. 157.

33 Poulopoulos et al, 'Technological Study of the Decoration on an Erard Harp from 1818', p. 99.

Figure 13. Left: Painted decoration on the soundboard of Erard N° 333, built in 1800. Royal College of Music, London (Inv. No. RCM 298). Right: Decoupage prints on the soundboard of Erard N° 2631, built in 1818. Deutsches Museum, Munich (Inv. No. 16147).

most expensive, ranging from £157 10s to £168. Several London harp makers imitated Erard by employing decoupage prints for the decoration of their instruments. These include, for example, Johann Andreas Stumpff (1769–1846), as evidenced by a harp built by him in 1819 and housed at the Henry Francis du Pont Winterthur Museum, Delaware (Inv. No. 57.748), which is decorated with decoupage printed with etched copperplate,[34] or Jacob Erat (1758–1821), whose use of decoupage is confirmed by surviving harps and references in Erat's ledgers.[35]

Under the Influence of Neoclassicism

The development of the Erard harp was affected as much by technical as by aesthetic advances, which were marked by the decline of Baroque and Rococo and the rise of

---

[34] For more details of this harp see Mark J. Anderson and Sally Malenka, 'The characterization and treatment of gilded surfaces on an early nineteenth-century harp', in Deborah Bigelow (ed.), *Gilded Wood: Conservation and History* (Madison, Connecticut: Sound View Press, 1991), pp. 319–330, at p. 324. Apart from this harp, double-action harps by Stumpff survive in the Münchner Stadtmuseum, Munich (Inv. No. 41–269) and the Kunstgewerbemuseum Dresden, Dresden (Inv. No. 32798); both of these instruments closely resemble Erard Grecian harps. For more information see Gunther Joppig, 'Die Stumpffharfe im Kunstgewerbemuseum Dresden', in Wolfram Steude and Hans-Günter Ottenberg (eds), *Theatrum instrumentorum Dresdense – Bericht über die Tagungen zu Historischen Musikinstrumenten, Dresden, 1996, 1998 und 1999* (Schneverdingen: Verlag der Musikalienhandlung Wagner, 2003), pp. 99–107. For Stumpff's biography and work see Pamela J. Willetts, 'Johann Andreas Stumpff, 1769–1846', *The Musical Times* 118/1607 (1977), pp. 29, 31 and 32.

[35] Baldwin, 'The Erat Harp Manufactory', p. 160.

Neoclassicism towards the end of the eighteenth century. A style that dominated European art, architecture and fashion from about 1760 to 1830, Neoclassicism had its roots in the archaeological discoveries that took place in southeastern Europe and the Near East and the subsequent dissemination of ancient Greek and Roman antiquities through collecting, exhibiting and publishing activities, firstly of private individuals and later of public institutions.[36]

Neoclassicism also had a strong influence on the musical instrument business. This was exemplified by various new instruments which evoked classical Greece due to their name or shape, such as the orphica or the lyre guitar,[37] or due to their ornamentation, such as Erard's 'popular, newly improved harp retailing as the "Grecian" model because of its Neoclassical decoration'.[38] The adoption of neoclassical features in the design and ornamentation of Erard harps, which was initiated from the late 1790s onwards, may have resulted from aesthetic trends as well as from social and political factors. Until the end of the eighteenth century, the harp was a favourite instrument of the French royalty and aristocracy, with the Queen of France, Marie Antoinette, being its most prominent advocate. However, the French Revolution in 1789 instigated a growing aversion towards the *Ancien Régime* and its customs. By the end of the eighteenth century, the frivolous, opulent appearance of French harps in Rococo style seemed largely outdated. In order to be approved and embraced by a more liberal middle-class clientele, the harp needed an urgent facelift, which found its expression in the emerging neoclassical style.[39]

Erard was a pioneer in the visual transformation of the harp. Not only did the firm implement new decorative materials and techniques, such as the composition ornaments and decoupage prints discussed earlier, but it also introduced a new style of harp design and decoration that was heavily influenced by the neoclassical movement. To begin with, the design of the harp pillar as an ancient fluted column with a capital was a direct reference to Neoclassicism. As a symbolic architectural element of classical antiquity, the column was 'to play a significant role in Neoclassical design as both a temporary and as a permanent structure', with 'the freestanding monumental column' becoming 'one of the most popular means of expressing a triumphant celebration'.[40] The fluted column was gradually integrated in the shape of various household objects, from candlesticks to clocks. Erard was probably the first harp manufacturer to introduce a fluted column with a capital instead of a scroll, which was a distinct trait of French harps. This change from scroll to capital is also shown

---

[36] For a comprehensive overview on the development and establishment of the neoclassical style see David Irwin, *Neoclassicism* (London: Phaidon, 2000), pp. 4–386.

[37] For more details on the orphica and lyre guitar see Panagiotis Poulopoulos, 'Musik im Freien in der Zeit des Biedermeier: Die Beispiele der Orphica, der Gitarre und des Csakans', *Phoibos: Zeitschrift für Zupfmusik* 8/1 (2015), pp. 43–68, and Panagiotis Poulopoulos, 'The Guitar as an "Open-air" Instrument in the Early Romantic Era', *Soundboard Scholar: Journal of the Guitar Foundation of America* 1 (2015), pp. 4–15.

[38] Irwin, *Neoclassicism*, p. 361.

[39] Michael Parker, *Child of Pure Harmony: A Source Book for the Single-Action Harp* (London: Parker, 2005), p. 10.

[40] Irwin, *Neoclassicism*, pp. 81–82.

in Erard's patent drawings: for example, his 1794 patent showed a harp column with a scroll, whereas the 1801 patent depicted a column with a capital. Furthermore, in Erard's 1810 patent for the double-action harp, the outline of the capital became more detailed and closer to the shape observed on surviving double-action harps, reminiscent of the Ionian pillar found in ancient Greek temples.

A second point worth analysing is the three-dimensional decoration of the column and pedalbox with a variety of neoclassical composition ornaments. These may have been inspired from drawings of ornaments on antique Greek and Roman monuments that were published in the second half of the eighteenth century. One highly influential publication, and a potential source of inspiration for Erard, was *The Antiquities of Athens* by James Stuart (1713–1788) and Nicholas Revett (1721–1804), which appeared in four volumes between 1762 and 1816.[41] For example, the mermen on the capital of Erard harps are reminiscent of the figure of Triton on the octagonal tower of Andronicus Cyrrhestes in Athens (called The Tower of the Winds or the Horologion),[42] while the male face on the front of the pedalbox evokes the male faces on the Ionic temple of the Illisus.[43] In addition, anthemia, palm leaves and flowers similar to those observed on Erard harps are depicted on the choragic monument of Lysicrates[44] as well as on the Parthenon and Erechtheion temples on the Acropolis of Athens.[45]

Arguably the most emblematic among the composition ornaments of Erard's Grecian model are the three winged caryatids resembling Nike, the Greek goddess who personified victory, on the harp's capital.[46] It is notable that although the composition ornaments on the pedalbox varied, the three figures of Nike remained a constant feature throughout the production of the Grecian model, indicating their popularity. This feature was extensively imitated by Erard's competitors, since in March 1819, Pierre informed his uncle that 'all of the makers are now copying your capital with three faces', as quoted earlier.[47]

Erard may have modelled these figures inspired by the Nike on *Incantadas* ('The Enchanted Ones'), an ancient Greek monument in Thessaloniki, which was described and depicted in the third volume of *The Antiquities of Athens*, published in 1794.[48] The Incantadas monument had provided the inspiration for the decoration

---

[41] James Stuart and Nicholas Revett, *The Antiquities of Athens* (4 vols; London: Haberkorn, 1762–1816). Some of the Greek monuments documented by Stuart and Revett had also been depicted in David Le Roy, *Les ruines des plus beaux monuments de la Grèce* (Paris, 1758).

[42] Stuart and Revett, *The Antiquities of Athens*, vol. 1 (1762), Ch. III, Pl. III.

[43] Stuart and Revett, *The Antiquities of Athens*, vol. 1 (1762), p. 11.

[44] Stuart and Revett, *The Antiquities of Athens*, vol. 1 (1762), Ch. IV, Pl. VI.

[45] Stuart and Revett, *The Antiquities of Athens*, vol. 2 (1762), Ch.1, Pl. VI, and Ch.2, Pl. V, VI, VIII, IX, XI, XII and XVIII.

[46] Roslyn Rensch, *Harps and Harpists* (Bloomington and Indianapolis: Indiana University Press, 1989), p. 183.

[47] L 251, 2 March 1819. Adelson et al, *The History of the Erard Piano and Harp*, pp. 708–710, at p. 710.

[48] See Stuart and Revett, *The Antiquities of Athens*, vol. 3 (2nd edn; London: Priestley and Weale, 1827), Ch. XI, Pl. XLV and XLVI.

in the Painted Room at Spencer House, London, designed in 1759 by James Stuart.[49] Unfortunately, in 1864 the monument was brutally dismantled by the French paleographer Emmanuel Miller, with its sculptures being transported to France and now housed at the Louvre Museum in Paris.[50] Several neoclassical ornaments that are quite similar to those found on Erard harps were also included in a set of drawings for musical instruments designed by Robert Adam (1728–1792) for Catherine II, Empress of Russia (1729–1796).[51] These include, for instance, the figure of Nike,[52] the mermen[53] and the lyre held between them.[54]

A third point of remark concerns the two-dimensional decoration of the soundboard, soundbox and neck with coloured coatings, decoupage prints and gilding. In comparison to earlier harps, the appearance of Erard's harps was more austere and uniform, as exemplified by the Grecian model. Regarding colour, the most common finish of Erard harps was a glossy black coating with gilded composition ornaments and reddish-gold decoupage prints. On extant harps with a black-gold decoration, these prints usually consisted of human figures on the bottom of the soundboard and on the shutters on the back of the soundbox, as well as of wide bordures on the outer edges of the soundboard.

On the earliest Grecian harps, built between 1811 and 1813, the bottom of the soundboard is decorated on each side with a large single decoupage print depicting a female figure in antique costume, with the left figure (from the viewer's side) playing a lyre and the right holding a wreath. In addition, the four lowest shutters on the back of the soundbox are embellished with male and female figures, which are dancing or playing instruments, while the top one bears a musical trophy. The bordures depict intersecting vines surrounding male and female masks as well as animal figures.

However, from around 1816 a new set of decoupage prints that was slightly different from the one described above began to be applied on black-gold harps. As can be seen on Erard N° 2631, built in 1818, the bottom of the soundboard on the left side is adorned with a female figure playing a tambourine, while the right with a female figure playing a triangle. Surviving examples, such as Erard N° 3070, N° 4561 or N° 5369, show that the same decoupage prints were occasionally applied on harps

---

49　John Wilton-Ely, 'Pompeian and Etruscan Tastes in the Neo-Classical Country-House Interior', *Studies in the History of Art* 25; *Symposium Papers X: The Fashioning and Functioning of the British Country House* (1989), pp. 51–73, at p. 54.

50　For more details on the history of this monument see Michel Sève, 'La colonnade des Incantadas à Thessalonique', *Revue archéologique* 1 (2013), pp. 125–133, and Benjamin Anderson '"An alternative discourse": Local interpreters of antiquities in the Ottoman Empire', *Journal of Field Archaeology* 40/4 (2015), pp. 450–460, at pp. 454–456.

51　Laurence Libin, 'Robert Adam's Instruments for Catherine the Great', *Early Music* 29/3 (2001), pp. 355–367. Interestingly, in the 1770s the Adam brothers presented a variety of neoclassical ornaments in their *Works in Architecture of Robert and James Adam* (London: Adam, 1773–1779).

52　Libin, 'Robert Adam's Instruments for Catherine the Great', pp. 356 and 361, drawings 7 and 11.

53　Libin, 'Robert Adam's Instruments for Catherine the Great', p. 360, drawings 8 and 10.

54　Libin, 'Robert Adam's Instruments for Catherine the Great', pp. 356 and 361, drawings 7 and 11.

with no coloured coating on the soundboard. In addition, the four lowest shutters of Erard Nº 2631 are embellished with images of female musicians holding wind or percussion instruments, whereas the top one bears a military trophy (Figure 14). The bordures on the soundboard depict intersecting vines surrounding masks, vases, animals and human figures, some holding musical instruments. Moreover, contrary to Erard harps built between 1811 and 1813, on later Grecian harps the vertical sides of the pedalbox are not fluted.

There were also diversions to the standard decoration described above. For instance, two Grecian harps, Erard Nº 1705 and Nº 1753, both built c.1813–1814, are decorated with more intricate patterns, which are mirrored on the left and right side of the soundboard. Each side includes, from bottom to top: a winged female figure playing the tambourine; a diamond-shaped emblem depicting a human head; the Prince of Wales's badge with three ostrich feathers; a young boy holding a bow and arrow; and a winged boy holding a wreath and a lyre. The five shutters on the back of Erard Nº 1753 bear images which include, from bottom to top: a tambourine and drum; a viol; a lyre and trumpet; a vase; and a trumpet, with all objects surrounded by ribbons, foliage and flowers. Additionally, the outer edges of the soundbox and shutters are decorated with wide bordures bearing floral and geometrical patterns. Erard Nº 1705 and Nº 1753 are the only known harps with this particular decoration, suggesting that the decorative pattern was presumably custom-ordered for particular Erard clients and that it was applied c.1813–1814 on only a few Erard harps. In this context it is noteworthy that Erard Nº 1705 (Figure 15) was acquired in 1813 by the Princess of Wales, as will be mentioned in Chapter Five.

Another extant harp, Erard Nº 2419, built c.1817, has an olive green coating and is decorated on the soundboard and neck with decoupage prints depicting spiral foliage, while the outer edges of the soundbox and shutters are adorned with a golden square meander with intersecting olive leaves (Figure 16). Several other surviving Erard harps display a diversity of decorative patterns with paintings or decoupage prints, although in most cases it is quite difficult to determine without further material and stylistic analysis whether they are original or the results of later redecoration or restoration.

Decorative work was quite significant as it could transform harps from rather plain structures of wood and metal to stunning pieces of art. Decoration could not only hide any imperfections in materials or construction techniques, but could also make harps more marketable. As early as 1797 Erard informed two dealers that the firm produced 'instruments to special order, as richly decorated as one would like, and whose prices vary according to the decoration'.[55] By the end of the 1810s the Erard firm had expanded its palette, adding more coloured finishes in order to cater for customers who purchased harps not only as musical instruments, but as elegant pieces of furniture.

Apart from the standard black-gold finish, Grecian harps were offered in at least five different colours, including ultramarine blue, smalt blue, green, red and rosewood. Also available were harps in grey or yellow transparent finishes. As mentioned

---

[55] L 7.388, 24 February 1797, and 7.389 (undated). Adelson et al, *The History of the Erard Piano and Harp*, pp. 178–179 and pp. 179–180 respectively, at p. 179.

Figure 14. Decoupage prints with neoclassical embellishments on the shutters of two Erard Grecian harps. Left: Erard Nº 1587, built c.1813. Museum of Fine Arts, Boston (Inv. No. 2012.991). Right: Erard Nº 2631, built in 1818. Deutsches Museum, Munich (Inv. No. 16147).

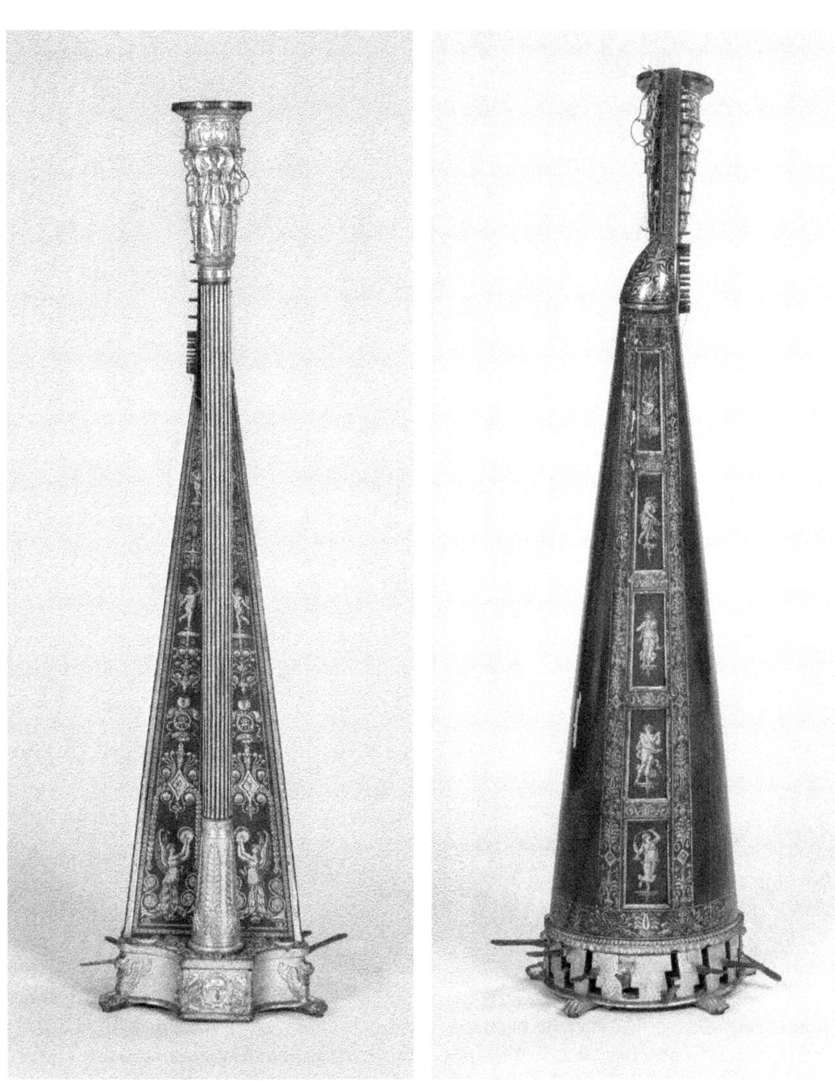

Figure 15. Erard N° 1705, an ultramarine blue double-action harp decorated with uncommon, possibly custom-ordered, decoupage prints on the soundboard and back. Notably the harp was acquired in 1813 by the Princess of Wales. Château de Fontainebleau, Fontainebleau (Inv. No. F 2465 C).

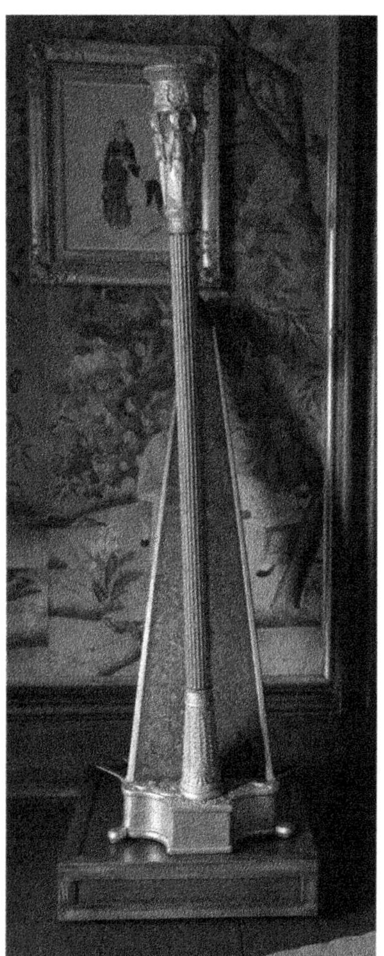

Figure 16. Front and side views of Erard Nº 2419, built c.1817. Abbotsford, The Home of Sir Walter Scott (Inv. No. T. AT. 3665). This harp has an olive green coating and is decorated on the soundboard and neck with decoupage prints depicting spiral foliage, while the outer edges of the soundbox and shutters are adorned with a golden square meander with intersecting olive leaves.

earlier, the blue, green or red harps, which were the most expensive in Erard's product line, could be embellished at an additional cost with more elaborate painted decoration, usually referred to as 'Raphael's Arabesks'.[56] An example of the decorative pattern with Arabesks can been observed on the soundboard, neck and shoulder on Erard N° 3704, an ultramarine blue harp built in 1825 and housed in the Fernanda Giulini Collection, Milan (Inv. No. 52).[57]

From an aesthetic viewpoint, the standard black-gold finish of Erard harps described above closely resembled the ancient black-red pottery that had been unearthed during archaeological expeditions and excavations in southern Italy, Greece and the Near East in the late eighteenth century. Often erroneously labelled as 'Etruscan', fine examples of Greek pottery with red figures on a black background had been imported to Britain mainly by private collectors and art dealers, and subsequently became known through exhibitions and publications. One the most influential of these publications was the *Collection of Etruscan, Greek and Roman antiquities from the cabinet of the Honourable William Hamilton*.[58] This richly illustrated book presented the collection of Sir William Hamilton (1730–1803), who as the British ambassador at the Court of Naples had amassed a large number of ancient Greek and Roman vases.[59]

The book helped to promote and establish the neoclassical style in Britain during the late eighteenth century, since the images it contained were widely circulated and imitated by designers and artists. Such publications had strong commercial potential, since they could be used 'as "pattern books" for craftsmen mass-producing a whole range of luxury collectibles after the antique for an elite English market'.[60] One notable example is the potter Josiah Wedgwood, whose painters copied the engravings in the book rather than the depictions on the ancient vases themselves, 'feeling free, however, to change the scene to better suit the intended audience, or to change border patterns and other decoration'.[61] Commenting on the impact of the antiquities in Hamilton's collection, a contemporary writer stated that 'the national taste has received a rapid improvement from them [...] We now have the pleasure

---

56 Erard Harp Catalogue (c.1819–1821), p. 1.

57 For more details of this harp see Dagmar Droysen-Reber, 'Schedules of the harps from no. 42 to no. 52', in John Henry van der Meer (ed.), *In Search of Lost Sounds: Art and Music in the Instruments Collection of Fernanda Giulini* (Milan and Briosco: Villa Medici Giulini, 2006), pp. 432–501, at pp. 492–497.

58 Baron d' Harcanville (Pierre François Hugues), *Collection of Etruscan, Greek and Roman antiquities from the cabinet of the Honourable William Hamilton* (4 vols; Naples: Morelli, 1766–1767).

59 For more details on Hamilton's collecting activities see Nancy Hirschland Ramage, 'Sir William Hamilton as Collector, Exporter, and Dealer: The Acquisition and Dispersal of His Collections', *American Journal of Archaeology* 94 (1990), pp. 469–480.

60 Viccy Coltman, 'Sir William Hamilton's Vase Publications (1766–1776): A Case Study in the Reproduction and Dissemination of Antiquity', *Journal of Design History* 14/1 (2001), pp. 1–16, at p. 5.

61 Nancy Hirschland Ramage, 'The English Etruria: Wedgwood and the Etruscans', *Etruscan Studies* 14 (2011), pp. 187–199, at p. 194.

of seeing new embellishments in the elegant manner of the ancients. The furniture of even the houses is already changed.'[62]

Equally important as Sir William Hamilton for the diffusion of the neoclassical style was his second wife, Emma Hamilton (1765–1815). In the late 1780s, young Emma began staging artistic performances that became known as 'Greek Attitudes', during which she re-enacted the poses depicted on the ancient vases collected by Hamilton. According to a visitor's account, during these performances Emma 'would provide herself with two or three cashmere shawls, an urn, a scent-box, a lyre and a tambourine. With these few properties and her classical costume she took up her position in the middle of the room.'[63]

Twelve of these Greek Attitudes were documented in drawings by Friedrich Rehberg (1758–1835),[64] with some of them bearing a striking resemblance to the figures on the vases in Hamilton's collection.[65] In this way, Emma's Greek Attitudes, 'engraved in 1794 and widely disseminated, gave a living presence to the classical art and literature'.[66] It has been further argued that 'both Sir William's collections and Emma's animation of its figures contributed to the neo-classical movement in its many forms of art, drama, dress, furnishing and designs, at once a re-presentation of the past and an augury of a future style'.[67]

The printed visualisation of Sir William's vase collections and Emma's performances may have also provided the themes for the decoupage prints on Erard harps. Sébastien Erard and the firm's decorators, who were most likely aware of these widely circulated images, may have selected and adapted some of them to suit the decoration of harps. For example, the female figure with a tambourine on the soundboard of Erard Nº 2631 may have been inspired by similar depictions of Emma Hamilton as a Bacchante holding a tambourine in Rehberg's Plate VIII (itself inspired by Plate 33 in d'Harcanville's third volume), as well as in a portrait by Elizabeth Vigée le Brun (1755–1842), painted c.1790–1792.[68] Likewise, the dancing female figure with a curved trumpet on the lowest shutter of Erard Nº 2631 (or with a similarly-shaped shawl on earlier harps built between 1811 and 1813), is similar to Emma's depiction as *The Muse of Dance* in Rehberg's Plate VI or as Mirth in her portrait by George Romney (1734–1802).[69] Moreover, the female figure with cymbals on the second shutter from the bottom is similar to Emma's depiction as a Bacchante holding cymbals by Richard Westall (1765–1836), painted in 1805.[70]

---

[62]   Quoted in Alicia Craig Faxon, 'Preserving the Classical Past: Sir William and Lady Emma Hamilton', *Visual Resources* 20/4 (2004), pp. 259–273, at p. 260.

[63]   Quoted in Faxon, 'Preserving the Classical Past', p. 264.

[64]   Friedrich Rehberg, *Drawings Faithfully copied from Nature at Naples* (Naples: 1794).

[65]   See Faxon, 'Preserving the Classical Past', pp. 264–269.

[66]   Faxon, 'Preserving the Classical Past', p. 272.

[67]   Faxon, 'Preserving the Classical Past', p. 272.

[68]   In the Lady Lever Art Gallery, Port Sunlight (Inv. No. LL 3527).

[69]   In private collection.

[70]   In private collection.

Emma's depictions with musical instruments were not imaginary, since she had learned to play the harp and harpsichord.[71] Thus, it is possible that Erard built upon the popularity of these depictions, as well as upon Emma's fame, to increase the attractiveness of Grecian harps. Several other figures on Erard harps built between 1811 and 1813 can be linked to the Hamiltons. One example is the female figure playing a lyre on the left side of the soundboard, which may have been inspired by a similar figure with a lyre on a tombstone that is included in d'Harcanville's first volume,[72] while in this context it is also worth noting Romney's sketch 'Lady Hamilton Playing a Lyre' (c.1785).[73] Moreover, the theme of a female figure with a lyre can be observed on the composition ornaments at the top of the pedalbox of Grecian harps, which typically consist of a winged female figure holding a lyre that is mirrored on the left and right side and is connected in the middle with a floral band, as seen on Erard N° 2631 (Figure 17).

That the appearance of such an advanced, modern instrument as the double-action harp was influenced by antiquity should come as no surprise. Neoclassicism had a strong impact on the design of numerous newly invented, state-of-the-art devices, ranging from timepieces to steam engines, which were often disguised in antique Greek or Roman styles.[74] In 1822, while he was in Paris, the piano maker Johann Baptist Streicher (1796–1871) witnessed a steam engine making chocolate, built with iron and brass in the form of an ancient temple; two sides of the pavilion rested on four-foot-high Doric columns of iron, with the chocolate being rolled on the bottom of the pavilion.[75] Regarding the novelty of the neoclassical style, one author has stated that 'it is one of the paradoxes of the spirit of continual invention that something ancient could appear new',[76] while another has likewise argued that 'it is one of the paradoxes of the age that the increasingly industrialized society of the 1770s and 1780s should have been obsessed with the culture of Classical antiquity and should have sought to express its ideals of progress in the imagery of classical art.'[77]

71 Jesse M. Hellman, 'Lady Hamilton, Nelson's Enchantress, and the Creation of Pygmalion', *Shaw* 35/2 (2015), pp. 213–237, at pp. 219–220.

72 d'Harcanville, *Collection of Etruscan, Greek and Roman antiquities*, vol. 1, p. 168.

73 National Gallery of Art, Washington (Inv. No. 1984.3.55).

74 See Irwin, *Neoclassicism*, pp. 360–386, and Ben Russell, *James Watt: Making the World Anew* (London: Reaktion Books, 2014), pp. 170–202.

75 '<u>Dienstag 5t</u> *Febr.* […] In der *Rue Richelieu* eine Dampf=Maschine gesehen, welche *Schokolade* bereitet. Sie ist äußerst schön gearbeitet, in Form eines Tempels; 2 Seiten [des] Pavillons ruhen auf 4 Fuß hohen Dorischen Säulen von Eisen, und unten, auf dem Boden der Pavillons wird der *Schocolat* gewaltzt. in der Mitte ist der *Cylinder* und das Räderwerk. Das Ganze, von Eisen und Messing gearbeitet, gewährt einen schönen Anblick.' Uta Goebl-Streicher, *Das Reisetagebuch des Klavierbauers Johann Baptist Streicher 1821–1822: Text und Kommentar* (Tutzing: Schneider, 2009), p. 110. I am grateful to Katharina Preller for bringing this source to my attention.

76 Coltman, 'Sir William Hamilton's Vase Publications', p. 6.

77 Hilary Young (ed.), *The Genius of Wedgwood* (London: Victoria and Albert Museum, 1995), p. 13.

Figure 17. Detail of the neoclassical motives depicted on the decoupage prints of the soundboard and on the composition ornaments of the pedalbox on Erard N° 2631. Deutsches Museum, Munich (Inv. No. 16147).

Similar ornaments like those found on harps were commonly applied to interior spaces decorated in neoclassical style in many country houses in Britain.[78] One of the finest examples is the Etruscan Room at Osterley Park, Middlesex, designed by Robert Adam in the early 1770s. The room's painted decoration was executed 'on sheets of paper pasted onto canvas' and was 'carried out in terra-cotta color and black on a pale blue-gray ground',[79] thus resembling in concept the decoupage prints used on Erard harps. The contrasting bright embellishments on a dark background applied on Erard harps corresponded also to the contemporary taste in home furnishing. In 1796 an architect's employee observed that:

[78] Wilton-Ely, 'Pompeian and Etruscan Tastes in the Neo-Classical Country-House Interior', pp. 57–65.

[79] Wilton-Ely, 'Pompeian and Etruscan Tastes in the Neo-Classical Country-House Interior', pp. 62–63.

you can scarce imagine how successful and new such ornaments appear – they are used in the way of our modern paper hangings, & are suited as well to the walls of a room as to the whole furniture throughout – figures, ornaments, symbols of every kind are copied from the real vases, representing them in their exact colours – the bordures are for panelling etc, (as I have sent you a scrap) and the figures are destined for the centre of pannells in a wide open field of dark colour.[80]

The neoclassical images chosen for the two- and three-dimensional decoration of Grecian harps demonstrate above all Erard's ingenious marketing and awareness of fashion. As already described, the images of the composition ornaments and decoupage prints display a variety of music-related scenes, including musicians, dancing figures and musical trophies, which were particularly appropriate for the embellishment of a musical instrument. Such images had a symbolic or allegorical character, acting as visual representations of music and the arts, and could thus greatly amplify the appeal of Erard's harps to customers passionate for neoclassically styled objects. For instance, judging from their iconographic attributes, several figures on the decoupage prints and composition ornaments of Erard Nº 2631 could be identified as the Muses, the patron goddesses of the arts in Greek mythology, while the composition ornament with the male face on the front of the pedalbox presumably depicts Apollo, the leader and protecting god of the Muses.[81]

Through its distinctive neoclassical decoration, Erard's Grecian model did not only reflect the elegance of classical Greece, but also the ideals of democracy, heroism and freedom, which helped to boost its popularity during the Napoleonic Wars and after. The harp's association with classical antiquity, strongly promoted by Erard's Grecian model, was frequently employed in European Philhellenism, which supported the Greek War of Independence against the Ottoman Empire (1821–1830). One characteristic example is the poem 'Grecian Triumph; Or, the Harp of Victory', written by a certain 'Utopia':

> Strike the harp for Ispara and Marathon's glory! / And strike, strike again, for the *Ottoman's* fall!
> For the valiant in song, and the deathless in story, / And the heroes that conquer'd at *liberty's* call! […]
> Strike the harp while the heart of the Musulman shrinketh, / Strike it loud for the *warriors* and *patriots* of *Greece*!
> The despot-star glimmers – in darkness sinketh, / And leaves to its conquerors – freedom and peace![82]

---

[80] Quoted in Coltman, 'Sir William Hamilton's Vase Publications', p. 6.

[81] For an analysis of the neoclassical ornaments on Erard Nº 2631 see Luise Eva-Maria Richter, *Fassungsuntersuchung der Doppelpedalharfe No. 2631 von Sébastien Erard aus dem Deutschen Museum München: Ein Beitrag zur Harfenforschung* (BA Diss., Studiengang Restaurierung, Kunsttechnologie und Konservierungswissenschaft, Munich: Technische Universität München, 2016), pp. 27–32.

[82] 'Grecian Triumph; Or, the Harp of Victory', *The Mirror of Literature, Amusement, and Instruction* 4 (London: J. Limbird, 1824), p. 339.

A reference to harps is likewise included in a poem written about the sacrificial exodus of Missolonghi on 10 April 1826:

They have perish'd! but they still / Shall live in the years to come,
When, on the noontide sunny hill, / Away from the cam's deep hum,
Some martial minstrel's song shall tell / How true they fought – how true they fell
They have perish'd! but not in vain; / For, when Liberty's high command
Comes like a battle-trumpet's strain / To the sons of some other land,
 They shall rush to the field, or leaguer'd wall, / And cry, 'Like them, we live or
    fall!' [...]
To them more sweet shall be, / At twilight's lonely hour,
The sound of the gale, sighing mournfully, / Through ivied wall and tower,
Than the thousand harps of a royal hall / At mighty monarchs festival. [...]
When there breathes not on the earth / One patriot heart,
When Freedom dies, and truth and worth / From the base world depart,
Then Missolonghi, – not till then, / Thy name shall perish amongst men. [83]

Missolonghi (or Messolonghi) is the place where the great philhellenist George Gordon Byron (1788–1824), better known as Lord Byron, had died in 1824 while helping the Greek rebels. Byron's tragic death created a strong wave of support for the Greek cause in Britain and other European countries. It is likely that the familiar image of the Erard Grecian harp, combined with the harp's celestial or sacred connotations, may have been the trigger for the insertion of the instrument in revolutionary poems and texts, a topic that will be further discussed in Chapter Seven.

The Establishment of Brand Identity

Another distinctive feature of Erard's Grecian harps concerns their conspicuous and consistent branding with inscriptions on the brass plates housing the mechanism. This differed considerably from the branding of earlier harps, on which the maker's signature and other inscriptions were relatively small and not easily detectable. In most cases, inscriptions included the maker's name and address, occasionally also the date of the instrument's manufacture. These inscriptions were usually written in ink, painted, or stamped on the wooden parts of the harp, such as the soundboard or the neck. Some makers also used small handwritten or printed paper labels glued inside the soundbox or pedalbox that could only be seen by dismantling certain instrument components.

Erard was not the first manufacturer to apply branding on the metal mechanism of pedal harps. This idea originated from Cousineau, and was introduced on single-action harps equipped with the béquilles mechanism, which Cousineau was building in the 1780s. On these harps, apart from Cousineau's common stamped or painted inscriptions on the wooden parts, the words 'COUSINEAU PERE ET FILS A PARIS' were cut on a thin brass sheet that was screwed on the mechanism and was visible through a glass panel on the harp's neck.

---

83 Bernard Wycliffe, 'Missolonghi', *The Oriental Herald, and Journal of General Literature* 10 (London: J. M. Richardson, 1826), p. 304.

However, Sébastien Erard took Cousineau's idea to the next level by having his name and other inscriptions engraved on the outer side of the brass plates enclosing the mechanism. The branding of Erard's harps thus became more prominent and easily recognisable. Moreover, since the inscriptions were engraved on metal rather than written or stamped on wood or paper, they were also more permanent, more reliable and more difficult to misinterpret or to fake. Apart from identification purposes that were required, for instance, in the hire, resale or repair of Erard's instruments, such inscriptions were warranty symbols, offering protection against counterfeit, which was quite common in the field of musical instruments during the late eighteenth and early nineteenth centuries.[84] An analysis of Erard's branding is therefore important because the applied inscriptions, in combination with the serial numbers discussed earlier, can facilitate the documentation, authentication, attribution and dating of Erard's Grecian harps.[85]

The first Grecian harps built from 1811 to 1813 were typically engraved on the right brass plate towards the capital with the inscription 'Sebastian Erard's // Patent Harp N XXXX // 18 Great Marlborough Street // London', where XXXX was the four-digit serial number of the instrument. This inscription informed the public not only about the manufacturer's name and address, but also about the imposing fact that he was the holder of a patent, thus boosting Erard's public image as an inventor. Around 1813 the inscription was moved from the right brass plate to the left one above the forked discs. Moreover, an image with the British coat of arms was added to the left of the inscription, and the layout and wording were also slightly altered, reading: 'Sebastian Erard's // Patent N XXXX // 18 Great Marlborough Street London'. This inscription remained standard on all double-action harps of the Grecian model produced subsequently by Erard, with the main noticeable change being the use of 'LONDON' (written in upper case) instead of 'London' from around 1814.

Erard's motivation for moving the inscription from the right to the left plate is unclear. The right plate offered more free space for engraving and the inscription there was more visible compared to the left one, which provided a narrower space due to the mechanism's parts and where the inscription was less readable, as it was partly covered by the strings. One possible explanation is that the double-action mechanism with forked discs was the most visually arresting area of the harp as well as Erard's crowning achievement, so placing the inscription there maximised its prominence. Moreover, from around 1812 the inscription 'SERARD // PUBLISH // APRIL 19 // 1811' was occasionally encircled in two of the four wreaths held by the winged caryatids on the front of the capital, which was another eye-catching area of the harp. This inscription, which most likely referred to the official announcement or publication of Erard's 1810 patent, further illustrated Erard's marketing skills.

---

[84] Panagiotis Poulopoulos, *New Voices in Old Bodies: A Study of 'Recycled' Musical Instruments with a Focus on the Hahn Collection in the Deutsches Museum. Deutsches Museum Studies 2* (Munich: Deutsches Museum, 2016), pp. 88–91.

[85] Erard's branding practices have been discussed in Panagiotis Poulopoulos, 'Shedding New Light on the Production Strategies of Erard', unpublished paper presented at the joint conference of the Galpin Society and the American Musical Instrument Society (AMIS), Musical Instrument Museums Edinburgh (MIMEd), Edinburgh, 1 to 4 June 2017.

Erard soon increased publicity using Grecian harps as a vehicle for self-marketing. Apart from the standard inscription on the left brass plate, from around 1816 the firm began using a promotional inscription engraved on the right brass plate, which read 'Maker // To H.R.H. the Princess Charlotte of Wales // His Most Christian Majesty the King of France // And H.I.M. the EMPEROR of all the Russias'. This inscription demonstrated Erard's strong contacts with the royal families in Britain, France and Russia. Following the defeat of Napoleon Bonaparte (1769–1821) in 1814–1815, which led to the Bourbon Restoration in France, these three superpowers now pulled the strings of international politics. As a fervent royalist himself, Erard was apparently eager to associate his business with the new European leaders through such advertising measures.

In the following years, this inscription was altered four times. It is interesting to observe how the changes in the inscription also reflect the changes in British monarchy, starting with Erard's self-reference as maker to the Princess of Wales. Charlotte Augusta of Wales (1796–1817) was the only child of George, Prince of Wales, who later became King George IV (1762–1830), and his wife, Caroline of Brunswick (1768–1821). Caroline played the harp, and her daughter, who reportedly 'sang, and performed on the piano, the harp and the guitar, with exquisite skill',[86] was most likely familiar with the instrument from an early age. This is evidenced by a portrait dated 1801 by Thomas Lawrence (1769–1830) that depicts young Charlotte holding a music sheet for her mother, who is tuning a harp.[87]

Caroline and Charlotte played upon Erard harps, since Erard N° 357, a black single-action harp, was acquired by 'Her Roy^l High^ss the Pr^ss of Wales' in 1800,[88] while Erard N° 1705 (the ultramarine double-action harp shown in Figure 15), was likewise obtained by 'Her Royal Highness // The Princess of Wales' in 1813, as will be discussed in Chapter Five.[89] However, with the death of young Charlotte in 1817 the inscription referring to her was no longer appropriate. Therefore, from around 1818 Erard used a slightly modified inscription that read 'Maker // TO THE ROYAL FAMILY // His Most Christian Majesty the King of France // And H.I.M. the EMPEROR of all the Russias', as illustrated on Erard N° 2631 (Figure 18).

Around 1821 Erard introduced a third and shorter inscription reading 'MAKER // By Special Appointment // to his Majesty and the // ROYAL FAMILY'. Again, the reasons for change lay in political developments: on 19 July 1821 George, Prince of Wales and from 1811 to 1820 Prince Regent, was officially crowned King George IV, and the inscription had to acknowledge the new sovereign. The event was reported in the Erard correspondence, since in June 1821 Pierre mentioned that 'everyone is preoccupied with the coronation, which will certainly be held on

---

86 Robert Desilver, *Memoirs of the late Princess Charlotte Augusta, of Wales and Saxe Cobourg* (Philadelphia: Robert Desilver, 1818), p. 9.

87 In the Silk Tapestry Room at Buckingham Palace, London (Inv. No. RCIN 407292).

88 Erard London Harp Ledgers, vol. 1, p. 90.

89 Erard London Harp Ledgers, vol. 2, p. 34. This harp survives together with the original stool and resonating board in the Château de Fontainebleau, Fontainebleau (Inv. No. F 2465 C.1).

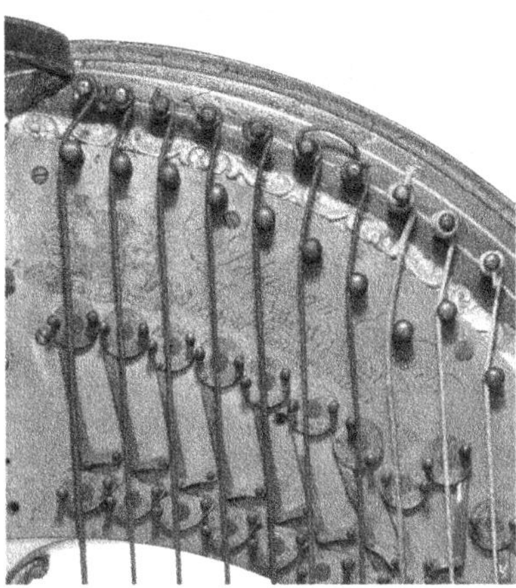

Figure 18. The engraved inscriptions 'Sebastian Erard's // Patent N 2631 // 18 Great Marlborough Street LONDON' (left) and 'Maker // TO THE ROYAL FAMILY // His Most Christian Majesty the King of France // And H.I.M. the EMPEROR of all the Russias' (right) on the left and right brass plates of Erard Nº 2631. Deutsches Museum, Munich (Inv. No. 16147).

the 19th of next month'.[90] In 1820 'His Majesty The King George IVth' had already endorsed Erard harps, purchasing Erard N° 3002, a smalt (blue) double-action harp.[91] This may have been the same harp as the one the king had gifted to his mistress Elizabeth Conyngham (1769–1861), with Pierre stating in March 1821: 'As I know that your harp was tried and kept by Lady Conyngham, who was given the harp as a gift from the king, I immediately requested the title of the Harp Maker to the King for my uncle Sébastien Erard'.[92] By this time, Erard had rather focused on the domestic market, since the references to the rulers of France and Russia were abandoned. For the next ten years, this inscription remained essentially the same, apart from the addition of Sébastien Erard's name around 1824. The new inscription read 'Sebastian Erard // MAKER // By Special Appointment // to his Majesty and the // ROYAL FAMILY.'

From around 1831 the inscription was modified again, this time reading 'Sebastian Erard // Harp & Piano Forte Maker in Ordinary // to her Majesty and the // ROYAL FAMILY'. This was due to two facts. The first is that Erard had started building pianos in his London branch from about 1825, and this new side of the business had to be mentioned in the revised inscription. The second fact highlights

90 L 302, 12 June 1821. Adelson et al, *The History of the Erard Piano and Harp*, pp. 772–773, at p. 772.

91 Erard London Harp Ledgers, vol. 2, p. 163.

92 L 295, 2 March 1821. Adelson et al, *The History of the Erard Piano and Harp*, pp. 759–762, at p. 761. It is worth noting that in her portrait by Thomas Lawrence, painted between 1821 and 1824 and housed in the Museu Calouste Gulbenkian, Lisbon, Elizabeth Conyngham is depicted tuning a small portable harp rather than an Erard double-action harp.

a further change in the British crown: the 'Her Majesty' in the inscription could refer to Adelaide of Saxe-Meiningen (1792–1849), the consort of King William IV (1765–1837), who acceded to the throne on the death of his brother George IV in 1830. However, it is more likely that it refers to George IV's niece, Victoria (Alexandrina Victoria 1819–1901), who became heir presumptive (the main candidate for the British throne), which she occupied on William's death in 1837, initiating the Victorian era in Britain. This inscription can be found on the last Grecian harps produced by Erard in the early 1840s.

The branding of harps with noticeable inscriptions was part of Erard's broad and intensive marketing scheme. As will be discussed in Chapter Five, similar inscriptions printed in the firm's bills[93] and catalogues[94] acted as powerful advertising tools for Erard, whose customers included members of the European royalty and aristocracy as well as celebrities and public figures. For example, in February 1816 Pierre wrote to his uncle Sébastien that the application of such inscriptions on Erard instruments and bills 'adds nothing to your reputation that it is so well done, but it makes a very good impression in the eyes of the public'.[95]

Although it is not known who was responsible for the engravings on Grecian harps, between 1807 and 1809 Erard regularly paid a certain 'Mr Adolpho' for engraving harp plates.[96] This must have been Francis Adolpho, a seal engraver working at 133 Oxford Street in 1818;[97] according to a surviving trade card, at some point his business was at 134 Oxford Street.[98] It is worth mentioning that Erard's branding practice was widely adopted by his contemporaries, as confirmed by the majority of surviving pedal harps from the early nineteenth century that bear engraved inscriptions on the brass plates of the mechanism.

As was typical in many businesses, even though Sébastien Erard had died in 1831, his name remained in the inscriptions of Grecian harps well into the 1840s, apparently to exploit his lasting fame as a harp maker and inventor. This is not surprising, since it was normal that the name of the male head of the firm was often, but not always, the one inscribed on the instrument, even after they themselves were no longer involved in the business. The identity of this individual and that of the firm are often conflated, partly for marketing reasons and partly due to the patriarchal nature of both the family and society at this time. Other examples include makers of pianos, such as Broadwood, or of woodwind and brasswind instruments, like Boosey & Hawkes.[99]

93 See, for example, the Erard Harp Bill dated 27 May 1818, held at Attingham Park Collection, Shropshire Archives, Shrewsbury, 112/6/54/381.

94 See, for example, Erard Harp Catalogue (c.1819–1821), p. 1.

95 L 169, 2 February 1816. Adelson et al, *The History of the Erard Piano and Harp*, pp. 623–624.

96 Nex, *The Business of Musical-Instrument Making in Early Industrial London*, pp. 393–434.

97 'Adolpho, Francis, Seal engraver'. Johnstone, *Johnstone's London Commercial Guide and Street Directory*, p. 368.

98 Metropolitan Museum of Art, New York (Inv. No. 26.28.365). For more details see 'Trade Card for Adolpho, Seal Engraver', available at https://www.metmuseum.org/art/collection/search/820838, accessed 3 June 2022.

99 I am thankful to the second anonymous reviewer for this observation.

Originals and Counterfeits

The trademarking of Erard harps can be compared to that of other branded goods, which became increasingly widespread in the course of the eighteenth century. In the luxury markets of urban centres, such as London or Paris, new as well as second-hand items, and originals as well as imitations and fakes, were commonly circulated.[100] For example, different types of counterfeit products abounded in the watch and clock industry, and therefore dealers and customers had to be extremely careful. Not only did continental makers often manufacture and distribute forgeries of English watches, but also prominent English watchmakers produced inferior timepieces signed with fictitious names for a less wealthy clientele. One representative case is George Prior (1735–1814), who manufactured watches predominantly for the eastern market. Prior's watches were widely copied by Swiss makers, while the Prior firm signed the lower-quality watches it produced with the imaginary name 'George Charles', thus adding a degree of deception to these items, since 'Ironically some thought Prior's name was fictional'.[101]

Branding became gradually of paramount importance for trade networks that included makers, suppliers, dealers and customers. In the case of proprietary medicines, which were one of the earliest types of branded products, branding was 'a means of establishing a distinct product identity which held out to the consumer a (highly questionable) guarantee of standards and effectiveness. It enabled the owners of the brands to distinguish their products from the generic medicines sold by apothecaries and other local retailers, and thereby both to establish larger national and international markets and to command a price premium.'[102]

Several measures for product differentiation were implemented, such as the packing of medicines in small glass bottles blown in brand-specific forms and bearing the brand details embossed on the glass surface, which allowed the brand owners 'to establish a distinct product identity among consumers', while reducing 'the constant threat of piracy'.[103] One of the pioneers of trademarking was Josiah Wedgwood, whose products were distinctively branded from the early 1770s onwards. Wedgwood 'was the first earthenware potter to consistently mark his wares, and the use of his own name impressed in clay set him apart from other English or Continental

---

[100] See, for example, Maxine Berg, 'From Imitation to Invention: Creating Commodities in Eighteenth-Century Britain', *The Economic History Review* 55/1 (2002), pp. 1–30, at pp. 17–26, as well as Natacha Coquery, 'The Language of Success: Marketing and Distributing Semi-Luxury Goods in Eighteenth-Century Paris', *Journal of Design History* 17/1 (2004), pp. 71–89, at pp. 81–87.

[101] Ian White, *English Clocks for the Eastern Markets: English Clockmakers Trading in China and the Ottoman Empire 1580–1815* (Ticehurst: Antiquarian Horological Society, 2012), p. 68; see also Artemis Yagou, 'Novel and Desirable Technology: Pocket Watches for the Ottoman Market (late18th c.–mid 19th c.)', *ICON: Journal of the International Committee for the History of Technology* 24 (2018/2019), pp. 78–107, at pp. 92–93.

[102] John Styles, 'Product Innovation in Early Modern London', *Past & Present* 168 (2000), pp. 124–169, at p. 149.

[103] Styles, 'Product Innovation in Early Modern London', p. 153.

manufacturers, who used a painted device such as the anchor of Chelsea or the crossed swords of Meissen.'[104]

The practice of branding with the name and logo of a prominent master or entrepreneur could also help to hide the complicated and divided manufacture of objects which often involved people and materials that originated from different locations being employed in crowded, noisy and dirty workshops. Discussing construction plans for the firm's store, Pierre noted characteristically in 1819: 'we could put the store in the place of the warehouses, to connect to the little house. But we would need to build everything. And then if we divide it to rent the house, the workshops would not please a <u>gentleman</u>. The horses and the carriages should pass by the door of the workshops.'[105] As one author has argued, 'Brands can be seen as a way of "disguising" the complexity of the productive process and the unpleasantries of cellars and garrets, by showing and guaranteeing quality through a process of trust: brands are the paper money of solid-gold quality', adding that '"Labelled" goods, such as furniture or shoes guaranteed provenance.'[106]

Nevertheless, the application of visible labels and trademarks could not prevent forgeries, as was well known to Erard, who was already aware of counterfeit Erard pianos in the late 1790s. In 1797 Erard warned a dealer in Madrid about this issue, stating 'We can not tell you enough to be wary of all the Erard labels stuck on pianos in Paris by numerous newly established instrument dealers who are trying to profit from our name in order to deceive the public with counterfeit instruments.'[107] Erard's harps were also widely copied by other makers in London, leading the firm to occasionally take measures against imitators. For instance, as early as 1798 Erard had announced a generous reward to those who would expose the illegal imitators of his new patent mechanism for the single-action harp:

> *Erard's new Patent Harp, One Hundred Guineas Reward.* Mr. Sebastian Erard is informed that attempts have been made to counterfeit the mechanism of his new Patent Harp: whoever will bring information against the culpable to No. 18, Great Marlborough-street, shall, on his or their conviction, receive a reward of 100 guineas. Although Mr. Erard is certain that every attempt to imitate must fall infinitely short of the perfection to which he has brought his new Patent Harp, yet he thinks it a duty he owes to himself and the public to punish this bare violation of the rights of property.[108]

The hundred guineas that Erard was offering was a considerable amount of money, much higher than the price of a single-action harp. A year later, in 1799, a similar announcement was published in another newspaper, suggesting that the issue was still troubling Erard:

---

[104] Young, *The Genius of Wedgwood*, p. 51.

[105] L 258, 17 May 1819. Adelson et al, *The History of the Erard Piano and Harp*, p. 718.

[106] Giorgio Riello, 'Strategies and Boundaries: Subcontracting and the London Trades in the Long Eighteenth Century', *Enterprise & Society* 9/2 (2008), pp. 243–280, at pp. 260–261.

[107] L 7.383, 10 February 1797. Adelson et al, *The History of the Erard Piano and Harp*, pp. 175–176, at p. 176.

[108] *The Morning Chronicle* (London), 2 March 1798.

ERARD'S NEW PATENT HARP.– One Hundred Guineas Reward.– Messrs. Erard and Co. are informed that attempts have been made to counterfeit the Mechanism of their New Patent Harp: Whoever will bring information against the culpable to No. 15, Great Marlborough-Street, shall, on his or their conviction, receive a Reward of 100 guineas.[109]

Erard was facing the same problems after he introduced his new patent double-action harp, since the Grecian model was soon imitated by other London makers. As already mentioned, in March 1819 Pierre warned his uncle that 'all of the makers are now copying your capital with three faces',[110] urging him to come up with a new design in Paris. Nevertheless, with the firm's reputation growing considerably in the 1810s after the establishment of the double-action harp, Erard seems to have been less afraid of imitation, since he probably understood that copies could only add to the firm's prestige. In February 1821 Pierre wrote to his uncle that 'the harp is becoming each day more popular, and I am pleased to be able to assure you that your inventions are more and more appreciated all the time. The copies only serve to emphasise the value of the original.'[111]

Regarding an essay that Pierre proposed to publish in order to promote Erard's double-action harp, he similarly claimed: 'The only disadvantage that could result from the publication of this essay would be to make everything too public! But your harps are in the hands of everyone, and if gentlemen factors could copy, nothing would be easier than obtaining an instrument. I do not see why that reason can stop us.'[112] One month later Pierre stated that 'it would be good to make the improvements you believe that your harp is capable of. Everyone is happy with it as is, but if it is possible to do even better, it would mark even more difference between the original and the copies.'[113]

Erard's attitude towards counterfeits was shared by other pioneering manufacturers. For example, Wedgwood considered imitation as 'a tribute to his standards of design and workmanship', declaring that 'so far from being afraid of other people getting our patterns, we should glory in it, throw out all the hints we can, and if possible have all artists in Europe working after our models. This would be noble, and would suit both our dispositions and sentiments better than all the narrow mercenary selfish trammels.'[114]

---

[109] *The Times* (London), 10 May 1799.

[110] L 251, 2 March 1819. Adelson et al, *The History of the Erard Piano and Harp*, pp. 708–710, at p. 710.

[111] L 294, 13 February 1821. Adelson et al, *The History of the Erard Piano and Harp*, pp. 758–759, at p. 759.

[112] L 297, 16 March 1821. Adelson et al, *The History of the Erard Piano and Harp*, pp. 763–767, at p. 764.

[113] L 300, 10 April 1821. Adelson et al, *The History of the Erard Piano and Harp*, pp. 770–771, at p. 771.

[114] Richard Tames, *Josiah Wedgwood: An Illustrated Life of Josiah Wedgwood, 1730–1795* (2nd edn; Aylesbury: Shire Publications Ltd, 1984), pp. 32–33.

Conclusions

The decoration and branding of the Erard Grecian harp show that the Erard firm was aware of the current developments not only in the musical instrument business but also in related luxury trades, ranging from furniture-making and horology to pottery and printing. This is exemplified by the introduction of composition ornaments and decoupage, two innovative techniques that provided inexpensive, flexible and consistent alternatives to woodcarvings and paintings, which had been common in harp making for centuries. Moreover, the neoclassical style that was integrated in the structural and decorative elements of Erard Grecian harps radically changed both the appearance and the identity of the harp. The Grecian model thus adopted a highly symbolic character, which resonated with post-revolutionary audiences that often looked back to the classical past of ancient Greece for guidance and inspiration. Furthermore, the instantly visible and recognisable inscriptions on Erard Grecian harps served effectively as an identification tool, a means of advertising and a measure against forgeries, as was the case with other branded commercial products. Additionally, the distinctive trademarking of these harps mirrored the developments in British and European politics as well as in the marketing schemes of the Erard firm during the first decades of the nineteenth century. The next chapter will shed new light on the manufacture of Erard Grecian harps, presenting various details about the organisation, management and operation of the firm's London branch, in which these instruments were produced.

CHAPTER FOUR

Manufacturing the Erard Grecian Harp: Aspects of Organisation, Management and Operation

'I have taken on lots of workers and have arranged it so that we can finish at least four double harps each week!'[1]

Erard N° 2631 is one of 160 double-action harps of the Grecian model known to have been produced by Erard in London in 1818. Although these harps proudly bear Sébastien Erard's signature, it is inconceivable that he could have handled all of them – let alone crafted them on his own – especially since from 1814 he was resident in Paris. How were then so many harps built during that year, who supervised their production and who was directly involved in their manufacture? Was this number typical of the firm's annual production or an exception? Who supplied Erard with materials, equipment and tools, and to what extent did the firm collaborate with subcontractors? And in what ways was the organisation, management and operation of the Erard London branch similar or different to other contemporary musical instrument makers as well as to producers in related manufacturing sectors? By investigating a variety of sources, this chapter will discuss the business administration, workshop arrangement, workforce, supply chain and working practices of the Erard firm, allowing us to be virtually transferred inside Erard's London harp manufactory and to discover the people, premises and processes behind Sébastien Erard in the background of Regency London.

The Organisation of Harp Manufacture at the Erard London Branch

The London branch of the Erard firm, where Grecian harps were made from 1811 to the mid-1840s, was situated at 18 Great Marlborough Street in Soho, a fashionable district in London's West End.[2] Erard's choice to establish the firm's site in this area was not random: during the end of the eighteenth and the beginning of the

---

[1] L 294, 13 February 1821, in Robert Adelson, Alain Roudier, Jenny Nex, Laure Barthel and Michel Foussard (eds), *The History of the Erard Piano and Harp in Letters and Documents, 1785–1959* (Cambridge: Cambridge University Press, 2015), pp. 758–759, at p. 759.

[2] For more details on the history of 18 Great Marlborough Street see 'Great Marlborough Street Area', available at https://www.british-history.ac.uk/survey-london/vols31-2/pt2/pp250-267#h3-0013, accessed 3 June 2022.

nineteenth centuries Soho was 'an important meeting point for émigrés', while 'The combination of its location in central London and its traditionally international population set it apart from other London districts.'[3] Soho was a geographically strategic point for many musical instrument makers in London, including those building harps,[4] since it provided easy access to suppliers of materials and equipment, to dealers and subcontractors, as well as to numerous upper-class customers who lived around this area. In Soho, Erard could easily meet and socialise with former French aristocrats as well as with fellow French royalists, like the painter Henry Pierre Danloux (1753–1809), who, like Erard, had many customers within the *Ancien Régime* and had left France in 1792 because he did not approve of the new republican state.[5]

Although Erard was the leading harp manufacturer, and one of the most prominent manufacturers of musical instruments in London, the information that we have about the actual production of harps at the Erard London branch is fragmented and incomplete, especially concerning the first years after the introduction of the double-action harp. The rich material contained in the Erard workshop accounts between 1807 and 1809[6] as well as in the surviving correspondence between Pierre and Sébastien Erard, which stretches from 1814 to 1831,[7] provides valuable glimpses into the firm's workshop organisation, workforce and daily operation. Yet, no thorough account that could enable a more detailed reconstruction of Erard's London harp manufactory during the early 1810s, when the firm entered a new, challenging phase with the launching of the Grecian model, has survived.

However, valuable insight into the setup and operation of Erard's business comes from the firm's Paris branch, which was directed by Sébastien's elder brother, Jean-Baptiste Erard (1749–1826). In contrast to the London branch, which was set up for the manufacture of harps, Erard's branch in the French capital focused on the manufacture of pianos (Figure 19), with harps being produced in relatively small numbers.[8]

---

3   Kirsty Carpenter, 'London: Capital of the Emigration', in Kirsty Carpenter and Philip Mansel (eds), *The French Émigrés in Europe and the Struggle against Revolution, 1789–1814* (London: Palgrave MacMillan, 1999), pp. 43–67, at p. 43.

4   Mike Baldwin, *The Harp in Early Nineteenth-century Britain: Innovation, Business, and Making in Jacob Erat's Manufactory* (PhD Diss., London: London Metropolitan University, 2017), pp. 52–62.

5   Kirsty Carpenter, *Refugees of the French Revolution: Émigrés in London, 1789–1802* (Basingstoke: MacMillan, 1999), pp. 52–53 and 73.

6   Erard London Harp Ledgers, vol. 1, 'Expenses' section, pp. 1–62. A transcription of these accounts is included in Jenny Nex, *The Business of Musical-Instrument Making in Early Industrial London* (PhD Diss., London: Goldsmiths College, 2013), pp. 393–434.

7   Annotated transcriptions of these letters in English are included in Robert Adelson, Alain Roudier, Jenny Nex, Laure Barthel and Michel Foussard (eds), *The History of the Erard Piano and Harp in Letters and Documents, 1785–1959* (Cambridge: Cambridge University Press, 2015), pp. 541–842.

8   For more details on the development of Erard pianos see Robert Adelson, *Erard: A Passion for the Piano* (Oxford and New York: Oxford University Press, 2021).

Figure 19. Erard N° 980, a typical example of the square pianos produced at the
Erard Paris branch. The instrument bears the inscriptions 'Sebastien Erard et Frere
/ Compag. Privilegiees du rói. Rué du Mail N 37 / Paris 1790' on the nameboard and
'Erard Freres à Paris 1790 / No. 980' on the soundboard. Deutsches Museum, Munich
(Inv. No. 24219).

As early as 1802, the German composer, writer and music critic Johann Friedrich
Reichardt (1752–1814) visited the Erard establishment in Paris, recording his observations in a letter that is worth discussing in detail. As Reichardt noted, by the beginning of the nineteenth century the Erard brothers enjoyed a reputation as large-scale
piano and harp manufacturers, whose high-quality and costly instruments were sold
all over Europe:

Paris, 22 November 1802.

The way that here many things, which among us always remain small-scale even
for the best workers, are being driven to a large scale, I experienced in the establishment of the Erard brothers, who are now making such perfect fortepianos and
harps as to be done anywhere. And in what incredible amount! without regarding
the high price, which exceeds even the price of English instrument makers. From
small fortepianos in clavichord format, at forty Louis neuf (or Carolinen, as we
call them, to six and a half Thaler) up to the largest highly tastefully decorated
fortepianos in grand piano format, which are paid for with one hundred and up

to two hundred Louis neuf. To all the countries of Europe, where water transport allows it, they send their instruments in large numbers.[9]

Most importantly, Reichardt's report provides a vivid description of Erard's business organisation and workforce. The details reveal a firm that can be labelled as 'comprehensive', that is, one that employs division of labour, with many workers of various specialisations occupied in appropriately equipped workshops under the same roof.[10] Apart from craftsmen engaged in woodwork and metalwork that were necessary for the building of pianos and harps, Erard also hired a variety of artisans for the ornamentation of instruments. This ensured that all stages of construction and decoration could be executed in-house:

> The establishment occupies though almost two sizable houses in one of the best areas of Paris. Everything that belongs to the most complete finishing of the most ornate instrument is processed in the house itself to a great extent. Not only the actual instrument makers, carpenters, wood turners, locksmiths and metal-workers have their fully equipped workshop there, but also the bronzesmith, the painter, the varnisher, the ebonist and the enamellist, the gilder, the wire drawer, and who knows who else, work there in spacious, well-equipped workshops.[11]

In several rooms Reichardt noticed numerous instruments in various stages of manufacture that included the making of instrument frames and cases, the assembly of the various parts and the finishing, which were reportedly carried out under the eyes or the hands of Jean-Baptiste Erard himself. High-quality wood of all kinds that was required for the building of fine pianos and harps was stored in the courtyards.

---

9 'Paris, den 22sten Novemb. 1802. Wie hier so manches, das bei uns auch für die besten Arbeiter, immer im Kleinen bleibt, ins Große getrieben wird, erleb' ich auch an dem Etablissement der Brüder Errard, die jetzt so vollkommene Fortepiano's und Harfen machen, als nur irgendwo gemacht werden. Und in welcher unglaublichen Menge! ohnerachtet des hohen Preises, der noch den Preis der englischen Instrumentenmacher übersteigt. Von kleinen Fortepiano's in Clavierformat, zu vierzig Louis neuf (oder Carolinen, wie wir sie nennen, zu sechs und einen halben Thaler) bis zu den größten höchst geschmackvoll verzierten Fortepiano's in Flügelformat, die mit hundert und bis zweyhundert Louis neuf bezahlt werden. Nach allen Ländern Europa's, wohin irgend der Wassertransport es begünstigt, senden sie ihre Instrumente in großer Anzahl.' Johann Friedrich Reichardt, *Johann Friedrich Reichardt's vertraute Briefe aus Paris geschrieben in den Jahren 1802–1803* (Hamburg: B. G. Hoffmann, 1805), pp. 150–151.

10 The term 'comprehensive' to describe the Erard firm is employed here in the context that has been used by design historian Pat Kirkham in her study of furniture-making companies in London. For more details on the development of comprehensive firms see Pat Kirkham, 'The London Furniture Trade, 1700–1870', *Furniture History* 24 (1988), pp. 57–71.

11 'Das Etablissement nimmt aber auch fast zwei ansehnliche Häuser in einer der besten Gegenden von Paris ein. Alles, was zur kompletesten Vollendung des verziertesten Instruments gehört, wird im Hause selbst ins Große verarbeitet. Nicht nur die eigentlichen Instrumentenmacher, Tischler, Drechsler, Schlösser und Stahlarbeiter haben da ihre vollständig eingerichtete Werkstatt, auch der Bronzierer, der Maler, der Lackierer, der Ebenist und Emaillist, der Vergolder, der Drathzieher, und wer weiß wer noch alles, arbeiten da in geräumigen, wohleingerichteten Werkstätten.' Reichardt, *Johann Friedrich Reichardt's vertraute Briefe aus Paris*, pp. 151–152.

Once completed, the instruments would be moved to spacious, elegant showrooms for display or packing:

> Whole large forecourts and halls are full of finished mahogany cases; others full of instruments, the assembly of which occupies the various workers, under the supervision of the master himself; others again full of those, to which he lays only the last hand. Larger, elegantly decorated halls are filled with completed instruments that await their enthusiasts, or their cases for travel. Several workers are seen day in and day out occupied with the packing of instruments. The courtyards are surrounded by containers full of exquisite wood of all kinds.[12]

An important part of the Erard Paris branch was the accounting department, which was responsible for managing the financial transactions as well as the correspondence of the firm: 'A complete counter with its accountant and his clerk manages, in the English manner, the accounts and correspondence; an associated pay desk takes care of the payments and calculates expenditure and revenue.'[13] As will be mentioned later, the systematic bookkeeping and the correspondence between the firm's managers as well as their written communication with professional associates or clients were vital also for the London branch, as confirmed by the ledgers, workshop accounts, letters and numerous other business documents that have survived.

The Erard family lived comfortably close to the Paris manufactory. The family's premises included Sébastien Erard's own painting gallery, as well as an apartment in which esteemed customers could select their instruments:

> Nearby resides and lives this well-mannered, well-educated family, as befits respected citizens in a wealthy, luxury-driven state. Not only does each of the brothers have their own well-furnished apartment, in which the one, who is a friend of paintings, also has his little select gallery. The felicitous sister, who lives with her amiable daughters in the same house, and looks after the family household, also lives in a very comfortable dainty apartment, whose main rooms simultaneously serve for the daily unification of society; just as a larger, completely detached, apartment serves for the reception of the distinguished strangers, who often visit this rare establishment to choose their own instruments; and on festive

---

[12] 'Ganze große Vorplätze und Säle stehen voll fertiger Mahagonikasten; andere voll Instrumente, mit deren Zusammensetzung die verschiedenen Arbeiter, unter der Aufsicht des Meisters selbst, beschäftigt sind; andere wieder voll solcher, an welche dieser nur noch die letzte Hand legt. Größere, elegant verzierte Säle sind mit vollendeten Instrumenten angefüllt, die ihre Liebhaber, oder ihre Kasten zum Verreisen erwarten. Mehrere Arbeiter sieht man Tag aus Tag ein mit dem Einpacken von Instrumenten beschäftigt. Die Höfe sind mit Schoppen voll köstlichen Holzes aller Art umgeben.' Reichardt, *Johann Friedrich Reichardt's vertraute Briefe aus Paris*, p. 152.

[13] 'Ein vollständiges Comtoir mit seinem Buchhalter und seinem Commis führt, nach englischer Weise, die Rechnungen und Correspondenzen; eine damit verbundene Casse besorgt die Zahlungen und berechnet Ausgabe und Einnahme.' Reichardt, *Johann Friedrich Reichardt's vertraute Briefe aus Paris*, p. 152.

days, when this family, constantly practicing the old and exceptional French hospitality, also sees a more solemn society.[14]

The information about Erard's painting gallery is quite significant. As evidenced in several letters in the Erard correspondence, Sébastien Erard was a keen collector of paintings by old masters of the Renaissance and Baroque, which apart from their aesthetic value were kept as a financial investment and were occasionally sold to generate money for the harp and piano business. Reichardt's report shows that by 1802 Erard had already built a 'select gallery' of masterpieces, which he must have later expanded, since in the 1820s his private collection comprised about 260 paintings, including works by Dürer, Titian, Velasquez and Rembrandt, some of which are now housed in major art museums worldwide.[15] This clearly illustrates Erard's contacts with the world of fine arts, which may have influenced the aesthetics of his harps, as pointed out in Chapter Three. Reichardt also confirms Erard's contacts with renowned German musicians, which may be attributed to the family's origins from Alsace, a German-speaking region:

> I have already spent such a homely festive day with this felicitous family very pleasantly on Sunday, in celebration of the marriage of the older daughter to the well-mannered, amiable painter Bonnemaison. To my delight I found many good German artists there, such as our excellent violoncellist Romberg, whose great talent is also well-known among us, and who has very much perfected himself here; the good piano teachers and composers, Adam, Wiederkehr, Pfeffinger and many others.[16]

---

[14] 'Dabey wohnt und lebt diese brave, feingebildete Familie, wie es angesehenen Bürgern in einem wohlhabenden, luxustreibenden Staate zusteht. Nicht nur hat jeder der Brüder sein eigenes sehr wohl eingerichtetes Apartement, in welchem der Eine, der ein Freund von Gemälden ist, auch seine kleine auserlesene Gallerie hat. Die treffliche Schwester, die mit ihren liebenswürdigen Töchtern dasselbe Haus bewohnt, und den Familienhaushalt besorgt, bewohnen auch ein sehr angenehmes zierliches Apartement, dessen Hauptzimmer zugleich zur täglichen Vereinigung der Gesellschaft dienen; so wie ein größeres, ganz freistehendes, Apartement zum Empfange der angesehenen Fremden dient, die dieses seltene Etablissement oft besuchen, um selbst sich Instrumente auszuwählen; und zu festlichen Tagen, an welchen diese Familie, die beständig die alte, selten gewordene französische Gastfreiheit übt, auch größer gebetene Gesellschaft bei sich sieht.' Reichardt, *Johann Friedrich Reichardt's vertraute Briefe aus Paris*, pp. 152–153.

[15] For more details see Ann Griffiths, 'A Dynasty of Harp Makers' (available at http://www. adlaismusicpublishers.co.uk/pages/harpists/erard.htm, first published in World Harp Congress Review 2002, accessed 3 June 2022.); see also Adelson et al, *The History of the Erard Piano and Harp*, p. 10.

[16] 'Ich habe mit dieser trefflichen Familie schon einen solchen häuslichen Festtag, zur Feier der Vermählung der ältern Tochter mit dem braven, liebenswürdigen Maler Bonnemaison, am Sonntage sehr angenehm verlebt. Zu meiner Freude fand ich da auch viele brave deutsche Künstler, als unsern vortrefflichen Violoncellisten Romberg, dessen großes Talent auch bei uns bekannt genug ist, und der sich hier noch sehr vervollkommnet hat; die braven Clavierlehrer und Componisten, Adam, Wiederkehr, Pfeffinger u. a. m.' Reichardt, *Johann Friedrich Reichardt's vertraute Briefe aus Paris*, pp. 153–154.

As will be discussed in the next chapter, several eminent musicians and music teachers acted as Erard's agents, promoting the firm's instruments to their pupils and potential Erard customers, usually receiving a commission for their services. The female members of the Erard family were not excluded from artistic and commercial initiatives; according to Reichardt, Erard's nieces were competent musicians who were also involved in the music business:

> The young ladies of the house are themselves very interesting singers and pianists and have also established their own music-selling business, which has also found its hall in this artistic home. All this will give you roughly an idea of the size of this great establishment. The excellence of the instruments is difficult to express in words. They have, however, everything that can make such an instrument brilliant and pleasing, and concerning the treatment and the thankful ease with which they follow the player are far preferable to English instruments.[17]

Remarkably, Reichardt's report includes a brief mention of Erard's London branch. Under the management of Sébastien Erard, the London branch manufactured single-action harps based on Erard's 1794 patent, the cost of which largely depended on the gloss of their finish:

> The brothers also have a sizable establishment in London, for which the older brother, whom I resentfully miss here, is staying there. This English establishment is based especially on a new improvement of the harp, which is now built by these artists according to their own idea more perfectly and beautifully than anywhere. It is a pleasure to see such a harp in the hands of the beautiful, so tasteful, magnificent and accomplished is the work. These harps, however, cost from sixty to a hundred Louis neuf and above, depending on whether appearance is more or less shiny.[18]

The structure and operation of Erard's branches in the British and French capitals must have been quite similar, at least as far as the manufacture of harps was concerned, since the harp workshop in Paris had been based on that established

[17] 'Die jungen Damen des Hauses sind selbst sehr interessante Sängerinnen und Clavierspielerinnen und haben auch einen eigenen Musikhandel etablirt, der auch noch in diesem kunstvollen Hause seinen Saal gefunden hat. Alles dieses wird dir ohngefähr einen Begriff von dem Umfange dieses großen Etablissements geben können. Von der Vortrefflichkeit der Instrumente ist es schwer mit Worten einen Begriff zu geben. Sie haben indeß alles, was ein solches Instrument brillant und gefällig machen kann, und sind in der Behandlung und der dankbaren Leichtigkeit, mit der sie dem Spieler folgen, den englischen Instrumenten weit vorzuziehen.' Reichardt, *Johann Friedrich Reichardt's vertraute Briefe aus Paris*, pp. 154–155.

[18] 'Die Brüder haben auch ein ansehnliches Etablissement in London, wofür sich der ältere Bruder, den ich sehr ungern hier vermisse, eben dort aufhält. Dieses englische Etablissement gründet sich besonders auf eine neue Vervollkommmnung der Harfe, die von diesen Künstlern nun nach eigner Idee vollkommner und schöner gebaut werden als irgendwo. Es ist schon eine Freude eine solche Harfe in den Händen der Schönen zu sehen, so geschmackvoll, prächtig und vollendet ist die Arbeit. Diese Harfen kosten aber auch, nachdem das Aeussere mehr oder weniger glänzend ist, von sechzig bis hundert Louis neuf und darüber.' Reichardt, *Johann Friedrich Reichardt's vertraute Briefe aus Paris*, pp. 154–155.

in London during the early 1790s. This is confirmed in a letter from 1797, in which Sébastien Erard informed a French customer that 'we will set up the manufacture of our harps with the new mechanism, patterned after our workshops in our firm in London'.[19] Considering this fact, and without ignoring any differences that may have existed in the manufacturing sectors of the two countries, we can assume that several of the above-mentioned details concerning the Erard Paris branch could also apply to the firm's London branch.

In addition, evidence from the Erard correspondence shows that the Paris and London branches often acted like communicating vessels, with materials, instruments, funds and people being occasionally sent from one branch to the other when this was needed. For example, in 1814 Pierre reported that 'The wood that we bought here recently is not dry enough. There is a good batch of wood set aside for the harps in our Paris branch. It would be very helpful if you could send us a small amount of it. They have the model for your new harp and they could cut it up in Paris.'[20] Likewise, in 1818 Pierre intended to let Delveaux, one of his foremen who had worked in both Paris and London, 'wait until next year' before paying him money that he owed to him, with his plan 'being to not pay the first six months of 1818, only what is absolutely necessary', in order to give his uncle 'the means to completely finish the business in Paris'.[21]

Further information about both the Paris and London branches is provided in the travel diary of the Viennese piano maker Johann Baptist Streicher, who toured various European countries between 1821 and 1822.[22] During his stay in Paris he was invited on 13 January 1822 by Jean-Baptiste Erard to the firm's premises. Streicher claimed that Erard pianos were richly decorated, but found that their sound was not equally satisfactory. Erard apparently boasted about the size of his workforce, stating that he employed 150 workers, whereas Streicher himself estimated about 80. Streicher further mentioned that part of the staff was occupied with the building of harps, adding that Sébastien Erard, who was also present during the meeting, had an establishment for the manufacture of harps in London:

> Sunday 13th January. [...] I was invited to dine with Mr Erard. He talked a lot about pianos, criticising the little taste that the Germans used on the external shape of their instruments. His pianos are decorated with enamel gilding on the wrestplank and with bronze on the feet, but there is still much to be desired in the sound. Erard may have about 80 workers, although he said to me incidentally that he has 150. However, he uses a team of journeymen for the manufacture of harps. His brother, who has the establishment of harps in London, was here today, and

---

[19] L 7.411, 29 April 1797. Adelson et al, *The History of the Erard Piano and Harp*, p. 194.

[20] L 111, 11 November 1814. Adelson et al, *The History of the Erard Piano and Harp*, pp. 562–564, at p. 563.

[21] L 216, 29 January 1818. Adelson et al, *The History of the Erard Piano and Harp*, p. 674.

[22] For more details see Uta Goebl-Streicher, *Das Reisetagebuch des Klavierbauers Johann Baptist Streicher 1821–1822: Text und Kommentar* (Tutzing: Schneider, 2009).

promised me to bring a letter to London. Mrs. Erard, a German, seems to have forgotten her language, like most Germans who are here.[23]

Streicher noted further details about Erard's workforce after a meeting he had a couple of weeks later with one of Erard's employees, mentioning that the Paris branch employed 12 harp makers, which was only about one tenth of his total personnel. He pointed out the firm's strict regulations, which prevented workers from different departments visiting one another, and thus exchanging trade secrets. He also compared Erard's business scheme to that of the piano maker Jean-Henri Pape (1789–1875), whose staff was about half the size of that at Erard's and who, in contrast to Erard, undertook administrative tasks alone:

> *Erard* indeed has over 100 workers, of which currently only 12 are harp makers. The journeymen of a workshop are not allowed to go into another; Erard himself often only comes around every 6 weeks. He has a *counter* with 4 *clerks*. *Pape* has 44 workers, but manages the purchases and *correspondence* himself.[24]

Additionally, when Streicher was visited by one of Erard's keyboard makers on 26 February he was informed that he would have a much better opportunity in London than in Paris to inspect the machine used to cut ivory – presumably for piano keys and other ivory parts used on pianos and harps – indicating that both branches were equipped with similar equipment.[25]

One month later Streicher was in London. Although during his stay in the British capital he met with several prominent instrument makers, who provided various details about their businesses, he did not describe the Erard London branch, probably because he was more interested in pianos than in harps. However, Streicher visited Stumpff, one of Erard's competitors, on 27 March 1822. In his diary he included a brief reference to the invention of the double-action harp, and the patents applied

---

23 'Sonntag 13t *Jänner*. […] Bey H *Érard* zu Tische geladen gewesen. Er sprach viel über *Claviere*, und tadelte den wenigen Geschmack, den die Deutsche auf die äussere Form ihrer Instrumente verwendeten. Seine *Claviere* sind an den Stimmstocken mit *Emaille* Vergoldungen, die Füsse mit Bronze verziert, aber doch bleibt im Ton viel zu wünschen über. *Erard* mag ungefähr 80 Arbeiter haben, obwohl er mir *en passant* sagte, er habe 150. Er verwendet aber einen Theil der Gesellen zur Verfertigung von Harfen. Sein Bruder, welcher das *Etablissement* von Harfen in *London* hat, war heute hier, und versprach mir einen Brief nach *London*. Ma^dme Érard, eine Deutsche, *affectirt* ihre Sprache vergessen zu haben, so wie die meisten Deutsche, welche hier sind.' Goebl-Streicher, *Das Reisetagebuch des Klavierbauers Johann Baptist Streicher*, p. 102.

24 'Dienstag 29t *Jänner*. […] Zu Hause bey *Kisting* den Stiefbruder von *Lunau*, und einen Arbeiter von *Érard* getroffen; mit ihnen in das *Café de la paix* gegangen. *Érard* soll doch über 100 Arbeiter haben, worunter gegenwärtig nur 12 Harfenmacher sind. Die Gesellen einer Werkstätte dürfen in keine andere gehen; *Érard* selbst kommt oft nur alle 6 Wochen überall herum. Er hat ein *Comptoir* mit 4 *Commis*. *Pape* hat 44 Arbeiter, besorgt aber Einkäufe und *Correspondenz* selbst.' Goebl-Streicher, *Das Reisetagebuch des Klavierbauers Johann Baptist Streicher*, pp. 107–108, at p. 108.

25 'Dienstag 26t *Feb*. […] Zu Hause besuchten mich *Lunau's* Bruder, der *Claviatur* Macher von *Érard* u noch ein Instrumentenmacher. Die Maschine um Elfenbein zu schneiden soll ich viel besser in *London* als hier sehen können.' Goebl-Streicher, *Das Reisetagebuch des Klavierbauers Johann Baptist Streicher*, p. 123.

for this instrument by Erard and Stumpff, claiming that the main difference was that Erard used an external connection for the fourchettes, whereas Stumpff used an internal one, both producing essentially the same effect. Moreover, he compared the quality of the harps built by the two makers. As in the case of Erard's pianos, which according to his comments looked nice but did not sound as well as their look suggested, Streicher observed that Stumpff's harps had a better, fuller tone than those of Erard, especially in the treble, which resulted from Stumpff's construction of the harp soundboard with unequal thicknesses.[26]

Although Streicher may have been simply repeating Stumpff's propaganda, his observation was similar to that of John Broadwood (1732–1812), the prominent London piano manufacturer. In 1803 Broadwood wrote to a customer who was interested in selling a piano and in buying a harp:

> We will allow you 35 guineas for your Gd. Pianoforte in exchange for a new one wt add.l keys which we sell at 75 Gu … A Lady has a harp to sell made by Erat … for which she asks 35 Gu … Erard is the most fashionable maker – but we know of no secondhand instrument of his at present. Mr Stumph [Stumpff] we think makes the best Harp – his price is 75 G. If you chose to have one of his, we think we can perswade [sic] him to throw off to you the music masters premium which is 12 G.[27]

This letter not only shows that a harp was as expensive as a grand pianoforte, but also provides a comparison by a contemporary author between three different harp makers working in London at that time: Erard, 'the most fashionable maker'; Erat, a maker without any noteworthy attributes; and Stumpff, who, according to Broadwood, 'makes the best Harp'.

Despite the subjectivity of such comments, they indicate that the success of Erard harps may have been based more on their attractive decorative and mechanical features than on their sound. Recommending that Sébastien open a piano manufactory in London, Pierre stated in 1819: 'I have to tell you that we are constantly refining the decorative aspect, and that the pretty shapes you give your instruments would constitute an advantageous contrast to the hideous forms of the other makers; and that they would not be able to rectify so quickly'.[28] Interestingly, Stumpff was a previous

---

[26] 'Mittwoch 27t *März*. […] H *Stumpff* besucht. Lange mit ihm über Instrumente gesprochen. Er hat eine Erfindung an der Harfe gemacht, auf welche er ein Patent hat. Diese besteht darin, durch ein Pedal eine Saite um 2 halbe Töne zu erhöhen. *Erard* hat dieselbe Erfindung auf eine weniger vollkommne Art gemacht. Bey *Erard* ist es durch aussere Verbindung, bey *Stumpff* wahrscheinlich durch Innere. Der *Effekt* mag derselbe seyn. Unstreitig haben aber die *Stumpffische* Harfen einen viel schöneren Ton, als die *Erardische*. *Stumpff* sagt, die ganze Kunst des Tons geben, lieg im Verhältniß und der Ausarbeitung des *Resonnazbodens*, welcher immer gleiche Schwingungen mit der Saite machen muß. Alle Böden zu den Harfen arbeitet er selbst aus und keine Stelle daran hat gleiche Dicke mit der anderen. Sein[e] Harfen haben im *Discant* viel mehr Boden als die *Erardischen*.' Goebl-Streicher, *Das Reisetagebuch des Klavierbauers Johann Baptist Streicher*, p. 143.

[27] Quoted in Dorothy Jean Deval, *Gradus ad Parnassum: The Pianoforte in London, 1770–1820* (PhD Diss., London: University of London, 1991), p. 45.

[28] L 245, 22 January 1819. Adelson et al, *The History of the Erard Piano and Harp*, pp. 702–704, at p. 703.

employee of Sébastien Erard, since a letter by James Shudi Broadwood (1772–1851) reports that Stumpff 'long worked with Old Erard',[29] and therefore it is not coincidental that Stumpff's instruments resembled (and according to Broadwood surpassed) those of his former master.

Additional information showing that there were parallel structures between the two Erard branches is contained in Pierre's letters. As in Paris, Erard's branch in London consisted of three main departments, namely the harp-making workshops, the accounting department and the showroom or shop, all housed in a rented property at 18 Great Marlborough Street that included 'the house, the garden and the stables'.[30] The three departments are clearly mentioned in the correspondence between 1817 and 1820, when the property was under extensive renovation due to its deteriorating state, which had been already confirmed in 1815. During this time the firm moved the accounting department and showroom to 53 Wigmore Street, while the workshops were relocated to nearby Portland Street. In July 1817 Pierre reported that 'I am writing to you from Wigmore Street where I have rented apartments for six months while we renovate Marlborough Street. We have here just the shop and the books; all of our workers are in Portland Street',[31] while a year later he similarly stated 'So here is where we stand: the store at n° 53 Wigmore Street and all the workshops in Little Portland Street.'[32] Therefore, although Erard N° 2631, a harp completed in 1818, is inscribed with the address '18 Great Marlborough Street' on the right brass plate, it is actually one of the many harps built between 1817 and 1820 at Portland Street rather than at Great Marlborough Street (Figure 20).

Interestingly, several harps built in 1818 are registered in the ledgers with the remark '370. Oxford Street // Covered with a plate'.[33] This was the address favoured by Pierre when in 1818 he asked his uncle to choose a location for the London branch, suggesting that some harps were stored temporarily at 370 Oxford Street.[34] Although the permanent relocation of the branch to new premises in Oxford Street was considered during the renovation, the building at 18 Great Marlborough Street eventually remained the headquarters of the firm in London throughout the production of the Grecian model.

As in Paris, the branch's director, Pierre, resided in close proximity to the business, since he lived in two rooms 'next to the store'.[35] A description of the build-

---

[29] Quoted in David Wainwright, *Broadwood, by Appointment: A History* (London: Quiller Press, 1982), p. 143.

[30] L 166, 27 December 1815. Adelson et al, *The History of the Erard Piano and Harp*, pp. 621–622, at p 621.

[31] L 204, 25 July 1817. Adelson et al, *The History of the Erard Piano and Harp*, pp. 661–662, at p. 661.

[32] L 234, 7 October 1818. Adelson et al, *The History of the Erard Piano and Harp*, pp. 691–692, at p. 692.

[33] Erard London Harp Ledgers, vol. 2, pp. 120–126.

[34] L 230, 8 July 1818. Adelson et al, *The History of the Erard Piano and Harp*, pp. 686–687, at p. 686.

[35] L 161, 1 November 1815. Adelson et al, *The History of the Erard Piano and Harp*, pp. 617–618, at p. 617.

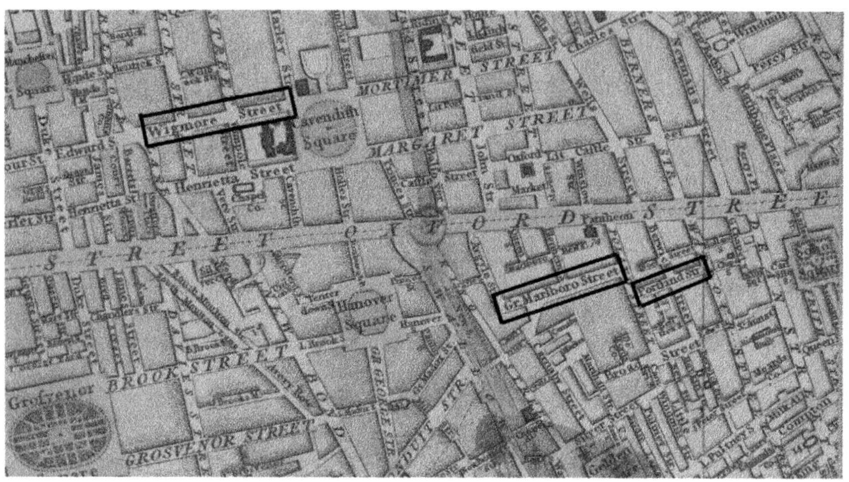

Figure 20. Detail from 'CARY'S New and Accurate Plan of LONDON', a London map published in 1818 (15th edition; first edition published 1787), showing the district where the Erard London branch operated in the 1810s. The marked areas show Great Marlborough Street, as well as Wigmore Street and Portland Street, where the branch had relocated temporarily between 1817 and 1820.

ing at Marlborough Street from November 1817 mentions a large room that was an 'elongated square 22 feet across by 34 in the length' (approximately 70 m²) on the first floor, which most likely served as the showroom. Provision of adequate light through large windows was included on the ground floor, where the harp workshops would have been arranged: 'Three large windows on the street, two on the garden and a door to go into the pavilion in front of the third window. The fourth window on the street will light up the stairway.'[36]

Additional workshops must have been located at the back of the garden. In September 1817 Pierre wrote: 'I think it would be highly desirable that the workshops at the back of the garden be built in the spring so that when we go back into the house we can install the workers at the same time', a wish that he repeated in 1820 when he wanted to 'have the workshops at the rear of the garden'.[37] Probably because of the increasing production demands, Pierre also wanted to expand the manufactory by 'having the tailor's house',[38] most likely referring to the adjoining property at 17 Great Marlborough Street, which had already been offered to Erard

---

[36] L 213, 18 November 1817. Adelson et al, *The History of the Erard Piano and Harp*, pp. 671–672, at p. 671.

[37] L 211, 23 September 1817, and L 280, 9 June 1820. Adelson et al, *The History of the Erard Piano and Harp*, pp. 669–670, at p. 669, and pp. 743–744, at p. 743, respectively.

[38] L 280, 9 June 1820. Adelson et al, *The History of the Erard Piano and Harp*, pp. 743–744, at p. 743.

in 1815.[39] Furthermore, as in Paris, the business included a gallery with paintings collected by Sébastien. From 1815 customers would have the chance to view a selection of these artworks, since that year Pierre removed some paintings from the gallery to the staircase due to humidity issues, keeping the largest ones in his lodgings.[40]

By combining the information in the two reports by Reichardt and Streicher as well as that in Pierre's letters presented above, it is clear that both in London and in Paris the Erards were at the head of a comprehensive firm, employing diverse crafts in a large manufactory comprising various specialised workshops.[41] The production of Erard harps in both cities therefore resulted from the fruitful interaction between many different groups of artisans working under the same roof, with each of them contributing to a specific stage of manufacture under the regular supervision of the firm's masters. Although some subcontractors would have been employed occasionally for specific tasks, the Erard firm was organised to function as an autonomous production system. This is indicated by Pierre's preference 'to have the whole manufacture in one place'[42] and also by his affirmation that 'The house in Malborö offers all one needs for the harp business'.[43]

As already mentioned in Chapter Two, comprehensive firms operating with modular systems of manufacture, and involving division of labour and subcontracting, were already known in various trades, including musical instrument making, from the mid-eighteenth century and probably earlier.[44] Numerous objects could be produced with flexible techniques in small manufacturing units, in which 'workforces were skilled, machinery multi-purpose and products varied', while even bigger firms, employing more than 50 workers, 'were more like a collection of artisanal workshops under one roof than the organizational innovation represented by the factory system'.[45] In Britain the comprehensive firm became a business model that was widely adopted in the production of diverse luxury goods and commodities, such as furniture,

---

[39] See L 134, 15 February 1815, L 265, 13 July 1819 and L 271, 23 February 1820. Adelson et al, *The History of the Erard Piano and Harp*, pp. 585–586, at p. 586; pp. 724–725, at p. 725; and pp. 729–734, at p. 731, respectively.

[40] L 161, 1 November 1815. Adelson et al, *The History of the Erard Piano and Harp*, pp. 617–618, at p. 617.

[41] Although the available information about Erard's London manufactory is limited, it must have shared similarities with that of Erat, a harp maker who imitated Erard's instruments and whose business is discussed in detail in Baldwin, *The Harp in Early Nineteenth-century Britain*, pp. 276–324.

[42] L 213, 18 November 1817. Adelson et al, *The History of the Erard Piano and Harp*, pp. 671–672, at p. 672.

[43] L 257, 13 May 1819. Adelson et al, *The History of the Erard Piano and Harp*, pp. 715–717, at p. 717.

[44] For more details see Geerten Verberkmoes, *Boussu Inside Out: A multifaceted organological study of the life, instruments and methods of the violin maker Benoit Joseph Boussu (1703–1773)* (PhD Diss., Ghent: Ghent University, 2020), pp. 288–290.

[45] Maxine Berg, 'Markets, Trade and European Manufacture', in Maxine Berg (ed.), *Markets and Manufacture in Early Industrial Europe* (London and New York: Routledge, 1991), pp. 3–27, at pp. 10–11.

coaches, clocks and shoes.[46] By the early nineteenth century several London firms had grown immensely, occupying hundreds of workers engaged in the serial production of standardised, uniform items; for example, '1500 people were employed in Christy's hat factory, 600 by Harwood and Co's wallpaper manufactory, up to 800 by the shipbuilders Green and Wigram and 400 by Seddons the cabinet makers.'[47] The increasing scale of businesses demanded appropriate methods of administration, and harp making was no exception, as confirmed by the case of Erard.

Business Administration: Pierre's Prudent Conducting under the Shadow of Sébastien

As mentioned in Chapter One, the original founder and leader of the Erard London branch was Sébastien Erard, who was in charge from the early 1790s – when the branch was established – until 1814, three years after the introduction of the double-action harp. In 1814 Sébastien's young nephew, Pierre-Orphée, took over as manager of the firm in London after his uncle had moved to Paris (Figure 21). Despite Sébastien's reputation as a prolific inventor and manufacturer, it was largely Pierre's professional devotion, persistence and acumen that helped the firm survive, and eventually thrive, during the mid- to late 1810s. These crucial years for the establishment of the double-action harp were marked by constant financial difficulties and strong competition from rival instrument makers in Britain and abroad, exacerbated by the unstable political, social and economic backdrop of Europe during and after the long Napoleonic Wars.

The twenty-year-old Pierre undertook his demanding tasks as director and representative of the London branch with fervour, serving exemplarily in this role, as demonstrated in the surviving correspondence between the two men. As already mentioned, the immense costs and effort invested by Erard in the development of the double-action harp and the preparation of the London manufactory for its production had exposed the firm to existential danger. From the very beginning, Pierre's aim was to control the branch's expenses and to secure enough money to continue building instruments as planned. In 1815, while mentioning various financial matters to his uncle, Pierre noted that 'I was always guided by the same principle, which is above all to reserve the necessary funds each month to keep your manufacturing in the flourishing state that your last invention has created for it', apparently referring to the double-action harp.[48] Although under his direction the new instrument was selling quite well, mainly due to the firm's aggressive promotional agenda, its

---

[46] Indicative examples of comprehensive firms are mentioned in Kirkham, 'The London Furniture Trade', pp. 57–71; in Michael Snodin and John Styles, *Design & the Decorative Arts. Georgian Britain 1714–1837* (London: V&A Publications, 2004), pp. 137–144; and in Giorgio Riello, *The Boot and Shoe Trades in London and Paris in the Long Eighteenth Century* (PhD Diss., London: University College London, 2002), pp. 205–230.

[47] David Colin Barnett, *The Structure of Industry in London, 1775–1825* (PhD Diss., Nottingham: University of Nottingham, 1996), p. 462.

[48] L 157, 10 October 1815. Adelson et al, *The History of the Erard Piano and Harp*, pp. 613–614, at p. 613.

Figure 21. Left: Sébastien Erard, lithography of a portrait by Charles Achille d'Hardivillier, printed by C. Motte, Paris, 1830. Right: Pierre-Orphée Erard, lithography by Wilhelm Heuer, after a portrait by Jean-Urbain Guerini, printed by C. Motte, Paris, 1820. Bibliothèque nationale de France, Paris, département Musique, Est. ErardS.004 (left) and Est.ErardP.001 (right), respectively.

production was costly, with Pierre arguing that 'there has been an enormous amount of money that has passed through the firm since you left, but the manufacturing costs are quite expensive.'[49] However, a few years later in 1823 Pierre remarked that 'the manufacturing expenses are proportionally less'.[50]

As will be described later, the firm's cost-cutting actions usually involved the reduction of staff, but occasionally extended to measures that affected working conditions. In autumn 1816 Pierre decided to reduce the working hours to avoid burning candles, claiming that 'I will keep our workers as long as I can by making them work only two-thirds of a day; we will not light the candles, which will also reduce the danger of a fire.'[51] Before the introduction of gas lighting, candles was the most common, but also most expensive, method of providing artificial light. Wax candles were the most pricey, with some members of the aristocracy reportedly spending enormous sums of money on wax candles in order to illuminate their evening social

<hr>

49 L 151, 25 July 1815. Adelson et al, *The History of the Erard Piano and Harp*, p. 607.

50 L 339, 30 May 1823. Adelson et al, *The History of the Erard Piano and Harp*, pp. 803–805, at p. 804.

51 L 182, 9 October 1816. Adelson et al, *The History of the Erard Piano and Harp*, pp. 636–638, at p. 637.

gatherings.[52] But even cheaper materials employed at industrial sites increased business costs significantly because 'factories worked long hours, and consequently used considerable quantities of oil and tallow in winter months [...]. In 1806 one of the largest of Manchester's spinning factories, McConnel & Kennedy, burned candles for at least eight hours on the shortest days and averaged four hours lighting a day for six months of the year', while 'In 1809 another Manchester cotton factory, Messrs. Burleigh, burned some 800 candles a night for six months of the year, which represented an annual expenditure of nearly £400.'[53] Besides, candles and oil lamps 'were most inconvenient where large areas needed lighting, for then the labour involved in constant snuffing, the smoke and heat, and the dangers from sparks, were at their greatest'.[54]

Considering the above details, the available lighting methods were 'not only expensive for factories – and shops and offices – but produced excessively hot and smoky conditions.'[55] Detailed work in workshops building musical instruments, including harps, demanded ample light, which during daytime would have been provided mainly by large windows facing south,[56] but in the evening hours this would not suffice. This is why between 1807 and 1809, the Erard London branch regularly purchased wax and tallow candles, as well as oil, from a certain 'Hailes' and 'Mr Green'. Light was also needed in the firm's showroom, where customers could inspect the finished harps. In February 1820, while reporting on the ongoing renovation work at Marlborough Street, Pierre noted that 'I do not find, as Bruzaud wrote, that the Counting House much obscures the large room, it seems to me that it would be better for the instruments to have the light stronger on one side than the other.'[57]

However, in a musical instrument manufactory where substantial quantities of dry wood were stored, candles, lamps and stoves posed a constant fire threat. The Erards were aware of accidents involving fire happening to their colleagues: when in 1807 a fire had damaged the premises of Clementi & Co on Tottenham Court Road, Erard reportedly 'contributed £3 to the subscription fund set up for the workers' of this firm.[58] Therefore, every night Pierre and his associates made sure that all lighting sources were extinguished because the danger of fire was great, as he stated in 1815: 'There are fires almost everyday. I never go to bed without checking all over the

---

[52] Hannah Greig, *The Beau Monde: Fashionable Society in Georgian London* (Oxford: Oxford University Press, 2013), pp. 42–43.

[53] Malcolm E. Falkus, 'The Early Development of the British Gas Industry, 1790–1815', *The Economic History Review* 35/2 (1982), pp. 217–234, at p. 219.

[54] Falkus, 'The Early Development of the British Gas Industry', p. 219

[55] Falkus, 'The Early Development of the British Gas Industry', p. 220.

[56] Robert Barclay, *The Art of the Trumpet-maker: The Materials, Tools, and Techniques of the Seventeenth and Eighteenth Centuries in Nuremberg* (Oxford: Clarendon Press, 1992), pp. 78–79.

[57] L 271, 23 February 1820. Adelson et al, *The History of the Erard Piano and Harp*, pp. 729–734, at p. 731.

[58] Jenny Nex, *The Business of Musical-Instrument Making in Early Industrial London* (PhD Diss., London: Goldsmiths College, 2013), p. 218.

house; Wilhelm also makes his rounds every evening at the workshop.'[59] In October 1818 Pierre amended the business insurance, stating 'I was horrified by the terrible fires that we have just had, and I am insuring the *stock in trade in Little Portland Street* for £6,000 more, which will make £10.000. With that sum, along with what will be on the books, we would at least be able to put the business back on its feet.'[60] Thus, in Pierre's operational scheme, sensible health and safety precautions could help the firm to avoid disasters, while, in the worst-case scenario, insurance policies could enable it to survive them.

The regular communication between Pierre and Sébastien was fundamental for consultancy and decision-making on a variety of administrative, social and technical matters, such as the purchase of materials and tools, the recruitment of personnel, the interactions with clients, acquaintances and rivals or the development and improvement of instruments. The correspondence also provided an overview of the production and sale of instruments, and of the general state of the Erard business through the years. For example, 1818, when Erard N° 2631 was built, must have been quite a busy year for the Erard firm; at least 26 letters were written that year by Pierre to his uncle, reflecting the firm at its peak. In his first letter from 6 January 1818 Pierre presented to his uncle the sales and income for 1816 and 1817, foreseeing 'a rosy outlook for 1818'.[61] His prediction was confirmed for the first months of 1818, since he wrote on 2 June that 'The sales were very nice! This month too will be terrific. If sales continue in this way, we will need to proceed differently.'[62] However, on 9 September he remarked that 'Sales are poor as they normally are at this time of the year',[63] while in his last letter for that year on 31 December he stated that 'The sales, that were slow for the past six weeks, are now starting to turn around!'[64]

This fluctuating pattern in the annual sale of harps was influenced by the London season, usually resulting in high sales in the late winter, spring and early summer months, when polite society was in London, and in low sales in the late summer, autumn and early winter months, when the beau monde retreated to their country estates, as will be described in the next chapter. A similar sale pattern has been identified in the study of double-action harps sold by Erard in 1812.[65] Despite the considerable profits from the sale of harps, the firm frequently had to borrow money and was constantly in need of funds; in 1816 Pierre complained 'I am still always so short

---

[59] L 163, 29 November 1815. Adelson et al, *The History of the Erard Piano and Harp*, pp. 618–619, at p. 619.

[60] L 235, 13 October 1818. Adelson et al, *The History of the Erard Piano and Harp*, pp. 692–693, at p. 692.

[61] L 215, 6 January 1818. Adelson et al, *The History of the Erard Piano and Harp*, p. 673.

[62] L 224, 2 June 1818. Adelson et al, *The History of the Erard Piano and Harp*, p. 682.

[63] L 232, 9 September 1818. Adelson et al, *The History of the Erard Piano and Harp*, p. 688.

[64] L 241, 31 December 1818. Adelson et al, *The History of the Erard Piano and Harp*, pp. 698–699, at p. 699.

[65] Nex, *The Business of Musical-Instrument Making in Early Industrial London*, pp. 114–115.

on money'.[66] Thus, keeping the business running often relied on the strong contacts of the Erard family with eminent bankers, sponsors and patrons, to whom the Erards turned for help in times of crisis. As evidenced in numerous letters, it was mainly about impending financial issues that Pierre often turned to his uncle for assistance, instruction and approval.

Aside from his uncle's advice, for the administration of the London branch Pierre relied on trusted employees who had been working in the firm for many years under Sébastien's guidance. Two of them were Wilhelm, mentioned above, and John Horn, both probably of German origin, about whom Pierre declared in 1815: 'Wilhelm is still making himself useful to you in Portland Street. Horn is still a very good man. These two are really precious servants.'[67] For Wilhelm, who eventually returned to France in 1817, Pierre informed his uncle that 'since your departure he has conducted himself as an honest and good man, full of attachment for you.'[68] Both men must have been experienced woodworkers, since in at least two occasions they helped Pierre select wood for harps.[69] Moreover, apart from finishing and repairing harps, Horn was assigned to the firm's bookkeeping, while Horn's wife also played an important role in the everyday organisation of the Erard business, being occupied with the firm's various household duties.[70]

Considering its complex structure and operation, as well as its large and international clientele, it is not surprising that the Erard firm kept meticulous workshop accounts and sale ledgers, which were updated by Horn and others, including Pierre himself. For example, in 1821 Pierre informed his uncle that he had transcribed in a single book the accounts of debtors that were previously included in six different books, adding that 'I keep the papers and the ledger myself, not being satisfied with the person I had assigned to perform this task, a man named Dawes, whom I will get rid of when I no longer need him.'[71] A year later Pierre noted that 'there have been delays in our bookkeeping. The young man who kept the journal and the ledgers did not suit me, not working as I wanted him to. I replaced him by a competent person and this change is causing a brief delay. I must also work on it and I am so busy with things right now.'[72] The various transactions of the Erard London branch are further

---

[66] L 182, 9 October 1816. Adelson et al, *The History of the Erard Piano and Harp*, pp. 636–638, at p. 637.

[67] L 150, 7 July 1815. Adelson et al, *The History of the Erard Piano and Harp*, pp. 606–607, at p. 606.

[68] L 210, 18 September 1817. Adelson et al, *The History of the Erard Piano and Harp*, p. 669.

[69] L 122, 16 December 1814, and L 204, 25 July 1817. Adelson et al, *The History of the Erard Piano and Harp*, pp. 575–576, at p. 575, and pp. 661–662, at p. 661, respectively.

[70] Nex, *The Business of Musical-Instrument Making in Early Industrial London*, p. 216.

[71] L 293, 26 January 1821. Adelson et al, *The History of the Erard Piano and Harp*, pp. 757–758, at p. 758.

[72] L 324, 13 February 1822. Adelson et al, *The History of the Erard Piano and Harp*, pp. 788–790, at pp. 788–789.

revealed in a surviving financial statement prepared by Pierre for the year 1822, which provides interesting details about the firm's clients, suppliers and stock.[73]

In the early nineteenth century bookkeeping had become essential for the efficient running of manufacturing businesses, especially those producing and distributing goods at both a regional and a global scale, usually involving division of labour and subcontracting. This is evidenced by other leading manufacturers, such as the Swiss-born watch-maker Abraham-Louis Breguet (1747–1823), one of Erard's close friends, who also had customers in numerous countries.[74] Like Erard, Breguet maintained scrupulous production registers, sales ledgers and repair books, now preserved among various archives relating to the company's history at the Breguet Museum in Paris.

These documents record valuable details on the fabrication, sale and repair of Breguet's timepieces, listed by serial number. For instance, the first wristwatch made by Breguet, bearing the number 2639, was commissioned in 1810 by the Queen of Naples, Caroline Murat (1782–1839), the youngest sister of Napoleon Bonaparte. This intricate watch took almost two and a half years to make, involving 17 artisans, who carried out 34 separate operations, all chronicled in the ledgers under the entry 2639.[75] Detailed sale ledgers were also kept by two of Erard's business associates, namely Jean-Jacques Holtzapffel, whose firm supplied Erard with various tools and equipment, and George Jackson, who provided Erard with composition ornaments and moulds for the decoration of harps, as mentioned in Chapters Two and Three respectively, further highlighting the role of bookkeeping in various manufacturing sectors.

Erard's Staff, Subcontractors and Suppliers: Precision Work on Wood and Metal

One of the key demands of harp manufacture was precision. The building of Erard Grecian harps in particular, with their compound construction, complex mechanics and elaborate decoration, required precision work on wood and metal with a variety of tools, materials and techniques. For this reason, the Erard firm employed several skilled craftsmen, many of whom were not luthiers, but belonged to other trades. In addition, the firm maintained a wide network of subcontractors and suppliers of materials, equipment and tools.

Erard's staff can be divided into three main groups, namely woodworkers, machinists and decorators. Valuable evidence about Erard's workforce and workshop layout can be obtained from an inventory compiled in Paris when Sébastien

---

[73] See Robert Adelson, *Erard: Empire of the Harp* (Ancenis: Les Harpes Camac, 2022), pp. 174–209.

[74] For more details see Emmanuel Breguet, 'Das Gewicht der Welt: Breguets Internationales Vertriebsnetz', in Emmanuel Breguet, Nicole Minder and Rodolphe De Pierri (eds), *Abraham-Louis Breguet: Die Uhrmacherkunst erobert die Welt* (Paris: Somogy, 2011), pp. 78–137.

[75] See Emmanuel Breguet, 'Breguet Makes the First Wristwatch fit for a Queen', *Le Quai de l'Horloge* 1 (2011), pp. 33–39, at pp. 34–39.

died in 1831. This document shows that at that time, the Erard Paris branch employed 18 workers involved in the manufacture of harps, occupied in three harp-making workshops, each including four woodworkers, a machinist and a decorator.[76] These 18 workers correspond to about one third of the personnel in the London branch during the mid-1810s, which employed about 50 to 60 workers of different professions.[77] Moreover, in the late 1810s and early 1820s, when the production of the Grecian model was at its peak, the Erard workforce consisted of about 70 to 80 workers.[78] Considering these numbers, and the similarities of the harp workshops in the two branches mentioned earlier, the London branch in the 1810s may have comprised at least nine harp-making workshops, in which 36 woodworkers, nine machinists and nine decorators undertook all the stages of harp manufacture, from beginning to end.

Different kinds of woodwork were needed for the construction of the harp's triangular wooden frame, consisting of the soundbox, neck and column. This demanded the thorough knowledge and handling of various woods with good mechanical and acoustic properties that were necessary for musical instruments. For example, the wood identification of Erard N° 2631 has shown that its soundbox, pedalbox and column are made of maple, its neck and bridge of beech, its soundboard and tone bars of spruce and the supporting braces of the soundbox of white oak.[79] Moreover, the workshop accounts and letters of the London branch reveal that various types of woods, such as sycamore, beech, burr walnut, lime, mahogany, ebony and deal, were purchased, and in some cases also sold, by the firm.[80] Although the Erard firm had several supply channels, obtaining appropriate materials was sometimes difficult and expensive due to trade restrictions and embargos imposed by the Napoleonic Wars, with Sébastien claiming as early as 1797 that 'The only problem is the continual increase in prices of raw materials we need, especially in France.'[81]

Erard's staff, subcontractors and suppliers included several woodworking specialists, such as cabinetmakers, joiners, carpenters, turners and carvers, who were assigned to the construction and assembly of the various wooden harp parts or related products. For example, between 1807 and 1809, 'Mr Prockter' was listed as 'turner' and 'Mr Allison' as 'carpenter', while 'Hensler', 'Johns', 'Clemens', 'Townsend', 'Scott', 'Thurston' and 'Kirkman' supplied 'belly boards', which refers to harp soundboards. Some of Erard's workers were also occupied in the building of other wooden items that the firm produced, such as harp cases, music stands,

---

[76] Ann Griffiths, Robert Adelson and Jenny Nex, 'Erard', in Laurence Libin (ed.), *The Grove Dictionary of Musical Instruments,* (2nd edn; New York: Oxford University Press, 2014), Vol. 2, pp. 234–237, at p. 235.

[77] Nex, *The Business of Musical-Instrument Making in Early Industrial London,* pp. 220–223.

[78] See Adelson, *Erard: Empire of the Harp,* pp. 97 and 127.

[79] Volker Haag, 'KO/1385/18: Holzartenbestimmung Erard Harfe (London 1818, Inventarnummer DM 16147), Deutsches Museum München' (unpublished report; Hamburg: Thünen-Institut für Holzforschung, 2019).

[80] Nex, *The Business of Musical-Instrument Making in Early Industrial London,* p. 228.

[81] L 7.388, 24 February 1797. Adelson et al, *The History of the Erard Piano and Harp,* pp. 178–179, at p. 179.

stools, sounding boards and, later, pianos, as well as with repairs, as will be discussed in Chapters Five and Eight. For example, in April 1818 Pierre, commenting on the branch's monthly production, remarked that 'there are the repairs, music stands, etc … which took time from several workers',[82] while in March 1822 he similarly noted that 'there are the music stands, stools, repairs, and repairs of rented harps that are quite considerable'.[83] Likewise, in 1824 he remarked that 'For the cases, keyboards, I have an excellent man in the firm whom I do not need for the harps.'[84]

Although the names of most workers employed in the Erard London branch during the production of the Grecian model remain unknown, a few workers are occasionally mentioned in the Erard correspondence. As usually happens, these were employees who stood out either because of their virtues or their vices (or both). Regarding woodworkers, who comprised the majority of Erard's workforce, archival evidence suggests that most came from continental Europe. As reported in a letter from 1815, most of the cabinetmakers working at Erard could 'speak German or French',[85] indicating that they may have been of German or French origin.

One characteristic case is John Zacharias Siegling (1791–1867), from Erfurt in Thuringia. According to Pierre, Siegling was a 'very smart young German who has worked for a long time in our Paris firm and more recently in London'.[86] In 1818 Siegling was put by Pierre 'in charge of the <u>Cabinet makers</u>', being described as 'someone a cut above the working class, thanks to his education and his knowledge', but also as someone who 'has ambitions', 'is not easy to lead and is not short of vanity'.[87] Siegling worked for Erard until 1819, when he emigrated to America, settling in Charleston, South Carolina, where he opened a prosperous music store.[88]

Two other employees most likely involved in woodwork are Zeiter, probably another German, and Green, both of whom had been recruited in 1818; Pierre referred to them as 'excellent', with their work being 'at very high level'. In contrast, a woodworker named Frayer (or Freyer), presumably also a German, who was working for Erard from at least 1807 until the beginning of 1819, was mentioned

---

82 L 220, 10 April 1818. Adelson et al, *The History of the Erard Piano and Harp*, pp. 677–678, at p. 677.

83 L 330, 8 March 1822. Adelson et al, *The History of the Erard Piano and Harp*, pp. 794–795, at p. 795.

84 L 356, 22 June 1824. Adelson et al, *The History of the Erard Piano and Harp*, pp. 822–823, at p. 822.

85 L 159, 26 October 1815. Adelson et al, *The History of the Erard Piano and Harp*, pp. 615–616, at p. 616.

86 L 185, 3 December 1816. Adelson et al, *The History of the Erard Piano and Harp*, pp. 639–640, at p. 639.

87 L 262, 2 July 1819. Adelson et al, *The History of the Erard Piano and Harp*, pp. 720–722, at pp. 721–722.

88 Candace Bailey, *Charleston Belles Abroad: The Music Collections of Harriet Lowndes, Henrietta Aiken, and Louisa Rebecca McCord* (Columbia: University of South Carolina Press, 2019), pp. 15–16.

as 'a cobbler' whose labour was of poor quality.[89] Frayer is mentioned several times in the Erard workshop accounts between 1807 and 1809, mainly building music stands and even having 'a labourer turning the lathes wheel' for him, suggesting he was a wood turner. It is tempting to assume that someone with the skills of Siegling, Zeiter or Green (but not of Frayer!) may have been involved in the construction and completion of Erard Nº 2631 in November 1818, even though such a scenario cannot be verified.

If information about the woodworkers that built Erard Grecian harps is scarce, even less is known about the firm's decorators. Some stages of decoration would be executed in-house by various artisans, such as plasterers, gilders, painters, printers and engravers, as mentioned in Reichardt's descriptions of the Erard Paris branch. However, more specialised work was probably carried out by subcontractors. The practice of subcontracting 'was the norm throughout the high-design sector, especially in London' since it 'provided access to skills that were not required frequently enough to justify employment of a full-time specialist worker in the master's workshop'.[90] Subcontracting essentially allowed businesses to handle 'rapid changes in demand for skilled labour', since 'it was more efficient to shunt commissioned work to semi-independent producers than to engage men permanently who could not work at low points of demand.'[91]

As mentioned in Chapter Three, the Erard London branch relied on various external specialists for the decoration of harps: for example, composition ornaments were supplied by Thorpe and later by Jackson, while the inscriptions on brass plates were engraved by Adolpho. The workshop accounts between 1807 and 1809 list payments to various other persons that were involved in decorative work, such as 'Collier', who carved eagles fixed on the harp's capital, 'Tillier' (Tillyer, Tillyard, Tillyerd), a gilder, or 'Kluth' and 'Riley' (Reyly), both labelled as varnishers. Although it cannot be corroborated, it is possible that these craftsmen continued to offer their services to the Erard firm during the production of the Grecian model in the 1810s.

Although the woodwork and decoration required in the production of pedal harps was quite demanding, the most difficult task in their manufacture was the construction of the mechanism. The mechanisms on these harps were usually built by professionals with mechanical or engineering expertise, such as those trained in the making of clocks and watches, automata, mechanised furniture or scientific instruments.[92] Given the fact that the Erards dealt in the export of copper, as reported in several letters from 1817,[93] the firm apparently had several connections within the metalworking trades.

---

[89] L 263, 4 July 1819. Adelson et al, *The History of the Erard Piano and Harp*, pp. 722–723, at p. 722.

[90] Snodin and Styles, *Design & the Decorative Arts*, p. 142.

[91] Matthew Craske, 'Plan and Control: Design and the Competitive Spirit in Early and Mid-Eighteenth Century England', *Journal of Design History* 12/3 (1999), pp. 187–216, at p. 206.

[92] For example, Jacob Erat, one of Erard's competitors was trained as a clock maker, as mentioned in Baldwin, *The Harp in Early Nineteenth-century Britain*, p. 244.

[93] See L 202 to 207, 11 July 1817 to 8 August 1817. Adelson et al, *The History of the Erard Piano and Harp*, pp. 658–666.

This is evidenced by the description of purchased materials as well as by the business nature of numerous suppliers who are listed in the workshop accounts between 1807 and 1809. For instance, 'Sainsbury' (Seinsbury, Sensbury), who supplied Erard with cast brass, steel (including 'Steel for pedals') and files, was most likely John Sainsbury (1766–1822), a clock and watch-tool manufacturer located at 2 Cowcross Street between 1806 and 1823.[94] John Philips, a brazier and coppersmith at 42 White Street, Borough, provided Erard with flattened or rolled brass, wire and glue,[95] whereas George Knight, an ironmonger at 41 Foster Lane, Cheapside, supplied steel letters that were used for marking brass.[96] The application of steel letters has been revealed on several examined Grecian harps, since small capital letters (A, B, C, D, E, F, G), referring to musical notes and the corresponding strings, are punched on the inside of the mechanism, usually on the left brass plate; some harps also bear punched numbers, usually identical to a harp's serial number, on various parts of the mechanism, that were probably executed with similar steel numbers (Figure 22).

The supply chain of the Erard London branch additionally extended to the furniture and textile industries for materials seemingly unrelated to pedal harps, but quite important for the proper function and protection of the instruments and their mechanisms. For instance, William Lonsdale, a cabinet maker and upholder at 7 Broad Street, provided various fabrics, mostly 'green baise'.[97] Together with felt from old hats, which were also bought by the Erard firm, baize would have been used to cover certain metal parts of the pedal mechanism or to line wooden surfaces in order to prevent mechanical damage and unwanted noises; baize would have also been used for lining cases and for harp covers. Skins and leather, used to make leather bags for the pedals as well as harp covers, were delivered by Abraham Hitchin, a leather seller at 1 Nassau Street.[98]

Considering that the mechanisms on Erard double-action harps consisted of more than 1,000 delicate metal components linked together with mechanical

<hr>

94 'Sainsbury, J. Watch tool manufacturer'. Andrew Johnstone, *Johnstone's London Commercial Guide and Street Directory* (London: Barnard & Farley, 1818), p. 146. See also Frederick James Britten, *Old Clocks and Watches & Their Makers* (5th edn; London: E. & F. N. Spon, 1922), p. 771. Interestingly, in the early 1820s Sainsbury's son, John, collaborated with Bochsa, one of the main advocates of Erard's double-action harp, for the publication of a music dictionary. For more details see Leanne Langley, 'Sainsbury's Dictionary, the Royal Academy of Music, and the Rhetoric of Patriotism', in Christina Bashford and Leanne Langley (eds), *Music and British Culture, 1785–1914: Essays in Honor of Cyril Ehrlich* (Oxford: Oxford University Press, 2000), pp. 65–97.

95 'Philips, John, Brazier & copper smith'. Johnstone, *Johnstone's London Commercial Guide and Street Directory*, p. 523.

96 'Knight, R. & G. Ironmongers & cutlers', Johnstone, *Johnstone's London Commercial Guide and Street Directory*, p. 209.

97 'Lonsdale, W. Cabinet Maker and Upholder'. Roger Wakefield, *Wakefield's Merchant and Tradesman's General Directory* (London: T. Davison, 1794), p. 195. Lonsdale is also listed as 'Cabinet Maker' in William Cobbett, *Cobbett's Political Register* (London: Cox and Baylis, 1811), vol. 19, pp. 483 and 495.

98 'Hitchin, Abraham, Leather seller'. Johnstone, *Johnstone's London Commercial Guide and Street Directory*, p. 344.

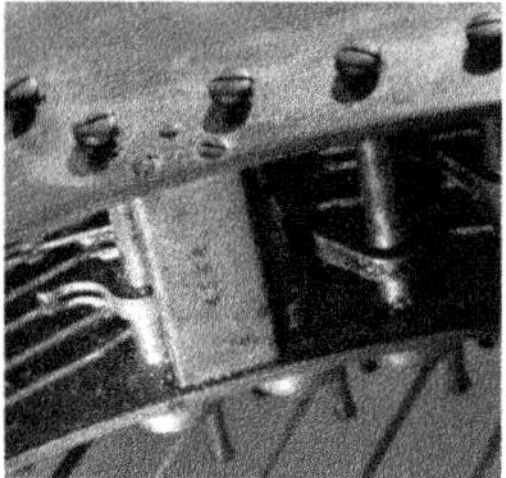

Figure 22. Detail of letters (left) and numbers (right) punched on the inside of the mechanism of Erard Grecian harps. Left: Erard N° 1945. Hospitalfield, Arbroath. Right: Erard N° 4568. Musical Instrument Museums Edinburgh (MIMEd), Edinburgh (Inv. No. 176).

connections, their construction depended on machinists with experience and skills in metalworking. Most information we have on Erard's machinists comes from the Erard workshop accounts between 1807 and 1809. During this period Erard repeatedly paid Edward Lydiatt (fl.1709–1809), as well as Christoph Rogala and one 'Colleman', for 'Machines', apparently referring to the machinery used on Erard harps.

However, the investigation of surviving harps provides valuable complementary evidence. For example, Lydiatt's signature is engraved on the rail of the mechanisms of four surviving harps dated between 1799 and 1809, confirming that Lydiatt was employed by Erard as a machinist at least during these ten years.[99] In some cases, the instruments offer the only clues for identifying Erard's employees. For instance, the previously unknown J. (Johann or John?) Schneegans was building mechanisms for single-action Erard harps in 1800, since the rail of the mechanism on Erard N° 333 is signed 'J. Schneegans. // 30. April, 1800' (Figure 23).[100] During the examination of Erard N° 2914, a double-action harp built in 1820, the undecipherable word 'SMILL..' was found engraved on one pedal arm inside the pedalbox, probably referring to the name of a person occupied in metalwork for harp pedals during that year. Likewise, the inscription 'July 1813 // Barker' on the inside of the brass plate of Erard N° 1747, a double-action harp built in 1813, indicates that Barker was constructing the action on Grecian harps produced in 1813.

---

99 These include Erard N° 281 ('Lydiatt // Sept 1799'); Erard N° 470 ('Lydiatt // March, 1802.'); Erard N° 1187 ('Lydiatt 1809 4'); and Erard N° 1224 ('LYDIATT 1809 7').

100 It is worth mentioning that a 'Mr William Schneegans' is listed in the 1822 financial statement of the Erard London branch, but without a description of his profession; it is possible that he was a relative of J. Schneegans. See Adelson, *Erard: Empire of the Harp*, p. 205.

Figure 23. Left: Detail of the inscription 'J. Schneegans. // 30. April, 1800', engraved on the mechanism of Erard N° 333. Royal College of Music Museum, London (Inv. No. RCM 298). Right: Detail of the inscription 'Lydiatt // March, 1802.', engraved on the mechanism of Erard N° 470. The Fitzwilliam Museum, Cambridge (Inv. No. M.8-1941).

In contrast, although it is known that as early as 1808 Christian Haarnack (1774–?) was head machinist at Erard,[101] with Pierre stating in April 1818 that 'the machines are going well with Haarnack',[102] his name has not been found on any examined Erard harps. As mentioned in Chapter Two, various parts on Erard Grecian harps made from the 1810s to the 1840s usually bear initials that may point to particular workers, subcontractors or suppliers of the Erard firm, but names or dates are rarely detected on these instruments. This is probably an indication of the growing tendency towards uniformity and anonymity that characterised the large-scale manufacture of standardised products, including musical instruments, from the early nineteenth century onwards.

The Erards most likely had little trouble finding and employing such artisans for the firm's London manufactory. In the decades around 1800, London was a pool of accomplished craftsmen who were able to carry out precision work with wood and metal. The majority of them were located in the Clerkenwell area and included 'clock and watch makers; scientific, surgical and optical instrument makers; and trades making a host of small metal parts such as locks, keys, candle snuffers and harness

---

[101] Moira Bonnington, 'The Oldest Harp Maker in the World!', *The Galpin Society Journal* 54 (2001), pp. 45–55, at p. 50.

[102] L 220, 10 April 1818. Adelson et al, *The History of the Erard Piano and Harp*, pp. 677–678.

fittings'.[103] When they could not be occupied in their usual jobs, and with a growing demand for precision work in emerging factories, these craftsmen were highly sought after because they could easily use and adapt their skills in other trades.[104]

One representative example is Heinrich Johannes Kessels (1781–1849), a prominent maker of chronometers and observatory regulators.[105] The Dutch-born Kessels, who had initially been trained as a blacksmith, moved to England in 1807 to learn the craft of clock making. In 1815 he returned to Paris to work for the famous watch maker Abraham-Louis Breguet until 1821, when he established his own workshop in Altona, in northern Germany. Very little is known about Kessels's activities in England between 1807 and 1815. Although in a letter from 1821 Kessels himself reported that he had worked for eight years in London in the most famous workshops,[106] he did not mention under whom he served his apprenticeship or for whom he worked during this time.

However, important evidence concerning Kessels's activities in London is found in the surviving correspondence between Sébastien and Pierre Erard. For example, in 1814 Kessel is mentioned as the 'young watchmaker' who helped Sébastien Erard construct the action for a new wind instrument on which Erard wanted to experiment.[107] The same year Kessels left London for Paris, intending to continue working for Erard there.[108] The fact that from 1815 he started working instead for Breguet may not be coincidental. Erard was well acquainted with Breguet, who is mentioned by Pierre as Sébastien's 'excellent and worthy friend',[109] so it is likely that Erard may have personally recommended Kessels to him.

---

[103] Anthony P. Woolrich, 'The London Engineering Industry at the time of Henry Maudslay', in John Cantrell and Gillian Cookson (eds), *Henry Maudslay and the Pioneers of the Machine Age* (Stroud: Tempus, 2002), pp. 39–53, at p. 40.

[104] Woolrich, 'The London Engineering Industry at the time of Henry Maudslay', p. 40. Woolrich mentions that 'as late as 1825 the engineer John Martineau claimed that he would respond to a sudden upsurge in demand by recruiting from the depressed handicraft trades such as watchmakers and mathematical instrument makers', arguing that these men required little practice before they could perform various tasks in an engineering factory.

[105] For a comprehensive account of Kessels's biography and work see Günther Oestmann, *Heinrich Johann Kessels: Ein bedeutender Verfertiger von Chronometern und Präzisionspendeluhren. Biographische Skizze und Werkverzeichnis* [Acta Historicae Astronomomiae 44] (Frankfurt am Main: Harri Deutsch, 2011).

[106] 'J'ai travaillé huit ans à Londres dans des ateliers les plus célèbres'. Letter dated 25 June 1821, quoted in Oestmann, *Heinrich Johann Kessels*, p. 143.

[107] 'M. Kessel, this young watchmaker, has finished the action for the wind instrument on which you wanted to experiment. He would like to know if you will continue when you return, because if not he would be obliged to find work elsewhere.' L 111, 11 November 1814. Adelson et al, *The History of the Erard Piano and Harp*, pp. 562–564, at pp. 562–563.

[108] 'M. Kessel, having finished his work and unwilling to look elsewhere in London, will leave in a few days for Paris. He hopes you will give him work, or recommend him to others. I will give him £5 to help him to make his journey.' L 122, 16 December 1814. Adelson et al, *The History of the Erard Piano and Harp*, pp. 575–576, at p. 575.

[109] 'I immediately went to see M. Breguet, your excellent and worthy friend, to give him your two letters and to tell him about your accidents'. L 98, 19 September 1814. Adelson et al,

In the following years, Kessels travelled back and forth between London and Paris, occasionally carrying out work for Erard. For instance, Kessels was in London in September 1818, when he was asked by Pierre to deliver a letter to his uncle Sébastien,[110] suggesting that he was a person of confidence, while in 1820 Kessels's name was included in a memorandum listing bills of the Erard London firm.[111] In 1822, Pierre reported to Sébastien that Kessels might have been sending information about Erard harps to the harp maker Delveaux; the letter reads: 'Would you by chance have revealed something of your new ideas for the harp to Kessell. He was always writing to Delveaux! I think it wise to watch out for him. He is devious.'[112]

Therefore, even while working for Breguet, Kessels maintained a close professional relationship with Erard, which may have influenced and benefitted the work of both sides. On the other hand, that Kessels was suspected of revealing Erard's secrets to a competitor, as expressed in Pierre's 1822 letter, may also explain his absence from the Erard correspondence in later years.

Preparing Harps for the Market: Finishing, Supervision and Quality Control

Once the basic construction and embellishment of Erard's Grecian harps had been completed by the woodworkers, machinists and decorators described above, the instruments would be ready for the finishing touches, which included stringing, regulating and tuning. Between 1807 and 1809 Erard purchased gut strings from local makers such as William Fossey and Samuel Weisbart (?–1818), while 'Mr Duff' regularly supplied 'Silverd Strings', which most likely refers to overwound strings for the bass; the firm also imported Italian gut strings, which were considered superior.[113] In 1814 Pierre noted: 'As for the strings, I think I will do business with Philips, Burey St City. They have a crate of them in the Thames. We are in dire need of them because we cannot continue to sell only English strings.'[114]

The History of the Erard Piano and Harp, pp. 547–549, at p. 547. On this occasion, Pierre Erard had turned to Breguet for financial help. It is worth mentioning that Sébastien Erard owned several clocks by Breguet, which were listed in Erard's posthumous inventory, as mentioned in Adelson et al, *The History of the Erard Piano and Harp*, p. 95, note 1.

[110] 'M. Kessels, who will be giving you the present letter, will be able to give you more information because he has just visited the site. He will tell you how much this matter disturbs me!' L 233, 27 September 1818. Adelson et al, *The History of the Erard Piano and Harp*, pp. 689–691, at p. 689.

[111] '3 September 1820. Memorandum of money paid for M. S. Erard in the London firm from 1 January 1820. [...] June 12 Bill payable to Kessels 17– 5–.' L 285, 8 August 1820. Adelson et al, *The History of the Erard Piano and Harp*, pp. 748–750, at p. 749.

[112] L 323, 8 February 1822. Adelson et al, *The History of the Erard Piano and Harp*, p. 788.

[113] Nex, *The Business of Musical-Instrument Making in Early Industrial London*, p. 230. For more details on suppliers of gut strings for harps see Jenny Nex, 'Gut String Makers in nineteenth-century London', *The Galpin Society Journal* 65 (2012), pp. 131–160.

[114] L 122, 16 December 1814. Adelson et al, *The History of the Erard Piano and Harp*, pp. 575–576, at p. 575.

The finishing tasks were undertaken by the firm's more experienced staff, usually those with musical skills who could also play the harp. Senior workers, like Horn, who was mentioned earlier, had dual roles in finishing and supervising during the production of Erard Grecian harps. In July 1819 Pierre argued that 'we absolutely need a foreman, without his having that title; Horn can barely finish the double harps and the repairs, he cannot supervise and work at the same time!'[115] Another skilled and multitasking employee involved in the finishing of Erard harps was James Delveaux (or Delveau) who worked in both the Paris and London branches. In 1815 Pierre wrote, 'Would you do me a great favour, my dear uncle, to send us back Delveaux if he is still in Paris, because I am wasting a great deal of time trying to replace him so that no harp leaves the workshop unless it is the way it should be. At this moment we are packing up 4 of them to send to St Petersburg.'[116]

Pierre thought so highly of Delveaux as to suggest that this 'very honest man' could become the firm's representative in Brussels, as well as in America, Brazil or Russia.[117] In June 1818 Delveaux was assigned to 'assemble the single-action instruments',[118] while in May 1820 he was 'very busy with part of the repairs, tunings, and instruments for rent'.[119] Delveaux's importance is illustrated in a letter which shows that after his resignation in 1821, Pierre was desperate: 'I have written to you that Delveaux left! The instruments are not finished when they leave Horn's hands. He is a really good man who works very hard, but he does not have what it takes to finish a harp well. I need to find someone and until I can count on him, I will do it myself!'[120]

Before they could be offered for sale, the finished harps had to be tested and evaluated. On several occasions, Pierre himself personally checked each instrument before it left the shop to ensure the high level of quality. For instance, in 1821 he stated, 'I examine all the instruments that leave the workshop and do not let anything pass.'[121] A year later he similarly remarked that:

> I am obliged to inspect them all myself because when one gives them to me as finished, they are in fact not. The jangling, this will be a very nice thing on your new model, all the action is on the outside, the little rods in the top are very prone to jangling. The pedals, whose mechanisms on the inside are mounted one on top of the other, are also prone to problems and do not work very freely

---

[115] L 263, 4 July 1819. Adelson et al, *The History of the Erard Piano and Harp*, pp. 722–723, at p. 722.

[116] L 156, 18 September 1815. Adelson et al, *The History of the Erard Piano and Harp*, pp. 612–613, at p. 613.

[117] L 212, 29 September 1817. Adelson et al, *The History of the Erard Piano and Harp*, p. 670.

[118] L 224, 2 June 1818. Adelson et al, *The History of the Erard Piano and Harp*, p. 682.

[119] L 279, 5 May 1820. Adelson et al, *The History of the Erard Piano and Harp*, p. 742.

[120] L 309, 21 August 1821. Adelson et al, *The History of the Erard Piano and Harp*, pp. 776–777, at p. 776.

[121] L 308, 8 August 1821. Adelson et al, *The History of the Erard Piano and Harp*, pp. 775–776, at p. 776.

or they jangle. Not a single harp leaves the workshop that is not absolutely in good working order.[122]

Pierre was able to judge the features of the new harps first-hand since he had taken harp lessons from the harpist Jean-Aimé Vernier (1769–1840).[123] Studying the harp also permitted Pierre to demonstrate the firm's instruments to customers or to perform in front of patent committees, as recorded in several letters.[124] Although in 1815 Pierre claimed that he intended 'to practise the harp 4 hours a day this summer in order to play the unisons in public next season if necessary',[125] he must have not enjoyed playing at public events. When asked to perform at Drury Lane in 1816 he confessed to his uncle that 'I will do it for the harp sake and in order to take care of your instruments, because I do not like to play in such a public hall.'[126]

'Hire-and-Fire': Workforce Fluctuation and Mobility at the Erard Firm

Apart from being 'jack of all trades' in the harp manufactory, Pierre was also obliged to act as an accountant, always keeping an eye on the firm's finances. Employing a large workforce that included numerous talented artisans, who had to be paid accordingly, imposed a great challenge on the budget of the Erard firm. Despite the substantial costs for materials, tools and other supplies, the firm's major continuous expenditure was the workers' wages.[127] As documented in several occasions in the Erard archives, the firm paid its workers once a week, usually on Saturday, which frequently proved to be a struggle for the management. For instance, in 1815 Pierre was 'fearing that the Saturday payrolls would become too expensive', while in 1822 he claimed that 'At this moment I only have what is needed to pay the workers on Saturday.'[128]

Erat, one of Erard's main competitors, also paid his workers on a weekly basis, as evidenced in his account books.[129] Other musical instrument manufacturers similarly settled and recorded their financial transactions every week. One notable example is Charles Wheatstone (1802–1875), the famous scientist and important

---

[122] L 330, 8 March 1822. Adelson et al, *The History of the Erard Piano and Harp*, pp. 794–795, at p. 795.

[123] L 110, 8 November 1814. Adelson et al, *The History of the Erard Piano and Harp*, pp. 561–562, at p. 562.

[124] See, for example, L 140, 9 June 1815, or L 328, 27 February 1822. Adelson et al, *The History of the Erard Piano and Harp*, pp. 604–606, at p. 605, and pp. 792–793, at p. 793, respectively.

[125] L 148, 1 June 1815. Adelson et al, *The History of the Erard Piano and Harp*, pp. 603–604, at p. 603.

[126] L 171, 27 February 1816. Adelson et al, *The History of the Erard Piano and Harp*, pp. 625–626, at p. 626.

[127] Nex, *The Business of Musical-Instrument Making in Early Industrial London*, p. 220.

[128] See L 157, 10 October 1815, and L 338, 21 November 1822. Adelson et al, *The History of the Erard Piano and Harp*, pp. 613–614, at p. 614, and pp. 802–803, at p. 802, respectively.

[129] Baldwin, *The Harp in Early Nineteenth-century Britain*, p. 392.

manufacturer of concertinas and other free-reed instruments in Victorian London. Like Erard, Wheatstone registered in ledgers 'weekly payments to employees, suppliers and other tradesmen who performed works and services for the Wheatstone workshops' from the mid- to late 1840s.[130]

Regarding the growing adoption of a weekly wage system in industrial workplaces, such as factories and dockyards, during the early nineteenth century, it has been claimed that 'the essence of the wage system is accountability. This meant that the worker was predictable; it meant that the worker's value was capable of quantitative measurement; it meant that the worker was responsible for losses of materials during production; it meant that money rationalized class society.'[131]

Since wages were usually calculated by the numbers of completed pieces rather than by the hour, it is possible that, with the exception of a few foremen, Erard's workers were paid by piece rate, as was the case at Broadwood, the piano manufacturer.[132] The majority of workers involved in the building of pianos 'were not employed directly by a small- or medium-sized piano-making firm but operated in the many stages of piano manufacture on casual basis, paid by the piece', with 'only a few "core" workers' being 'on the payroll of larger firms'.[133] This method of payment seems to have been customary not only in musical instrument-making, but in other trades, such as in the field of scientific instruments[134] or in the building industry.[135] In July 1819 Pierre proposed 'giving 2 or 2/6 per harp to one of the good workers'.[136] Rewarding diligent employees was a clever scheme in order to increase the staff's motivation and to maintain the required product uniformity and quality.

A noteworthy aspect regarding the operation of the Erard London branch was the frequent workforce fluctuation and mobility, which depended on the firm's production goals and financial situation, as well as on the overall condition of the harp market. For example, the considerable business expansion required in the critical years shortly before and after the arrival of the double-action harp is vividly reflected in the number and variety of Erard's personnel.

---

[130] Neil Wayne, 'The Wheatstone English Concertina', *The Galpin Society Journal* 44 (1991), pp. 117–149, at p. 144.

[131] Quoted in William J. Ashworth, '"System of Terror": Samuel Bentham, Accountability and Dockyard Reform during the Napoleonic Wars', *Social History* 23/1 (1998), pp. 63–79, at pp. 78–79.

[132] Alastair Laurence, *The Evolution of the Broadwood Grand Piano 1785–1998* (PhD Diss., York: University of York, 1998), p. 68; see also Nex, *The Business of Musical-Instrument Making in Early Industrial London*, pp. 237–238.

[133] Francesca Carnevali and Lucy Newton, 'Pianos for the People: From Producer to Consumer in Britain, 1851–1914', *Enterprise & Society* 14/1 (2013), pp. 37–70, at p. 46.

[134] Alison D. Morrison-Low, *Making Scientific Instruments in the Industrial Revolution* (Aldershot: Ashgate, 2007), p. 286.

[135] Linda Clarke, *Building Capitalism: Historical Change and the Labour Process in the Production of Built Environment* (London and New York: Routledge, 2011), pp. 56–58.

[136] L 263, 4 July 1819. Adelson et al, *The History of the Erard Piano and Harp*, pp. 722–723, at p. 722.

A comparison of the expenses for wages has shown that between the late 1800s and the mid-1810s the Erard firm may have doubled in size in terms of its in-house workforce, thus growing from about 30 to about 60 workers of various specialisations,[137] presumably to cope with the more complicated and demanding manufacture of the new harp. This number corresponds to a statement by Pierre showing that in 1815 the firm's staff comprised 70 workers.[138] The growth of Erard's workforce in the 1810s was comparable to that of other prominent manufacturers as their businesses expanded. For example, in the 1800s the machine and tool maker Henry Maudslay employed about 80 workers; by 1814 his workforce was over 200, a number retained and probably increased in the 1820s.[139]

Since workers' wages was Erard's main financial burden, the occasional hiring of staff was a common measure to increase production when demand was great, whereas their firing could spare costs when money was scarce. This is exposed in several letters in which Pierre informed his uncle about the current state of the London branch. For example, in September 1814 Pierre stated that 'the pay for the workers will be healthy [on] Saturday because we are getting rid of some of them. Horn and I thought that there was no problem because we have many orders and sales are rather calm this season.'[140] However, in April 1815 the firm urgently needed more hands, with Pierre asserting that 'we have so many harps on rent that we are very short for harps. The small amount of advance work that there was before your departure for machinery and wood is completely exhausted. It would be necessary to hire a dozen more workers, but the payrolls are already too burdensome in the current situation?'[141]

Decreasing the expenses for personnel seems to have been a constant preoccupation for Pierre. In October 1815, he stated: 'I hesitate to take on a few more workers, fearing that the Saturday payrolls would become too expensive.'[142] In January 1818, he announced that 'there will also be reductions to make in our workforce; I will make cuts everywhere I can',[143] while in April of the same year he wrote to his uncle, 'I am convinced that you could dramatically reduce your labour costs [...]. For the moment you have to rely on me, my dear uncle, to do my best to

---

[137] Nex, *The Business of Musical-Instrument Making in Early Industrial London*, p. 222.

[138] L 149, 9 June 1815. Adelson et al, *The History of the Erard Piano and Harp*, pp. 604–606, at p. 605.

[139] John Cantrell, 'Henry Maudslay', in John Cantrell and Gillian Cookson (eds), *Henry Maudslay and the Pioneers of the Machine Age* (Stroud: Tempus, 2002), pp. 18–38, at pp. 19–21. Cantrell refers to an advertisement in *The Times* from 25 May 1826, according to which Maudslay employed about 500 men at that time.

[140] L 99, 22 September 1814. Adelson et al, *The History of the Erard Piano and Harp*, pp. 549–550, at p. 549.

[141] L 142, 7 and 12 April 1815. Adelson et al, *The History of the Erard Piano and Harp*, pp. 594–595, at p. 594.

[142] L 157, 10 October 1815. Adelson et al, *The History of the Erard Piano and Harp*, pp. 613–614, at p. 614.

[143] L 216, 29 January 1818. Adelson et al, *The History of the Erard Piano and Harp*, p. 674.

reduce expenses in all ways.'[144] In contrast, in February 1821 he pointed out that 'Sales are very good. We have several harps on order that cannot yet be delivered. I have taken on lots of workers and have arranged it so that we can finish at least four double harps each week.'[145]

This practice of 'hire-and-fire' according to seasonal demand was not unusual among instrument makers. For Erat, 'The monthly fluctuations in total wages paid suggest that the number of employees rose and fell, probably in response to the number of customer orders.'[146] Likewise, at Broadwood, the largest piano manufacturer in Regency London, the same labourers who would be employed to boost production when sales were high, would be dismissed when orders were low.[147] On the other hand, it is worth noting that Adolphe Sax (1814–1894), inventor and maker of the saxophone and other wind instruments in Paris, refrained from dismissing employees because of fears of a strike, despite facing financial difficulties that eventually led to his first bankruptcy in 1852.[148]

The rather cruel measure of unregulated 'hire-and-fire', if considered from a modern perspective of working rights, must have been essential for the survival of businesses, albeit not without its shortcomings. Particularly in times of financial crisis, this was an unavoidable yet undesirable tactic not just for large-scale musical instrument manufacturers, such as Erard or Broadwood, but also for other leading industrialists: facing a severe financial depression in 1772, the pottery manufacturer Josiah Wedgwood regretted having to discharge several of his workers, fearing that they would be recruited by his antagonists.[149]

Erard must have shared the same worries as Wedgewood, since, not surprisingly, some of the fired men would seek employment at Erard's competitors. For instance, after being laid off by Pierre due to poor work, the above-mentioned Frayer (or Freyer) found shelter at the workshop of Jacob Erat (1758–1821), one of Erard's main rivals.[150] Likewise, the cabinetmaker John Rider, who in 1809 was Erard's employee, apparently also worked in later years for the harp maker Edward Dodd (1791–1843),

---

[144] L 220, 10 April 1818. Adelson et al, *The History of the Erard Piano and Harp*, pp. 677–678, at p. 677.

[145] L 294, 13 February 1821. Adelson et al, *The History of the Erard Piano and Harp*, pp. 758–759, at p. 759.

[146] Baldwin, *The Harp in Early Nineteenth-century Britain*, p. 395.

[147] Laurence, *The Evolution of the Broadwood Grand Piano*, p. 67.

[148] Adrian von Steiger, 'Sax figures: can we deduce details of Adolphe Sax's instrument production from the sources?', *Revue belge de Musicologie / Belgisch Tijdschrift voor Muziekwetenschap* 70, Issue 'Adolphe Sax, his influence and legacy: a bicentenary conference' (2016), pp. 129–148, at p. 140.

[149] Neil McKendrick, 'Josiah Wedgwood and Cost Accounting in the Industrial Revolution', *The Economic History Review* 23/1 (1970), pp. 45–67, at p. 63.

[150] L 263, 4 July 1819. Adelson et al, *The History of the Erard Piano and Harp*, pp. 722–723, at p. 722.

before returning to Erard in 1817.[151] Another woodworker named Webb, who had left Erard to work for the piano maker Robert Wornum (1780–1852), returned in 1820.[152]

Inevitably, this frequent movement of workers from one employer to another could not prevent incidents of industrial espionage or the stealing of intellectual property. In at least two cases, previous employees used the experience they had gained at the Erard London branch to set up their own businesses and even register patents for the harp. The first was John Charles Schwieso, who was made redundant by Pierre in October 1815 due to his bad behaviour.[153] Schwieso went to work for Dodd before forming a partnership with a certain Meyer in 1819.[154] In the 1820s, Schwieso made harps in collaboration with John Frederick Grosjean and was granted two patents relating to harps in 1826 and 1831.[155] The second was James Delveaux (or Delveau), discussed earlier, who was assembling and finishing harps for Erard as early as 1815.[156] Having quitted Erard in 1821, Delveaux was reportedly working with Erat's eldest son Jacob in 1822,[157] when he took a patent for 'an improvement on harps'.[158] As already mentioned, Delveaux may have been secretly informed about Erard's latest ideas by Kessels, while Pierre asserted that 'Delveaux benefitted from what he saw in the workshop.'[159]

The transition from foreman to master seems to have been a typical career move for ambitious employees in the instrument-making business. For instance, several talented craftsmen working for Wheatstone, the concertina manufacturer mentioned earlier, left him to become independent concertina makers.[160] A similar phenomenon has been observed in the furniture trade, where 'The experience of working as a foreman gave some men the confidence to set up on their own' and often 'the fact of having trained or worked as a craftsman in an important firm was used for publicity'.[161]

---

[151] L 214, 16 December 1817. Adelson et al, *The History of the Erard Piano and Harp*, pp. 672–673, at p. 672.

[152] L 279, 5 May 1820. Adelson et al, *The History of the Erard Piano and Harp*, pp. 742–743, at p. 742.

[153] L 159, 26 October 1815. Adelson et al, *The History of the Erard Piano and Harp*, pp. 615–616, at p. 616.

[154] L 253, 23 March 1819. Adelson et al, *The History of the Erard Piano and Harp*, p. 711.

[155] Patents Nº 5404, 22 August 1826, and Nº 6069, 2 February 1831. For more details see Bennett Woodcroft, *Patents for Inventions, Abridgements of Specifications relating to Music and Musical Instruments, AD. 1694–1866* (facsimile edn of the original 1871 edn; London: Bingham, 1984), pp. 100 and 112.

[156] L 156, 18 September 1815. Adelson et al, *The History of the Erard Piano and Harp*, pp. 612–613, at p. 613.

[157] L 317, 5 January 1822. Adelson et al, *The History of the Erard Piano and Harp*, pp. 782–783, at p. 782.

[158] Patent Nº 4672, 24 April 1822. For more details see Woodcroft, *Patents for Inventions*, p. 91.

[159] L 326, 19 February 1822. Adelson et al, *The History of the Erard Piano and Harp*, p. 791.

[160] Wayne, 'The Wheatstone English Concertina', p. 144.

[161] Kirkham, 'The London Furniture Trade', p. 84.

Registration System and Production Rate of Erard Grecian Harps

Equally important as the controlling of the workforce at the Erard London branch was the monitoring of the firm's output. Apart from workers' payments, another task carried out on a weekly basis was the registration of completed harps in the firm's ledgers, a practice which started in 1818, the year Erard N° 2631 was made. In previous years, only the date of sale of a harp, listed by serial number, along with the details of the buyer, was usually written in the ledgers. However, from 1818 onwards, both the date of registration, which corresponded roughly with the date of completion of a harp, and the date of sale or other transaction (e.g. hire or shipment) of the instrument were typically noted in the ledgers. This was important for controlling the firm's orders and stock, while enabling estimations of production and sales rates.

Since the interpretation of the harp entries in the Erard ledgers is an important tool for the better understanding of the firm's administrative system during the production of the Grecian model, it is useful to discuss them in greater detail, focusing on the year 1818. The fact that Erard N° 2631 was built in 1818 is confirmed by its entry in the second volume of the Erard ledgers, according to which the instrument was completed and registered in the ledgers on 30 November 1818, and was then sold to Chappell & Co, a prominent music selling and publishing company, on 18 January 1819 (Figure 24).[162]

As already mentioned, this volume contains the entries for harps Erard N° 1375 to N° 4214, covering the first 18 years in the manufacture of the Grecian model from 1811 to 1829. Each page of the second volume typically lists ten harps with serial numbers XXX5 to XXX4 (e.g. N° 2625 to N° 2634). The first column on the left of each entry includes the serial number and type of instrument, with S for single-action and D for double-action harps; in some cases a brief description of a particular model (e.g. 'old', 'Small. / N°. 1.', '3.^d Size') or finish (e.g. 'Red', 'Yellow', 'Burnished') is provided.

The date of entry for the year 1818 is written perpendicularly on the right side of the first column ('N°'); in later years it is also written horizontally below the serial number and model. The second column ('*Sold*') usually contains the title, name and address of the customer, as well as the date of sale of a harp. As will be described in the next chapter, this was usually the date when the Erard firm took an order, simultaneously issuing the customer's invoice, and not necessarily when it actually received the money from the customer. There are also three columns (two labelled '*Folio*', one '*Journal Folio*') that include numbers, which presumably refer to other files and records kept by Erard; as cited earlier, in 1821 Pierre mentioned six different books with debtors' accounts. Five additional columns (labelled '*Let*', '*Lent*', '*Ret^d*', '*Remarks*', '*Taken in exchange*') contain notes regarding the return, repair, replacement, modification, hire, lending or resale of a harp (usually summarised under the column '*Remarks*').

A survey of the harp entry dates in the Erard ledgers for the year 1818, in which Erard N° 2631 was built, has revealed that during that year Erard produced in total 184 harps, including 160 double-action and 24 single-action harps, with three to four

---

[162] Erard London Harp Ledgers, vol. 2, p. 126.

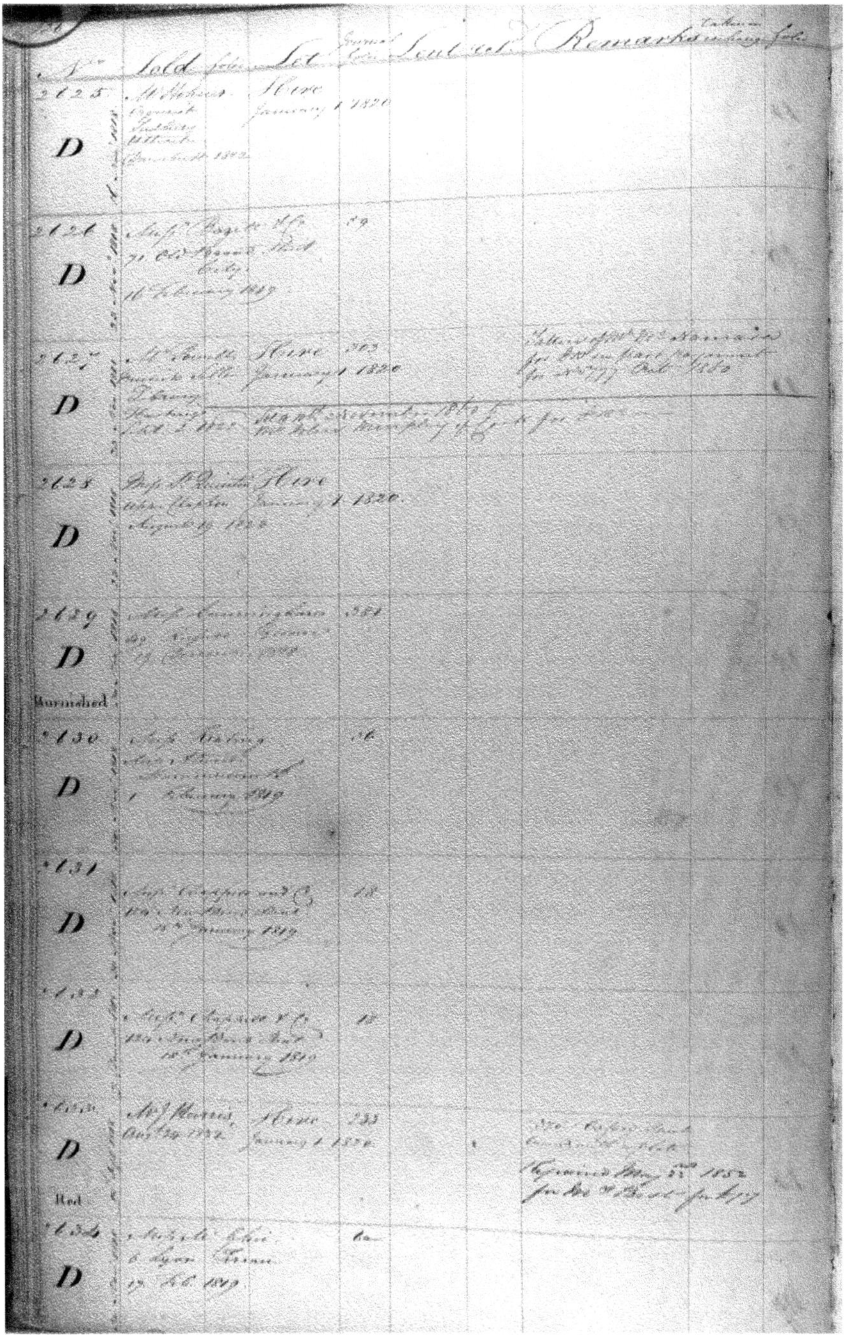

Figure 24. The page listing harps Erard N° 2625 to N° 2634, including Erard N° 2631, in the Erard London Harp Ledgers, vol. 2, p. 126. Royal College of Music, London, Special Collections, (RCM 497).

harps being completed every week. The 20 pages in the Erard ledgers spanning the year 1818 actually list only 179 harps, including 160 double-action harps and 19 single-action harps.[163] However, to these should be added five single-action harps (Erard N° 2275 to N° 2279), all having dates of entry within 1818, but registered earlier in the ledgers.[164] It is also important to note that there are ten harps with no entry date, but which according to their serial numbers could have been built in 1818. These include two single action-harps (Erard N° 2455 and N° 2456), as well as eight double action-harps (Erard N° 2471 to N° 2474 and Erard N° 2475 to N° 2478). Nevertheless, since these harps do not have a confirmed date of registration in the ledgers, they were excluded from this analysis for 1818. Such discrepancies are common in the Erard ledgers, which were working papers rather than official documents, thus requiring particular attention when they are examined. In some cases, two different harps have been given the same number, while others have been renumbered, making their identification difficult. For example, the same serial number 1458 was given to a double-action and to a single-action harp; next to the serial number the entry in the Erard ledgers reads 'These 2 harps are of the same N°'.[165]

The first entry for a double-action harp in 1818 was Erard N° 2479, registered on 19 January 1818, while the last was Erard N° 2642, registered on 28 December 1818. During these 12 months, the harps were usually registered in the ledgers on Mondays, with the exception of September and October, in which they were registered on Saturdays. This practice seems to have been repeated in the following years. This may explain why some harps appear to have been sold earlier than the date of their registration; for example, a finished harp may have been sold to a customer on a Friday, but was registered in the ledgers on the coming Monday.

The average output of three to four harps per week estimated for 1818 is further confirmed by the study of the Erard ledgers and correspondence during the late 1810s and early 1820s. This production rate is mentioned as early as April 1815 by Pierre, who stated that 'we finish about 4 harps a week.'[166] Three years later, in April 1818, Pierre reported that 'In March, we made 19 harps',[167] while in June 1818 Pierre argued that Horn, an employee who worked principally on double-action harps, 'can scarcely finish four harps a week'.[168] This number must have been a constant production target, as corroborated in 1821 by Pierre, who mentioned that 'I have taken on lots of workers and have arranged it so that we can finish at least four double harps each week!'[169] Pierre almost achieved this goal, since that year the Erard London branch produced

---

[163] Erard London Harp Ledgers, vol. 2, pp. 108–127.

[164] Erard London Harp Ledgers, vol. 2, p. 91.

[165] Erard London Harp Ledgers, vol. 2, p. 9.

[166] L 142, 7 and 12 April 1815. Adelson et al, *The History of the Erard Piano and Harp*, pp. 594–595, at p. 594.

[167] L 220, 10 April 1818. Adelson et al, *The History of the Erard Piano and Harp*, pp. 677–678, at p. 677. A study of the Erard ledgers for March 1818 proves that the firm indeed built 19 harps, including 17 double-action and two single-action instruments.

[168] L 224, 2 June 1818. Adelson et al, *The History of the Erard Piano and Harp*, p. 682.

[169] L 294, 13 February 1821. Adelson et al, *The History of the Erard Piano and Harp*, pp. 758–759, at p. 759.

193 harps in total, out of which 180 were double-action harps, implying that about three and a half double-action instruments were completed every week.[170]

The production rate of the Erard firm was relatively high when compared to other musical instrument manufacturers. For example, in the mid- to late 1810s, when the Erard London branch produced four double-action harps a week employing about 70 workers, Broadwood, who was London's largest piano manufacturer, produced six to seven grand pianos a week employing about 75 workers.[171] This reveals two noteworthy facts: firstly, that the productivity of the Erard firm roughly equalled that of the most prolific piano firm in London, and secondly, that building an Erard Grecian harp took almost as long (if not longer) as building a Broadwood grand piano, not least because of the harp's complex pedal mechanism and its elaborate decoration. It is also worth noting that between 1821 and 1824 Erat, one of Erard's rivals, produced 6.7 harps per month (or about 1.6 harps per week), albeit employing a smaller workforce than Erard.[172]

As will be discussed in the next chapter, the majority of harps built in 1818 were sold within days or weeks after completion, a factor which indicates both their great popularity and the hurry which which they had to be made. Similar sales patterns have been observed for other years in the 1810s and 1820s. The great demand for Erard harps, which imposed several challenges on their manufacture, had already started in the late 1790s, when Erard's single-action harp with the new fourchettes mechanism was becoming fashionable. For example, in 1797 Sébastien Erard informed a dealer in Madrid about the appeal of harps with the new mechanism, claiming that 'we cannot make enough of them in England',[173] while to a client in Amiens he remarked that 'We have no finished harps at the moment; they are sold as they are made, and we even have a waiting list.'[174] Writing to a client in Bordeaux about the growing approval of the firm's single-action harps with fourchettes, Erard noted that 'in London, we can barely build enough of them, and we sell them for 70 guineas';[175] in two other letters he similarly argued that 'we cannot respond to all of the orders and we sell them regularly for 70 guineas.'[176]

In the case of Erard double-action harps, which rapidly became popular during the 1810s, production was accelerated by the implementation of standardised, interchangeable parts for their construction as well as by the use of composition ornaments and decoupage prints for their decoration, as described in the previous chapters. The speed required for the manufacture of these harps is further

---

[170] L 330, 8 March 1822. Adelson et al, *The History of the Erard Piano and Harp*, pp. 794–795, at p. 795.

[171] Laurence, *The Evolution of the Broadwood Grand Piano*, pp. 66–67.

[172] Baldwin, 'The Erat Harp Manufactory', p. 151.

[173] L 7.383, 10 February 1797. Adelson et al, *The History of the Erard Piano and Harp*, pp. 175–176, at p. 176.

[174] L 7.409 (undated). Adelson et al, *The History of the Erard Piano and Harp*, p. 193.

[175] L 7.411, 29 April 1797. Adelson et al, *The History of the Erard Piano and Harp*, p. 194.

[176] L 7.388, 24 February 1797, and L 7.389 (undated). Adelson et al, *The History of the Erard Piano and Harp*, pp. 178–179, at p. 179, and pp. 179–180, at p. 180, respectively.

demonstrated in the application of their coatings. The irregularities detected by microscopic inspection in the various coating layers, as well as the pigment migration between coloured coatings and subsequently applied transparent varnishes on examined Erard Grecian harps, indicate that there was not sufficient drying time between the different working steps.[177] Since these irregularities are not visible macroscopically, and taking into account the general high-quality finishing of Erard harps, this must have been an intentional measure aiming to shorten the overall production time without compromising the appearance of the instruments.

Conclusions

In the late 1810s the Erard firm could annually produce about 180 double-action harps of the Grecian model, employing approximately 70 workers. The study of the Erard London branch during the early years of the production of the Grecian harp reveals the meticulous business planning and organisation that was required for the manufacture of such a complex and expensive instrument, whose construction and decoration involved diverse materials, techniques and skills, as discussed in the previous chapters. Hitherto-unnoticed evidence found in surviving instruments and archives reflects the close collaboration between different specialists that was indispensable for the manufacture of these harps, most of whom have remained unknown or have been obscured by the dominant personalities of the branch's directors during this period, first Sébastien and then Pierre. The Erard archives also reveal the broad network of suppliers on which the firm relied for materials, equipment and tools, as well as the various subcontractors that carried out specialised work for Erard, especially relating to harp decoration. As presented in various examples, by the prudent use of staff, facilities and resources, with practices that were common in other industrial sectors in Britain, the Erard firm managed to adapt successfully to the fluctuating conditions and demands of the musical instrument trade during the first decades of the nineteenth century. Moreover, the systematic bookkeeping and written communication with long-distance correspondence allowed the Erard firm to have a regular overview of expenses and revenue as well as to effectively monitor the production and distribution of instruments. The next chapter will explore the marketing of Erard Grecian harps, analysing the advertising and sales methods as well as the customer profile of the Erard firm.

---

[177] Panagiotis Poulopoulos, Marisa Pamplona, Luise Richter and Elke Cwiertnia, 'Technological Study of the Decoration on an Erard Harp from 1818', *Studies in Conservation* 65/2 (2020), pp. 86–102, at pp. 91–97; see also Panagiotis Poulopoulos, Marisa Pamplona and Luise Richter, 'The Industrialisation of the Early Pedal Harp: Detecting Evidence on Wood and Metal', in Marco A. Pérez and Sandie Le Conte (eds), *Making Wooden Musical Instruments: An Integration of Different Forms of Knowledge. Proceedings of the 3rd Annual Conference of the COST Action FP1302 WoodMusICK* (Barcelona: Museu de la Música, 2016), pp. 185–190, at p. 188. An early version of this article had been presented by the authors at the 3rd Annual Conference of the COST Action FP1302 WoodMusICK (Wooden Musical Instrument Conservation and Knowledge), 'Making Wooden Musical Instruments: An Integration of Different Forms of Knowledge', Museu de la Música, Barcelona, 7 to 9 September 2016.

CHAPTER FIVE

Marketing the Erard Grecian Harp: Promotional Strategies and the Establishment of a Refined Clientele

'The nobility and the landowners are very short of money. This class of society was the one that did the most business with us for the past eighteen months or two years; now on our ledgers we can find scarcely a few names from this class. Our customers now come from the merchant class and instrument dealers.'[1]

The first owner of Erard N° 2631, the harp housed at the Deutsches Museum, is unfortunately unknown. Although, as mentioned in the previous chapter, the Erard ledgers show that the harp was sold to the London music retailers Chappell & Co on 18 January 1819, there are no traces of the instrument between this date and its acquisition by the Deutsches Museum in 1908. However, we can get an impression of the persons who purchased and used similar Erard Grecian harps by analysing two surviving harp bills issued for different customers, the first dating from 1818 – the same year that Erard N° 2631 was made – and the second dating from 1817. Additionally, by identifying and linking the items included in the two bills with those listed in a harp catalogue by Erard, and by comparing them to extant Erard instruments and accessories, we can examine the product range and services offered by the Erard London branch in the late 1810s. Moreover, by discussing a harp tutor and harp music published around 1818 for the double-action harp, we can further explore the marketing schemes of the Erard firm and the role that music composers, performers, teachers, publishers and sellers played in the diffusion of the Erard Grecian harp in Britain and abroad.

Erard Harps for the Polite Society: A Harp Bill for a Lord, a Grecian Harp for a Lady

For the majority of Erard Grecian harps which have survived, like Erard N° 2631, there is limited information about their consumption and distribution. Apart from the name and address of the customers recorded in the Erard ledgers, usually noth-

---

[1] L 339, 30 May 1823, in Robert Adelson, Alain Roudier, Jenny Nex, Laure Barthel and Michel Foussard (eds), *The History of the Erard Piano and Harp in Letters and Documents, 1785–1959* (Cambridge: Cambridge University Press, 2015), pp. 803–805, at p. 804.

ing else is known about the context in which a harp was purchased and used, and one can only make assumptions based solely on the surviving instrument. For instance, many Erard harps have visible signs of use and modification, while some also bear inscriptions indicating repair and restoration, which can be attributed to their various owners and users, as will be discussed in Chapter Eight. Yet, there are a few examples of Erard harps where the opposite is true: there is sufficient archival evidence about a harp's purchase, ownership and usage, but the actual instrument has disappeared.

This is exactly the case with Erard Nº 2524, an ultramarine double-action harp registered in the Erard ledgers on 20 April 1818.[2] Although the harp is presently missing, the bill regarding its purchase has miraculously survived (Figure 25).[3] Since the identity of the buyer and the details of the purchase are recorded in detail in this bill, they can help us to reconstruct the everyday transactions between the Erard firm and its clientele.

The bill reveals that on 27 May 1818 Lord Berwick (Thomas Noel Hill, 2nd Baron Berwick of Attingham, 1770–1832) purchased a double-action harp and several harp-related accessories from the Erard London branch. Apart from 'a new patent double movement Harp elegantly ornamented' at £168, the items listed in the bill included 'a Music Stool to correspond' at £10 10s; 'a Music Stand D[o]' at £9 9s; 'a String box D[o]' at £4 4s; 'a Leather Cover' at £5 15s 6d'; 'a Set Strings' at £3 3s; 'a Set Silver D[o]' at £1 18s; 'a Harp Packing Case' at £3 10s; and 'a Stool D[o]' at 15s. The total costs of £207 4s 6d were reduced by £10 7s, so the final price amounted to £196 17s and 6d. In comparison, in 1818 a six-and-a-half octave grand piano or an upright grand piano, the two most expensive items in Broadwood's product list, cost £105.[4]

It is also interesting to compare these prices with contemporary wages and the cost of living. The price of around £197 for the Erard harp together with accessories that Lord Berwick purchased in 1818 was a considerable sum for that time, almost equal to the annual salary of a surgeon,[5] or the annual expenses of a gentleman's family, including himself, his wife, three children and a maid-servant.[6] As a further comparison, the household expenses of a country estate show that in the mid-1820s a 'French Man-Cook' earned £80, a 'Butler' £50, a 'Gardener' £40, while a 'Female Teacher' only £30 per year.[7] Even excluding any harp-related accessories,

[2] Erard London Harp Ledgers, vol. 2, p. 115.

[3] The bill, now held at the Attingham Park Collection, Shropshire Archives, Shrewsbury, 112/6/54/381, was previously kept together with other documents at Attingham Park.

[4] Jenny Nex, *The Business of Musical-Instrument Making in Early Industrial London* (PhD Diss., London: Goldsmiths College, 2013), p. 199.

[5] In the 1810s the average annual wage of a surgeon was £217, whereas that of an agricultural labourer was £42; see Nex, *The Business of Musical-Instrument Making in Early Industrial London*, p. 111.

[6] See 'Practical Estimates on Household Expenses: Part 1', in Colburn and Company, *A New System of Practical Domestic Economy* (London: H. Colburn and Company, 1823), p. 37.

[7] Samuel and Sarah Adams, *The Complete Servant: Being a Practical Guide to the Peculiar Duties and Business of All Descriptions of Servants* (London: Knight and Lacey, 1825), p. 7.

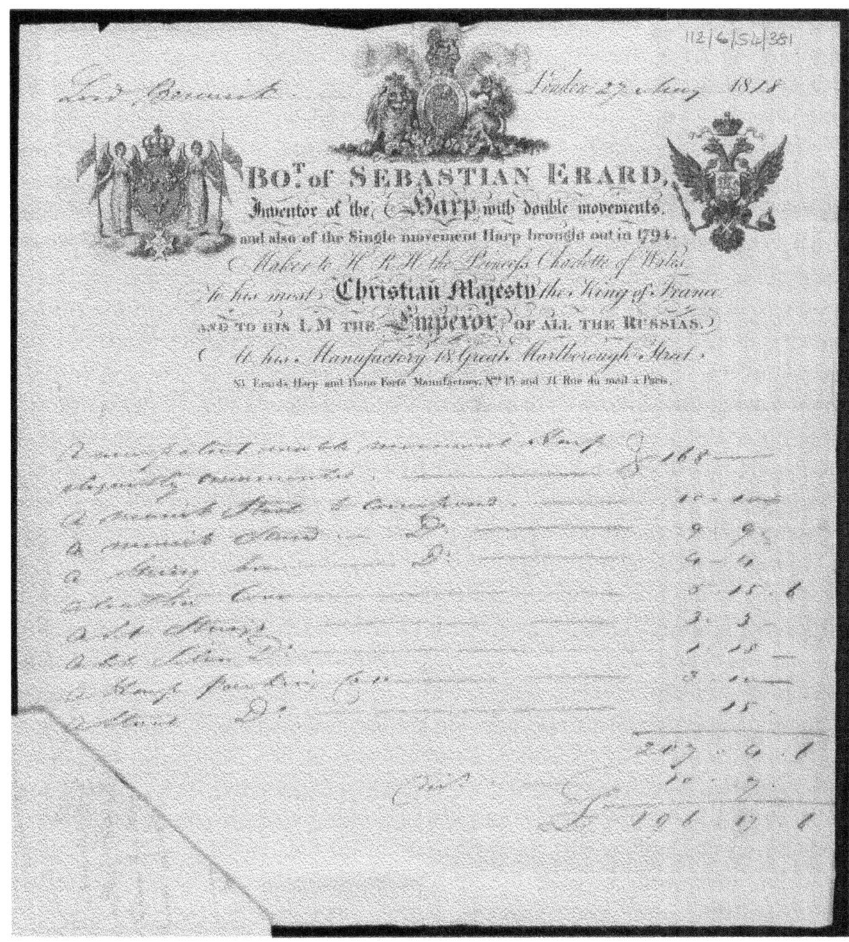

Figure 25. A bill dated 27 May 1818 regarding the purchase of 'a new patent double movement Harp elegantly ornamented', along with several harp-related accessories, by Lord Berwick. Attingham Park Collection, Shropshire Archives, Shrewsbury, 112/6/54/381.

one can assume that the Erard harp that Lord Berwick bought would be unaffordable for most people.

Whereas the purchased items are handwritten, the top part of the Erard bill bears various printed details, essentially resembling a trade card and illustrating Erard's close links to the printing and publishing industries, as mentioned in Chapter Three. Even though they were used primarily for financial purposes, bills, invoices, receipts and similar documents were important for raising the public image and prestige of the firm. In this bill Sébastien Erard proudly informed the public that he was 'Inventor of the Harp with double movements' as well as 'of the Single movement

Harp brought out in 1794'. The first description refers to Erard's 1810 patent for the double-action harp, while the second description refers to his first patent from 1794 for a single-action harp with fourchettes. Erard also prominently demonstrated his connections to British and European royalty, since he declared himself to be maker 'to H. R. H the Princess Charlotte of Wales', 'to his most Christian Majesty the King of France', as well as 'TO HIS I.M the Emperor OF ALL THE RUSSIAS', additionally depicting the coats of arms of England, France and Russia on the top of the bill.

After the definitive defeat of Napoleon Bonaparte in 1814–1815 and the Bourbon Restoration, these were three of the most powerful states in Europe. Sébastien Erard's political views were rather conservative and his sympathy to the *Ancien Régime* is indicated by the fact that he only permanently returned to Paris in 1814, after Napoleon's reign in France had practically ended. In July 1815, during the military campaign that followed the Battle of Waterloo, Pierre became quite worried about his uncle's well-being, stating that 'we were told here for the past two days that Paris was in flames' and adding 'Thank God it is not, but it seems that the surrounding areas greatly suffered'.[8] Therefore, as a fervent royalist himself, Erard was apparently eager to associate his business with the new European leaders through appropriate advertising measures.

Moreover, the bill includes Erard's address not only in London at '18. Great Marlborough Street', but also in Paris at 'N°s. 13 and 21 Rue du mail', where the manufacture of both harps and pianos was carried out, thus highlighting the international profile and broad scope of the firm. It seems that the Erard firm started using such inscriptions, which are also found in the harp catalogue that will be discussed later, around 1816. This is evidenced in a letter from 1816 in which Pierre wrote to his uncle Sébastien that 'the engraving plate for the *Bills* is quite worn down; I am having a new one made'.[9] Pierre then proposed an inscription almost identical to that on the bill from 1818, adding that the application of such inscriptions on Erard instruments and bills would be good for publicity purposes.[10] As described in Chapter Three, similar inscriptions were engraved on the brass plates of Grecian harps that were built from around 1816 onwards.

A receipt written on a small paper kept together with the bill, states that a certain J. J. Bruzaud received from Lord Berwick the amount of £196 17s and 6d on behalf of Sébastien Erard on 29 May 1818, proving that Lord Berwick paid for the harp two days after the issuing of the bill.[11] This is not unusual, since buying instruments on credit was quite common in Regency Britain, and therefore the date of sale of a harp did not always coincide with the date of payment.[12] The sale of goods on the principle of credit was a practice that mostly suited large firms, since 'In a period where the gentry and nobility were notorious for running up credit on tradesmen, powerful

---

8　L 150, 7 July 1815. Adelson et al, *The History of the Erard Piano and Harp*, pp. 606–607, at p. 606.

9　L 169, 2 February 1816. Adelson et al, *The History of the Erard Piano and Harp*, pp. 623–624.

10　L 169, 2 February 1816. Adelson et al, *The History of the Erard Piano and Harp*, pp. 623–624.

11　Attingham Park Collection, Shropshire Archives, Shrewsbury, 112/6/54/381A.

12　Nex, *The Business of Musical-Instrument Making in Early Industrial London*, p. 243.

manufacturers could sustain a violation of contract which might break a smaller competitor'.[13] Additionally, 'those who produced on a large scale were able to use their suppliers as bankers, running up credit which financed their continuity of trade.'[14]

Nevertheless, even prominent manufacturers like Erard were not immune to the effects of credit, and the limited cash flow often exposed businesses to the dangers of mounting debts and bankruptcy. One should not forget that the Erard Paris branch was declared bankrupt in 1813, augmenting the severe financial difficulties which the London branch faced throughout the mid- to late 1810s due to economic stagnation in Britain, as will be described below. The seasonal fluctuation of sales and the lack of cash could severely disrupt the arrangement and operation of the firm, calling for brave adjustments. In July 1821 Pierre reported that 'sales are very weak, especially for this season', further stating that 'I would regret having to make changes in the workshops, because they are very well set up, especially for the woodwork, but if sales do not meet expenses, I will be compelled to do so!'[15]

Since most transactions were based on the principle of credit, it was important for firms to know which clients still owed money for goods or services they had purchased, and, if needed, to pursue them until they had settled their debts. From this perspective, Bruzaud's name on the receipt is notable. John Joseph Bruzaud (1780–1849) was a trustworthy Erard employee who was occasionally responsible for the firm's administration and correspondence, as evidenced by several letters written and signed by him on behalf of the firm.[16] Bruzaud's involvement in the firm's management is further demonstrated by the fact that his son, George John (c.1814–1887), became director of the Erard London branch in 1855.[17] In 1819 Pierre praised John Joseph Bruzaud to Sébastien, writing: 'Bruzaud, whom I have come to know during the five years that we are together everyday, has some excellent qualities. He is a perfectly honest man, to whom one could confide everything, and whose character and manners are very well suited to his position!'[18]

Confidence and trust were important, especially for the financial side of the Erard business, because apparently not every worker behaved as honourably as Bruzaud. Pierre experienced this in October 1819, when upon his return from a trip to Wales he discovered 'that the shop assistant who was assisting Bruzaud is a <u>thief</u>. He received money on your account, and he kept it […] He used my name to borrow money from our friends, even from some workers.'[19]

---

[13] Matthew Craske, 'Plan and Control: Design and the Competitive Spirit in Early and Mid-Eighteenth Century England', *Journal of Design History* 12/3 (1999), pp. 187–216, at p. 207.

[14] Craske, 'Plan and Control', p. 207.

[15] L 304, 6 July 1821. Adelson et al, *The History of the Erard Piano and Harp*, pp. 773–774, at p. 774.

[16] See 'Correspondance diverse (1816–1842)', available at http://www.sebastienerard.org/fr/?m=cdiverse, accessed 3 June 2022.

[17] Adelson et al, *The History of the Erard Piano and Harp*, p. 13.

[18] L 265, 13 July 1819. Adelson et al, *The History of the Erard Piano and Harp*, pp. 724–725, at p. 725.

[19] L 270, 13 October 1819. Adelson et al, *The History of the Erard Piano and Harp*, pp. 728–729, at p. 729.

Probably due to his morality and reliability, Bruzaud was frequently assigned to financial duties. These included dealing with payments to the firm's workers and suppliers,[20] as well as occasionally chasing customers for pending bills, because evidence in the Erard correspondence shows that not all customers paid as promptly as Lord Berwick did when he bought the double-action harp. For instance, in February 1816 Pierre informed Sébastien that he 'just hired a young man to collect the small debts, as Bruzaud and Baugh are extremely busy at the firm',[21] while in January 1817 he reported that 'Sales are very good, but with hardly any cash. This is not without going to see the people and writing to them, because at this time two workers do almost nothing else but run around trying to collect money.'[22] As one of the most experienced and trustworthy members of the Erard staff, Bruzaud was obviously the appropriate person to settle a payment involving both a great amount of money and an esteemed customer such as Lord Berwick. The fact that the handwriting in the bill is the same as in the receipt suggests that Bruzaud most likely wrote both documents himself, a further proof of his authority within the Erard London branch.

The transaction between the Erard firm and Berwick is also corroborated in the Erard ledgers, albeit with some discrepancy concerning the client's identity and gender. According to the ledgers it was 'Lady Berwick 4 Stratford Place' who on 27 May 1818 bought Erard N° 2524, and not Lord Berwick. A study of the individuals who bought the first 100 double action-harps by Erard between 1811 and 1812 has shown that it is difficult to ascertain whether the firm's male customers purchased the instruments for themselves; presumably most of them would have procured the harps for their wives, daughters, mistresses or other female acquaintances.[23] So, like the majority of Erard's male customers, although Lord Berwick paid for the harp, he was not the actual user of the instrument, even though he was an enthusiastic patron of the arts. Instead, the Lord purchased the harp for his young wife, Sophia Dubochet (1794–1875), who he had married in 1812.

When Sophia became Lady Berwick she was able to enter London's aristocratic circles despite her humble origins. Sophia and her sister, Harriette Wilson (1786–1845), were famous courtesans in Regency London. It is noteworthy that references to the harp are included in Harriette's memoirs published in 1825, suggesting that the older of the two sisters was also familiar with the instrument. Most importantly, Harriette provides evidence that her younger sister took harp lessons with the renowned harpist Robert Nicolas-Charles Bochsa (1789–1856), mentioning that one day Sophia experienced 'a multiplicity of disasters', one of which was that she

[20] 'Bruzaud is behind for several acceptances being held by suppliers and also for several payrolls for the workers'. L 188, 3 February 1817. Adelson et al, *The History of the Erard Piano and Harp*, p. 643.

[21] L 170, 14 February 1816. Adelson et al, *The History of the Erard Piano and Harp*, pp. 624–625, at p. 624.

[22] L 187, 19 January 1817. Adelson et al, *The History of the Erard Piano and Harp*, pp. 642–643, at p. 642.

[23] Nex, *The Business of Musical-Instrument Making in Early Industrial London*, p. 110.

'could not match the silk she wanted to finish a purse she happened to be netting for her handsome harp-master Bochsa, of – notoriety'.[24]

Bochsa, an eminent advocate of the Erard double-action harp, was harp tutor to several members of the nobility, as evident in the Erard correspondence.[25] Interestingly, in 1818 Bochsa married Amelie Wilson (1781–1838), the eldest sister of Harriette and Sophia, who was also a courtesan. Sophia most likely began having lessons with Bochsa that year, shortly after Lord Berwick had procured the Erard harp for her. The teacher-pupil relationship between Bochsa and Sophia is further revealed by the fact that around the same time, Bochsa composed *Preludes for the Harp*, which were 'composed & dedicated to Lady Berwick'[26] and published by Chappell & Co, music publishers and sellers who retailed Erard harps, among which was Erard Nº 2631. Moreover, although not mentioning a name, a handwritten note recording a payment of £4 12s and 9d to 'the Harp Master for her Ladyship' on 30 May 1821 in Lord Berwick's archives must have referred to Bochsa's wages for Sophia's harp tuition.[27]

Sophia apparently liked her Erard harp so much that the instrument must have been occasionally transported from London to Lord Berwick's country estate at Attingham Park, Shropshire. For instance, a bill in Lord Berwick's archives shows that a harp, most likely the one that was purchased in 1818, was returned to London on 15 January 1819,[28] possibly to be used by Lady Berwick during the London season, as will be described later. Probably in the late 1820s the harp was sent to Italy, where the couple moved in 1827 to escape the consequences of Lord Berwick's bankruptcy.[29] Of all the items listed in Lord Berwick's bill, only the harp stool and music stand are known to have survived, now on display at Attingham Park.[30]

Sophia's love for the harp is also evidenced by a music automaton, which is believed to have been gifted to her by Lord Berwick. The automaton, made around 1820 by Moulinie Aine and Co. of Geneva, depicts a chained monkey seated before a harp and music stand.[31] The fact that the harp was commonly featured in the designs

---

24   Harriette Wilson, *The Memoirs of Harriette Wilson: Written by Herself* (2 volumes; London: Eveleigh Nash, 1909), vol. 2, p. 645.

25   For more details on Bochsa see Adelson et al, *The History of the Erard Piano and Harp*, pp. 648–649.

26   Robert Nicolas-Charles Bochsa, *Preludes for the Harp, composed & dedicated to Lady Berwick* (London: Chappell & Co, c.1818), Pendlebury Library of Music, University of Cambridge, XRa.850.18A.X22.

27   Attingham Park Collection, Shropshire Archives, Shrewsbury, 12/6/64/98.

28   Attingham Park Collection, Shropshire Archives, Shrewsbury, 12/6/63/341.

29   For more details see 'Musical Instruments at Attingham – The Harp', available at https://attinghamparkmansion.wordpress.com/tag/harp/, accessed 3 June 2022.

30   In Attingham Park, Shropshire, National Trust (Inv. No. NT 608181.1 and NT 608181.2 respectively). For details of the stool and stand see 'Music stool', http://www.nationaltrustcollections.org.uk/object/608181.1 and 'Duet stand', http://www.nationaltrustcollections.org.uk/object/608181.2, both accessed 3 June 2022.

31   In Attingham Park, Shropshire, National Trust (Inv. No. NT 608416). For details of the automaton see 'Automaton', http://www.nationaltrustcollections.org.uk/object/608416, accessed 3 June 2022.

of fashionable household devices, such as automata and clocks, further indicates the instrument's popularity in contemporary society.

Made in London, Played in Baltimore: Buying an Erard Harp for an American Home

A surviving bill similar to the one issued for Lord Berwick presents the captivating story of another Erard Grecian harp. The bill relates to Erard Nº 2372, a double-action harp purchased in 1817 for Eliza Eichelberger Ridgely (1803–1867).[32] Eliza was the only child of Nicholas Greenbury Ridgely (1770–1829), a wealthy wine merchant in Baltimore. Since her mother had died shortly after giving birth, Eliza's father sent his daughter at the age of 13 to Miss Lyman's Institution, a boarding school for young women in Philadelphia, intending to offer her a fine education. At Miss Lyman's, Eliza took singing, dancing, piano and harp lessons among other subjects, such as deportment, natural history, botany, grammar, literature, French and drawing. Eliza was 'a professionally trained and talented musician who took her playing very seriously'; Hampton National Historic Site, where Eliza's harp is presently housed, 'preserves several hundred pieces of her original manuscript and printed sheet music for harp, pianoforte, and voice'.[33]

As an accomplished harpist, Eliza made good use of the Erard harp she received in 1817; her father's surviving papers from 1820 to 1826 contain 96 bills for music lessons as well as numerous others for harp repairs and strings. The Erard harp was probably the instrument that Eliza played upon to entertain the famous Marquis de Lafayette (1757–1834) when he visited Baltimore in 1824.[34]

Dated 26 June 1817, the bill for Eliza's harp is prepared on paper with the same printed letterhead as the bill of Lord Berwick and bearing the same handwriting, suggesting it was written by Bruzaud. Interestingly, the bill was not issued to Elisa's father, as would be expected, but to J. C. Nielson, an agent who obtained the harp for the 14-year-old Eliza; the purchase of the harp is also documented in the Erard ledgers, with the relevant entry reading, 'Mr. J. C. Nielson // Baltimore U.S. America // 27 June 1817'.[35] The items listed in the bill included 'a new patent double movement Harp' at £110 5s, 'a leather Cover' at £4 4s, 'a Set of Roman Strings' at £3 3s, 'Silver Strings' at £1 16s, as well as 'a Packing Case' at £3 10s. A reduction of £12 4s on

---

[32] Ridgely Family Papers, Maryland Historical Society (Inv. No. MS 692). I am thankful to Gregory Weidman for providing me with a copy of this bill and with information on Eliza's harp-related activities.

[33] Gregory Weidman, 'Eliza Ridgely's historic Erard Harp', *American Harp Journal* 26/1 (2017), p. 52.

[34] Robert Wilson Torchia, 'Eliza Ridgely and the Ideal of American Womanhood, 1787–1820', *Maryland Historical Magazine* 90/4 (1995), pp. 405–423, at pp. 406–407.

[35] Erard London Harp Ledgers, vol. 2, p. 100. For more details of the harp and its recent conservation see Weidman, 'Eliza Ridgely's historic Erard Harp', p. 52, as well as 'Restoration Project for Eliza Ridgely Harp', at https://www.baltimoreharp.org/historic-eliza-ridgely-harp-restoration/, accessed 3 June 2022.

the total price of £122 18s meant that Nielson eventually had to pay £110 14s for the objects he purchased on behalf of Ridgely.

Investigating the Product Line of the Erard Firm through a Harp Catalogue

The types and prices of the various items which are included in the two bills discussed above can be identified and compared with the products listed in a harp catalogue issued by the Erard firm (Figure 26). Although the catalogue is undated, it must have been published around 1821 and certainly no earlier than 1819. This dating is due to two facts: the first is that the 'Rosewood' finish listed in the catalogue is first mentioned in the Erard ledgers in the entry for Erard N° 2708, a harp built in May 1819, while the second is that a wording similar to the title of the catalogue, which advertises Erard as 'Harp Maker, // (By special Appointment) // 'TO HIS MAJESTY AND THE ROYAL FAMILY' began to be used in the engravings of Erard harps in 1821.

The details in the two Erard bills and this catalogue indicate that at least during the late 1810s there were no major changes in the variety and prices of harps and harp-related accessories available from Erard. Moreover, the similarities between the product descriptions and prices in the two bills and catalogue confirm that, although dating from c.1819–1821, the catalogue is representative of the firm's product line from 1817 and 1818, when Erard N° 2631 was made. Therefore, as already described in Chapter Three, Erard N° 2631 was most likely the second cheapest double-action harp in Erard's catalogue, labelled as 'Black, with double gold vignettes, burnished gilding' and costing £126.

The study of the catalogue reveals the wisely calculated marketing policy of the Erard firm, which offered a wide variety of products and services for clients with different budgets. The first three product categories relate to harps. The catalogue starts with the most expensive product of the firm, the double-action harp, listing one full-sized model available in five different price levels and seven finishing options. These depended on the type and complexity of the decoration, including eight coloured finishes, decoupage vignettes, burnished gilding and painted ornaments labelled as 'Raphael's Arabesks'; these decorative features have been analysed in Chapter Three.

The second category in the catalogue includes small harps in three different sizes (No. 1, 2 and 3) addressed to young ladies between seven and fifteen years old, since 'from that age any person can play with the greatest facility on the full-sized Harp'. According to the catalogue, these harps could be 'exchanged from size to size should it be required', a practice that presumably helped to keep young Erard clients loyal to the firm's instruments as they grew older. Single-action harps, the third category, were offered either in the 'Former Shape' or in 'The same shape as the Double Movement', to which 'the Double Movement can be introduced' for an additional cost. This illustrated the ingenious standardisation measures of the firm, by which the same moulds and templates could be used for two different harp models with single- and double-action mechanisms.

Both single- and double-action harps could be lent or hired per month in 'either town or country', thus allowing clients both in the capital and in the provinces to familiarise themselves with the firm's instruments before deciding upon buying an

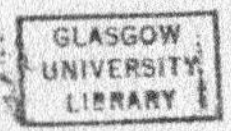

CATALOGUE.

SEBASTIAN ERARD,

Harp Maker,

(By special Appointment)

TO HIS MAJESTY AND THE ROYAL FAMILY,

18, GREAT MARLBOROUGH STREET, LONDON;

And Nos. 13 & 21, RUE DU MAIL, PARIS, where PIANO-FORTES are also manufactured.

DOUBLE MOVEMENTS.

(The first Patent obtained in England for the Double Movement Harps was granted to Mr. S. ERARD, the 16th June, 1801.)

FULL SIZE.

	£	s.	d.
Light ultramarine blue, painted with Raphael's Arabesks, and decorated with burnished gilding	168	0	0
Double smalt blue, green, or red, painted with Raphael's Arabesks, burnished gilding	157	10	0
Dark blue, green, or red, with double gold vignettes, but burnished gilding	136	10	0
Transparent grey or yellow, without any other painting but burnished gilding	126	0	0
Rosewood without any other ornament but burnished gilding	126	0	0
Black, with double gold vignettes, burnished gilding	126	0	0
Black, with single gold vignettes (generally called plain ones)	110	5	0

SMALL HARPS.

	£	s.	d.
No. 1, 2, 3. black, with gold vignettes	89	5	0

No. 1 is adapted to the use of young ladies from 7 to 10 years of age.

No. 2 to the use of young ladies from the age of 10 to 13—and

No. 3 to the use of young ladies from 13 to 15 years of age; from that age any person can play with the greatest facility on the full-sized Harp.

These Harps will be exchanged from size to size should it be required.

SINGLE MOVEMENTS.

	£	s.	d.
The same shape as the Double Movement	89	5	0

To which instruments the Double Movement can be introduced for £31. 10s.

	£	s.	d.
Former Shape	73	10	0

Harps, with the Double or Single Movements, lent on Hire for either town or country.

	£	s.	d.
The Double Action, at per month	2	12	6
The Single Action, ditto	2	2	0
Ditto ditto	1	11	6

MUSIC STOOLS.

	£	s.	d.
Light or dark blue, green, red, &c. and painted with Arabesks to correspond with Harps of 160 to 150 guineas, velvet seat, &c.	10	10	0
Dark blue, red, green, yellow, grey, with gold lines; rosewood, and black, with vignettes to correspond with Harps of 130 to 120 guineas, velvet seat	9	9	0
Mahogany, with Turkey leather seat	6	6	0

The above stool has an iron screw and brass cap, by which the seat can be raised or lowered at pleasure.

Figure 26. Erard harp catalogue listing prices for various models of double- and single-action harps, as well as for harp-related accessories, such as music stools, music stands, sounding boards, string boxes, gut and silver strings, harp covers and packing cases. Erard Harp Catalogue (London: Erard, c.1819–1821), pp. 1–2. University of Glasgow Archives & Special Collections, A.x.24.

MUSIC STANDS.

	£.	s.	d.
Light ultramarine blue, dark blue, red, green, painted with Raphael's Arabesks, burnished gilding to correspond with Harps of 160 to 150 guineas	9	9	0
Dark, blue, red, green, yellow, grey, with gold lines; rosewood, and black, with vignettes to correspond with Harps of 130 and 120 guineas	8	8	0
Black with lines, to correspond with Harps of 105 to 85 guineas	7	7	0
Mahogany	5	5	0

The above Stands have brass poles, candlesticks, and branches, and are so constructed
as to admit of being packed up in the same case with the Harp.

SOUNDING BOARD.

Any colour with gold lines	10	10	0

STRING BOXES.

Square, with a drawer, containing tuning-key, tuning-fork, string-gage, and scissars, &c.	5	5	0
Ditto, with room inside for tuning-key, tuning-fork, and string-gage, light or dark blue, green, red painted with Arabesks	4	4	0
Black, less ornamented	3	3	0
Plain, with gold lines	2	2	0
Common ones	1	5	0

GUT STRINGS.

A set of Italian strings	3	3	0
A set of English ditto	2	5	0

SILVER STRINGS.

(Made in the manufactory on a particular machine.)

A Set (8)	1	18	0

Gut and Silver Strings may be had by the single String.

HARP COVERS.

Red, purple, or green leather, lined with calico, with a neat plated lock, and buttons	5	15	6
Brown leather . . . ditto	4	4	0
Purple or green, morine	2	10	0
Leno	1	1	0

PACKING CASES.

Wooden Harp Case, lined with green baize, with lock and key	3	10	0
Ditto ditto, lined with tin	3	10	0
Packing Case for Sounding Board	1	10	0
Packing Case for a Music Stool	0	15	0
Packing Case for Music Stand	0	12	0
Packing Ditto, Eagle	0	6	0
Packing in Mats, Straw, Cords, &c.	0	15	0
A Tuning-Key	0	5	6
An Octave of Tuning-Forks	2	2	0
A Tuning-Fork	0	4	6
A String Gage or Measure	0	6	0

ADDITIONAL ORNAMENTS TO THE HARP; an Eagle, carved and gilt	6	6	0
a Coronet, carved and gilt	6	6	0
a Swan, carved and gilt	6	6	0

J. Matthews, Printer, 6, Noel-street, Soho, London.

Erard harp, which required a more serious commitment and financial investment. This is quite important, especially if one compares the price of the double-action harp with that of the second most popular plucked instrument of the period, the guitar. Most imported or locally-made guitars cost less than ten guineas, with the price of the finest guitars by Louis Panormo, the most prominent maker in early nineteenth-century London, being 15 guineas,[36] whereas Erard double-action harps cost between 120 and 160 guineas.

The next nine catalogue categories list various harp-related accessories. The first four include music stools, music stands, sounding boards and string boxes offered in finishes matching those of the different harps. These accessories were designed to assist and improve harp performance to the maximum. For example, the velvet or leather seat of the music stools could be 'raised or lowered at pleasure' by means of an iron screw and brass cap. Music stands were equipped with candlesticks to help harpists read music scores at night, while their construction with folding parts allowed them to be 'packed up in the same case with the Harp'. In addition, the sounding board demonstrates one of the earliest devices for the acoustic amplification of harps and other stringed instruments. The sounding board was essentially an oval wooden hollow resonator resting on small feet that aimed to amplify the volume of the harp. Two rectangular areas with a grid on the left and right side of the sounding board enabled players to rest their feet securely and to prevent slipping when holding the instrument, whereas three protruding iron studs on the back of the board permitted the secure attachment of the stool, so that it could not move during performance.

This acoustic harp amplifier must have been introduced by Erard around 1812, if not earlier, since payments for the ornamenting of sounding boards for Erard during that year are listed in the accounts of George Jackson, the composition maker mentioned in Chapters Three and Four.[37] Erard's sounding board is depicted in the harp tutor *A Complete Demonstration of the Advantages afforded by Mr. Sebastian Erard's New Invented Harp, with Double Action in the Pedals*, published by John Baptist Mayer in 1816.[38] The image on the frontispiece (Figure 27) shows a young woman in neoclassical costume holding a Grecian harp quite similar to Erard N° 2631, while standing on a sounding board next to a round stool.

The next two categories of the Erard catalogue concern harp strings, which could be purchased in sets or as single strings. Gut strings were of Italian or English manufacture, with the latter being the cheapest, while 'Silver Strings', referring to overwound bass strings, were 'Made in the manufactory on a particular machine', further confirming the extensive use of specialised machinery at the Erard London branch, as discussed in Chapters Two and Four.

---

[36] Christopher Page, *The Guitar in Georgian England: A Social and Musical History* (New Haven and London: Yale University Press, 2020), pp. 153–155.

[37] George Jackson and Sons Ledger, V&A Archive of Art and Design, London, AD/2012/1/2/1, pp. 1–2.

[38] Mayer's tutor must have been published in early 1816, since a review is included in Sylvanus Urban, *The Gentleman's Magazine: and Historical Chronicle. From January to June 1816. Vol. 86* (London: Nichols, Son, and Bentley, 1816), p. 539.

Figure 27. The frontispiece of J. B. Mayer's *A Complete Demonstration of the Advantages afforded by Mr. Sebastian Erard's New Invented Harp, with Double Action in the Pedals* (London: Mayer, 1816). University of Glasgow Archives & Special Collections, Ca10-a.26.

Two further categories include leather harp covers of various types, colours and prices, as well as wooden cases for packing and transporting harps and their accessories, using 'Matts, Straws, Cords, &c.' for extra protection. This was essential, especially considering the available means of transport and the poor state of the roads, which encompassed great risks for fragile objects like harps (this is why transport on water was often preferable when possible). A harp treatise from 1802 advised harpists to take precautions when transporting their instruments, stating that 'When travelling, one must put the harp in its case (and unstrung) in the top compartment of a carriage'.[39] The Erard firm also sold tuning keys, tuning forks and string gauges which enabled harpists to string and tune their harps, while the final category in the catalogue regarded additional ornamentation with carved and gilt figures of an eagle, a coronet or a swan that were fixed on the top of the harp's capital, as evidenced on a few surviving instruments.[40]

Most importantly, the two bills and the catalogue allow us to examine two different cases of Erard's customers. In the first case it is worth noting that Lady Berwick acquired almost the entire harp package offered in Erard's catalogue, except for the sounding board and the additional ornamentation of the harp column. Moreover, all the items that Lady Berwick selected, from the 'elegantly ornamented' harp to the leather cover and packing case, correspond to the most expensive pieces in the catalogue. This demonstrates the success of Erard's marketing strategy, since affluent customers and persons of distinction who could afford to purchase Erard instruments apparently bought the best and most complete of the firm's product range. In contrast to Lady Berwick, Eliza Ridgely, a customer of more modest means, chose the cheapest double-action harp model in the catalogue, the 'Black, with single gold vignettes', which at £110 5s was still quite an expensive instrument. Moreover, Eliza did not purchase the full range of accompanying harp accessories offered by Erard, but only the most necessary items, such as a brown leather cover and strings, as well as the 'Wooden Harp Case, lined with green baize, with lock and key', obviously to enable the safe transport of the harp to the other side of the Atlantic.

That the social elite usually purchased not only the most expensive Erard harps, but also an extended range of the firm's costliest products, is further illustrated by the example of Erard Nº 1705. In 1813 this ultramarine double-action harp, the priciest harp in the Erard catalogue, was acquired by 'Her Royal Highness // The Princess of Wales'.[41] Like Lady Berwick, Charlotte, the Princess of Wales, apparently ordered an entire set of the most expensive Erard products, since along with her harp, she obtained a music stool, music stand, sounding board and string box in matching ultramarine finish, all of which have fortunately survived together as an ensemble (Figure 28). Ironically, Charlotte's harp and accessories are currently preserved not

---

[39] Quoted in Robert Adelson, 'The Viscountess de Beaumont's Harp and Music Album (1780)', *The Galpin Society Journal* 62 (2009), pp. 159–166, at p. 164.

[40] For instance, a rare specimen of an Erard double-action harp decorated with a coronet has been presented in Robert Adelson, *Erard: Empire of the Harp* (Ancenis: Les Harpes Camac, 2022), p. 99. The harp, housed in the private collection of Jerry Monks, was built in Paris in 1818 and bears the serial number 26.

[41] Erard London Harp Ledgers, vol. 2, p. 34.

Figure 28. Erard Nº 1705, an ultramarine double-action harp acquired in 1813 by the Princess of Wales, with accompanying music stool, music stand, sounding board and string box in matching finish. Château de Fontainebleau, Fontainebleau (Inv. No. F 2465 C).

in a royal building or institution in Britain, as one would expect, but in the Château de Fontainebleau in France, once the residence of Napoleon Bonaparte and the place where he spent the last days of his reign.[42]

Customer Profile and Geographical Diffusion of Erard Harps: Class, Gender, Address

Lady Berwick and Charlotte, the Princess of Wales, are only two noteworthy examples among Erard's many distinguished customers. The firm's clientele included members of the royalty and aristocracy, influential public figures and celebrities and successful businessmen and entrepreneurs, as well as renowned musicians, artists, authors and intellectuals. The Erard ledgers list numerous persons of political, economic and social prominence in Britain and abroad, the most esteemed being members of the British royal family.[43] Yet, although the Erards boasted in every possible way about their connections to those who led fashion and taste, the average Erard customer was mainly characterised by a respectable financial and social standing rather than by noble birth or public visibility.

By the beginning of the nineteenth century the Erard firm had already developed a strong customer base for harps, capitalising upon the success of Sébastien Erard's single-action harp with fourchettes. As early as 1802 Johann Friedrich Reichardt, who had visited the Erard Paris branch, as mentioned in the previous chapter, observed in his report that the majority of Erard's harps, whose high prices depended on their finish, were purchased by Russian and English customers, adding that the 'new rich' often bought harps as pieces of furniture. Reichardt also pointed out the limited musical activity in the French capital due to the absence of wealthy patrons, a result of most aristocrats being in exile after the French Revolution:

> These harps, however, cost from sixty to a hundred Louis neuf and above, depending on whether the appearance is more or less shiny. Russians and Englishmen, who know to appreciate the accomplished work best, and always have enough money and good will to pay better for the better work, receive the most and prettiest of them. But you see them often enough in the houses of the new rich, who buy all the same as a beautiful, fashionable piece of furniture, if they are not musical at the same time, and their children less eager to stop music, as happened before, since all, rich and great, lived and wove in the arts and especially in music. But these have left Paris, if not the world, and now

---

[42] According to the records of the Château de Fontainebleau, the harp and accessories were purchased in 1934 at a public sale. I am grateful to Patricia Kalensky for sending me information on and images of these artefacts.

[43] As already mentioned in Chapter Two, Erard Grecian harps were acquired in 1813 by Charlotte, Princess of Wales (Erard N° 1705) and in 1820 by King George IV (Erard N° 3002). In 1824 Princess Sophia Matilda of Gloucester (1773–1844) followed the example of her relatives, purchasing Erard N° 3558; for this harp see Erard London Harp Ledgers, vol. 2, p. 219. Apart from the family of King George IV, Erard's customer list included the families of the Duke of Wellington, Sir Joseph Paxton, Sir Walter Scott and Jane Austen, to name but a few.

those who have returned lately have neither the fortune nor the calm of the mind which is required in order to surrender to the enjoyment of the pleasant arts. That is the reason why there is very little music here except the theatre. Otherwise one hardly knew how to save himself for it; almost every morning one could hear music quartets in several large houses, and almost every evening there was a small or large concert somewhere. One was often embarrassed by the choice between good and better, now none of them.[44]

The same year, another German writer included the Erard brothers among the best harp manufacturers in Paris, along with Nadermann, the Cousineau father and son and Holzmann.[45] Like Jean-Henri Nadermann and Georges Cousineau, most French makers of the late eighteenth century, such as Godefroy Holzman (c.1736–1799), Jean Louvet (c.1728–1793), Edmond Saunier (c.1730–c.1783), Pierre Krupp (fl.1777–1791), Sébastien Renault (c.1745–after 1827) or Pierre Challiot (c.1775–1839) had made their names largely as producers of the single-action harp, building a devoted noble clientele in France and further afield. However, as we saw in Chapter One, initially Georges Cousineau and later Sébastien Erard were the only exceptions among Parisian harp makers to become genuinely interested and intensely involved in the development of the double-action harp. In the case of Erard, who had entered the harp trade as an established keyboard manufacturer, it is possible that this was motivated as much by his engineering background and curiosity as by the profitable prospects of a new instrument in a market saturated by the appealing but rather limiting single-action harps with crochets.

---

44 'Diese Harfen kosten aber auch, nachdem das Aeussere mehr oder weniger glänzend ist, von sechzig bis hundert Louis neuf und darüber. Russen und Engländer, die die vollendete Arbeit am besten zu schätzen wissen, und immer Geld und guten Willen genug haben, die bessere Arbeit auch besser zu bezahlen, erhalten davon die meisten und schönsten. Doch sieht man sie auch häufig genug in den Häusern der neuen Reichen, die alle dergleichen schon als schönes, modisches Meuble anschaffen, wenn sie gleich nicht musikalisch sind, und ihre Kinder weniger eifrig zur Musik anhalten, als ehedem wohl geschah, da alles, Reiche und Große, in Künsten und besonders in Musik lebte und webte. Diese haben aber, wo nicht die Welt, doch Paris verlassen, und die nun auch in der letzten Zeit zurückkehrten, haben weder das Vermögen noch die Ruhe des Gemüths, die dazu gehört, um sich ganz und gerne dem Genusse der angenehmen Künste zu überlassen. Daher kommt es denn auch, daß man hier, ausser dem Theater, sehr wenig Musik zu hören bekommt. Sonst wußte man sich dafür kaum zu retten; fast jeden Vormittag konnte man in mehrern großen Häusern Quartettenmusik hören, fast jeden Abend war irgendwo ein kleines oder großes Concert. Man kam oft in die Verlegenheit der Auswahl zwischen dem Guten und Bessern, jetzt nichts von alle dem.' Johann Friedrich Reichardt, *Johann Friedrich Reichardt's vertraute Briefe aus Paris geschrieben in den Jahren 1802–1803* (Hamburg: B. G. Hoffmann, 1805), pp. 155–156.

45 'Sollten sich Liebhaber finden, die gute Pedalharfen zu haben wünschen, so dürfen sie sich nur an den berühmten Herrn Nadermann in Paris wenden, der sie zu 25, 30, 40, 50 und so fort bis 100, 150 Louisdor verfertigt; doch sind diejenigen von 25 bis 30 Louisd'or von dem nehmlichen wesentlichen Werth als die von 100. Auch verdienen die Gebrüder Errard, Coussineau Vater und Sohn und Holzmann, als geschickte Harfen-Verfertiger hier genannt zu werden.' Johann David Scheidler, 'Ueber Harfen und die besten Verfertiger dieses Instruments', *Journal des Luxus und der Moden* 17 (1802), pp. 85–86, at p. 86.

The public corresponded accordingly. With his patents first for the improved single-action harp with fourchettes in 1794 and then for the double-action harp in 1810, Erard strengthened and expanded his reputation as the finest harp manufacturer, which helped the firm to attract new customers. 'If ever I want a harp I will go to Erard's because I know he is the first maker', declared Lord Lyddle, whose wife acquired an Erard double-action harp in 1815.[46] The approval and exposure of the Erard Grecian harp in the hands of the upper classes was crucial for its establishment, since the instrument soon became an object of desire among the wealthy middle classes, who were keen to imitate those at the top of society. An analysis of the first 100 double-action harps sold by Erard between 1811 and 1812 has shown that, as was expected, a number of these instruments were bought by titled persons belonging to the aristocracy and landowning gentry, who led fashion and could afford the high prices. However, the majority were sold to prosperous merchants, bankers, industrialists and professionals of the clergy and army, who neither possessed a title, nor influenced fashion, but who had enough money to support the musical activities of their families.[47]

This tendency continued in the late 1810s and early 1820s. During this time the sales of the Erard firm were affected by a financial stagnation in Britain, which lasted from the end of the Napoleonic Wars in 1815 until 1821.[48] The economic recession, which is mentioned in several letters by Pierre,[49] seems to have brought further changes to the firm's customer base, indicating the increasing consumption power of the middle classes. In May 1823 Pierre complained to his uncle about low harp sales, stating that 'the nobility and the landowners are very short of money. This class of society was the one that did the most business with us for the past eighteenth months or two years; now on our ledgers we can find scarcely a few names from this class. Our customers now come from the merchant class and instrument dealers.'[50]

A case study of the Erard ledgers for 1818 – the year Erard N° 2631 was produced – confirms that the social and financial characteristics of the persons who bought Erard harps remained essentially the same throughout the 1810s. The study has a narrow focus, since it includes only the double-action harps made and sold by the Erard London branch in 1818, as documented by their completion and sales entries in the Erard ledgers. Stocked double-action harps that had been built in previous years, but sold in 1818, as well as double-action harps made in 1818, but sold later, were not included in the study. According to the results, out of the 160 double-action

---

46 L 144, 30 April 1815. Adelson et al, *The History of the Erard Piano and Harp*, pp. 596–600, at p. 598.

47 Nex, *The Business of Musical-Instrument Making in Early Industrial London*, pp. 109–116; see also Adelson et al., *The History of the Erard Piano and Harp*, pp. 525–534.

48 For more details about the economic depression in Britain after the defeat of Napoleon see Gash Norman, 'After Waterloo: British Society and the Legacy of the Napoleonic Wars', *Transactions of the Royal Historical Society* 28 (1978), pp. 145–157, at pp. 152–157.

49 See for example, L 176, 6 May 1816, or L 252, 9 March 1819. Adelson et al, *The History of the Erard Piano and Harp*, p. 710, and pp. 630–631, at p. 630, respectively.

50 L 339, 30 May 1823. Adelson et al, *The History of the Erard Piano and Harp*, pp. 803–805, at p. 804.

harps built in 1818 by Erard, 120 were sold during the same year. Although the main aim of the study was to investigate the sale rate of Erard Grecian harps, which will be discussed later, the results have also revealed interesting details about the customer profile and geographical distribution of these instruments.

The first remarkable observation concerns the social position and class of Erard's customers. Out of the 120 Erard Grecian harps built and sold in 1818, only 12 harps (10%), were purchased by titled persons, including two males ('Sir' and 'Duke') and ten females (one 'Countess' and nine with the title 'Lady', one of whom was the above-mentioned Lady Berwick, whose harp was paid for by her husband, Lord Berwick).[51] In contrast, the largest proportion (90%) of these 120 harps were sold to untitled individuals of diverse social backgrounds, with about one third being bought by men ('Mr.' or 'Esq.') and about two thirds by women ('Mrs.' or 'Miss'). In seven instances, we know more about the occupations of the male customers because they are listed as professionals. These include two clients with clerical designations ('Rev' and 'Revd.', referring to Reverend), four with military ranks ('Gen.', 'General', 'Colonel', and 'Captn.'), and one with a medical or academic description ('Dr.').

Although the biographies and finances of most of these customers remain unknown, they undoubtedly belonged to well-to-do families. One representative example is 'Miss Ricardo' who purchased Erard N° 2479, a yellow Grecian harp, in January 1818.[52] According to her recorded address at 56 Upper Brook Street, she must have been the daughter of David Ricardo (1772–1823), a wealthy financier and highly influential economist of Jewish origin, who was also a Member of Parliament from 1818 until his death in 1823.[53] Interestingly, about a year after the procurement of Erard N° 2479, the Ricardo household acquired another yellow Grecian harp, since 'Mrs. Ricardo', residing at the same address, presumably Ricardo's wife, purchased Erard N° 2617 in March 1819.[54] Obtaining the two yellow Grecian harps, each costing £126 according to the Erard catalogue presented earlier, within less than 18 months imposed a considerable financial burden that only families of great fortune such as that of David Ricardo could possibly bear.

Notably, about a tenth of the above-mentioned 120 harps were sold to music sellers in London and the provinces, a fact that confirms Pierre's statement from 1823 regarding the sale of harps to instrument dealers. The firm Chappell & Co purchased five harps – Erard N° 2497, N° 2561, N° 2590, N° 2601 and N° 2606 – in the last three

---

51 It should be pointed out that it is sometimes difficult to know who the actual customer was. For example, the female customers in the entries of Erard N° 2515 and N° 2527 are listed as 'Miss Paul // Lady Anne Simpson' and 'Mrs. Mytton Junr // Lady Jones'. This may suggest that the untitled customers were temporarily hosted by the ladies Simpson and Jones at the time of purchase. However, it could also be that the harps were intended to remain at the ladies' households after their guests had gone.

52 Erard London Harp Ledgers, vol. 2, p. 111.

53 For an overview of the biography and work of David Ricardo see John P. Henderson with John B. Davis [Warren J. Samuels and Gilbert B. Davis, (eds)], *The Life and Economics of David Ricardo* (Boston: Kluwer Academic, 1997).

54 Erard London Harp Ledgers, vol. 2, p. 125.

cases acting as an agent for individual customers, whose names were also listed in the relevant sales entries in the Erard ledgers. Clementi & Co bought one harp – Erard Nº 2540 – while the piano manufacturer Robert Stodart (1748–1831), procured two harps – Erard Nº 2568 and Nº 2557 – the latter of which was on behalf of 'Gen. Dunlop Esq.' A smaller number of harps were sold to music professionals outside of London. For instance, in Bath, the favourite spa resort of London society, one harp, Erard Nº 2528, was purchased by William Owen, who is listed both as *'Harp Teacher'* and 'Music-seller' in a travel guide from 1825.[55] Further north, three harps – Erard Nº 2484, Nº 2529 and Nº 2596 – were obtained by Robert Purdie, music seller at 70 Princes Street, Edinburgh, who in 1828 advertised the sale of 'ERARD'S BEST DOUBLE ACTION HARPS'.[56]

Regarding the customer gender of the 120 Grecian harps made and sold in 1818, almost two thirds of the total clients (both titled and untitled) were female (76 harps) and one third male (44 harps). However, as mentioned earlier, most male customers would have bought harps for female acquaintances or members of their families, meaning that the actual consumers of these instruments were women. In some cases this is clearly stated in the ledgers: for example, 'Captn. Boileau' procured Erard Nº 2564 not for himself, but 'for Mrs. Kinnian // 62 Thornhaugh Street'.[57] Concerning the age and marital status of the female customers, the figures are balanced. About half of them are listed as 'Mrs', referring to married women whose social and financial position provided them with enough leisure time for playing the harp, while the other half are listed as 'Miss', suggesting that they were young, unmarried girls who probably learned the harp as a means to achieve upwards social mobility through a successful marriage, as will be described in the next chapter.

Equally illuminating about the consumption of Erard Grecian harps is the geographical distribution of Erard's clientele. Although the main public for the Grecian harp was in London, the instrument's vogue was not restricted to the capital, but reached ports, manufacturing centres and watering places all over Britain. Concerning the location of customers who acquired the 120 Grecian harps made and sold in 1818, almost two thirds were residing in London, while about a third was living in the British provinces. The concentration of Erard's clientele in London should come as no surprise since, due to urbanisation, economic growth and market expansion, the metropolis was 'the centre of mass consumption and set the fashion and tastes for the whole country'.[58] On the other hand, the recorded addresses of Erard customers in provincial regions were mostly in large cities, such as Bristol, Liverpool, Sheffield or Edinburgh, where music-selling businesses were usually

---

55　*New Guide. An historical and descriptive account of Leamington and Warwick; to which are added, short notices of the towns, villages, etc. within the circuit of ten miles* (Warwick, 1825), unnumbered page in the Appendix entitled 'Professional Gentlemen'.

56　Quoted in John Leonard Cranmer, *Concert Life and the Music Trade in Edinburgh c.1780–c.1830* (PhD Diss., Edinburgh: University of Edinburgh, 1991), p. 246.

57　Erard London Harp Ledgers, vol. 2, p. 119.

58　Maxine Berg, 'Markets, Trade and European Manufacture', in Maxine Berg (ed.), *Markets and Manufacture in Early Industrial Europe* (London and New York: Routledge, 1991), pp. 3–27, at p. 21.

situated, but also in smaller towns, such as Norwich, Derby, Bath or Cheltenham, while one harp, Erard N° 2544, was purchased by the Duke of Leinster, residing in Maynooth, Ireland.

It is also noteworthy that two harps registered in the ledgers on 16 March 1818 – Erard N° 2507 and N° 2508, a yellow and grey double-action harp respectively[59] – were sent to Sébastien Erard in Paris at Pierre's command; these were probably used as demonstration pieces at the Paris shop, or may have been sold or gifted to individuals personally acquainted to Sébastien. In addition, three of the 120 Grecian harps were sold to overseas customers from the British Colonies: two of them – Erard N° 2580 and N° 2581 – were sent to Calcutta in India, and one – Erard N° 2577 – to Charleston, South Carolina, in the United States of America, thus revealing Erard's extended international network. As evidenced by the places mentioned in the Erard ledgers and correspondence, although the majority of Erard Grecian harps were sold to customers in Britain, the Erard firm also exported harps to global destinations stretching from Russia in the north, to Spain, Portugal and Italy in the south,[60] and from India, Australia and New Zealand in the east[61] to North America in the west.

Sales Rate and Consumption Patterns of Erard Grecian Harps

The great popularity of the Erard double-action harp translated into high and fast sales. The above-mentioned study of the Erard Grecian harps made and sold in 1818 has shown that these instruments were selling rapidly: out of 160 harps built in 1818, 120 (75%) were sold in the same year, suggesting a short shelf life. For example, Erard N° 2479, the harp purchased by Miss Ricardo mentioned earlier, was registered in the ledgers on 19 January 1818 and was sold only ten days later, on 29

---

[59] Erard London Harp Ledgers, vol. 2, p. 114.

[60] See indicatively the instruments discussed in Cristina Bordas, 'Erard Pianos and Harps in Spain and Portugal', in Rudolf Frick (ed.), *Sébastien Erard: ein europäischer Pionier des Instrumentenbaus. Internationales Erard-Symposium Michaelstein 13.–14. November 1994, Michaelsteiner Konferenzberichte 48* (Blankenburg: Stiftung Kloster Michaelstein, 1995), pp. 30–32; in Romà Escalas i Llimona, (ed.), *Museu de la Música: 1/Catàleg d'instruments* (Barcelona: Ajuntament de Barcelona, 1991); in Giovanni Paolo Di Stefano, Selima Giorgia Giuliano and Sandra Proto (eds), *Strumenti musicali in Sicilia* (Palermo: CRICD-Regione Siciliana, 2013); in Alessandro Restelli, *Museo degli Strumenti Musicali del Casello Sforzesco a Milano* (Milan: Skira, 2014); and in Luigi Sisto, Emanuele Cardi and Sergio Tassi, *Il Museo della Musica. Strumenti Antichi e Documenti del Conservatorio di S. Pietro a Majella: Guida alla mostra a cura di Luigi Sisto, Emanuele Cardi, Sergio Tassi* (Naples: Conservatorio di S. Pietro a Majella, 2002).

[61] For more details see Ian Woodfield, *Music of the Raj: A Social and Economic History of Music in Late Eighteenth-Century Anglo-Indian Society* (Oxford: Oxford University Press, 2000), pp. 30 and 203; Rosemary Margaret Hallo, *Erard, Bochsa and their impact on harp music-making in Australia (1830–1866): An early history from documents* (PhD Diss.; Adelaide: The University of Adelaide, 2014), pp. 37–58; and Geoffrey Haimes, 'New Zealand, an Erard island', in Rudolf Frick (ed.), *Sébastien Erard: ein europäischer Pionier des Instrumentenbaus. Internationales Erard-Symposium Michaelstein 13.–14. November 1994, Michaelsteiner Konferenzberichte 48* (Blackenburg: Stiftung Kloster Michaelstein, 1995), pp. 34–36.

January. Likewise, Erard Nº 2524, the harp acquired by Lady Berwick, was entered in the Erard ledgers on 20 April 1818 and was sold a few weeks later on 27 May 1818. A similar sales percentage applies to single-action harps, since out of 24 single-action harps produced in 1818 by Erard, about two thirds (15 harps) were sold during that year. This high sales rate appears to be typical for that year, since most of the 120 Grecian harps were purchased only a few days or weeks after they were finished and registered in the ledgers.

Similar conclusions can be drawn by examining the total sales of Erard in 1818, which include double-action harps from stock as well as single-action harps that were not considered in the above-mentioned study, and which amount to 155 instruments. As a means of comparison, in 1818, Erat, one of Erard's main competitors, sold in total 60 harps,[62] while four years later, in 1822, he sold 67 harps.[63] This suggests that during the late 1810s, and possibly later, Erard sold on average more than twice as many harps as Erat. The popularity and rapid pace of sale of Erard harps is also indicated in Pierre's letters. For example, comparing the quality of Erard harps to those by other makers, in July 1819 Pierre commented to his uncle that 'Yours, as they are today, are superior to all others that are made, and they sell well',[64] while in August 1820 he similarly remarked 'The harp is becoming more popular every day and seems to be the rage!'[65]

However, the dispersal of sales was not equal throughout the year. As discussed in the previous chapter, harp sales fluctuated according to the London season, which particularly affected the luxury trades. The London season usually lasted from February to July, when British peerage was in London because of their parliamentary duties as representatives of their constituencies. The London season generated a variety of social activities, such as evening galas, dinners, balls and parties, concerts and theatrical productions, art exhibitions and other public events, where the rich could display their money and extravagance. In contrast, from August to January most of the aristocracy lived outside of London in their country houses, and therefore their social activities, and the purchase of luxury goods, were relatively limited.[66] As a result, harp sales increased considerably during the London season, when the fashionable society was in town, whereas they declined once the aristocracy had left the city.

---

[62] L 242, 8 January 1819. Adelson et al, *The History of the Erard Piano and Harp*, pp. 699–700, at p. 700.

[63] Mike Baldwin, *The Harp in Early Nineteenth-century Britain: Innovation, Business, and Making in Jacob Erat's Manufactory* (PhD Diss., London: London Metropolitan University, 2017), p. 306.

[64] L 264, 9 July 1819. Adelson et al, *The History of the Erard Piano and Harp*, pp. 723–724, at p. 724.

[65] L 285, 8 August 1820. Adelson et al, *The History of the Erard Piano and Harp*, pp. 748–750, at p. 749.

[66] For an overview of the London season and its impact on culture during the Georgian era see Hannah Greig, *The Beau Monde: Fashionable Society in Georgian London* (Oxford: Oxford University Press, 2013), pp. 1–31.

The above-mentioned study concerning the 120 Grecian harps made and sold in 1818 by Erard clearly illustrates the effect of the London season on the firm's sales. According to the results, the highest and fastest sales of these 120 instruments were observed from February to July, while the lowest and slower sales were documented from August to December (the only exception being October). A closer look at the figures reveals the rising and falling demand for harps depending on the season. For instance, out of 15 Grecian harps registered in the Erard ledgers in February 1818, nine were sold during the same month, while the other six were sold no later than mid-April of that year. The following month shows a similar pattern, since out of 17 Grecian harps built in March, the largest percentage (about 60%) were sold during that month, while most of the remaining instruments (35%) were purchased no later than mid-June. The busiest month was May, when out of 15 Grecian harps which Erard produced, 13 were sold in May and the other two no later than the beginning of June. In contrast, out of the 31 Grecian harps built in August and September, only one was sold during those two months, with the rest being traded at a slower rate up to December or during the following year.

Despite its limitations,[67] this study provides an objective indication of the great demand for Erard Grecian harps, because the fact that during the London season most of these instruments were sold shortly after they were completed suggests that the firm's stock of harps was insufficient to meet the market needs. However, in order to yield more objective results about the consumption patterns of Erard harps and to further investigate the changes in seasonal demand, it is necessary to repeat the study over several years of production and sale, which was outside of the scope and timeframe of this book.

The impact of the London season on the harp market is also vividly reported in the Erard correspondence. For instance, in February 1815 Pierre stated that 'The business season has now arrived, there are already many people in town'.[68] However, in August of the same year Pierre noted that 'we are in the time of the year when the income is weak'.[69] A similar situation is documented in the correspondence four years later. In February 1819 Pierre maintained that 'Sales are going well!',[70] whereas

---

[67] As already noted, since the study focuses on Grecian harps built and sold in 1818, it does not take into account stocked Grecian harps built in previous years but sold in 1818, or of those made in 1818 but sold in later years. For example, Erard N° 2631 was built on 30 November 1818, but was sold about two months later in 18 January 1819, so it has been excluded from the study. Although it does not represent the annual total sales of the Erard firm, the study has the advantage that it reflects the workshop's finished output within a year, meaning not just building parts for stockpiling, but assembling and finishing a harp to have it ready for sale. I am thankful to Julin Lee for her assistance with the analysis and interpretation of Erard harp sales.

[68] L 134, 15 February 1815. Adelson et al, *The History of the Erard Piano and Harp*, pp. 585–586, at p. 585.

[69] L 152, 7 August 1815. Adelson et al, *The History of the Erard Piano and Harp*, pp. 608–609, at p. 608.

[70] L 244, 21 January 1819. Adelson et al, *The History of the Erard Piano and Harp*, pp. 701–702, at p. 702.

in July 1819 he wrote that 'The season is almost over'.[71] In August of that year he observed that 'we are in the slow season', adding that 'Our gentlemen the workers are fairly relaxed. All the work we do is well done, and we find ourselves ahead of the schedule for the season.'[72]

Thus, during the quiet months the firm apparently tried to produce more harps and keep them in stock in order to cover the growing demand for instruments, maintenance and repairs during the busier London season. For example, in November 1815 Pierre reported that 'Horn and I have prepared the coloured harps and the brownish-black harps for the season.'[73] Discussing his business endeavours in Ireland, in October 1816 he similarly remarked that 'We have a large quantity of harps already built. I will reduce this stock by about thirty or so that I will send to Dublin, in order to have a full selection.'[74]

The Novelty Factor of the Grecian Harp and the Expansion of Erard's Customer Base

The commercial success of the Erard Grecian harp was largely due to its novel features. During the early nineteenth century novelty was an important factor in the trade of luxury objects, and musical instruments were no exception.[75] The so-called 'Consumer Revolution' that took place during the seventeenth and eighteenth centuries created a new type of fashion-conscious customer, who was keen to acquire – and accordingly pay for – the latest and trendiest products.[76] The changing aspect in consumer habits resulted from the exculpation of pleasure and luxury, rather than from economic progress or a fascination with technology:

> The enthusiasm for variety and novelty in mid-eighteenth-century English élite culture cannot, however, be understood simply as a by-product of growth of world markets, and improvements in the mechanics of raw materials supply. More fundamentally, it was dependent upon profound alterations in polite society's attitude to visual pleasure, upon the emergence of a social ethos which dis-

---

[71] L 265, 13 July 1819. Adelson et al, *The History of the Erard Piano and Harp*, pp. 724–725, at p. 725.

[72] L 268, 7 September 1819. Adelson et al, *The History of the Erard Piano and Harp*, pp. 726–727.

[73] L 109, 3 November 1814. Adelson et al, *The History of the Erard Piano and Harp*, pp. 559–560, at p. 560.

[74] L 182, 9 October 1816. Adelson et al, *The History of the Erard Piano and Harp*, pp. 636–638, at p. 637.

[75] For a thorough discussion of musical instruments, including Erard harps, from the perspective of luxury see Panagiotis Poulopoulos, 'Aspects of Technology in Populuxe Musical Instruments of the Late Eighteenth and Early Nineteenth Centuries', in Artemis Yagou (ed.), *Novelty, Technology and Luxury. Deutsches Museum Studies 12* (Munich: Deutsches Museum, 2022), pp. 15–43.

[76] For the effects of the consumer revolution on the manufacturing sectors of London see David Colin Barnett, *The Structure of Industry in London, 1775–1825* (PhD Diss., Nottingham: University of Nottingham, 1996), pp. 464–466.

posed the public towards searching out the pleasures to be obtained from various and novel sensations.[77]

As a result, 'Retailers' competition to provide variety and novelty to their customers was a central motivating force behind the rise of design in the period. It obliged producers to concentrate upon the generation of novelties, new shapes, new textures and new functions.'[78]

As a novel, expensive and highly fashionable instrument, the Erard double-action harp attracted not only prosperous clients who were eager to demonstrate their wealth and status, but also those with more restricted means who were aspiring to behave, and thus consume, like their superiors. Since fashions were predominantly devised for and sustained by women, it was mainly female customers who were the driving force in the harp market. In 1818 Pierre claimed that 'The English like novelty and they need a really talented performer who plays the harp everywhere. When you bring out your new model, that won't hurt things either. If you would be able to add an <u>Index</u>, that could only help. <u>Women</u> love <u>little toys</u> like that. They cling to the shutters out of <u>habit</u>; an echo would be seen as new and would make them forget about the shutters.'[79] In several of his letters from the early 1820s Pierre referred to a new harp model that was being developed by his uncle, noting in 1823 that 'there are some people waiting for the new harp.'[80] This was just a decade after the launching of the double-action harp, suggesting the public's constant anticipation for new instruments.

The double-action harp was arguably the flagship of the Erard firm. However, Pierre had also recognised the demand for a 'budget' harp. In 1817 he wrote to Sébastien:

> I have always noticed that we are short of simple inexpensive harps to rent in the provinces or to sell to people who cannot give a hundred guineas but who would gladly give fifty. The harps that we take in exchange become more expensive than the manufacturing price and are not sufficient for the demand. I have therefore decided to have some simple harps made according to the old model. I will set the price as low as possible. All the little harp makers sell harps that are very cheap. I do not see why you do not do the same; the doubles are too much appreciated now for this measure to harm their sales, as these harps will sell as if they were *second hand*.[81]

Several single-action harps are listed in the Erard ledgers for the years 1817 and 1818, confirming that the firm indeed built cheap single-action instruments based on the older Empire model, which, together with the plainly decorated double-action harps, were addressed to less affluent customers.

---

[77] Craske, 'Plan and Control', p. 193.

[78] Craske, 'Plan and Control', pp. 194–195.

[79] L 221, 24 April 1818. Adelson et al, *The History of the Erard Piano and Harp*, pp. 678–679, at p. 679.

[80] L 339, 30 May 1823. Adelson et al, *The History of the Erard Piano and Harp*, pp. 803–805, at p. 804.

[81] L 208, 15 August 1817. Adelson et al, *The History of the Erard Piano and Harp*, pp. 666–667.

Erard thus followed a marketing strategy similar to that introduced some decades earlier by pioneering entrepreneurs such as Matthew Boulton, the renowned engineer and business partner of James Watt, or Josiah Wedgwood, the famous pottery manufacturer. Both Boulton and Wedgwood were aware of the hierarchical structure of fashion and realised that emulation could play a key role in the diffusion of new products. For instance, Boulton 'made commemorative issues of goods for royal birthdays, and sent new patterns to members of the aristocracy', subsequently producing 'a similar commodity in a variety of materials accessible to all levels of society', with the classic example being the shoe buckle, an ornament that was produced 'in every size and every material from diamonds to paste, from gold to pinchbeck'.[82] Likewise, Wedgwood initially made a name by selling spectacularly decorated, expensive pieces of earthenware to members of the royalty and nobility. However, once his reputation had been established through the dissemination of these objects among rich patrons who shaped fashion, he started producing pottery of the same quality, but which was less ornamented, and thus cheaper, for a middle-class clientele. Wedgwood's cunning marketing is illustrated in a letter from 1772, in which he argued:

> The great people have had Vases in their palaces long enough for them to be seen and admir'd by the <u>Middling Class</u> of People; which class we know are vastly, and I had almost said infinitely, superior in numbers to the great, & though a <u>great price</u> was I believe at first necessary to make the Vases esteemed <u>Ornaments</u> for <u>Palaces</u> that reason no longer exists. Their character is established, & the middling People would probably buy quantities of them at a reduced price.[83]

Although Wedgwood was one of the largest manufacturers in his field, his products were not cheaper than those of his competitors; on the contrary, Wedgwood 'charged what the market could bear, keeping prices consistently higher than others', in order 'to maintain quality' and also 'to cover the exceptionally high costs of his experiments, investments and showrooms'.[84] Erard, who presumably spent as much as Wedgwood in product research and development, must have imitated this practice: his harps were the most expensive among those offered by harp makers in London, a fact that paradoxically increased rather than diminished their appeal.

Marketing Tactics in the Promotion of Erard Grecian Harps

As described in Chapters Three and Four, the decorative features of Erard Grecian harps enhanced their attractiveness significantly. Coloured harps, in contrast to the standard black ones, seem to have been particularly impressive and were occasion-

---

[82] Berg, 'Markets, Trade and European Manufacture', p. 14.

[83] Hilary Young (ed.), *The Genius of Wedgwood* (London: Victoria and Albert Museum, 1995), p. 18.

[84] Young, *The Genius of Wedgwood*, p. 18; for an overview of Wedgwood's marketing tactics see also Neil McKendrick, 'Josiah Wedgwood: An Eighteenth-Century Entrepreneur in Salesmanship and Marketing Techniques', *The Economic History Review* 12/3 (1960), pp. 408–433.

ally used to promote the double-action harp to new customers. In May 1816, Pierre proposed to exchange the black harp of an esteemed client with a blue one, arguing that this would be a good promotional tactic, since the harp would augment the visibility and reputation of the firm's instruments to polite society. Pierre wrote:

> My friend Lady Macnamara is leaving tomorrow or later with the Count [...] She is also a very sincere friend of yours. I thought it is best to exchange the black harp for one in a fresh shade of blue. I thought that you would not find it so bad since it is so well able to showcase your beautiful instrument and because it will be often seen in society; it has a matching music stand and a box of strings that I have given him as a payment for a reduction we owed her.[85]

This blue harp must have been an ultramarine harp, such as Erard Nº 2524, belonging to Lady Berwick, or Erard Nº 1705, owned by the Princess of Wales, both described earlier. Since blue harps were the most expensive in Erard's catalogue, it meant that the persons who owned them, such as Lady Macnamara, unconsciously acted as Erard's best agents, exposing the firm's prettiest and costliest instruments to their upper-class peers, who could afford them.

The exchange of harps, which in most cases involved the replacement of single-action with double-action instruments, seems to have been common, as revealed in the Erard ledgers and correspondence. One characteristic example concerns Lady Lyddle, mentioned earlier. In April 1815, while her old single-action harp had been sent to the Erard firm for repair, Pierre visited her in order to persuade her to exchange it for a double-action harp. Pierre demonstrated the advantages of the new harp by playing preludes in all keys, stating that both the Lady and her husband, who was present, were 'delighted with the harp'.[86] Likewise, during preparations for a trip to Ireland in July 1816, Pierre wrote to his uncle: 'I will take a harp along with me that I will try to sell. I will see the various people who have your harps to see if there is anything they need and to try to convince them to exchange them for doubles. If needed, I could play.'[87]

In Chapter Three it was pointed out that with the launching of the Grecian model the branding of Erard harps became more perceptible, descriptive and detailed compared to earlier harps. However, it is worth noting that the date of manufacture on the firm's instruments was gradually omitted; the only known Erard harps bearing a visible date of manufacture are Empire harps built in Paris between c.1799 and 1809. Since Erard Grecian harps were produced using a standardised and consistent model, this would have enabled the firm to stock and sell older harps as if they were new. For example, in 1816 Pierre sent a harp to a certain 'M. Beerembruck', stating that 'There was a dark blue harp in the store from 200 numbers back. I did well to send it to him; it is very beautiful but not as fresh as the others'.[88]

---

[85]   L 176, 6 May 1816. Adelson et al, *The History of the Erard Piano and Harp*, pp. 630–631, at p. 630.

[86]   L 144, 30 April 1815. Adelson et al, *The History of the Erard Piano and Harp*, pp. 596–600, at pp. 597–598.

[87]   L 180, 31 July 1816. Adelson et al, *The History of the Erard Piano and Harp*, pp. 634–635.

[88]   L 177, 16 May 1816. Adelson et al, *The History of the Erard Piano and Harp*, pp. 631–632, at p. 632.

Another remarkable marketing practice of the Erard firm regards the hire and lending of instruments before sale. For example, some Erard harps made in 1818 were hired on 1 January 1820 before they were sold at a later date. The custom of hiring instruments before sale may seem unusual, even curious, by modern standards, yet it was not uncommon in the musical instrument trade during the early nineteenth century. For instance, the practice of 'pre-sale hire' of instruments was also employed by the piano manufacturer Broadwood.[89] It should also be pointed out that used harps were often traded in the second-hand market, much like other musical instruments, luxury household objects and scientific instruments,[90] while methods of payment extended to barter with consumable goods, such as wine.

As revealed in several letters from the 1790s, Sébastien Erard liked wine so much that he often received it as payment for instruments, especially from customers in Burgundy.[91] In 1791 he had asked a friend in Dijon to select and send him 'about 600 livres of good ordinary wine, which is not expensive considering that I drink a lot of it'.[92] The purchase of wine is also listed in the Erard workshop accounts from 1807 to 1809, indicating the frequent consumption of alcohol, most likely by the firm's owner rather than by its employees. According to an inventory from the early 1820s, Sébastien Erard kept more than 2,000 bottles of wine stored in the cellar of the Château de la Muette at Passy near Paris, where he resided.[93] Like Erard's vast collection of paintings, it is possible that the stored wine may have been kept as much as a financial investment as for the keeper's private pleasure.

Erard's Ambassadors and Advocates: Composers, Performers, Teachers and Publishers

As already noted, although Erard double-action harps were initially met with scepticism, if not criticism, by a few instrument makers, musicians and music instructors, they were wholeheartedly embraced by numerous distinguished members of polite society and the wider music-loving public. This was mainly due to a tireless promotional campaign led by Pierre Erard, who wasted no opportunity of presenting and championing his uncle's inventions, and who engaged renowned virtuosi, such as

---

[89] Alastair Laurence, *The Evolution of the Broadwood Grand Piano 1785–1998* (PhD Diss., York: University of York, 1998), pp. 101–104.

[90] See, for example, Nex, *The Business of Musical-Instrument Making in Early Industrial London*, pp. 94–95; Natacha Coquery, 'The Language of Success: Marketing and Distributing Semi-Luxury Goods in Eighteenth-Century Paris', *Journal of Design History* 17/1 (2004), pp. 71–89, at pp. 84–87; and Simon Werrett, *Thrifty Science: Making the Most of Materials in the History of Experiment* (Chicago: University of Chicago Press, 2019), pp. 140–147.

[91] See, for instance, L 7.148, L 7.209, L 7.218, L 7.354 and L 7.463, dating between 1792 and 1797, in Adelson et al, *The History of the Erard Piano and Harp*, at pp. 100, 121, 124, 167 and 219, respectively.

[92] See, for example, L 7.99, 1 August 1791. Adelson et al, *The History of the Erard Piano and Harp*, p. 84.

[93] Ann Griffiths, 'A Dynasty of Harp Makers' (available at http://www.adlaismusicpublishers.co.uk/pages/harpists/erard.htm, first published in World Harp Congress Review 2002, accessed 3 June 2022.).

Robert Nicolas-Charles Bochsa, to compose, perform, teach and publish for the double-action harp. As one of Erard's main ambassadors, in 1819 Bochsa praised Erard's new harp in his new harp method, stating that 'From this short account of the advantages which are derived from the Harp with the Double Movement, one may anticipate that it will become as fashionable as the Piano-Forte',[94] while in 1823 he reportedly assured Pierre that 'he would never play on another harp'.[95]

Concerts and public performances by famous harpists were arguably the most important advertising events for the double-action harp. In 1815 Pierre wrote to his uncle: 'I heard Horn last night in a concert. He played very well and was enthusiastically applauded. The double action was announced.'[96] Like Bochsa, Henry Horn (1789–1862?) was a keen performer of the double-action harp; it is worth a reminder that his father John was a trustworthy Erard employee who was occupied with the finishing of double-action harps, as mentioned in Chapter Four. According to a contemporary music dictionary, when Horn returned to London after a successful tour in Scotland and Ireland in 1812, he was 'immediately engaged for the Bath concerts, where he had the honour of first introducing to the public, Erard's double movement harp, the mechanism of which was the admiration of all the artists and amateurs. On his return to the metropolis, he had an opportunity of introducing this beautiful instrument before a London audience at the King's theatre, and was received with the most flattering applause.'[97]

The firm's publicity events usually involved renowned harpists, such as Bochsa or Horn, but sometimes even Pierre himself. In January 1817, while in Dublin, Pierre informed his uncle that he played 'for a gathering of professors and amateurs at a dinner for a Philharmonic group, in such a way as to be not so unworthy of your harp.'[98] Besides, as already mentioned, Pierre often demonstrated the advantages of the double-action harp to old and new customers, either at the firm's premises or at their homes, while the firm's store was occasionally used for harp concerts.[99] Prospective Erard clients thus learned about the new harp mostly by seeing and hearing the instrument in the hands of eminent musicians or of the firm's director himself, and by word-of-mouth rather than by systematic advertising in the press.

Apart from any purely artistic motivations, the music professionals who were persuaded to endorse Erard Grecian harps mainly did so because of financial reasons. As confirmed in the Erard correspondence and workshop accounts, the firm offered

---

94 Robert Nicolas-Charles Bochsa, *A New and Improved Method of Instruction for the Harp* (London: Chappell & Co, c.1819), p. 9.

95 L 339, 30 May 1823. Adelson et al, *The History of the Erard Piano and Harp*, pp. 803–805, at p. 804.

96 L 133, 7 February 1815. Adelson et al, *The History of the Erard Piano and Harp*, pp. 584–585, at p. 585.

97 John Sainsbury, *A Dictionary of Musicians, from the Earliest Ages to the Present Time*, Vol. 1 (2nd edn; London: Sainsbury, 1827), p. 376.

98 L 187, 19 January 1817. Adelson et al, *The History of the Erard Piano and Harp*, pp. 642–643, at p. 642.

99 See, for example, L 177, 16 May 1816. Adelson et al, *The History of the Erard Piano and Harp*, pp. 631–632, at p. 632.

attractive commissions and discounts to music composers, performers, teachers, publishers and sellers who recommended the new harps to their audiences, pupils and customers. For example, in January 1815 Pierre mentioned to Sébastien that 'One of Clementi's colleagues came to ask what discounts we would give them on harps, as they wish to send double actions to India', noting that 'The arrangement you made with Chappell has been my guide, I give them 25% and they give us credit for four months'.[100]

In October of that year Pierre informed the pianist Johann Baptist Cramer (1771–1858), who wanted to obtain a double-action harp from Erard for his daughter, about the reduction of 30 guineas that the firm offered to teachers 'when the harp is for their use', adding that 'the harp is being reduced by that to 75 guineas.'[101] A few weeks later Pierre reported to his uncle that he intended to offer the harpist Frederic Charles Meyer a 20% discount on harp strings, the same percentage he gave for harps.[102] Notably, a year earlier Meyer had requested to know what discount Erard was willing to offer him on the coloured harps, claiming that 'if you give 20 G for a harp of 105, you will give 30 for one of 150.'[103]

Therefore, by offering varied discount schemes to music professionals, Erard enabled the distribution of Grecian harps to a diverse range of customers, including those who would acquire instruments through their teachers as well as those who would buy them directly from a music dealer, thus bypassing Erard's own shop. However, this practice was not without disadvantages, since it was not always easy to control the actions of dealers, especially in the provinces, or to maintain neutrality among the firm's agents. In 1816 Pierre argued that 'Sending instruments on commission is a poor gamble, the harps become damaged and often they are rented. And if one gives preference to a dealer or a teacher all the others become jealous.'[104]

The shrewd methods of Erard and his associates in enforcing the transition from the single- to the double-action harp is further demonstrated in an extant harp tutor entitled *Forty Studies Expressly Composed for Sebastian Erard's Double Movement Harp*, published in 1818 (Figure 29).[105]

---

[100] L 129, 17 January 1815. Adelson et al, *The History of the Erard Piano and Harp*, pp. 581–582, at p. 581.

[101] L 158, 13 October 1815. Adelson et al, *The History of the Erard Piano and Harp*, pp. 614–615, at p. 615.

[102] L 163, 29 November 1815. Adelson et al, *The History of the Erard Piano and Harp*, pp. 618–619.

[103] L 99, 22 September 1814. Adelson et al, *The History of the Erard Piano and Harp*, pp. 549–550, at p. 549.

[104] L 182, 9 October 1816. Adelson et al, *The History of the Erard Piano and Harp*, pp. 636–638, at p. 637.

[105] Robert Nicholas-Charles Bochsa, *Forty Studies Expressly Composed for Sebastian Erard's Double Movement Harp* (London: Chappell & Co, 1818). A copy of Bochsa's *Forty Studies* is included in a bound volume entitled '48 Exercises or Fantasias / Dizi', held in the Pendlebury Library of Music, University of Cambridge, XRa.850.18A.X22, which was examined by the author during a research visit at Pendlebury Library.

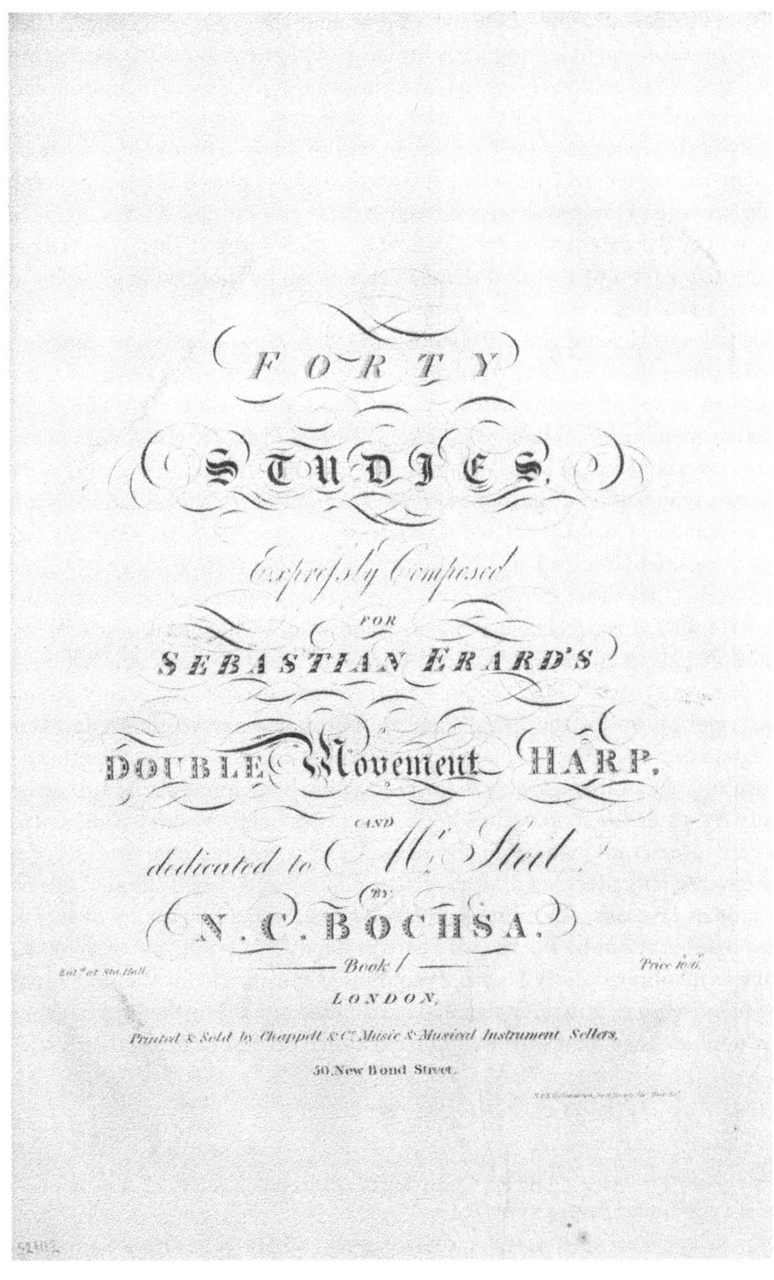

Figure 29. The front page of Robert Nicholas-Charles Bochsa's *Forty Studies Expressly Composed for Sebastian Erard's Double Movement Harp* (London: Chappell & Co, 1818). Pendlebury Library of Music, University of Cambridge, XRa.850.18A.X22.

Written by Bochsa, one of the most prominent advocates of the Erard Grecian harp, this method includes 40 pieces for harp, with instructions for specific fingering and pedalling techniques, as well as indications for the use of a metronome. As with many early methods for the double-action harp, despite the tutor's title, the majority of the music could still be played on the single-action harp, therefore not excluding the large number of harpists who owned and played single-action instruments. However, a few pieces were written explicitly for the new double-action harp, requiring pedal combinations unattainable by earlier harps.[106] This rendered necessary the acquisition of an Erard double-action harp by those willing to play all of Bochsa's 40 studies.

Bochsa must have prepared the studies in spring 1818, possibly with Erard's consent and cooperation, since in April of that year Pierre wrote that Bochsa 'is at work composing a method for the new harp for Chappell, as well as études for the double-action harp', further stating that 'They are very beautiful and are as good and perhaps even better' than those composed by Dizi, another famous harpist and rival of Bochsa, who will be discussed below.[107] That a tutor for the double-action harp was published by Chappell & Co is no coincidence, since as already mentioned, the firm also retailed Grecian harps by Erard. Bochsa's tutor is only one of the many examples that illustrate the intersecting links between instrument makers, performers, composers, music teachers, publishers and sellers, which were essential for the promotion and commercial success of a new instrument like the double-action harp.

Until now, relatively little research has been carried out concerning the music written specifically for the Erard Grecian harp compared to its predecessors.[108] However, a thorough discussion on aspects of composition techniques, performance practice and repertoire regarding the double-action harp during the early nineteenth century is outside the scope of this book. It is, nevertheless, worth noting that there is a wealth of relevant material in libraries and archives around the world waiting to be discovered and interpreted, although the filtering and classification of this material is not an easy task. For example, the British Library online catalogue lists more than 500 publications by Bochsa with harp in the title, but only one of these works, the above-mentioned *Forty Studies*, is composed specifically for the double-action harp (mentioned as 'double-movement harp' in the title). A further search using the terms 'double-movement harp' or 'double-action harp' results in less than ten works

---

[106] I am grateful to Maria Christina Cleary for her observations on Bochsa's compositions from a performing harpist's viewpoint.

[107] L 221, 24 April 1818. Adelson et al, *The History of the Erard Piano and Harp*, pp. 678–680, at p. 679.

[108] For an overview of the music and performance practice relating to single- and double-action harps, as well as for information on the main composers and players of these instruments, see Roslyn Rensch, *The Harp: Its History, Technique and Repertoire* (London: Duckworth, 1969); see also Rensch, *Harps and Harpists*; Hallo, *Erard, Bochsa and their impact on harp music-making in Australia*; and Maria Christina Cleary, *The 'harpe organisée', 1720–1840: Rediscovering the lost pedal techniques on harps with a single-action pedal mechanism* (PhD Diss., Leiden: Leiden University, 2016).

written for this instrument during the early nineteenth century, thus highlighting the need for a more systematic study of such sources.[109]

Erard's Rivals and Opponents:
The Harp Market in Regency London Beyond Erard

Although Erard was the first maker to introduce the double-action harp in London, within a few years similar instruments developed by other manufacturers appeared. The Erard Grecian model should thus be considered as the most cherished, but not exclusive, product in an expanding, competitive market, in which double-action harps co-existed with single-action harps that Erard and these other manufacturers produced. In 1818, the year in which Erard N° 2631 was built, apart from Erard there were at least five harp makers in London, whose ateliers were concentrated in the fashionable West End of the capital. A London trade directory published in 1818[110] lists in total six musical instrument makers whose workshops built harps, including in alphabetical order: Alexander Barry at 17 Frith Street;[111] Thomas Dodd at 92 St Martin's Lane;[112] Sébastien Erard at 18 Great Marlborough Street;[113] John Erat at 100 Wardour Street;[114] and Johann Andreas Stumpff at 44 Great Portland Street,[115] all of whom are well-known, as well as the previously unknown H. Stephens working at 10 George Street.[116]

The descriptions of the above-mentioned instrument makers in this directory reveal several interesting facts about Erard and his competitors in Regency London.[117] For example, apart from Erard, who is listed as 'Erard, Seb. *Patent harp*

---

[109] The majority of the listed works for harp are published collections and arrangements of solo music. These works are presumably just the tip of the iceberg, with the role of the Erard Grecian harp in chamber music and orchestral music still open to exploration. The last point is of particular importance, since the introduction of the harp as a regular member of the orchestra was one of the most significant developments in orchestral music of the early nineteenth century, making a powerful contribution to the soundscape of theatrical music of that period. I am thankful to the first anonymous reviewer for this observation.

[110] Andrew Johnstone, *Johnstone's London Commercial Guide and Street Directory* (London: Barnard & Farley, 1818).

[111] 'Barry, Alexander, *Harp manufacturer*'. Johnstone, *Johnstone's London Commercial Guide*, p. 212.

[112] 'Dodd, Thomas, *Music. instru. Maker*'. Johnstone, *Johnstone's London Commercial Guide*, p. 431.

[113] 'Erard, Seb. *Patent harp manufacturer*'. Johnstone, *Johnstone's London Commercial Guide*, p. 325.

[114] 'Erat, John, *Patent harp maker*'. Johnstone, *Johnstone's London Commercial Guide*, p. 515.

[115] 'Stumpff, J. A. *Pedal harp manufact.*'. Johnstone, *Johnstone's London Commercial Guide*, p. 390.

[116] 'Stephens, H. *Harp and organ builder*'. Johnstone, *Johnstone's London Commercial Guide*, p. 215.

[117] For an overview of harp makers in early nineteenth-century London see Baldwin, *The Harp in Early Nineteenth-century Britain*, pp. 52–62.

manufacturer', the only other harp manufacturer with reference to a patent is Erat, who was granted a patent for a double-action harp in 1813.[118] Moreover, Stumpff is listed as a 'Pedal harp' manufacturer, suggesting that he was exclusively building pedal harps, in contrast to Barry, who is mentioned simply as a 'Harp manufacturer', and who is known to have produced various types of harps or harp-like instruments, such as harp lutes. On the other hand, the entry for Dodd does not explicitly refer to harps, although his son Edward (1791–1843) produced the so-called 'perpendicular harp', a double-action harp which had been patented in 1813 by the Belgian harpist François Joseph Dizi (1780–1847) and Charles Gröll.[119]

As evidenced in the Erard correspondence, Dizi, and his partner Dodd, were, along with Erat and Stumpff, Erard's three main rivals during the late 1810s, producing instruments that were largely based on Erard harps and frequently challenging, but never really threatening, Erard's dominance in the harp trade. In contrast, Barry or Stephens seem not to have been significant players in the harp market of Regency London. Apart from their individual entries, the harp manufacturers Barry, Dodd, Erard, Erat and Stumpff are also listed in Johnstone's directory in the section of musical instrument makers (Figure 30).

However, Stephens is included among organ makers, suggesting that the making of harps was a rather secondary activity in his workshop, further confirmed by the fact that no harps by him are known to have survived. Johnstone's directory additionally provides the details of three manufacturers of harps strings, namely Christopher Siems at 4 Castle Street,[120] John Glessing at 18 Bell Lane[121] and Sebastian Schwartz at 3 White's Row.[122] Furthermore, the directory lists numerous significant musical instrument manufacturers and dealers in the section on piano makers. As noted in the previous chapters, some of them, such as Chappell & Co and Clementi & Co, retailed harps by Erard or other makers, while others, such as Broadwood, were personally acquainted with the Erards and may have also kept business contacts. Moreover, the

---

[118] British Patent Nº 3693, 8 May 1813. See Woodcroft, *Patents for Inventions*, pp. 72–73. For Erat's patent see also Baldwin, *The Harp in Early Nineteenth-century Britain*, pp. 201–206.

[119] British Patent, Nº 3642, 22 January 1813. See Woodcroft, *Patents for Inventions*, p. 71. For more details on Dizi's perpendicular harp see Robert Adelson, *The Harp, from Marie-Antoinette to the Present* (Ancenis: Editions Camac, 2017), p. 11; see also Adelson et al, *The History of the Erard Piano and Harp*, pp. 560–561, footnote 5. Surviving examples of Dizi's perpendicular harp are housed in the following collections: Victoria and Albert Museum, London (Inv. No. 382-1907); Musikmuseum Basel (Inv. No. 2008.290); Musée de la musique, Paris (Inv. No. E.2000.5.1); Musée Condé, Chantilly (Inv. No. OA 2085); and Camac Collection, Ancenis. Another specimen in a private collection was reported at Pilgrim Harps, Surrey. On 1 November 1817 Dizi took a second patent relating to the perpendicular harp (British Patent Nº 4171); see Woodcroft, *Patents for Inventions*, pp. 82–83. For more details on Dizi's patents see also Baldwin, *The Harp in Early Nineteenth-century Britain*, pp. 198–200 and 206–209.

[120] 'Siems, Chr. *Violin & harp-string manuf.*'. Johnstone, *Johnstone's London Commercial Guide*, p. 100.

[121] 'Glessing, J. *Violin and harp string manu.*'. Johnstone, *Johnstone's London Commercial Guide*, p. 34.

[122] 'Schwartz, S. *Harp & violin string manufacturer*'. Johnstone, *Johnstone's London Commercial Guide*, Addenda, p. 19.

Residence.	See Page
126 Evans and Randle	49
10 Gallant, Matt.......	111
175 Lyon, N..........	10
42 Mowbray and Co.	364
51 Nickolls, Wm.....	443
14 Nunn, Eliz........	278
44 Poole and Sampson	452
164 Robertson, Thomas	467
25 Robson and Co.....	318
5 Stantons and Co....	70
20 Stephens, S.......	81
13 Thwaits, T. & J.A.	295
46 Walford, H........	137
58 Wilson, Peter......	432
4 Young, M.	80
18 Younie, Jane......	278

MINERAL PAINT WAREHOUSE.

1 M'Adam, James ..	175

MINERAL WATER MERCHANTS.

54 Deane, John	341
79 Schweppe, J. & C.	322
2 Shipwash, R.......	421

MINERALOGISTS.

149 Brown and Co. ...	467

MINIATURE PAINTERS.

Burnett, John	179
17 Burrell, J.F.	436
31 Goddard, John....	402
14 Leslie, Peter.......	310
391 Lethbridge, W.S..	470
40 Mitchell, Thomas	466
12 Nerve, H.........	115
34 Patten, W. and Son	317
158 Polack, S.........	467
13 Saunders, Robert...	493
13 Sharp, M.........	277
69 Thwaites, William	393

MODELLERS AND FIGURE MAKERS.

197 Brown, N.	499
44 Mazzoni, J. M. ...	137

MONA MARBLE WORKS.

4 Bullock, George.....	481

MOROCCO AND SPANISH LEATHER DRESSERS.

Ball, J. and Co.....	530

Residence.	See Page
Cundall, Thomas..	505
Duerr, F...........	530
Flatbman, H.	16
Frere, James	530
Hayerdal, S. & Co.	418
Kent, William......	420
27 Semler, John	418
Spencer, R.	418
Tait, J. and Co. ...	346

MOURNING RING MAKERS.

11 Gibbs, John........	355
4 Glover, Samuel ..	84
17 Price, W. A.	320

MUSIC WAREHOUSES.

408 Ball, James........	371
32 Bevan, Silas.......	100
140 Birchall, Robert ...	54
11 Boag, William.....	504
75 Button and Co. ...	435
36 Christmes, Charles	373
9 Corrall, R.	427
Downing, William	265
3 Falkner, H.........	55
78 Fenton, J..........	466
12 Gallaway, William	398
37 Galloway, Daniel	398
20 Goulding and Co...	456
23 Halliday and Co....	44
221 Hamilton, James...	385
45 Hodsoll, Wm.......	249
364 Kennedy, Thomas	371
20 Key, Thomas	108
28 Lavenu, Lewis.....	53
44 Laverick, Thomas	140
60 Monro, James......	455
25 Phipps and Co. ..	172
77 Piercy, H.	114
20 Potter, Sam.	280
Preston, Thomas...	183
19 Robertson, W......	235
112 Rolfe and Co......	117
138 Skillern and Co....	368
106 Walker, George ...	390
87 Watts, Richard	49
128 Wheatstone, Wm.	374
436 Wheatstone & Co.	470
8 White, Thomas	521
29 Williams, Thomas	481

MUSICAL INSTRUMENT MAKERS.

79 Astor and Harwood	141
35 Bainbridge and Co.	255
17 Barry, Alexander	212
8 Betts, A.	345
2 Betts, J...........	498
76 Biggs, John	189
14 Briggs, J.	222

Residence.	See Page
124 Chappell and Co....	54
26 Clementi and Co....	115
8 Dale, William	391
92 Dodd, Thomas......	431
18 Erard, Seb.	325
100 Erat, John	515
87 Forster, Wm.	466
1 Geruck, Charles....	225
126 Holst, M...........	590
91 Keith, R.W........	9
5 Lawson, Henry	344
199 Lawson, Joseph ..	499
181 Longman and Co.	117
105 Metzler and Son...	515
357 Millhouse, W.......	370
159 Mitchell, W.	54
24 Monzani and Co....	168
44 Morrison, J.	395
35 Norris, John	146
89 Percival and Co....	427
9 Phillips, Wm.......	321
214 Phillips, Thomas...	500
5 Potter, R. and Son	272
34 Power, J.	466
97 Preston, T.	467
Prowse, T.	521
21 Shaw, Thomas.....	410
44 Stumpff, J.A.	380
84 Wigley, C.........	466
315 Wilkinson, G.	670
50 Wood, James	185
15 Wrede, Herman ...	497

MUSLIN AND GAUZE DRESSER.

117 Knight, W.L......	84

MUSLIN WAREHOUSES,

51 Andrews, James ..	435
3 Bickers, J. and Co.	56
52 Brouse and Co......	212
16 Brown and Co......	64
26 Carlile, E...........	516
25 Chipchase, R.	361
1 Connell and Co. ...	211
11 Cooper, J. and Co.	518
137 Farrer and Co......	117
9 Fultons and Co. ...	518
53 Gibbs, Thomas.....	134
9 Horrocks, J. & Co.	64
65 Jackson, J.B. & Co.	435
3 Kilgour and Co.....	211
46 Lazarus, Elia	120
30 Leighton and Co...	64
132 Lloyd, Thomas	368
13 Lloyd and Co......	285
127 Lowndes, J.T. & Co.	538
7 Lowndes, W. and J.	518
59 Nunn and Co.	212
30 Petty, Wm.........	64
2 Russell, W. and Co.	62
54 Stabb, T. and F....	212

Figure 30. Sébastien Erard listed along with the harp manufacturers Barry, Dodd, Erat and Stumpff in the section of musical instrument makers in Andrew Johnstone's *Johnstone's London Commercial Guide and Street Directory* (London: Barnard & Farley, 1818), p. 1040. Sammlung von Handschriften und alten Drucken, Österreichische Nationalbibliothek, Vienna, 213798-B.Alt-Mag, S. 1040.

directory includes several important entrepreneurs, from Holtzapffel, the machine and tool maker, to Jackson, the composition maker, who provided products or services to Erard and other harp makers, as mentioned in previous chapters. The directory thus offers an exceptionally panoramic view on musical instrument making in Regency London, demonstrating the extended professional networks upon which the harp trade was dependent.

Conclusions

As novel and fashionable instruments, Erard Grecian harps were selling like hot cakes, particularly during the London season. In 1818 the Erard London branch sold three quarters of its total production for that year, indicating the great popularity of the Erard double-action harp. High and fast sales resulted from the firm's aggressive marketing, which relied on prominent composers, performers, music teachers, publishers and sellers, who acted as Erard's advocates and ambassadors. Erard Grecian harps were frequently viewed and heard in concerts, public events and social gatherings, which helped to strengthen their reputation. Additionally, clever and flexible promotional strategies, including, for example, the hire or exchange of harps as well as the provision of varied accessories and services, enabled the firm to develop and sustain a market for these instruments, which were above all symbols of taste, affluence and status. With Erard harps being endorsed by London's polite society, it was not difficult for the firm to establish a devoted clientele consisting mainly of female customers who belonged to rich families from the upper and middle classes, and who were eager to consume Erard products according to their individual budgets and interests. Although Erard did not have a monopoly on harps, he managed to stay ahead of the competition from other London makers, largely because of the great success of the Grecian harps, which were highly sought after not only in Britain, but all over the world. The Erard double-action harp gradually became a global phenomenon, with the instrument being deeply integrated in the education, art and fashion of the early nineteenth century. This will be the topic of the following chapter, which will examine the sociocultural impact of the Erard Grecian harp in Regency Britain.

CHAPTER SIX

Erard and the Harp in
Education, Art and Fashion:
'Evening Dress' for a Private Concert

'The Harp – tis so commonplace. There's an inundation of them in the Exhibition all strumming St. Cecilias disgracing themselves and the Painters and all for the love of Mr. Erard.'[1]

With their elegant silhouette, elaborate decoration and fine sound, pedal harps like Erard Nº 2631, discussed in the previous chapters, were popular accessories in the lifestyle of Regency Britain. These harps were perceived not only as musical instruments, but as fashionable objects and status symbols that could add taste and prestige in affluent homes. Additionally, for young girls as well as for married women, who in contrast to men had limited options for entertainment and were obliged to stay mostly indoors, playing the harp was more than a private leisure activity, as it offered many possibilities for both musical and social interaction. This chapter will explore the impact of pedal harps, and Erard harps in particular, on the education, art and fashion of the Regency era.

'This elegant and delightful instrument': The Harp in Education

The public appeal of the pedal harp was not coincidental. Like other free-standing musical instruments, the harp was not just a sounding device, but a stylish and expensive piece of furniture, and thus a signifier of luxury, sophistication and social rank.[2] Moreover, as part of the musical education of upper- and middle-class girls, playing the harp was considered an essential female skill, serving, like other plucked or keyboard instruments, as a representation of cultivation, conformity and domes-

---

[1] Quoted in Martin R. F. Butlin, 'Lawrence's Portrait of Mrs Francis Robertson: Some New Letters', *The Burlington Magazine* 99/646 (1957), pp. 27–29, at p. 27.

[2] For an overview of the pedal harp as a piece of furniture in eighteenth-century France see Klaus-Peter Brenner, *Die Naderman-Harfe in der Musikinstrumentensammlung der Universität Göttingen. Ein französisches Instrument des 18. Jahrhunderts als Maschine, Skulptur, Möbel, Prestigefetisch, Ware und Klangwerkzeug. Orbis Musicarum 14* (Göttingen: Edition Re, 1998), pp. 128–155. See also Eve Zaunbrecher, *An Enlightened Instrument: The Design, Education, and Sociability of the Single Action Pedal Harp in* Ancien Régime *Paris, 1760–1789* (MA Diss., London: Royal College of Art, 2016), pp. 87–98.

ticity.[3] Furthermore, the harp was an important means of female seduction, since, apart from its majestic, enchanting sound, the instrument permitted young women to effectively expose their arms, hands and feet, thus winning many admirers and potential husbands.

The harp 'made its female performer the object of male attention and desire', since 'the posture which it demanded was seen by contemporary writers as showing the female form to its full advantage.'[4] The instrument 'allowed the person playing it (almost invariably a woman) to appear both talented and graceful at the same time',[5] while providing 'a most acceptable way to display pretty arms and a "well turned ankle"'.[6] This is confirmed in a letter written in 1818, the year Erard N° 2361 was made, by a lady informing her sister about her acquaintance in Brighton with a young girl named Harriet, in which she mentioned that 'The gentle Harriet [...] has the finest hand and arm you ever saw [...] and has the most beautiful foot and ancle in the world', further commenting that 'She is extremely slender, and light as a Sylph, and whenever she is called upon to perform on the harp, she puts herself into the most studied attitude, and gives a prelude to the song she is about to accompany, with such wonderful execution that you would think her a musician by profession.'[7]

The intense feminisation of the pedal harp, which took place in France during the third quarter of the eighteenth century, was due to the fact that the instrument 'struck a perfect balance between conformity to and transgression of contemporary ideas of feminine decency.'[8] The single-action harp, which became a favourite instrument of French ladies, was 'the perfect vehicle through which women's relegated role of natural, sensual and emotional moral being could be played out'.[9] The gendering of the harp as a feminine instrument is reflected in the large number of amateur and

[3] For more details see Richard Leppert, *Music and Image: Domesticity, Ideology and Socio-cultural Formation in Eighteenth-century England* (Cambridge: Cambridge University Press, 1988), pp. 176–200, and also Leppert, *The Sight of Sound: Music, Representation, and the History of the Body* (Berkeley and Los Angeles: University of California Press, 1993), pp. 91–118.

[4] Megan Fisher, 'Women and Harps in the Home in Early Nineteenth-century London: Part 1', *Harp* 2016/1 (2016), pp. 18–19, at p. 18.

[5] Jeffrey A. Nigro, '"Favourable to Tenderness and Sentiment": The Many Meanings of Mary Crawford's Harp', *Persuasions On-Line* 35/1 (available at http://www.jasna.org/persuasions/on-line/vol35no1/nigro.html, published 2014, accessed 3 June 2022).

[6] Roslyn Rensch, *The Harp: Its History, Technique and Repertoire* (London: Duckworth, 1969), p. 106.

[7] 'Fourth letter from a young married lady, to her sister in the country', *Belle Assemblée; being Bell's Court and Fashionable Magazine* (London: John Bell, 1818), pp. 39–40, at p. 39.

[8] Robert Adelson and Jacqueline Letzter, '"For a woman when she is young and beautiful": The Harp in Eighteenth-Century France', in Annette Kreutziger-Herr and Katrin Losleben, *History/Herstory: Alternative Musikgeschichten* (Cologne, Weimar, Vienna: Böhlau, 2009), pp. 314–335, at p. 320.

[9] Hannah Lane, 'L'orage des passions: Expressing Emotion on the Eighteenth-Century French Single-action Harp', *Ceræ: An Australasian Journal of Medieval and Early Modern Studies* 1 (2014), pp. 75–89, at p. 83.

professional female harpists that were active during the early nineteenth century.[10] In his advice on choosing an instrument for a young girl, an American writer compared the harp favourably to other instruments, such as the piano and guitar, claiming:

> The Harp, for instance? Decidedly – the finest of them all – the finest of all – the grand enchanter – the Prospero among these imprisoned spirits of sweet sound. Its richness, expressiveness, comparative facility of execution, capability of being kept in order by oneself, extreme portability, and, though last not least, in woman's eyes, its grace of form, raise it to unapproachable superiority. At once its music is full of beauty, – when 'married to sweet verse,' irresistible. As to its being a more expensive instrument than the Piano, the idea, though a common, is an erroneous one. The original cost is by the half less, and the stringing of the one about equal to the tuning of the other. With me, the chief objection to the harp is precisely what so generally recommends it: that grace required in its votaries, and which many of them seem to think it has the power of communicating, though the spectators do not always coincide in the opinion. To appear to advantage at the harp, a *certain* appearance is indispensable. But this certain appearance I shall leave in the same mystery, as the *certain* age is left in Beppo, merely observing, that no where does a good figure look better, nor a bad one worse. [11]

Thus the harp could greatly improve the public image of someone already pretty, as it could impair that of someone with less attractive features. The emblematic, theatrical qualities of performing upon the harp are highlighted in the following passage, in which the harpist is a young man:

> While I was eating an ice, which Sir Bingham had just handed to me, I observed a very elegant young man pass me, along with the lady of the feast. She led him to a raised platform, on which stood a splendid harp and a Grecian chair. He sat down in the one and began to tune the other. The groupe thus formed seemed perfectly attic; had the harp been changed to a lyre, I might have supposed that I saw the graceful Alcibiades about to strike its string 'to Peleus' son.[12]

As a result of its increased musical potential, social suitability and powerful symbolism, the pedal harp gradually occupied a prominent position among instruments addressed to women of status and fashion.[13] By the beginning of the nineteenth cen-

---

[10] For more details see Freia Hoffmann, *Instrument und Körper: die musizierende Frau in der bürgerlichen Kultur* (Frankfurt am Main: Insel, 1991), pp. 131–152, as well as Freia Hoffmann and Jannis Wichmann, 'Karrieren mit Hindernissen. Professionelle Harfen- und Gitarrenspielerinnen im 19. Jahrhundert', *Phoibos: Zeitschrift für Zupfmusik* 5/2 (2012), pp. 93–110, at pp. 101–109.

[11] John E. Hall, 'Choice of Musical Instruments for Females', in John E. Hall (ed.), *The Port Folio* 10, No. 1 (Philadelphia: Harrison Hall, 1820), pp. 91–93, at p. 92. The writer must have been referring to single-action harps, since double-action harps were as expensive, if not costlier, than a piano, as mentioned in Chapter Six.

[12] 'Hymenea in search of a husband', *La Belle Assemblée: being Bell's Court and Fashionable Magazine, Addressed Particularly to the Ladies* 4 (London: John Bell, 1811), pp. 7–11, at p. 10.

[13] For more details on the role of the harp in female culture see Mike Baldwin, *The Harp in Early Nineteenth-century Britain: Innovation, Business, and Making in Jacob Erat's*

tury the harp had become as popular as the piano or similar keyboard instruments and was listed as one of the necessary female accomplishments in education treatises and conduct manuals. In 1810 an author maintained that 'The harpsichord, the harp, are instruments often touched by female hands; nor would it be proper to forbid ladies to exercise their delicate fingers in calling forth the enchanting sounds of these instruments'.[14] Likewise, an essay on the education of young ladies published in 1815 stated that 'The word in female studies simply means the theory and performance upon the piano forte, (of late years) upon the pedal harp; and, finally, the culture of melody in the voice.'[15] Like most contemporary critics, who measured the harp against the piano, the author provided the following description:

> The Harp. – This elegant and delightful instrument is often attempted to be prac-tised by young people, who are only half way towards excellence upon the piano-forte. It is impossible to find time for both, consequently, neither is ever well understood.[16]

She also pointed out that 'The harp is generally considered rather an easy instru-ment to learn; this is a mistaken notion, for, to be a good performer upon it, requires as much time as does the piano-forte.'[17] The author apparently wrote with Erard's new double-action harp in mind, since she claimed that 'the instrument is now brought to such a pitch of excellence, that every modulation of key is perfectly prac-ticable', adding that 'Every whole tone, every semi tone, is complete'. She further argued that 'Persons used to be entirely confined to a few keys of the minor and major scales; but, upon the harps of which I am speaking, they may play in any one of the twenty-four.'[18] The praise of Erard, 'whose talents in architecture and mech-anism have been so appreciated in his own country' is expressed more openly in the next quotation:

> To mention here the indefatigable exertions of the gentleman, to whom all who practice the improved patent harp are so much indebted, is no more than common justice; and, I trust, that, should this page ever meet his observation, he will not disdain the trifling acknowledgement it offers to his merit. To Mr. Sebastian Erard, whose talents in architecture and mechanism have been so appreciated in his own country, the improvement of the harp is solely due. – After a very close application, and the most minute attention, he has succeeded in remedying the former defects of this instrument; and every friend of science and harmony cannot but unite in wishing him an ample remuneration for the pains he has taken, to the injury of his fortune and his health, in accomplishing his views,

---

Manufactory (PhD Diss., London: London Metropolitan University, 2017), pp. 65–82.

[14] John Dougall, *The Modern Preceptor; Or, a General Course of Education*, vol. 1 (London: Vernon, Hood and Sharpe, 1810), p. 29.

[15] Elizabeth Appleton, *Private Education; or a Practical Plan for the Studies of Young Ladies. With an Address to Parents, Private Governesses, and Young Ladies* (London: Henry Colburn, 1815), p. 135.

[16] Appleton, *Private Education; or a Practical Plan for the Studies of Young Ladies*, p. 162.

[17] Appleton, *Private Education; or a Practical Plan for the Studies of Young Ladies*, pp. 162–163.

[18] Appleton, *Private Education; or a Practical Plan for the Studies of Young Ladies*, pp. 164–165.

and at length completely triumphing over every difficulty, and rendering to this instrument the excellence it at present is entitled to.[19]

Apart from its augmented capabilities for modulation and expression due to Erard's contributions, the harp possessed another strong advantage over the piano. Contrary to keyboard instruments, which, due to their bulky size and fixed position within a room, sometimes prevented players from showing their body or from facing their audience directly, the slimmer and more portable harp allowed for a maximum display of beauty and talent. This is noted in a conduct manual published in 1830 by an unnamed 'Lady of Distinction', who advocated simplicity of actions in playing an instrument or singing:

> There are many young women who, when they sit down at the piano or the harp, or to sing, twist themselves into so many contortions, and writhe their bodies and faces about into such actions and grimaces, as would almost incline one to believe that they are suffering under the torture of the toothach, or the gout [...] Let their attitude at the piano or the harp be easy and graceful. I strongly exhort them to avoid a stiff, awkward, elbowing position at either; they must observe an elegant flow of figure at both. The latter certainly admits of most grace, as the shape of the instrument is calculated, in every respect, to show a fine figure to advantage. The contour of the whole form, the turn and polish of a beautiful hand and arm, the richly-slippered and well-made foot on the pedal stops, the gentle motion of a lovely neck, and, above all, the sweetly-tempered expression of an intelligent countenance; these are shown at one glance, when the fair performer is seated unaffectedly, yet gracefully, at the harp.[20]

Although the two instruments were competing against each other in terms of their public approbation, they were frequently collaborating in terms of performance practice. During the early nineteenth century, arrangements of popular pieces and songs as duets for piano and harp were the core of domestic repertoire. As has been pointed out, being 'Imprisoned by the expectations of society and their cumbersome instruments', female harpists 'sought freedom and emotion in the music they played at home'.[21] It was quite common for wealthy families who had two or more daughters to own both a piano and harp, as well as other instruments. This provided musical variety and flexibility, since the instruments could be distributed among the family members according to their interests and skills. A proposed selection of instruments for a family with several daughters consisted of 'Piano-forte, harp, guitar, or harmonica, harp-lute, castanets, and tambourine.'[22]

Playing the piano, harp or guitar was a common prerequisite for governesses, who were responsible for the private education of the daughters of well-off families.

---

19 Appleton, *Private Education; or a Practical Plan for the Studies of Young Ladies*, pp. 165–166.

20 'On the management of the person in dancing, and in the exercise of other female accomplishments', *The Mirror of the Graces: Or, The English Lady's Costume* (Edinburgh: A. Black, 1830), pp. 136–160, at pp. 151–154.

21 Megan Fisher, 'Women and Harps in the Home in Early Nineteenth-century London: Notes on Harp and Piano Duets', *Harp* 2016/2 (2016), pp. 12–13, at p. 13.

22 Appleton, *Private Education; or a Practical Plan for the Studies of Young Ladies*, p. 162.

In 1825 a couple who had allegedly worked for 50 years as servants in different families noted that a governess should 'be able to play on the PIANO FORTE, so as to give the first lessons, and to superintend the practice directed in the lessons of a master; and in cases where great perfection is not desired, to render a master unnecessary. If she can perform on the harp or guitar, these instruments will qualify her to accommodate her instructions to various tastes.'[23]

These governesses, many of whom were of French origin, were expected to teach the instruments currently in fashion, including Erard's new double-action harp. One example was Amélina Petit de Billier (1800–1876), nanny to the children of the scientist, inventor and photography pioneer William Henry Fox Talbot (1800–1877). In 1827 Amélina noted in her diary that 'a tuner came from Devizes to tune the piano, with the excellent harp by Erard, which Mr F. bought before leaving London. It is a perfect instrument; the piano is also very good.'[24] This harp was Erard Nº 1663, the so-called 'Angel' harp, bought in 1827 and now housed in Lacock Abbey, Fox Talbot Museum and Village, Wiltshire (Inv. No. NT 995846.1). This was probably the same instrument as that played by Horatia Feilding (1810–1851), Talbot's half-sister, as shown in a 'Calotype', a kind of early photograph, dating from c.1842.

The eminence of the harp and piano in the musical education of women is also revealed in a popular travel guide originally published by the influential harp teacher Caroline-Stéphanie-Félicité, Madame de Genlis (1746–1830) at the end of the eighteenth century, but appearing in numerous editions during the early nineteenth century. In a section labelled 'Various Questions and Answers' the guide contains the following questions, evidently helping a traveller to obtain information about the musical skills of a female acquaintance: 'Does she dance well? Does she sing well? Does she play or perform well on the harp or piano-forte?'[25] That the author was herself a harpist does not diminish the fact that the harp was seen as an effective tool of musical and social interaction.

'For the love of Mr. Erard': The Harp in Art

The pedal harp had a strong presence in contemporary art, since playing the harp was as much a visual as an aural experience. The harp's popularity as 'a symbol of delicate urbane luxury'[26] is evidenced in the countless portraits of elegantly dressed young women posing with their equally elegant harps. Interestingly, the earliest

---

[23] Samuel and Sarah Adams, *The Complete Servant: Being a Practical Guide to the Peculiar Duties and Business of All Descriptions of Servants* (London: Knight and Lacey, 1825), p. 273.

[24] For more details see 'The journal of Amélina Petit de Billier', http://amelina.dmu.ac.uk/diary_1827_talbot_finds_magna_carta_transcript.html, published 2012; accessed 3 June 2022.

[25] Pietro A. Cignani (ed.), *Manuel Du Voyageur, Or, the Traveller's Pocket Companion: Consisting of Familiar Conversations in English, French, and Italian; With Models of Letters, Notes etc. Also a Table of French and Italian Coins, and the Various Terms Used in Music. By Madame de Genlis* (12th edn, London: Samuel Leigh, 1819), p. 249.

[26] Nigro, '"Favourable to Tenderness and Sentiment"'.

known depiction of a pedal harp, dated 1759, is a painting of a male harpist, the art collector Ange Laurent de La Live de Jully (1725–1779) by Jean-Baptiste Greuze (1725–1805).[27] However, the majority of portrayed harpists during the late eighteenth century were women, with the earliest dated portrait of a woman with a pedal harp being a painting from 1761 by Jean-François Gilles Colson (1733–1803).[28]

This fashion began in France, where female members of the royalty and aristocracy were often depicted with harps, as evidenced by the painting of the Queen of France, Marie Antoinette, playing the harp at the French Court (c.1775) by Jean-Baptiste-André Gautier-Dagoty (1740–1786).[29] Another well-known example is the painting of Mademoiselle d'Orléans taking a harp lesson (1791) by Antoine Théodore Giroust (1753–1817).[30] This painting shows Louise Marie Adelaïde Eugénie de Bourbon d'Orléans (1753–1821), daughter of the Duc d'Orléans, playing a duet with her governess, Madame de Genlis, mentioned earlier. A notable detail of this painting is that the two harpists are using child- and full-sized harps as would have been common in harp tuition. Pedal harps gradually found their way into the works of renowned British artists, such as Thomas Gainsborough (1727–1788), who in 1778 portrayed Louisa Skrine, Lady Clarges (1760–1809) playing a single-action harp,[31] or George Romney (1734–1802), who painted the two daughters of the Duke of Marlborough, with the younger of them, Lady Elizabeth Spencer (1764–1812), sitting at the harp (c.1786–1792).[32]

The widespread use of the pedal harp as an artistic prop in Britain by the beginning of the nineteenth century seems to have been fuelled by the technical and aesthetic development of the instrument by Erard in the 1790s.[33] In 1801 Sir Thomas

[27] See Rensch, *The Harp: Its History, Technique and Repertoire*, p. 99, and Adelson and Letzter, '"For a woman when she is young and beautiful"', p. 332. The painting is in the National Gallery of Art, Washington (Inv. No. 1946.7.8). For more details see 'Ange Laurent de La Live de Jully', https://www.nga.gov/collection/art-object-page.32686. html, accessed 3 June 2022.

[28] Adelson and Letzter, '"For a woman when she is young and beautiful"', p. 329.

[29] In the Château de Versailles, Versailles (Inv. No. INV.DESS 854). For more details see Juliette Trey, 'Jean-Baptiste-André Gautier-Dagoty portraiturant la Reine dans sa chambre', http://collections.chateauversailles.fr/#7ca71495-248a-4386-88bc-8acae1ef7991, accessed 3 June 2022.

[30] In the Dallas Museum of Art, Dallas (Inv. No. F 2015.10.FA). For more details see 'The Harp Lesson', https://collections.dma.org/artwork/5340929, accessed 3 June 2022.

[31] In the Holburne Museum, Bath (Inv. No. L1988.1). For more details see 'Louisa Skrine, Lady Clarges', http://collections.holburne.org/object-l1988-1, accessed 3 June 2022. For an analysis of this painting see Ann Sumner, 'Gainsborough's "Portrait of Lady Clarges"', *The Burlington Magazine* 130/1027 (1988), pp. 761–763.

[32] In the Huntington Library, Art Museum and Botanical Gardens, San Marino (Inv. No. 11.44). For more details see 'Lady Caroline Spencer, later Viscountess Clifden, and her sister, Lady Elizabeth Spencer', http://emuseum.huntington.org/objects/197/lady-caroline-spencer-later-viscountess-clifden-and-her-si?ctx=ab108333-9f30-4e8f-9b4e-e1e51307d9af&idx=0, accessed 3 June 2022.

[33] Regarding depictions of harps in British paintings of the late eighteenth and early nineteenth centuries see Robert Wilson Torchia, 'Eliza Ridgely and the Ideal of American Womanhood, 1787–1820', *Maryland Historical Magazine* 90/4 (1995), pp. 405–423, at

Lawrence (1769–1830), a leading portrait painter, advocated one of his clients, Miss Laura Dorothea Ross, against the inclusion of a harp in her portrait, arguing contemptuously that 'The Drapery *shall* be yellow and for a thousand reasons but *principally because I know you will agree to my rubbing out the Harp*. The Harp – tis so commonplace. There's an inundation of them in the Exhibition all strumming St. Cecilias disgracing themselves and the Painters and all for the love of Mr. Erard.'[34] Lawrence presumably referred to images like the pastel drawing of Emily de Visme, Lady Murray (1787–1873), playing the harp as St Cecilia, patron saint of music (1794), by John Russell (1745–1806), which appeared as a print in 1795, enabling its dissemination to a wider public.[35]

Nevertheless, Lawrence himself contributed greatly to the trend he criticised, since in 1801 he produced one of the earliest, if not the earliest, depictions of an Erard harp in his portrait of Caroline, Princess of Wales (1768–1821) and her daughter Princess Charlotte (1796–1817).[36] This portrait shows Caroline tuning a harp, while her young daughter is showing her a music sheet. The harp depicted in the portrait was most likely Erard N° 357, a black single-action harp which had been sold to 'Her Roy[l] High[ss] the Pr[ss] of Wales' in 1800.[37] Around the same time (c.1798–1804), Lawrence painted the portrait of Miss Laura Dorothea Ross, mentioned above.[38] As in the portrait of Caroline and Charlotte, Miss Ross is not playing upon her harp, but standing next to it, with her face directed to the viewer and her left hand resting nonchalantly on the harp's neck.

The portraits of prominent women with harps in France and Britain inspired numerous similar paintings in America.[39] Arguably the most famous of them is the portrait of a lady with a harp (1818) by Thomas Sully (1783–1872).[40] The painting has been identified as the portrait of Eliza Eichelberger Ridgely (1803–1867), daughter of a wealthy Baltimore merchant, who was mentioned in Chapter Five. Eliza's portrait

---

pp. 412–413, and Pierre Dubois, *Music in the Georgian Novel* (Cambridge: Cambridge University Press, 2015), p. 226.

[34] Quoted in Martin R. F. Butlin, 'Lawrence's Portrait of Mrs Francis Robertson: Some New Letters', *The Burlington Magazine* 99/646 (1957), pp. 27–29, at p. 27.

[35] A print of this drawing survives in the British Museum, London, (Inv. No. 1953,0214.41). For more details see 'Portrait of Miss Emily de Visme', https://www.britishmuseum.org/collection/object/P_1953-0214-41, accessed 3 June 2022.

[36] In the Silk Tapestry Room at Buckingham Palace, London (Inv. No. RCIN 407292). For more details see 'Caroline, Princess of Wales, and Princess Charlotte', https://www.rct.uk/collection/407292/caroline-princess-of-wales-and-princess-charlotte, accessed 3 June 2022.

[37] Erard London Harp Ledgers, vol. 1, p. 90.

[38] In the Tate Gallery, London (Inv. No. N00136). For more details see 'Miss Laura Dorothea Ross (Mrs Francis Robertson)', https://www.tate.org.uk/art/artworks/lawrence-miss-laura-dorothea-ross-mrs-francis-robertson-n00136, accessed 3 June 2022.

[39] For more details on the presence of the harp in American portraits of the nineteenth century see Torchia, 'Eliza Ridgely and the Ideal of American Womanhood', p. 419.

[40] In the National Gallery of Art, Washington (Inv. No. 1945.9.1). For more details see 'Lady with a Harp: Eliza Ridgely', https://www.nga.gov/collection/art-object-page.32577.html, accessed 3 June 2022.

shows her in a standing pose wearing a white dress, holding a tuning key in her right hand and plucking a string of the harp with the left, while simultaneously depressing a pedal with her right foot. Notably, the depicted instrument is not Eliza's own Erard N° 2372, a double-action harp purchased for her in 1817,[41] but a single-action French harp, which Sully may have obtained for his Philadelphia studio.[42]

However, as double-action harps by Erard became established in the 1810s, more and more of these instruments were included in contemporary iconography. One of the earliest depictions of a double-action harp is shown in the portrait of Miss Jane Reade (Figure 31), painted in 1813 by Sir William Beechey (1753–1839).[43]

Miss Reade, who is portrayed wearing a white dress and standing next to her harp, like Miss Ross and Miss Ridgely mentioned above, is tuning her harp with her right hand, while plucking a string with her left one. The black-gold decoration of the depicted harp with decoupage vignettes and a fluted pedalbox is similar to that of Erard harps produced between 1811 and 1813; a representative example in a public collection is Erard N° 1587, built c.1813 and housed at the Museum of Fine Arts, Boston (Inv. No. 2012.991), shown in Chapter Three. Another depiction of a double-action harp is included in the undated portrait of a lady in a white dress by Sir Martin Archer Shee (1769–1850).[44] In this case, the harp is rather part of the room's decoration, since it is standing in the background far away from the portrayed lady. Here the depicted instrument bears a striking resemblance to the standard black-gold Grecian model produced by Erard in the late 1810s, a typical example of which is Erard N° 2631.

Although the majority of the paintings described above depict harpists standing next to their harps, seated harpists were not uncommon in early-nineteenth-century paintings. For instance, a seated harpist is shown in the portrait of a young lady playing a single-action harp by James Northcote (1746–1831), exhibited in 1814.[45] Another example is an undated watercolour of a seated lady with a double-action harp.[46] Although the watercolour is labelled as French, the depicted black-gold harp

[41] Erard London Harp Ledgers, vol. 2, p. 100.

[42] For a comprehensive analysis of this portrait see Robert Wilson Torchia, Deborah Chotner and Ellen G. Miles, *American Paintings of the Nineteenth Century, Part II* (Washington: National Gallery of Art, 1998), pp. 151–159.

[43] In the Spencer Museum of Art, University of Kansas, Gift of Walstein Findlay, (Inv. No. 1958.0126). For more details see 'Portrait of Miss Jane Reade', https://spencerartapps. ku.edu/collection-search#/object/10023, accessed 3 June 2022.

[44] The present whereabouts of this painting, which was sold on 14 July 2011, are unknown. For more details see 'Portrait of a lady in a white dress', http://www.artnet.com/artists/ sir-martin-archer-shee/portrait-of-a-lady-in-a-white-dress-with-a-yellow-h5wo-a9T-FYUwHTekJrfaA2, accessed 3 June 2022.

[45] In the Tate Collection, London (Inv. No. N04376). For more details see 'A Young Lady Playing the Harp', https://www.tate.org.uk/art/artworks/northcote-a-young-lady-playing-the-harp-n04376, accessed 3 June 2022.

[46] At the time of writing the watercolour was available for sale by the London musical instrument dealer Tony Bingham. For more details see 'French watercolour of a seated lady with a harp', https://www.oldmusicalinstruments.co.uk/iconography/icon_detail. php?id=37&cat=PS, accessed 3 June 2022.

Figure 31. Portrait of Miss Jane Reade painted by Sir William Beechey in 1813; the depicted double-action harp is similar to Erard Grecian harps from this time. Spencer Museum of Art, University of Kansas, Gift of Walstein Findlay (Inv. No. 1958.0126).

with decoupage vignettes on the soundboard is a London-made instrument, most likely by Erard or one of his imitators, since double-action harps built in Paris did not have this type of decoration. A seated harpist is also portrayed in an undated sketch by Elizabeth Rigby, Lady Eastlake (1809–1893).[47] Although the details of the harp are not clear, the instrument may have been an Erard harp belonging to Rigby's sister Matilda, since in one of her letters written in 1848 Elizabeth referred to it in a complaint drafted against Erard, stating that 'The object is to give Erard a thorough blowing up so that he may feel himself "the most blowed up man alive" & 2ndly that the bill may be materially reduced.'[48]

Also common were depictions of duets with young women sitting on stools and playing the harp and piano, with the harpist usually facing the viewer. One of the most well-known examples is the painting of the Grosvenor family (1833) by Charles Robert Leslie (1794–1859), which depicts Mary Margaret Stanley, Lady Wilton (1801–1858) playing seated at her harp, with Elizabeth Mary Grosvenor, Marchioness of Westminster (1797–1891) accompanying her at the piano.[49] The depicted harp may be Erard N° 1982, an ultramarine double-action harp that Mary Margaret had bought in 1815.[50] Likewise, a colour print by Thomas Lord Busby (fl.1804–1837), entitled 'Music' and dating from 1813, shows two girls in long white dresses seated on round stools next to each other, with one performing on a square piano, the other on a highly ornamented double-action harp.[51] Another print entitled 'The Musical Infant Sisters', made by John Doyle (1797–1868) and published in 1826, illustrates two small girls 'at 4 and 7 Years of Age', one playing on a grand piano and the other on a double-action harp.[52] An interesting feature of the image is the presence of a system with extensions attached to the harp's pedals, apparently to allow small children to perform on standard-sized double-action harps. Similar extensions have been fitted on the pedals of a double-action harp by Erard, built in Paris in 1835 and bearing the serial number 1273, housed at the Musée de la musique, Paris (Inv. No. E.0998).[53]

---

47 In the Tate Collection, London (Inv No. T09803). For more details see 'Elizabeth Rigby (Lady Eastlake)', https://www.tate.org.uk/art/artworks/rigby-title-not-known-t09803, accessed 3 June 2022.

48 Julie Sheldon (ed.), *The Letters of Elizabeth Rigby* (Liverpool: Liverpool University Press, 2009), p. 118.

49 For a reproduction of this painting see Rudolf Frick (ed.), *Sébastien Erard: ein europäischer Pionier des Instrumentenbaus. Internationales Erard-Symposium Michaelstein 13.–14. November 1994, Michaelsteiner Konferenzberichte 48* (Blankenburg: Stiftung Kloster Michaelstein, 1995), p. 5.

50 Erard London Harp Ledgers, vol. 2, p. 61.

51 In the British Museum London (Inv. No. 1887,0722.177). For more details see 'Two women sitting on stools and playing music', https://www.britishmuseum.org/collection/object/P_1887-0722-177, accessed 3 June 2022.

52 In the British Museum London (Inv. No. 1878,0511.1150). For more details see 'Two young girls, one sitting at a piano and the other a harp', https://www.britishmuseum.org/collection/object/P_1878-0511-1150, accessed 3 June 2022.

53 For more details and images of this instrument see 'Harpe à double mouvement', https://collectionsdumusee.philharmoniedeparis.fr/doc/MUSEE/0156103/harpe-a-double-

The artworks presented above exemplify the standardised, homogeneous iconography of the pedal harp. A recent study of more than 250 pictorial representations of harps from the late eighteenth and early nineteenth centuries has shown that these can be divided into three distinct categories, including images with harps in the background (more than 30 examples), images with the harpist in a standing pose (more than 120 examples) and images with the harpist in a sitting pose (over 100 examples).[54] It is worth noting that in most of these paintings the female harpists are shown in a stylised way: they are typically wearing fancy voluminous dresses, which may have been uncomfortable for harp performance, and are invariably facing the viewer rather than the instrument.

That the portrayed harpists are not looking at their fingers but gazing at their fictional audience suggests that they did not want to seem too focused on their playing; this would indicate their serious devotion to music-making, which was disapproved of for women.[55] Additionally, the harps and their female owners are usually shown in a domestic setting rather than in public buildings or outdoors, further emphasising contemporary notions of female obedience and domesticity. Moreover, in many cases the depicted instruments do not represent pedal harps in action, but static props, since the feet of the players are away from the pedals or the pedals are shown in the upper position.[56]

'Harmony before Matrimony' or 'March of Intellect'? The Harp in Fashion and Satire

Apart from their depictions in paintings, pedal harps were frequently illustrated in fashion magazines and comic art, which shaped public opinion and taste. One representative example is a fashion plate from 1805 entitled 'London fashionable full dress', which depicts a smartly clad lady resting her right hand on a harp's neck.[57] Two other fashion plates in magazines published in 1819 and 1826 show that the harp often accompanied images of female costumes and dresses designed for private concerts. The first plate (Figure 32), showing a finely dressed lady with a harp in the background, is entitled 'Evening dress' and corresponds to the description of a

---

    mouvement, accessed 3 June 2022.

[54] See Maria Christina Cleary, *The 'harpe organisée', 1720–1840: Rediscovering the lost pedal techniques on harps with a single-action pedal mechanism* (PhD Diss., Leiden: Leiden University, 2016), pp. 200–202.

[55] This fact has been analysed in Elise Kolle, *Feminine Portraits: Lady Harpists and Their Music in the Age of Enlightenment* (Masters Diss., Glasgow: University of Glasgow, 2020), pp. 17–34 and 49–51.

[56] A virtual gallery including numerous portraits with harps is presented in Elise Kolle, 'Portraits of Harpists: A database for portraits of people with their harps, from 1500 to 1900', available at https://historicalharpportraits.wordpress.com/, accessed 3 June 2022.

[57] 'London full dress', *The Lady's Magazine, Or, Entertaining Companion for the Fair Sex* 36 (London: G. and J. Robinson, 1805), p. 321. For more details, see 'London fashionable full dress', https://www.npg.org.uk/collections/search/portrait/mw279959/London-fashionable-full-dress-June-1805?LinkID=mp64662&role=art&rNo=12, accessed 3 June 2022.

Figure 32. Fashion plate showing an elegantly dressed lady with a harp in the background, included in Rudolph Ackermann, *The Repository of arts, literature, fashions, commerce, manufactures, &c.* (London: Rudolph Ackermann, 1819), plate 30.

'Private concert costume'.[58] The second plate, entitled 'Private concert dress', similarly illustrates a young lady in an elegant dress and hat holding a harp and plucking the strings with her left hand.[59] In all three plates the features of the harps are rather generic, lacking the detail usually observed in paintings. This suggests that the artists may have worked from memory and did not draw a particular harp, while the poses of the female models seem to have been inspired from some of the portraits mentioned above. Interestingly, the instruments in the 1819 and 1826 plates strongly resemble Erard harps, whose features were widely copied by several harp makers.

In addition to fashion plates, which mirrored the daily habits of the *beau monde*, there are many caricatures with harps that usually satirised the complications of married life, particularly for women. One example is the comic print 'Music hath charms, or a dull husband' (1789) by the eminent cartoonist Thomas Rowlandson (1757–1827), which shows a young woman playing the harp and singing, while her husband, who apparently has no interest in her performance, has fallen asleep.[60] Likewise, in 'Harmony before Matrimony' (1805) by James Gillray (1756–1815), a young man is singing passionately together with a young woman playing a pedal harp,[61] while in a companion caricature entitled 'Matrimonial Harmonics', the relationship of the couple seems to have deteriorated after several years of marriage: the wife is now more devoted to her piano than to her family and her household duties, while her husband listens to her, rather bored, being absorbed in his newspaper.

These caricatures ridiculed the social system that forced young girls to learn various artistic skills, such as playing the harp, which could help them find a husband, but which did not guarantee a happy marriage and rendered them socially and financially reliant on their spouses. This issue was recognised by a certain 'Father Abraham', who argued that it was acceptable for upper-class girls to 'let painting occupy their leisure hours, let the pallet, the maul-stick, and easel occupy one apartment, the forte-piano, the harp, or the guitar be seen in another', but who urged middle- and lower-class girls to gain financial independence through their training in male-dominated professions, stating that 'The study of surgery can be no bar to domestic felicity, nor can wire-working hurt the hand more than striking the strings of the harp.'[62] Indeed, the musical activities of female harpists were often diminished after marriage, with their instruments falling into neglect and adopting a rather

---

58 'Fashions. London fashions. Plate 30.– Private concert costume', in Rudolph Ackermann, *The Repository of arts, literature, fashions, commerce, manufactures, &c.* (London: Rudolph Ackermann, 1819), p. 306 and plate 30.

59 'Records of the Beau-Monde. Fashions for April 1826. Private concert dress', *La Belle Assemblée, or Court and Fashionable Magazine* 3 (London: George Whitaker, 1826), p. 168; the plate is on an unnumbered page between pp. 172 and 173.

60 For a reproduction of this image see Joseph Grego, *Rowlandson the Caricaturist: A Selection from His Works* (2 vols; London: Chatto and Windus, 1880), vol. 1, pp. 266–267.

61 In the British Museum, London (Inv. No. 1935,0522.4.132). For more details see 'Harmony before matrimony', https://www.britishmuseum.org/collection/object/P_1935-0522-4-132, accessed 3 June 2022.

62 'On the Preservation of the Independence of the Female Character', *Belle Assemblée*, pp. 164–165.

decorative character, as pointed out in the article 'The Young Wife's Harp', published in 1830 in the magazine *The World of Fashion*:

> I beheld, in the drawing-room of the youthful and pretty Mrs. Vernon, a splendid harp, adorned with all the brilliant devices of the nineteenth century, but put up in a solitary corner, where it seemed placed merely as an ornament, and not as a memento of the talent which once existed [...]. I approached the instrument with regret, so well adapted to female beauty, and lending such fresh attraction to her native charms, and my eyes immediately discovered that more than half of the strings were broken, and what remained of them twisted round their supporters, testifying, but too evidently, a determined neglect, a voluntary forgetfulness.[63]

The harp's feminine character as well as its novelty is further highlighted in a comic sketch from 1829 consisting of two images, the first entitled 'The 'Old way of performing a Concert', the second, 'The New way of performing a Concert'. In the two images an old-fashioned group of musicians playing instruments typical of the late eighteenth century is contrasted with a younger and more stylish ensemble performing on a new array of instruments.[64] Notably, whereas in the first image the harp is absent, in the second image it has adopted a prominent frontal place in the hands of a smartly dressed young lady sitting near a dandyish man playing the guitar.

As a representation of the female world and of polite cultivation, the harp was also depicted in satirical prints with an intellectual or social-class content, such as the 'March of Intellect among the Black-diamond Carriers' (Figure 33).[65] Published in 1828 by John Fairburn (fl.1789–1840), the caricature shows a coal-heaver who, transformed into a fairy with colourful butterfly wings, is playing on a pedal harp and singing a popular song, while being watched by his fellow coalmen and a surprised lady standing nearby. The humorous element of the image relies on 'incongruity, the transforming interruption of the ludicrously genteel', which is denoted by the pedal harp and the imagined, fairy-like features of the worker with butterfly wings, 'into the world of famously uncultured and traditionally comic coalmen'.[66] The satire of this print is 'directed as much at the sentimentality and over-refinement of popular parlour songs as at the unlikeliness of a coal-heaver being metamorphosed into an exotic butterfly', with 'The genteel presence of the ornate harp at the centre of the image' putting 'both the coal heavers and the fairies in perspective'.[67]

---

[63] Quoted in Baldwin, *The Harp in Early Nineteenth-century Britain*, p. 70.

[64] Both images have been reproduced in Christopher Page, *The Guitar in Georgian England: A Social and Musical History* (New Haven and London: Yale University Press, 2020), p. 209, fig. 47.

[65] In the British Museum, London (Inv. No. 1988,1001.17). For more details see 'March of Intellect', https://www.britishmuseum.org/collection/object/P_1988-1001-17, accessed 3 June 2022.

[66] Laurel Brake, Bill Bell and David Finkelstein (eds), *Nineteenth-Century Media and the Construction of Identities* (Basingstoke and New York: Palgrave, 2000), p. 108.

[67] Brake, Bell and Finkelstein, *Nineteenth-Century Media and the Construction of Identities*, p. 108.

Figure 33. Caricature entitled 'March of Intellect among the Black-diamond Carriers', published in 1828 by John Fairburn. British Museum, London (Inv. No. 1988,1001.17).

In the early nineteenth century the harp was occasionally featured in political satire, particularly as the national symbol of Ireland. This is demonstrated, for example, by the print 'The Mad Music Master, Or Unison No Harmony', published in 1801.[68] A rather bitter comment on the Act of Union, which united Great Britain and Ireland in 1801, the cartoon shows Ireland as a young lady in a green dress resting on her harp and refusing to perform under the direction of England, which is depicted as an authoritative music master in military uniform, with Scotland being represented in this music ensemble as a bagpiper in highland costume. A similar political caricature, in which the harp is linked with Ireland, is the 'Dissolution of the Association', drawn by William Heath (1795–1840) and published in 1829.[69] A green-clad Erin, the female personification of Ireland, with a golden harp shown behind her, is being violently thrown by the Duke of Wellington onto a bed bearing the Union Jack on its coverlet. The print was a satirical reference to the process

---

68 In the British Museum, London (Inv. No. 1868,0808.6918). For more details see 'The mad music master', https://www.britishmuseum.org/collection/object/P_1868-0808-6918, accessed 3 June 2022.

69 Copies of this print survive in the British Museum, London (Inv. No. 1868,0808.8920) and the National Portrait Gallery, London (Inv. No. NPG D48731). See 'Dissolution of the association', https://www.britishmuseum.org/collection/object/P_1868-0808-8920, and 'Dissolution of the association', https://www.npg.org.uk/collections/search/portrait/mw297448, accessed 3 June 2022.

of Catholic emancipation, which gradually reduced and removed the restrictions imposed on Roman Catholics in Great Britain and Ireland, and which was eventually settled with the Roman Catholic Relief Act of 1829. Interestingly, the column and neck of the depicted harp has the shape of a winged female figure, a feature which is found on harps by John Egan (fl.1797–1829), but which also evokes the decoration of Erard's Grecian harp with winged caryatids on the capital.[70]

Conclusions

During the late eighteenth and early nineteenth centuries the pedal harp was a prevailing icon of lifestyle. In Britain, largely due to the success of Erard's single- and later double-action instruments, the harp became central to the musical education of young women, providing them with the opportunity to demonstrate both their musical abilities and their physical features. For this reason, the harp was considered as both an essential female accomplishment and an effective means of seduction by contemporary instructors, who praised the instrument's potential for self-display and courtship. Moreover, as a recognisable signifier of femininity and sophistication, the harp strongly marked the art, fashion and satire of this era. The instrument appeared as a common prop not only in the works of renowned painters, but also in influential forms of popular art and printed media, such as fashion plates, prints, book illustrations and caricatures with social or political themes. Erard harps and their imitations were frequently depicted in the hands of celebrities and members of polite society, further consolidating the firm's reputation and esteem. The next chapter will discuss the role of harps, and of Erard harps in particular, in the literature of the Romantic era.

---

[70] For more details on Egan and his instruments see Nancy Hurrell, *The Egan Irish Harps: Tradition, Patrons and Players* (Dublin: Four Courts Press, 2019).

CHAPTER SEVEN

Erard and the Harp's Literary Footprint: From *Pride and Prejudice* to *War and Peace*

'And we agreed it would be best to have the harp, for it seems to amuse her more than the piano-forte.' [1]

The opening quotation is included in Jane Austen's novel *Persuasion*, published posthumously in 1818, the year Erard N° 2631 was built. This is just one of the numerous references to the harp found in Austen's writings, exemplifying the significance of the instrument in the literature of Regency Britain. Due to their symbolic character, pedal harps like Erard N° 2631 were used not only as artistic props, but also as literary devices. References to harps were commonly included in novels and poems by celebrated authors of the nineteenth century, ranging from Jane Austen and Sir Walter Scott to Charles Dickens and Leo Tolstoy. This chapter will discuss the important role of the pedal harp, and of the Erard harp in particular, in the literature of the Romantic era in Britain.

The Harp in the Novels and Letters of Jane Austen

Although the famous British novelist Jane Austen (1775–1817) may have never played the harp herself, her lifespan corresponds quite well to a period when the instrument witnessed unprecedented technical development and became very popular in a domestic context, especially for young women. Therefore, despite the fact that she learned the piano, an instrument that is also frequently mentioned in her works, the harp was certainly not unknown to Austen. In fact, she must have been immersed in the sounds and looks of the instrument, since at least two members of her family, with whom she spent a considerable amount of time, played the harp. The first was Eliza Hancock, formerly Comtesse de Feuillide (1761–1813), Austen's cousin and sister-in-law, while the second was Fanny Catherine Knight (1793–1882), Austen's niece, both of whom were accomplished harpists. [2] It is thus no coinci-

---

[1] Jane Austen, *Northanger Abbey: and Persuasion* (4 vols; London: John Murray, 1818), vol. 3, p. 114.

[2] For more details on the musical activities of Jane Austen and her family see David Selwyn, *Jane Austen and Leisure* (London and Rio Grande: The Hambledon Press, 1999), pp. 115–144, as well as Kathryn L. Libin, 'Daily Practice, Musical Accomplishment, and the Example of Jane Austen', in Natasha Duquette and Elisabeth Lenckos (eds), *Jane Austen*

dence that five of Austen's six published novels as well as many of her letters include references to the harp, as will be described below.

The harp already features in Austen's first novel *Sense and Sensibility* (1811), published in the same year that Sébastien Erard introduced his patent double-action harp in London. In this novel Elinor Dashwood, one of the protagonists, despite being 'neither musical, nor affecting to be so', does not fail to notice 'a grand pianoforte' as well as 'a harp, and a violoncello' at a musical party held by Mrs Dennison.[3] Interestingly, in a letter to her sister Cassandra written in 1811 Austen described a musical event organised by Eliza Hancock which may have been similar to that described in her novel, and which included a harp. Austen provided some details of the invited musicians, stating that 'one of the Hirelings, is a Capital on the Harp, from which I expect great pleasure',[4] a fact which indicates that by 1811 she was already familiar with the instrument and its music. The identity of the harpist Austen referred to is revealed in her next letter, in which she reported that 'Between the Songs were Lessons on the Harp, or Harp & Piano Forte together – & the Harp Player was Wiepart, whose name seems famous, tho' new to me.'[5] This must have been either John Erhardt Weippert (1776–1823) or his younger brother John Michael (1775–1831), both of whom were renowned players of the pedal harp.[6] As a young girl, Austen had probably heard other harp players, though not as prominent as Weippert: for example, as early as 25 July 1792 Jane and her family had been invited for lunch by the Hales family at Bekesbourne, where another guest, Penelope Cooke, 'played a great deal on the harp. All the Austens dined here likewise and it was very pleasant.'[7]

Austen also included a reference to the harp in her second and arguably most well-known novel, *Pride and Prejudice* (1813), in which during a discourse between the two main characters, Elizabeth Bennet and Fitzwilliam Darcy, the former asks the latter to 'tell your sister I am delighted to hear of her improvement on the harp'.[8] Austen is widely recognised as an author whose novels provide very sharp and accurate views of the tastes and customs of contemporary society, so the fact that she

---

   and the Arts: Elegance, Propriety, and Harmony (Bethlehem: Lehigh University Press, 2013), pp. 3–20.

3   Jane Austen, *Sense and Sensibility: A Novel* (3 vols; London: Thomas Egerton, 1811), vol. 2, p. 266.

4   Letter dated dated 18–20 April 1811, in Deidre Le Faye (ed.), *Jane Austen's Letters* (4th edn; Oxford and New York: Oxford University Press, 2011), p. 188.

5   Letter dated 25 April 1811, in Le Faye, *Jane Austen's Letters*, p. 191.

6   For more details on the Weipperts see Philip H. Highfill, Jr., Kalman A. Burnim and Edward A. Langhans, *A biographical dictionary of actors, actresses, musicians, dancers, managers & other stage personnel in London, 1660–1800* (Carbondale: Southern Illinois University Press, 1993), pp. 335–337. A 'Mr Weippert', presumably John Michael Weippert, is registered in the Erard ledgers as the purchaser in 1828 of Erard N° 2875, a single-action harp built in 1820; see Erard London Harp Ledgers, vol. 2, p. 151.

7   Quoted in Deidre Le Faye, *A Chronology of Jane Austen and Her Family: 1700–2000* (Cambridge: Cambridge University Press, 2006), p. 147.

8   Jane Austen, *Pride and Prejudice: A Novel* (3 vols; London: Thomas Egerton, 1813), vol. 1, p. 104.

includes learning the harp in the education of upper-class Georgiana Darcy provides more evidence of the instrument's elevated status in Regency Britain. It is worth noting that the harp citation in *Pride and Prejudice* is evoked in a letter by Austen to her niece, Fanny Knight, dating from 1814 in which Austen reported that 'Miss Lloyd came, as we expected, yesterday, & desires her Love. – She is very happy to hear of your learning the Harp.'[9] This example further indicates that Austen's fiction was largely based on incidents occurring within her close family circle and that the harp was not employed arbitrarily in her works.

However, it is in Austen's third novel, *Mansfield Park* (1814), that the harp is used not just to represent musical activity, but plays a major role in the book's plot. Here one of the female heroines, Miss Mary Crawford, is having her harp sent from London to the country house where she stays in order to continue her regular practice upon the instrument. Rather arrogantly Mary insists that the instrument should be transported as soon as possible with a cart, even though she is informed that it may be difficult 'in the middle of a very late hay harvest, to hire a horse and a cart'[10] as these are needed by the local farmers, leading her brother Henry to offer 'to fetch it in his barouche'.[11] The harp's arrival is eagerly anticipated by Edmund Bertram, who apparently being aware of the harp's popularity in London society, 'spoke of the harp as his favourite instrument, and hoped to be soon allowed to hear her', as well as by Fanny Price, who, living in the countryside and being cut off from the latest fashions, 'had never heard the harp at all, and wished for it very much'.[12] The following quotation is indicative of the attributes with which the harp represented an idealised, predominantly feminine image in the eyes of Austen's contemporaries:

> Miss Crawford's attractions did not lessen. The harp arrived, and rather added to her beauty, wit, and good-humour; for she played with the greatest obliging-ness, with an expression and taste which were peculiarly becoming, and there was something clever to be said at the close of every air. Edmund was at the Parsonage every day to be indulged with his favourite instrument: one morning secured an invitation for the next; for the lady could not be unwilling to have a listener, and every thing was soon in affair train. A young woman, pretty, lively, with a harp as elegant as herself, and both placed near a window, cut down to the ground, and opening on a little lawn, surrounded by shrubs in the rich foliage of summer, was enough to catch any man's heart. The season, the scene, the air, were all favoura-ble to tenderness and sentiment.[13]

The harp in *Mansfield Park* has highly symbolic connotations, being the object around which Mary Crawford, Edmund Bertram and Fanny Price, three persons of

---

[9] Letter dated 18–20 November 1814, in Le Faye, *Jane Austen's Letters*, p. 293.

[10] Jane Austen, *Mansfield Park: A Novel* (3 vols; London: Thomas Egerton, 1814), vol. 1, p. 119.

[11] Austen, *Mansfield Park*, vol. 1, p. 121. On the portability of Mary Crawford's harp and its possible connection to Erard see John Wiltshire, 'Exploring Mansfield Park: In the Footsteps of Fanny Price', *Persuasions* 28 (2006), pp. 81–100, at pp. 85–87.

[12] Austen, *Mansfield Park*, vol. 1, p. 121.

[13] Austen, *Mansfield Park*, vol. 1, p. 133.

different temperaments and moral values, interact in various scenes of the novel.[14]
It has been suggested that in Austen's era the harp was 'a complex cultural object,
resonant with multiple meanings, some of them mutually contradictory'.[15] The harp
was 'at once considered to be the most ancient and the most modish of instruments',
acting as 'a symbol of both romantic "primitivism" and urbane sophistication', while
being 'associated with virtuous people as well as less-than-virtuous ones'.[16]

Austen's decision to arm Mary Crawford with the harp as a means of attraction
and seduction was well grounded. Like Georgiana Darcy, she belonged to the higher
strata of society, and her education and taste, if not her manners, needed to follow
the prevailing trends, one of which was playing the harp. The harp's inclusion in the
upbringing of young ladies is revealed in another passage in *Mansfield Park*, when
during an inquiry about the musical skills of the three Miss Owens, Mary Crawford
states that 'two play on the piano-forte, and one on the harp – and all sing – or would
sing if they were taught – or sing all the better for not being taught – or something
like it.'[17] Likewise, in Austen's fourth novel, *Emma* (1816), the dialogue between Mrs
Elton and the young Jane Fairfax demonstrates that knowing how to play the harp
as part of a girl's musical training could be an important asset for positioning herself
favourably in social intercourse, eventually enabling upwards social mobility:

> … with your superior talents, you have a right to move in the first circle. Your
> musical knowledge alone would entitle you to name your own terms, have as
> many rooms as you like, and mix in the family as much as you chose; – that is – I
> do not know – if you knew the harp you might do all that, I am very sure; but you
> sing as well as play; – yes, I really believe you might, even without the harp, stipu-
> late for what you chose.[18]

Although not as important for the narrative as in *Mansfield Park*, the harp is nevertheless present in Austen's unfinished novel *Sanditon*, written in 1817, but edited
and published in 1925, more than a century after her death. In the seaside village
of Sanditon 'the sound of a harp', which 'might be heard through the upper case-
ment' of a baker's shop is considered as 'highly blissful' by Mr Thomas Parker, a
local inhabitant who seeks to gentrify Sanditon.[19] Lydia Beaufort, the eldest of the
fashion-conscious Beaufort sisters, who come to Sanditon on vacation, hires a harp
desiring 'praise and celebrity from all who walked within the sound of her instrument'.[20] On one occasion, the harp being rather 'an impediment' to her plans is
being 'magnanimously abandoned' in favour of a walk outside, although Charlotte

---

[14] For a comprehensive analysis of the harp's role in *Mansfield Park* see Jeffrey A. Nigro,
'"Favourable to Tenderness and Sentiment": The Many Meanings of Mary Crawford's
Harp', *Persuasions On-Line* 35/1 (available at http://www.jasna.org/persuasions/
on-line/vol35no1/nigro.html, published 2014, accessed 3 June 2022).

[15] Nigro, '"Favourable to Tenderness and Sentiment"'.

[16] Nigro, '"Favourable to Tenderness and Sentiment"'.

[17] Austen, *Mansfield Park*, vol. 2, p. 251.

[18] Jane Austen, *Emma: A Novel* (3 vols; London: John Murray, 1816), vol. 2, pp. 325–326.

[19] Jane Austen, *Sanditon* (New York: Simon and Schuster, 1998), p. 22.

[20] Austen, *Sanditon*, p. 67.

Heywood, who is visiting Sanditon as Mr Parker's guest, is later invited to the house where the Misses Beaufort reside to 'listen to the neglected harp'.[21] In another passage the addition of the harp to provide a fuller musical accompaniment is noted by Mr Parker's younger sister Diana during preparations for a local ball: 'Two violins, I said, were quite enough for a small Assembly – with the piano and violoncello as well; for I dare say there will be no more than sixteen couples. Now if we could have counted on twenty or twenty five, I might have added a harp –.'[22]

The harp is also mentioned in *Persuasion*, published posthumously in 1818 together with *Northanger Abbey*, one of Austen's earliest novels. It should be remarked that contrary to Austen's later novels, neither the harp nor the piano are mentioned in *Northanger Abbey*, which was completed in 1803; the only allusion to a musical instrument consists of 'the remains of a broken lute'.[23] This is not surprising, since during the late 1790s or early 1800s, when Austen wrote this novel, the popularity of the harp and piano was still relatively low in Britain. In contrast, *Persuasion*, which was Austen's last novel, was completed in 1817 when the harp and piano had become two of the most fashionable instruments.

In *Persuasion* the respectable Musgrove family owns both a piano and harp, played by their two daughters, Henrietta and Louisa. During a visit to their home, the novel's leading character, Anne Elliot, is invited to sit 'in the old-fashioned square parlour, with a small carpet and shining floor, to which the present daughters of the house were gradually giving the proper air of confusion by a grand piano forte and a harp, flower-stands and little tables placed in every direction'.[24] In one incident, the harp is employed to entertain the Misses Musgroves' mother, who feels depressed. After apologising for arriving late, Louisa, the youngest of the Miss Musgroves, states that she 'only came on foot, to leave more room for the harp, which was bringing in the carriage', adding that 'we agreed it would be best to have the harp, for it seems to amuse her more than the piano-forte.' (Figure 34).[25]

In another passage we are once again reminded of the significance of harp-playing as a female accomplishment, since Anne Elliot 'played a great deal better than either of the Miss Musgroves; but having no voice, no knowledge of the harp, and no fond parents to sit by and fancy themselves delighted, her performance was little thought of, only out of civility, or to refresh the others, as she was well aware'.[26]

Investigating Jane Austen's Links to Erard Harps

Despite the fact that Austen does not specify what type of harp her heroines played upon, it is most likely that they were performing on pedal harps, which by the begin-

---

[21]   Austen, *Sanditon*, pp. 135–136.

[22]   Austen, *Sanditon*, p. 237.

[23]   Jane Austen, *Northanger Abbey: and Persuasion* (4 vols; London: John Murray, 1818), vol. 2, p. 78.

[24]   Austen, *Northanger Abbey: and Persuasion*, vol. 3, pp. 90–91.

[25]   Austen, *Northanger Abbey: and Persuasion*, vol. 3, p. 114.

[26]   Austen, *Northanger Abbey: and Persuasion*, vol. 3, p. 106.

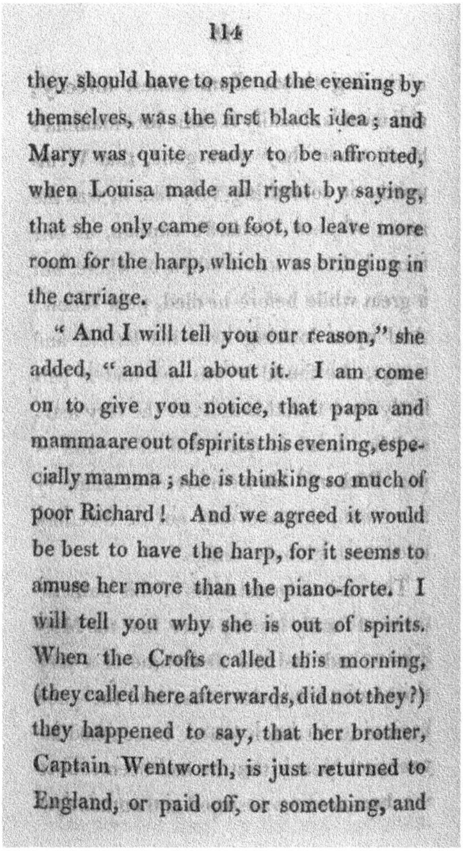

114

they should have to spend the evening by
themselves, was the first black idea ; and
Mary was quite ready to be affronted,
when Louisa made all right by saying,
that she only came on foot, to leave more
room for the harp, which was bringing in
the carriage.

" And I will tell you our reason," she
added, " and all about it. I am come
on to give you notice, that papa and
mamma are out of spirits this evening, especially mamma ; she is thinking so much of
poor Richard ! And we agreed it would
be best to have the harp, for it seems to
amuse her more than the piano-forte. I
will tell you why she is out of spirits.
When the Crofts called this morning,
(they called here afterwards, did not they?)
they happened to say, that her brother,
Captain Wentworth, is just returned to
England, or paid off, or something, and

Figure 34. Reference to the harp in the first edition of Jane Austen's novel *Persuasion*, published posthumously in London by John Murray in 1818.

ning of the nineteenth century were commonly used in Britain and which Austen must have witnessed first-hand at family gatherings and social events. As mentioned earlier, both her cousin Eliza Hancock and her niece Fanny Knight played the pedal harp; many harp pieces which may have been studied and performed by them are included among Austen's surviving music books.[27]

Most importantly, there is sufficient evidence to suggest that Austen was acquainted with Erard harps through her niece Fanny. In 1801 Edward Austen Knight (1768–1852), Fanny's father and the older brother of Jane, purchased Erard N° 369, a red single-action harp, most likely for his young daughter.[28] Ten years later Fanny wrote that she

---

[27] Jeanice Brooks, 'The Austen Family Music Books' (available at https://archive.org/details/austenfamilymusicbooks, published 2015, accessed 3 June 2022).

[28] Erard London Harp Ledgers, vol. 1, p. 93. Edward Austen Knight may have also bought a harp for Fanny from Erard in 1810, although this cannot be corroborated; see Le Faye, *A*

'was in ecstasies at hearing the Piano Forte Harp & Violin together' at her home,[29] while in 1814 she reportedly heard 'delicious harp music' during a visit to her friend Mary Oxenden (1794–1870).[30] This and similar events may have strengthened her motivation to commit to the harp, since in 1815 Fanny started taking harp lessons with 'Meyer', as repeatedly mentioned in her letters. This was either Philip James Meyer (1779–1849) or his brother Frederic Charles (1780?–1840), both of whom were celebrated harpists and harp teachers in London.[31] For instance, in 1815 Philip James Meyer was described as 'one of the most eminent harp professors now living'.[32] The Meyers had close personal and professional relations with the Erard family and are frequently mentioned in the surviving Erard ledgers and correspondence.[33]

Under Meyer's tuition Fanny's harp-playing intensified; on 14 April 1815 she noted: 'Had Meyer for the harp'[34] and, almost a week later, 'Meyer in the afternoon'.[35] A month later, Fanny's learning the harp even prevented her from meeting some visitors: she stated, 'I was taking my Harp lesson & did not see them.'[36] Jane Austen, who seemed to have disapproved of music teachers, described Meyer in rather negative terms:

> Mr. Meyers gives his three Lessons a week – altering his days & his hours however as he chuses, never very punctual, & never giving good Measure. – I have not Fanny's fondness for Masters & Mr. Meyers does not give me any Longing after them. The truth is I think, they are all, at least Music Masters, made of too much consequence & allowed to take too many Liberties with their Scholar's time.[37]

On 20 November 1815 Fanny informed her aunt that 'A Harp arrived fm. Chapels and Mr. Meyer gave my first lesson';[38] the new instrument must have been used a few days later when Jane reported that Fanny played 'from 7 to 8 the Harp'.[39]

    Chronology of Jane Austen and Her Family, p. 377.

[29] Letter dated 24 May 1811, in Le Faye, *A Chronology of Jane Austen and Her Family*, p. 404.

[30] Quoted in Margaret Wilson, *Almost Another Sister: The Family and Life of Fanny Knight, Jane Austen's Favourite Niece* (Canterbury: Kent Arts and Libraries, 1990), p. 23.

[31] For more details on the Meyers see Highfill, Kalman and Langhans, *A biographical dictionary of actors, actresses, musicians, dancers, managers & other stage personnel in London*, pp. 208–209.

[32] Elizabeth Appleton, *Private Education; or a Practical Plan for the Studies of Young Ladies. With an Address to Parents, Private Governesses, and Young Ladies* (London: Henry Colburn, 1815), p. 164.

[33] For more details see L 99, 22 September 1814, in Robert Adelson, Alain Roudier, Jenny Nex, Laure Barthel and Michel Foussard (eds), *The History of the Erard Piano and Harp in Letters and Documents, 1785–1959* (Cambridge: Cambridge University Press, 2015), pp. 549–550.

[34] Letter dated 14 April 1815, in Le Faye, *A Chronology of Jane Austen and Her Family*, p. 502.

[35] Letter dated 20 April 1815, in Le Faye, *A Chronology of Jane Austen and Her Family*, p. 504.

[36] Letter dated 3 May 1815, in Le Faye, *A Chronology of Jane Austen and Her Family*, p. 505.

[37] Selwyn, *Jane Austen and Leisure*, p. 128.

[38] Letter dated 20 November 1815, in Le Faye, *A Chronology of Jane Austen and Her Family*, p. 520.

[39] Letter dated 25 November 1815, in Le Faye, *Jane Austen's Letters*, p. 313.

This information is significant because like the Meyers, the firm Chappell & Co were professionally associated with Erard, as evidenced in the Erard ledgers and correspondence. A few months before Fanny received her harp, Pierre Erard had informed his uncle about offering a discount of 25% on harps sold to Clementi & Co.[40] Furthermore, in 1818 Chappell & Co published studies composed by Robert Nicolas-Charles Bochsa for Erard's double-action harp, as discussed in Chapter Five.[41] In addition, more than 50 Erard harps were sold to Chappell & Co in the 1810s and 1820s.[42] Therefore, it is possible that the harp sent by Chappell & Co to Austen's niece was built by Erard.

It is worth noting that until 1815, when Fanny was sent her harp, Chappell & Co had bought only four Erard harps, all of which were single-action instruments. However, considering the above-mentioned business arrangement, Chappell & Co, who were prominent music sellers and publishers, could have easily procured a double-action harp from Erard upon a client's request. Moreover, since Fanny already owned and played a single-action Erard harp, the new harp upon which she had her 'first lesson' on 20 November 1815 was presumably a double-action harp, perhaps recommended by her teacher, as was often the case with Erard customers. If this is the case, Austen's niece exemplified a large number of Erard's clients, who typically started out on the older single-action harp, but later moved on to Erard's new double-action model.

Fanny's approval of Erard double-action harps is further indicated by the fact that her husband, Sir Edward Knatchbull (1781–1849), who married Fanny in 1820, purchased Erard N° 3052, a double-action harp, in 1821. However, the harp may have been ordered not for Fanny, but for her younger sister Cassandra Jane (1806–1842), since 'Miss Cassandra Knight' is written under Knatchbull's name.[43] Another double-action harp, Erard N° 2367, which according to the Erard Ledgers had been sold in 1817 to 'Miss Alcock', is listed as 'Now Mrs Henry Austen'.[44] Henry Austen, Jane's older brother, had been married to his cousin, the harpist Eliza Hancock, who died in 1813. Since Erard N° 2367 was made around 1817, it was not purchased for Eliza, but presumably for Eleanor Jackson, Henry's second wife, who he married in 1820, suggesting that the harp was bought after this date.

[40] L 129, 17 January 1815. Adelson et al, *The History of the Erard Piano and Harp*, pp. 581–582, at p. 581.

[41] Robert Nicolas-Charles Bochsa, *Forty Studies Expressly Composed for Sebastian Erard's Double Movement Harp* (London: Chappell & Co, 1818). The studies are briefly mentioned by Pierre Erard in L 221, 24 April 1818. Adelson et al, *The History of the Erard Piano and Harp*, pp. 678–680, at p. 679.

[42] Erard London Harp Ledgers, vol. 2, pp. 36–278. The earliest transaction between Erard and Chappell & Co concerned Erard N° 1837, a single action-harp sold on 2 July 1813, while the latest regarded Erard N° 4114, a double-action harp sold on 28 April 1828.

[43] Erard London Harp Ledgers, vol. 2, p. 168.

[44] Erard London Harp Ledgers, vol. 2, p. 100.

Sir Walter Scott and his Connection to Erard Harps

As has been pointed out, 'Jane Austen's lifetime could be described as the Golden Age of the Harp';[45] this is confirmed by the strong presence of the harp in the literary works of her contemporaries. One renowned author whose writings contain many references to the harp is Sir Walter Scott (1771–1832). The harp is mentioned, for instance, in his poem *The Lady of the Lake* (1810),[46] as well as in several scenes of his historical novels *Waverley* (1814) and *Ivanhoe* (1820). For example, in *Waverley*, Flora, the sister of a highland chieftain, accompanies her enchanting singing with a harp,[47] while in *Ivanhoe* the Black Knight, discovering a harp in the hermit's possession, claims 'I see a weapon there (here he stooped and took out the harp) on which I would more gladly prove my skill with thee, than at the sword and buckler.'[48]

Scott was certainly aware of the harp's association with femininity, as he mockingly asks in the introduction of *Waverley* 'if I had rather chosen to call my work a "Sentimental Tale", would it not have been a sufficient presage of a heroine with a profusion of auburn hair, and a harp, the soft solace of her solitary hours, which she fortunately finds always the means of transporting from castle to cottage'.[49] Instead, Scott's use of the harp in his fiction is symbolic of ancient cultures and traditions and, from this viewpoint, quite different to Austen's, whose novels mirrored the habits and trends of contemporary British society. Yet, as in Austen's case, the harp, and more specifically the pedal harp, must have been a familiar object in Sir Walter Scott's home, since both of his daughters, Sophia (1799–1837) and Anne (1803–1833), were talented harpists. Playing the harp was an everyday pastime especially for Sophia, leading her younger sister to complain that 'Sophia is rather too much with her harp', adding, 'I wish she would take example of old times and hang it up.'[50]

Although there is no evidence for what kind of harp Sophia played as a young girl, we know that after her marriage she owned Erard Nº 2914, a double-action harp now housed at Abbotsford, The Home of Sir Walter Scott (Inv. No. T. AT. 1784) (Figure 35). This harp was purchased for her in 1820 by her husband, John Gibson Lockhart (1794–1854), presumably as a wedding present.[51]

This must have been the harp Sophia played upon as a married woman to entertain the family's guests, as described in an account by the poet William Wordsworth (1770–1850), who visited Scott in 1831, one year before he died:

---

45 Nigro, '"Favourable to Tenderness and Sentiment"'.

46 Walter Scott, *The Lady of the Lake: A Poem* (Edinburgh: John Ballantyne & Co, 1810).

47 Walter Scott, *Waverley; or, 'Tis Sixty Years Since* (3 vols; Edinburgh: John Ballantyne & Co, 1814), vol. 1, pp. 340–347.

48 Walter Scott, *Ivanhoe: A Romance* (3 vols; Edinburgh: Archibald Constable, 1820). vol. 2, p. 39.

49 Scott, *Waverley*, vol. 1, p. 6.

50 William Eric Kinloch Anderson (ed.), *The Journal of Sir Walter Scott* (Edinburgh: Canongate, 1998), p. xl.

51 Erard London Harp Ledgers, vol. 2, p. 154. I am grateful to Kirsty Archer-Thompson for providing me with information about the two Erard harps at Abbotsford, The Home of Sir Walter Scott.

Figure 35. Erard Nº 2914, the double-action harp built in 1820 that Sophia Scott, the eldest daughter of Sir Walter Scott, owned and played. Abbotsford, The Home of Sir Walter Scott (Inv. No. T. AT. 1784).

In the evening Mr. and Mrs. Liddell sang, and Mrs. Lockhart chanted old ballads to her harp; and Mr. Allan, hanging over the back of a chair, told and acted odd stories in a humorous way. With this exhibition, and his daughter singing, Sir Walter was much amused, and indeed, were we all, as far as the circumstances would allow.[52]

That Scott must have enjoyed the sounds of the harp is proven by the fact that in 1817 he had purchased Erard N° 2408, also a double-action harp, either for Sophia or for Anne, his youngest daughter.[53]

Moreover, Erard N° 3478, a yellow double-action harp which was sold on 2 December 1823 to a 'Mr Jobson', is registered in the Erard ledgers as 'now Mr Walter Scott'.[54] This suggests that Scott had acquired the harp after 1823, most likely for Anne, who remained unmarried and continued living with her parents. Thus, like Austen, Scott himself had frequently seen and heard Erard harps in his household and it is reasonable to assume that the inclusion of harps in his fiction may have been inspired by the Erard harps his two daughters played upon.

A Powerful Allegory: The Harp in the Literature of the Romantic Era

Apart from Austen and Scott, whose literary implementation of the harp can be to some extent attributed to Erard harps, many other writers of the Romantic era have employed the harp in its various representations in their works. Given the international reputation and clientele of the Erard firm, which in Europe extended from Dublin to Moscow and from Copenhagen to Naples, it is not unlikely that some of them had Erard instruments in mind when they referred to harps in their texts.

One book that is most relevant to the discussion of the harp as a vehicle of female expression and display is *The Wanderer* by Frances Burney (1752–1840), published in 1814, the same year as Austen's *Mansfield Park* and Scott's *Waverley*. It has been argued that the appearance of the harp in each of these three novels 'reveals some of the diverse cultural assumptions surrounding the instrument'.[55] In *The Wanderer*, which reflects the difficulties of those occupied in the music business in the decades either side of 1800, the harp has a central role as the instrument with which the heroine, Juliet Granville, strives to gain financial and social independence working as a harp teacher and performer.[56] Under a double identity as Ellis, Juliet gradually wins

52 Christopher Wordsworth, *Memoirs of William Wordsworth. Volume 2* (Cambridge: Cambridge University Press, 2014), p. 234.

53 Erard London Harp Ledgers, vol. 2, p. 104.

54 Erard London Harp Ledgers, vol. 2, p. 211.

55 Nigro, "'Favourable to Tenderness and Sentiment'".

56 Gillen D'Arcy Wood, *Romanticism and Music Culture in Britain, 1770–1840: Virtue and Virtuosity* (Cambridge: Cambridge University Press, 2010), pp. 56–57. For a discussion of Juliet's situation as a female musician see also Joseph Morrissey, *Women's Domestic Activity in the Romantic-Period Novel, 1770–1820: Dangerous Occupations* (Basingstoke: Pallgrave Macmillan, 2018), pp. 75–128.

the approbation of her audience by performing firstly on the piano and then on the harp, the instrument which she has mainly practised and which also allows her to demonstrate her singing skills:

> they soon learnt that she played also upon the harp; Lord Melbury instantly went forth in search of one; and it was then, as this was the instrument which she had most particularly studied, that Ellis completed her conquest of their admiration; for with the harp she was prevailed upon to sing; and the sweetness of her voice, the delicacy of its tones, her taste and expression, in which her soul seemed to harmonize with her accents, had an effect so delightful upon her auditors, that Mrs. Howel could scarcely find phrases for the compliments which she thought merited; Lord Melbury burst into the most rapturous applause; and Lady Aurora was enchanted, was fascinated.[57]

However, in the less talented hands of Juliet's pupils the harp could quickly expose handicaps and limitations; as is scornfully pointed out, the harp, 'because it shews beauty and grace to advantage, is often erroneously chosen for exhibiting those who have neither; as if its powers extended to bestow the charms which it only displays'.[58] For example, having listened to Sir Lyell Sycamore remarking that 'nothing added so much grace to beauty as playing upon the harp', the vain Miss Brinville, aiming to seduce him, decides 'to sit at the harp', an activity which 'became her principal study; and the glass before she tried her attitudes and motions, told her such flattering tales, that soon she began to think the harp the sweetest instrument in the world and that to practise it was the most delicious of occupations' even though 'she had total ignorance of music and a native dull distance to all the arts, save the millinery'.[59] The various scenes in which the harp is involved in Burney's novel illustrate 'the dichotomy between two contradictory images of the harp – worldly and superficial on the one hand, intimate and profound on the other'.[60]

The harp is mentioned in several books by Mary Wollstonecraft Shelley (1797–1851), another significant author of the Romantic era. Although in *Frankenstein* (1818), her first and most famous novel, it is not the harp, but the guitar that introduces Frankenstein's monstrous creature to the sounds of music,[61] the harp features prominently in Wollstonecraft Shelley's second novel *Mathilda*, written between 1819 and 1820, but published in 1959. For Mathilda, the novel's protagonist, who was urged by her aunt to learn the harp when she was a young girl, the harp gradually becomes 'a companion' and her 'only friend':

---

57 Frances Burney, *The Wanderer; or, Female Difficulties* (5 vols; London: Longman, Hurst, Rees, Orme and Brown, 1814), vol. 1, pp. 255–256.

58 Burney, *The Wanderer*, vol. 2, p. 87.

59 Burney, *The Wanderer*, vol. 2, pp. 100–101.

60 Pierre Dubois, *Music in the Georgian Novel* (Cambridge: Cambridge University Press, 2015), p. 258.

61 For references to the guitar in *Frankenstein* see Mary Wollstonecraft Shelley, *Frankenstein; or, The Modern Prometheus* (3 vols; London: Lackington, Hughes, Harding, Mavor & Jones, 1818), vol. 2, pp. 47–48, 51, 70, 74–75.

> When I was twelve years old it occurred to my aunt that I ought to learn music;
> she herself played upon the harp. It was with great hesitation that she persuaded
> herself to undertake my instruction; yet believing this accomplishment a neces-
> sary part of my education, and balancing the evils of this measure or of having
> some one in the house to instruct me she submitted to the inconvenience. A harp
> was sent for that my playing might not interfere with hers, and I began: she found
> me a docile and when I had conquered the first rudiments a very apt scholar. I had
> acquired in my harp a companion in rainy days; a sweet soother of my feelings
> when any untoward accident ruffled them: I often addressed it as my only friend;
> I could pour forth to it my hopes and loves, and I fancied that its sweet accents
> answered me. [62]

In Mathilda's narration the harp has a comforting, healing purpose, as she mentions
that 'I had besides many books and a harp with which when despairing I could
soothe my spirits, and raise myself to sympathy and love.'[63] It is worth mentioning
that the therapeutic qualities of harp playing are also remarked in French literature
of the early nineteenth century.[64]

Brief references to the harp are also included in Wollstonecraft Shelley's later
novels, such as *Valperga* (1823),[65] *The Last Man* (1826),[66] *Perkin Warbeck* (1830)[67]
and *Lodore* (1835).[68] Wollstonecraft Shelley's familiarity with the harp is further
revealed in one of her letters. Writing from Italy to Mrs Hunt in 1822 she observed
about her acquaintance with Jane Williams (1798–1884), who was a skilled harpist:
'I look forward to many duets with this lady and Hunt. She has a very pretty voice,
and a taste and ear for music which is almost miraculous. The harp is her favourite
instrument; but we have none, and a very bad piano.'[69]

As in the case of Wollstonecraft Shelley's *Mathilda*, the harp is a 'constant companion' for Ellinor St. Clare, a secondary character in *Glenarvon* (1816), a novel by
Lady Caroline Lamb (1785–1828).[70] Written about her relationship with George
Gordon Byron (1788–1824), better known as Lord Byron, this novel is, however,
more interesting for two other aspects relating to the harp. The first is that contrary
to the usual gendered pattern of portraying the harp as an accessory of female allure,
here it is a male harpist, Glenarvon, an Irish rebel, who seduces Calantha with his

---

[62] Mary Wollstonecraft Shelley, *Mathilda* (Auckland: The Floating Press, 2010), p. 33.

[63] Wollstonecraft Shelley, *Mathilda*, p. 97.

[64] See Eve Zaunbrecher, *An Enlightened Instrument: The Design, Education, and Sociability of
the Single Action Pedal Harp in Ancien Régime Paris, 1760–1789* (MA Diss., London: Royal
College of Art, 2016), pp. 112 and 115.

[65] Mary Wollstonecraft Shelley, *Valperga: or, The life and adventures of Castruccio, prince of
Lucca* (3 vols; London: G. and W. B. Whittaker, 1823).

[66] Mary Wollstonecraft Shelley, *The Last Man* (3 vols; London: Henry Colburn, 1826).

[67] Mary Wollstonecraft Shelley, *The Fortunes of Perkin Warbeck, a Romance* (3 vols; London:
H. Colburn and R. Bentley, 1830).

[68] Mary Wollstonecraft Shelley, *Lodore* (3 vols; London: R. Bentley, 1835).

[69] Letter dated 5 March 1822, in Julian Marshall, *The Life & Letters of Mary Wollstonecraft
Shelley* (2 vols; London: Richard Bentley & Son, 1889), vol. 1, p. 332.

[70] Caroline Lamb, *Glenarvon* (3 vols; London: Henry Colburn, 1816), vol. 3, p. 9.

harp-playing and singing.[71] Moreover, in *Glenarvon* the instrument is spoken about with nationalistic overtones, since it is maintained that 'the harp means Ireland',[72] an association which is frequently reflected in nineteenth-century Irish literature.[73]

Lamb's lover Lord Byron himself used the harp metaphorically in several of his lyrical works, such as 'The Harp the Monarch Minstrel Swept' or 'By the Rivers of Babylon We Sat Down and Wept' from *Hebrew Melodies*, a collection of poems published in 1815.[74] Although the adoption of the harp was probably due to its biblical association as King David's preferred instrument, Byron may have been equally inspired by the pedal harps he experienced through his interactions with London's aristocratic circles. For instance, in 1814, one year before the publication of the above-cited poems, Byron must have seen and heard an Erard double-action harp when he was invited to dine with Charles Grey (1764–1845), 2nd Earl Grey and future Prime Minister of the United Kingdom (1830–1834). Byron reported that 'the same evening I met Lawrence, the painter, and heard one of Lord Grey's daughter (a fine, tall spirit-looking girl, with much of the *patrician thorough-bred look* of her father, which I dote upon) play on the harp, so modestly and ingenuously, that she *looked music*.'[75] The harp that Byron heard that evening was most likely Erard No 1668, a double-action harp that Earl Grey had purchased in 1813, presumably for his daughter.[76] It is also noteworthy that Lawrence, the artist that Byron met during this dinner, painted several portraits of female harpists, with some depicting Erard instruments, as mentioned in the previous chapter.

Although the harp was employed by esteemed writers such as Austen, Burney, Scott or Byron, the instrument occasionally found its way into the less refined literature of the time. For example, the harp was included in the scandalous memoirs of Harriette Wilson, a celebrated London courtesan mentioned in the previous chapter, whose patrons included several eminent personalities from the Duke of Wellington to Lord Byron himself. Published in 1825, Harriette's memoirs created a shocking sensation, as they provided 'behind-the-scenes' glimpses into the sensual lifestyle and habits of polite society in Regency London. In one passage Harriette describes her visit to the house of Mrs Julia Johnstone, a Lady, stating that 'when I entered her drawing-room at the hour she had appointed, I was struck with the

---

[71] This is reminiscent of the often erotic relationship between a male harp teacher and his female pupil, as highlighted in the scandalous French novel *Dangerous Liaisons* (original title *Les Liaisons Dangereuses*) by Pierre Choderlos de Laclos, published in 1782.

[72] Lamb, *Glenarvon*, vol. 2, p. 370.

[73] For a discussion of the harp's role in the propagation of Irish nationalism in the nineteenth century see Julie Donovan, *Sydney Owenson, Lady Morgan and the Politics of Style. Irish Research Series 55* (Bethesda, Dublin and Palo Alto: Academica Press, 2009), pp. 89–130. For an overview of the harp within the social, political and cultural landscape of nineteenth-century Ireland see Mary Louise O'Donnell, *Ireland's Harp: The Shaping of Irish Identity c.1770–1880* (Dublin: University College Dublin Press, 2014).

[74] George Gordon Byron, *Hebrew Melodies* (London: John Murray, 1815), pp. 5–6, 44–45.

[75] Fitz-Greene Halleck (ed.), *The Works of Lord Byron, in Verse and Prose, Including his Letters, Journals, etc. with a Sketch of his Life* (New York: G. Dearborn, 1833), p. 252.

[76] Erard London Harp Ledgers, vol. 2, p. 30.

elegant taste, more than with the richness of the furniture. A beautiful harp, draw-ings of a somewhat voluptuous cast, elegant needle-work, Moore's poems, and a fine pianoforte, formed a part of it.'[77]

In another passage, which underlines the theatrical potential of the harp, Harriette maintains that 'there was something dramatic about Julia. I often surprised her, hanging over her harp so very gracefully, the room so perfumed, the rays of her lamp so soft, that I could scarcely believe this tout ensemble to be the effect of chance or habit. It appeared arranged for the purpose like a scene in a play.'[78] Harriette must have been familiar with Erard instruments, since her younger sister Sophia, Lady Berwick, owned Erard N° 2524, a Grecian harp, and took lessons with Bochsa, one of the main ambassadors of Erard's double-action harps, as described in the previous chapter.

References to the harp abound in the works of Charles Dickens (1812–1870), an author known for his intense study of human character and society as well as for his humour and satire. In his first novel, *The Pickwick Papers*, Samuel Pickwick, an affluent gentleman who is exploring provincial England, is dancing feverishly to the music provided by 'the two best fiddles, and the only harp, in all Muggleton'.[79] In *A Christmas Carol* (1843) we learn that 'Scrooge's niece played well upon the harp; and played among other tunes a simple little air (a mere nothing: you might learn to whistle it in two minutes)',[80] while in *Dombey and Son* (1848) a male figure, Dr Blimber, as well as two female characters, Edith Skewton and her mother, perform on the harp in different occasions and with diverse motivations.[81] Two female harp-ists also appear in *David Copperfield* (1850), the first being Miss Larkins, who enter-tains visiting officers by playing on the harp, the second being Rosa Dartle, who uses her harp to accompany her singing of an Irish song for James Steerforth.[82]

The image of the harp as a symbol of both female accomplishment and sexual attraction pertained to the literature of the early Victorian period. Published in the late 1840s, but describing the customs of English society at the time of the Battle of Waterloo (1815), *Vanity Fair* (1848) by William Makepeace Thackeray (1811–1863) portrays the harp as a powerful weapon of female seduction. The author lists various common activities of young girls, asking 'What causes them to labour at piano-forte sonatas, and to learn four songs from a fashionable master at a guinea a lesson, and to play the harp if they have handsome arms and neat elbows, and to wear green

---

[77] Harriette Wilson, *The Memoirs of Harriette Wilson: Written by Herself* (2 volumes; London: Eveleigh Nash, 1909), vol. 1, p. 26.

[78] Wilson, *The Memoirs of Harriette Wilson*, vol. 1, p. 29.

[79] Charles Dickens, *The Posthumous Papers of the Pickwick Club* (London: Chapman & Hall, 1837), p. 293.

[80] Charles Dickens, *A Christmas Carol. In Prose. Being a Ghost Story of Christmas* (London: Chapman & Hall, 1843), p. 110.

[81] Charles Dickens, *Dombey and Son* (London: Bradbury & Evans, 1848), pp. 144, 208, 210, 278 and 279.

[82] Charles Dickens, *The Personal History of David Copperfield* (London: Bradbury & Evans, 1850), pp. 191, 306 and 307.

Lincoln Green toxopholite hats and feathers, but that they may bring down some "desirable" young man with those killing bows and arrows of theirs?'[83]

Just as the harp's elegant image was 'supposed to represent the conventions of polite society and domestic harmony',[84] its distortion highlighted tensions in human relationships. This is vividly illustrated in *Helen* (1834) by the Irish novelist Maria Edgeworth (1767–1849). In one dramatic scene Helen, the protagonist, is driven into an embarrassing situation by Cecilia, her long-time friend, when Cecilia conceals the truth about her being the real author of some love letters erroneously attributed to Helen. The breaking of two strings while the bewildered Helen tunes her harp shortly after this incident indicates the breaking of trust between her and her friend, further underlined by Helen's mechanical, passionless performance once the harp has been restrung and retuned.[85]

In the conservative, restrictive environment of the Regency and Victorian periods, social interaction, especially for young girls, frequently focused around instruments such as the harp or piano. This is shown, for example, in *Jane Eyre: An Autobiography* (1847) by Charlotte Brontë (1816–1855), in which the heroine, Jane Eyre, excluded 'from every enjoyment' finds delight in 'listening to the sound of the piano or harp played below' in the drawing room by her cousins Eliza and Georgiana Reed.[86] The harp is the preferred instrument of Julie Karagina, a wealthy heiress in *War and Peace* (1869) by Leo Tolstoy (1828–1910), which provides a thorough description of Russian society during the Napoleonic Wars. During a social event hosted by the Rostovs, a noble family in Moscow, Julie performed 'a little air with variations on the harp' when 'the young people, at the countess' suggestion, gathered round the clavichord and harp',[87] whereas in a later scene she 'played most doleful nocturnes on her harp' for her husband Boris Drubetskoy.[88] The harp belonging to the Rostov household must have been used for the music education of young Natasha Rostova. However, having heard 'Uncle', a Russian peasant, performing on the guitar, she 'resolved to give up learning the harp and to play only the guitar'.[89] In another passage Mr Dimmler, a musician employed by the Rostovs, is asked by the countess Natalya Rostova 'to play a nocturne by Field' on a harp 'that stood there in a corner' – perhaps Natasha's neglected harp – and which 'gave out a jarring sound' when its cloth covering was removed.[90]

---

[83] William Makepeace Thackeray, *Vanity Fair: A Novel without a Hero* (London: Bradbury & Evans, 1848), p. 17.

[84] Dubois, *Music in the Georgian Novel*, p. 240.

[85] Maria Edgeworth, *Helen, a Tale* (3 vols; London: Richard Bentley, 1834), vol. 3, pp. 13–16.

[86] Charlotte Brontë, *Jane Eyre: An Autobiography* (3 vols; London: Smith, Elder & Co., 1847), vol. 1, p. 43.

[87] Leo Tolstoy, *War and Peace* (first published 1869; trans. from Russian by Louise and Aylmer Maude; Chicago, London and Toronto: Encyclopædia Britannica Inc., 1952), p. 35.

[88] Tolstoy, *War and Peace*, p. 311.

[89] Tolstoy, *War and Peace*, p. 290.

[90] Tolstoy, *War and Peace*, p. 295.

Finally, it is important to mention that the harp was frequently used as a metaphor not only for the natural, but also the supernatural world. This may be mainly due to the Aeolian harp, a stringed instrument which sounds with the aid of wind and which was eminent in the poetry and prose of the late eighteenth and early nineteenth centuries.[91] Within this context it is not surprising that the harp was inserted in early horror fiction, such as the *Walled-up Door* (original title *Das Majorat*, published in 1817), a short story by Ernst Theodor Amadeus Hoffmann (1776–1822). Secluded in a gloomy castle, the pretty baroness Seraphine states that 'I play pretty well on the harp; but that is a pleasure of which I must deprive myself here, for my husband detests music'.[92] The dreadful absence of music at the castle, exemplified by the lack of a harp, is temporarily remedied by the acquisition of a rather dysfunctional harpsichord from a nearby village. However, according to the baron, this instrument, and music-making in general, is thought to be detrimental for Seraphine's health, as she falls ill after playing upon it.

Conclusions

As evidenced by the countless examples included in many classic works cited in this chapter, the harp in its various representations played a significant role in the literature of the Romantic era. For many authors the harp was considered an indispensable accessory of female culture, acting as a sign of refined upbringing and intellectual cultivation. Moreover, the harp was perceived not only as a rewarding pastime but also as a steady companion for young girls growing up in the austere environment of Regency and Victorian Britain. Furthermore, the harp was seen as an effective means of female allure and seduction, enabling its players to display their musical skills as well as their beauty and elegance. Additionally, the harp was employed as an allegory for diverse concepts, ranging from gender identity, rank and social class, to historicism and nationalism, and even to spiritualism. Although not explicitly stated, pedal harps, and Erard harps in particular, may have been the source of inspiration for several writers who had experienced these instruments at their homes or at social events, as evidenced by the cases of Jane Austen, Sir Walter Scott and Lord Byron. In the next chapter we will examine the importance of the Erard harp as an artefact of cultural heritage, discussing the acquisition, preservation, documentation and exhibition of surviving Erard Grecian harps in public and private collections around the world.

---

[91] For an overview of the Aeolian harp and its use in literature see Kilian Jost, '"Daß Harmonie in der Natur tief gegründet (…) zeigt uns ganz besonders auch die Aeolsharfe". Eine vergessene akustische Ausstattung des frühen Landschaftsgartens', *Die Gartenkunst* 26/2 (2014), pp. 201–208.

[92] Ernst Theodor Amadeus Hoffmann, *Hoffmann's Strange Stories* (trans. from German by Burnham Brothers; Boston: Burnham Brothers, 1855), p. 125. Interestingly, Hoffmann also referred to the Aeolian harp in his short story *The Automata* (original title *Die Automate*), published in 1814.

CHAPTER EIGHT

The Erard Grecian Harp as an Artefact of Cultural Heritage: 'Self-destruction' and Resurrection

'repairs, and repairs of rented harps […] are considerable, because after five or six years the harps naturally wear out'[1]

Erard Nº 2631, the Grecian harp in the collection of the Deutsches Museum, is one of around 300 Erard Grecian harps known to have survived to date. As a musical instrument produced by the firm of a prominent inventor and manufacturer during a groundbreaking time for the development of musical instruments and music in Europe, it is an object of great organological and musicological value, especially because it is in relatively good condition and in its original state. However, this harp is also an important document of historical significance. As already described in the previous chapters, this instrument is a witness of several changes that took place in the late eighteenth and early nineteenth centuries on a musical, technological, aesthetic, economic, political, social, intellectual and cultural level. In addition, with its allocation to a museum through a process of cultural assessment and selection, as well as with its documentation, conservation and exhibition, this harp adopted a new identity. Therefore, what once had been a common, replaceable sounding device, began a new life as a distinguished historical object primarily for study and display. Focusing on Erard Nº 2631 and similar harps, this chapter will examine the transformation of Erard harps from functional instruments into artefacts of cultural heritage, discussing the challenges and opportunities regarding their preservation, display and use in public and private collections.

Acquisition, Distribution and Survival Rate of Erard Grecian Harps

Recent research on surviving Erard harps around the world during the preparation of this book has shown that Erard Nº 2631 is the earliest double-action harp surviving in a public collection in Germany. The instrument was purchased by the Deutsches Museum in 1908 for 500 M (German Marks) from J. W. Auerbach, an antique dealer at Wilhelmstrasse 94, Berlin (Figure 36).[2]

---

[1]   L 330, 8 March 1822, in Robert Adelson, Alain Roudier, Jenny Nex, Laure Barthel and Michel Foussard (eds), *The History of the Erard Piano and Harp in Letters and Documents, 1785–1959* (Cambridge: Cambridge University Press, 2015), pp. 794–795, at p. 795.

[2]   Letter dated 29 October 1908, Deutsches Museum, Munich, Archive, DMA VA 1755.

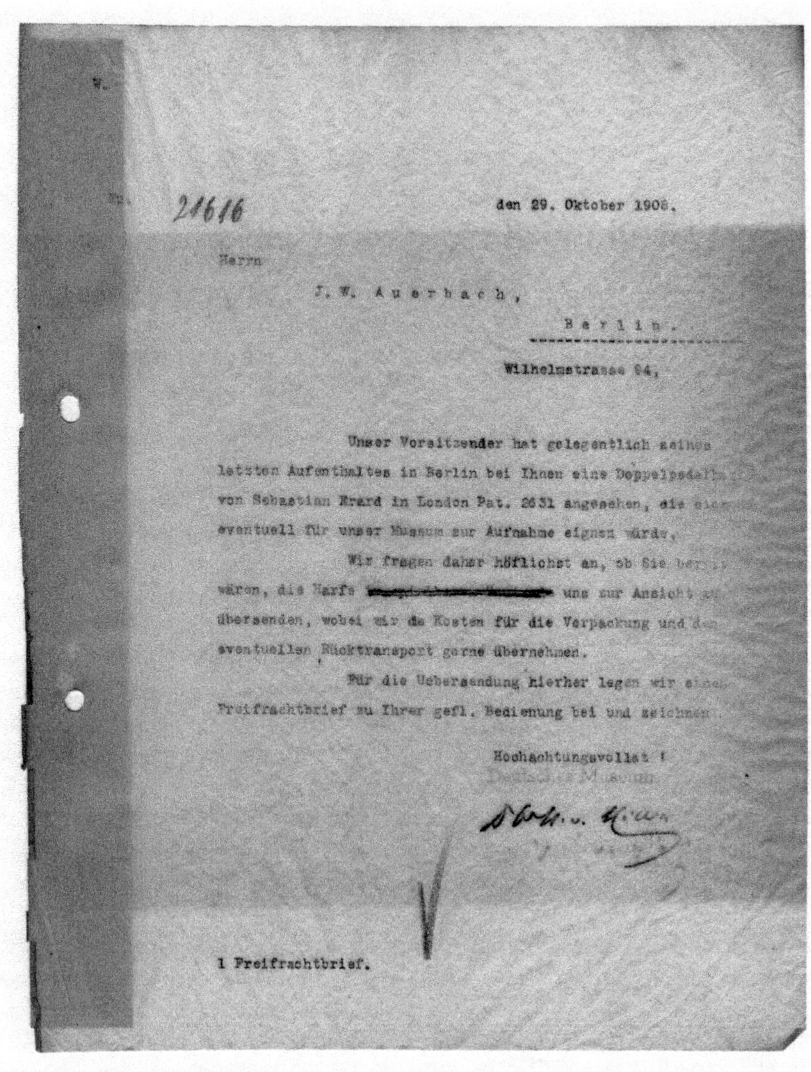

Figure 36. Letter dated 29 October 1908 regarding the acquisition of Erard N° 2631. Deutsches Museum, Munich, Archive, DMA VA 1755/1.

The acquisition history of this harp is related to a 'wish list' of musical instruments that the Deutsches Museum had prepared and published in 1905 shortly after its foundation.[3] According to the 'wish list' the museum desired to acquire a pedal harp in the form of an original instrument (i.e. not a copy, a model or a drawing).[4] Considering its unconventional acquisition through a 'wish list', the history of Erard N° 2631 is therefore different to that of many other Erard harps that ended up in museums mainly through donations or purchases during the late nineteenth and early twentieth centuries, when several major collections of musical instruments were established in Europe and North America.

Interestingly, Erard N° 2631 was the first double-action harp in the collection of the Deutsches Museum, but the second pedal harp, since in 1906 the museum had acquired an unsigned single-action harp.[5] The Erard harp was mentioned briefly in the guide of a provisional exhibition in Munich (c.1909) as 'Doppelpedalharfe nach Erhard'.[6] Erard N° 2631 was on display probably from 1925, when the present museum building was opened to the public (Figure 37), and until 2003; a technical description of the instrument had also been included in a museum catalogue published in the late 1990s.[7] In 2004 the harp was moved into storage, where it was examined by the author about ten years later, in 2013, during preparations for a new permanent exhibition of musical instruments at the Deutsches Museum as part of the museum's larger renovation project. This consequently led to new research, conservation, publication and exhibition activities concerning the instrument.

Erard N° 2631 is also one of the relatively few London-made Erard Grecian harps housed in a public collection worldwide. At the time of writing around 300 of these harps have been identified by the author, dispersed across 16 countries in four continents around the world (for more details see Appendix). These include, in alphabetical order, Australia, Austria, Belgium, Canada, Czech Republic, Finland, France, Germany, Italy, Japan, Netherlands, Spain, Sweden, Switzerland, UK and USA. Out of the c.300 listed extant instruments, only 67 belong to public institutions, such as

---

3   For more details on the 'wish list' see Panagiotis Poulopoulos, *New Voices in Old Bodies: A Study of 'Recycled' Musical Instruments with a Focus on the Hahn Collection in the Deutsches Museum. Deutsches Museum Studies 2* (Munich: Deutsches Museum, 2016), pp. 52–53.

4   See item 'i) Pedalharfe', section 'C. Saiteninstrumente. I. Zupfinstrumente mit freistehenden Saiten. 22. Entwicklung der Harfe', in 'Liste wünschenswerter Sammlungsgegenstände aus dem Gebiete des Musikinstrumentenbaues für das Deutsche Museum in München', *Zeitschrift für Instrumentenbau* 26/15 (1906), pp. 441–475, at p. 457, Nr. 22.

5   For more details see 'Inv. Nr. 6724. Pedalharfe mit einfacher Rückung und Zugrückenmechanik. Frankreich, ca. 1780/1790', in Bettina Wackernagel, *Europäische Zupf- und Streichinstrumente, Hackbretter und Äolsharfen. Deutsches Museum München. Musikinstrumentensammlung Katalog* (Frankfurt am Main: E. Bochinsky & Deutsches Museum, 1997), p. 182.

6   I am grateful to Silke Berdux for providing me with this information as well as for bringing to my attention other sources relating to the history of Erard N° 2631 since its acquisition by the Deutsches Museum.

7   Wackernagel, *Europäische Zupf- und Streichinstrumente, Hackbretter und Äolsharfen*, pp. 184–185.

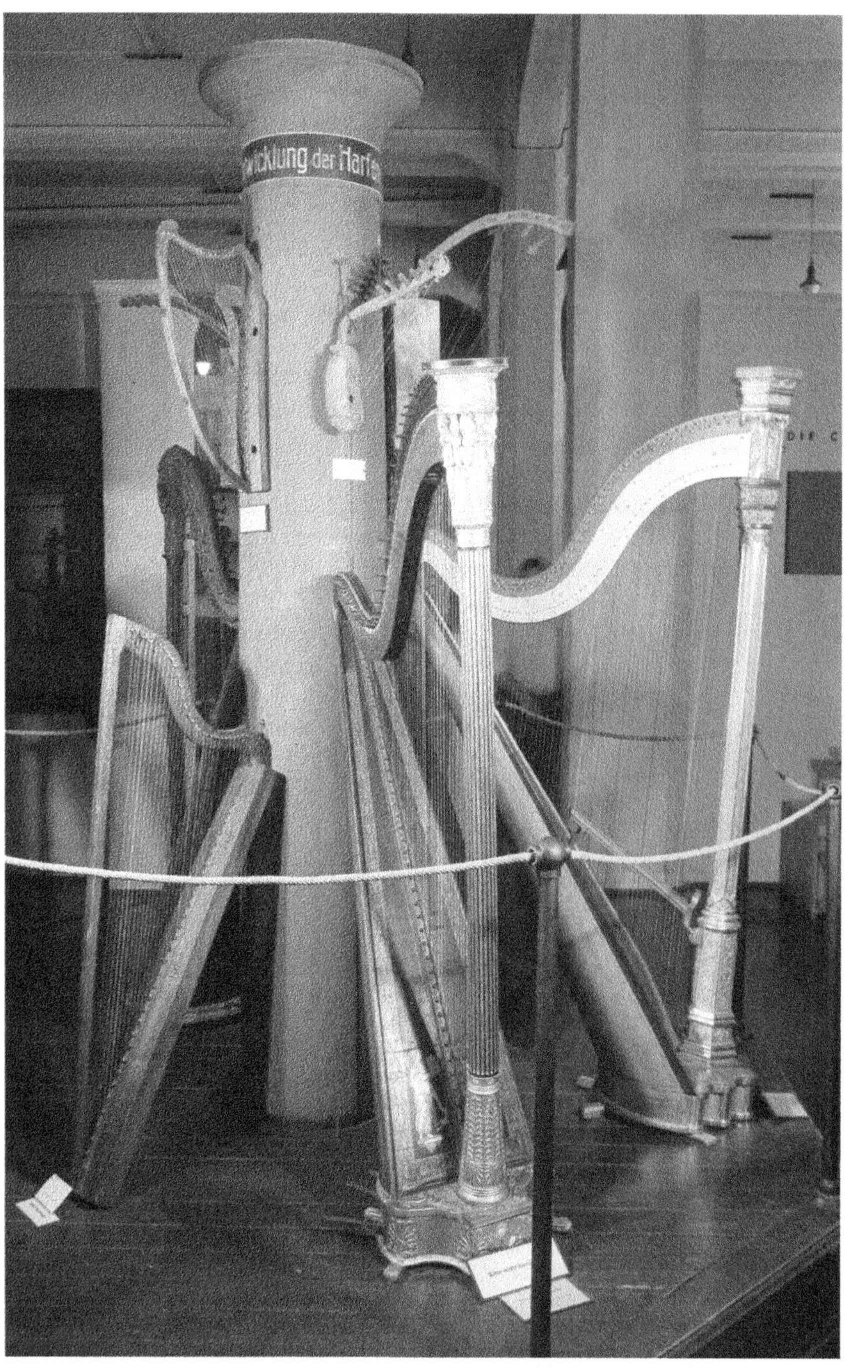

Figure 37. Erard N° 2631 (centre) displayed among other harps in an exhibition at the Deutsches Museum, Munich; the photograph dates probably from the early to mid-twentieth century and certainly before 1974. Deutsches Museum, Munich, Archive, L3102-13.

museums, universities or conservatoires, whereas the rest are in private collections. Among those harps in public institutions, about half (35) are kept in regional or city museums and historic houses, 24 in music or musical instrument museums, five in art museums and three in museums of science and technology. It is worth noting that very few public institutions or private owners have more than one Erard Grecian harp in their collection, a fact that makes the identification and comparison of these harps quite difficult.

On the other hand, the fact that Erard used a single numbering sequence for harps enables the quite accurate calculation of the survival rate for the firm's Grecian model. Since about 3,500 harps of this model were built by Erard in London from 1811 to c.1845, the c.300 known extant specimens indicate a survival rate of approximately 8.5%. In comparison, less than 60 harps produced by or attributed to the Naderman firm in Paris from the 1760s to the 1830s are known to have survived, although the firm must have built several hundreds or thousands of instruments.[8] However, the diverse numbering systems applied to Naderman harps do not allow for estimations of the survival rate for this firm.

The high survival rate of Erard Grecian harps can be explained by the fact that, in contrast to single-action harps, such as those manufactured by Naderman, they were more adaptable to new musical demands because of their double-action mechanism. Additionally, due to their decorative character, some of these harps may have been kept as pieces of furniture and were not destroyed even after they could not be played and had become obsolete. It is, nevertheless, worth noting that the percentage mentioned above is not uniform and can differ from year to year of production. For example, a survey for the year 1818, when Erard Nº 2631 was built, shows a similar survival rate of 10%, since out of 160 double-action harps produced by Erard in London that year, 16 harps are known to have survived. In contrast, in 1821 Erard made 180 double-action harps, out of which only 11 are known to have survived, indicating a lower survival rate of about 6%.

The Preservation of Erard Harps: Restoration and Conservation Approaches

The condition of preservation and the state of authenticity of surviving Erard Grecian harps is quite diverse. A few of them have remained untouched for decades, being in good, stable condition and retaining their original features intact, while others are in a fragile condition and bear inauthentic parts from various repairs and restorations that have occurred during their lifetime. The most obvious non-original material concerns strings as well as small movable components, such as tuning pins, endpins and screws, which can be easily lost during restringing or during adjustments to the pedal mechanism. Moreover, on numerous Erard harps, major struc-

---

[8]	Extant instruments by Naderman are listed in Klaus-Peter Brenner, *Die Naderman-Harfe in der Musikinstrumentensammlung der Universität Göttingen. Ein französisches Instrument des 18. Jahrhunderts als Maschine, Skulptur, Möbel, Prestigefetisch, Ware und Klangwerkzeug. Orbis Musicarum 14* (Göttingen: Edition Re, 1998), pp. 80–91, as well as in Beat Wolf, *Harp Archives* (Schaffhausen: Wolf, 2016), 330 Naderman 30 and 330 Naderman 31–33.

tural components, such as the soundboard, the neck or the pedalbox, as well as parts of the pedal mechanism, have been replaced due to irretrievable damage of the wood or the metal, as will be described below.

Like other historical instruments, many Erard Grecian harps have been maintained in or restored to playing condition. Several of these harps bear inscriptions on the back of the soundboard, inside the soundbox or inside the pedalbox, which point to restoration work carried out during the end of the nineteenth and the beginning of the twentieth centuries, when these instruments were already out of fashion, as they had been superseded by Erard's Gothic model, but were still considered worth preserving. These inscriptions may include names, places and dates pointing to a restorer, dealer or customer associated with a harp's restoration or resale. For example, the quite descriptive inscription 'Restored by J Miller Leeds / Dec 1894' is written with ink on the back of the soundboard of Erard Nº 4153, whereas on Erard Nº 3070 the only evidence indicating its restoration or purchase is the date '1896' written with pencil inside the pedalbox. Likewise, the repair of Erard Nº 1747 is evidenced by the words 'Repaired 1913 / M Coombs' written with pencil inside the soundbox, while the detailed inscription 'May 8th 1910 glasnevin / Irene Mc Kee', written with pencil on the back of the soundboard of Erard Nº 2672, allows for a precise dating of a transaction related to restoration or resale (Figure 38). In contrast, the name 'Celentano' and the inscription 'bgA 99', which are written inside the soundbox of Erard Nº 4534, are less informative.

A number of Erard Grecian harps reveal traces of uninformed restoration processes that took place more recently. The treatment of some of these harps during the last decades, when the demand for playable historical harps increased due to the early music revival, has often included the intentional application of historically inaccurate or incompatible materials and techniques, often with limited documentation of the procedures. Such restoration approaches have usually aimed to make antique objects, in this case pedal harps, capable of withstanding the operational standards of their modern equivalents, usually leading to the distortion or loss of original material. For example, the soundboard of Erard Nº 4534 was replaced during restoration in the early 1990s with a new, thicker soundboard, complemented by the addition of thicker bracing inside the soundbox. This affected the vibroacoustic behaviour of the instrument considerably, as it resulted in a much stiffer construction compared to the original, a fact that was proven when this harp was compared to other Erard harps retaining their original soundboards.[9]

In addition, Erard Grecian harps have been harmed over the years mainly from wrong stringing and tuning. This is largely due to the use of modern harp strings,

9   Panagiotis Poulopoulos, Marisa Pamplona, Luise Richter and Niko Plath, 'Conservation Issues on Historical Pedal Harps: Preserving Tangible and Intangible Properties', in Pascale Vandervellen (ed.), *Preservation of Wooden Musical Instruments: Ethics, Practice and Assessment. Proceedings of 4th Annual Conference of the COST Action FP1302 WoodMusICK* (Brussels: Muziekinstrumentenmuseum, 2017), pp. 69–72, at pp. 70–71. An early version of this article had been presented by the authors at the 4th annual conference of the COST Action FP1302 WoodMusICK (Wooden Musical Instrument Conservation and Knowledge), 'Preservation of Wooden Musical Instruments: Ethics, Practice and Assessment', Muziekinstrumentenmuseum, Brussels, 5 to 7 October 2017.

Figure 38. Details of inscriptions written on the back of the soundboard of two Erard Grecian harps. Left: Inscription 'Restored by J Miller Leeds / Dec 1894' on Erard N° 4153. Private collection, Germany. Right: Inscription 'May 8th 1910 glasnevin / Irene Mc Kee' on Erard N° 2672. Muziekinstrumentenmuseum, Brussels (Inv. No. 3952).

which have very different properties to those of the strings which would had been used originally, and which can have detrimental effects on historical harps. For example, modern bass strings usually consist of metal wound over a core of metal wire rather than of silk threads, as would be typical for bass strings in the early nineteenth century. Stringing with modern strings and tuning these harps to modern pitch, which is usually higher than that to which they were historically tuned, can increase the overall tension applied to an instrument and potentially cause severe damage to the soundboard, column and neck, calling for intrusive restoration measures.[10]

Another situation where invasive treatments have been used concerns the strengthening and static support of the wooden structure due to damage from woodworm attack. Because Erard harps were built using different types of wood, woodworm damage may have impaired only selected areas or components of a harp, leaving others unaffected. For example, woodworm had caused heavy damage only to the pedalbox of Erard N° 1945, housed at Hospitalfield, Arbroath, which was eventually replaced during a recent restoration of the instrument, whereas its soundbox, column and neck remained largely intact.[11] A further issue demanding drastic intervention concerns the retrieval of the mechanism's functionality. The pedal mechanism consists of numerous functional metal parts which may have stuck together and become immovable due to long periods of inactivity and the drying

---

[10] Rainer Thurau, 'Die Harfenmechanik Erards – ihre Funktion und Restaurierung', in Rudolf Frick (ed.), *Sébastien Erard: ein europäischer Pionier des Instrumentenbaus. Internationales Erard-Symposium Michaelstein 13.–14. November 1994, Michaelsteiner Konferenzberichte 48* (Blankenburg: Stiftung Kloster Michaelstein, 1995), pp. 28–29, at p. 29.

[11] For more details see 'Hospitalfield Harp Renovation', https://www.crowdfunder.co.uk/hospitalfield-harp-renovation, accessed 3 June 2022.

of lubricants, as well as the accumulation of dust and dirt.[12] Equally problematic and visually disturbing are metal surfaces that have become rusty after continuous exposure to high levels of humidity and the presence of corrosive elements in the environment in which a harp is stored.

Apart from alterations to a harp's structural or mechanical parts, restoration has often been accompanied with changes to the original decoration. For instance, the neoclassical ornaments on the capital of Erard Nº 3916, a harp bearing evidence of restoration kept at the Musikinstrumentenmuseum der Universität Leipzig, Leipzig (Inv. No. 4801), are different and less intricate compared to those normally found on Erard Grecian harps, while on Erard Nº 3574, housed at the Czech Museum of Music, Prague (Inv. No. E 1994), which bears the inscription 'Restored by J. George Morley, Harp Maker from Erard: / 6, Sussex Place, South Kensington London' on its neck, the ornaments on the capital and base of the column have been completely eliminated.

In some cases, Erard Grecian harps have been transformed into artworks or display pieces. One representative example is the 'O Ruin'd Harp', a sculpture consisting of Erard Nº 3264, a double-action harp in poor condition, upon the neck of which a taxidermy owl has been attached. The description of the object reads: 'The large and fine stuffed and mounted barn owl (Tyto alba) specimen with DOE and Cites certificate, spread-eagled amidst landing upon a distressed Regency period ebonised and giltwood and gesso harp by Sebastian Erard, maker by special appointment to his Majesty and the royal family.'[13] In this rather extreme case, the character of the object has been radically changed from a musical instrument to a collectible artistic item for display.[14]

Although several copies of eighteenth-century single-action pedal harps have been produced in the past in order to satisfy the growing need amongst musicians for these instruments,[15] until now there have been no known attempts to build copies of Erard Grecian harps. This may be due to the large number, availability and

---

[12] According to harp maker and restorer Beat Wolf, the first requests for repairs by the owners of new harps he builds are received on average 12–14 years from their manufacture, when parts of the mechanism may start to malfunction because of the drying of the lubricants. See Beatrix Darmstädter, Rudolf Hopfner and Alfons Huber (eds), *Die Sammlung alter Musikinstrumente / The Collection of Historic Musical Instruments - Die ersten 100 Jahre / The First 100 Years* (Vienna: Praesens, 2018), p. 419.

[13] For more details see 'O Ruin'd Harp, Unique', https://www.doeandhope.com/products/o-ruin-d-harp-unique, accessed 3 June 2022.

[14] It is important to note that apart from their depiction in numerous contemporary paintings, Grecian harps by Erard or other makers have also inspired modern artworks, such as the sculpture *Nicador's Nightmare* (1983) by Fernandez Arman (1928–2005), auctioned by Bonham's at New York on 14 May 2013 (lot 86). For more details see 'Nicador's Nightmare', https://www.bonhams.com/auctions/20945/lot/86/, accessed 3 June 2022. In addition, Grecian harps have been frequently used as props in films and television series, particularly those based on classical novels, from Stanley Kubrick's *Barry Lyndon* (1975) to Joe Wright's *Pride and Prejudice* (2005).

[15] See, for example, Beat Wolf, 'The Louis XVI–Harp' (available at https://www.harpspectrum.org/historical/wolf_long_updated.shtml, published 2009, accessed 3 June 2022).

constant circulation of these harps in the market, which enables harpists interested in historically informed performance to acquire original Erard instruments at reasonable prices. There are, however, some previously unnoticed but quite important aspects of Erard harps which are useful to know about before these instruments are put back in playing condition and which will be discussed in detail below.

'Self-destructive' and Unconventional Elements of Construction

A noteworthy feature of Erard Grecian harps concerns several 'self-destructive' and unconventional elements of construction, which often render their return to functioning order unwise and risky. For instance, a common problem with these harps is that the area at the end of the neck near the shoulder is structurally weak. On many extant Erard harps the wood has developed cracks or has broken exactly on this spot, a phenomenon that may have been accelerated on instruments which at some point were strung with modern strings of higher tension.

Interestingly, the Erard firm was aware of this issue. In 1819 Pierre Erard asked his uncle: 'Could we not give more strength to the neck, by continuing the metal plate and having it rest directly on the top part of the body? Does the gluing at the end of the neck, near the body, still come apart in India or other humid places?'[16] A few months later he repeated his question, writing: 'I still wanted to ask you if you believe that there would not be some way to have the plates rest on the body in such a way as to prevent the neck from cracking, something that always happens in precisely the spot where the plate is screwed. Near the heel, the screws weaken the wood and make it split.'[17] This damage is clearly demonstrated on Erard N° 3908, in the collection of The Fitzwilliam Museum, Cambridge (Inv. No. M.9-1941), on which the wood has split at the end of the brass plate near the shoulder (Figure 39).[18]

Another typical issue that can be observed on Erard Grecian harps is the formation of an arching or 'belly' at the bottom of the soundboard due to the tension of the bass strings, which pull the soundboard wood upwards. The arching of the soundboard in combination with the sinking of the neck due to the applied string force can cause considerable changes to the intonation of the harp, since the scaling (the vibrating string length) is shortened.[19] The sensitivity of the soundboard, which on Erard Grecian harps is quite thin, measuring from about 2 to 6 mm from treble to bass, probably explains why many of these harps were returned to the firm for a soundboard replacement, as will be described later. Additionally, several harps have horizontal cracks at the bottom end of the soundboard where it meets the pedalbox, which again can be attributed to the pulling force of the bass strings. These cracks

---

[16] L 251, 2 March 1819. Adelson et al, *The History of the Erard Piano and Harp*, pp. 708–710, at p. 709.

[17] L 264, 9 July 1819. Adelson et al, *The History of the Erard Piano and Harp*, pp. 723–724, at p. 724.

[18] For more details see 'Grecian harp', https://collection.beta.fitz.ms/id/object/77348, accessed 3 June 2022.

[19] Thurau, 'Die Harfenmechanik Erards – ihre Funktion und Restaurierung', p. 29.

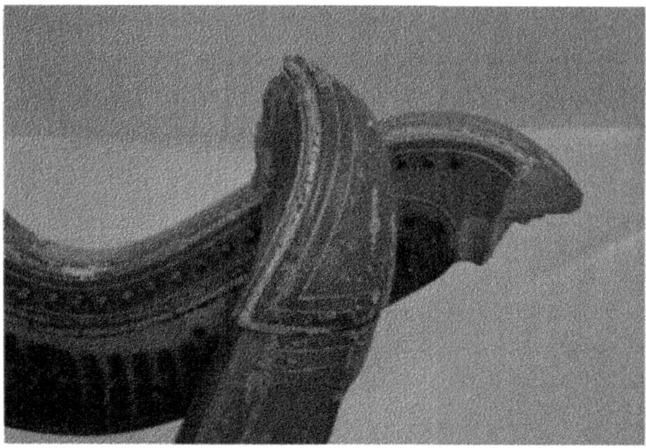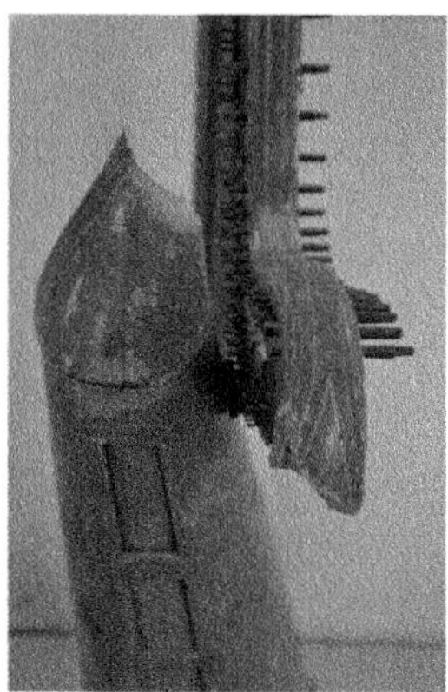

Figure 39. Detail of the damage on the shoulder of Erard N° 3908, built in 1826. The Fitzwilliam Museum, Cambridge (Inv. No. M.9-1941).

have developed even on harps with a new soundboard, like Erard N° 4534, the restoration of which was mentioned above.

A further inherent construction characteristic which can be mistaken for damage, but which was a deliberate design feature, is a torsion of the column towards the right side from the player's position, evident particularly when the strings are slack. In order to counteract the pulling force of the strings, which tend to move the column towards the left side, Erard intentionally built the column with a slight bend to the right of its vertical axis. This feature aimed to prevent the twisting of the column to the left under the high tension of the tuned strings, as was frequently observed on earlier harps. In an essay that Pierre Erard prepared in 1821 to promote his uncle's contributions to harp design, he stated that:

> On harps where the pillar is placed perpendicular to the horizon, all it takes is a slight variation of the neck of the harp made by the pull of the strings for the pillar to deviate from the centre point e, and as soon as it has moved from this point, it is powerless to stop it in opposition, so that it always tends to tilt towards the point f, as can be seen on older harps, and even on more recent harps built on this flawed principle. It is obvious that this defect would be much more evident if we removed the wood that connects the two metal plates, as they form a single firm and solid mass, while they would be subject to warping in different ways, following the contours of their curves, if they were not held strongly together, as on the neck of M. Sébastien Erard's harp.[20]

According to Pierre this design feature developed by his uncle 'rectified the warping of the pillar'.[21]

---

[20] L 297, 16 March 1821. Adelson et al, *The History of the Erard Piano and Harp*, pp. 763–767, at pp. 764–765.

[21] L 298, 30 March 1821. Adelson et al, *The History of the Erard Piano and Harp*, pp. 767–768, at p. 768.

As far as the mechanism is concerned, a common problem is that after several years of usage, and the resulting tension and friction, various spindles and bearings that secure mechanical parts, and the holes in which they are introduced, are worn out, requiring either the drilling of larger holes or the insertion of reams. This is essential in order to improve the attachment of movable parts on the brass plates and to prevent any unwanted noises when the vibration of strings is transferred onto parts that have become loose.[22] If a dismantling of the mechanism is necessary to allow basic maintenance or repair, it is advised to unscrew the mechanism, but not to open the two brass plates. With the mechanism is removed, the mechanical components enclosed between the two plates can then be adjusted, cleaned and oiled both from above and from below as well as from the outside. However, if opening the brass plates is unavoidable for further cleaning or repairs, only one plate should be removed at a time, leaving all mechanical components fixed on the other plate and vice versa.[23] The above-mentioned points should be taken into account in future conservation and restoration projects regarding Erard Grecian harps in order to assist the decision-making process and to prevent further damage.

Authorised Interventions: The Repair and Conversion of Erard Grecian Harps

Although many Erard Grecian harps have fortunately survived to date, they were clearly not made to last for 200 years. In fact, the average life expectancy of these instruments seems to have been less than a decade. As Pierre Erard characteristically stated in 1822, a significant amount of work at the Erard London branch concerned 'music stands, stools, repairs, and repairs of rented harps that are considerable, because after five or six years the harps naturally wear out'.[24] This is proven by various authorised interventions, such as repairs, adjustments or replacements that were carried out by the Erard firm and which can reveal significant information about how these harps were made and used.

A study of the Erard ledgers has shown that about one third of Grecian harps were repaired by the Erard firm at least once; some instruments were returned to the workshop for repair purposes several times. The most usual documented repair concerned the replacement of the soundboard. For example, Erard N° 1738, a black harp built c.1813 and sold in 1816, was hired to a new customer in 1832 after being

---

[22] Thurau, 'Die Harfenmechanik Erards – ihre Funktion und Restaurierung', p. 28.

[23] I am grateful to Beat Wolf for his remarks on the dismantling of the mechanism on Erard harps. For examples of recent conservation projects involving the removal of the mechanism of Erard harps see Sandra Walter, *Die Einfachpedalharfe 512 der Brüder Erard aus dem Couven-Museum Aachen: Untersuchungen zu Bestand, Zustand, historischer Kontextualisierung, sowie Durchführung der Konservierung, Restaurierung und Neubesaitung* (Diplomarbeit, Fachrichtung Konservierung und Restaurierung, Erfurt: Fachhochschule Erfurt, 2011), as well as Franziska Bühl, *Untersuchung einer Erard-Doppelpedalharfe von 1820–1825* (BA Diss., Studiengang Restaurierung, Kunsttechnologie und Konservierungswissenschaft, Munich: Technische Universität München, 2014).

[24] L 330, 8 March 1822. Adelson et al, *The History of the Erard Piano and Harp*, pp. 794–795, at p. 795.

'Thoroughly repaired with New Sound̃ Board'.[25] Likewise, Erard Nº 2235, a harp sold in 1816, was listed with 'New S. Board & thoroughly repaired' in 1837,[26] while Erard Nº 2494 was 'thoroughly repaired' in 1834, 'with new WSB' (SB referring to a soundboard) added in 1859.[27] Similar examples, which show that major repairs were often due after ten years of usage, include Erard Nº 2993, built and sold in 1820, on which 'a New S.B' was 'adjusted' in 1832,[28] and Erard Nº 3177, built and sold in 1821, on which a 'New Sounding Board' was added in 1831.[29]

A more drastic interference involving the replacement of the entire wooden structure was apparently required on Erard Nº 2888, a harp built and sold in 1820, that was 'thoroughly rep.ᵈ with new Frame' in 1833.[30] It is also worth mentioning that repairs to the soundboard were occasionally accompanied by a refinishing in a different colour. For example, Erard Nº 1643, a green harp sold in 1814 and now kept at the Scenkonstmuseet, Stockholm (Inv. No. M2281), was at some point returned to the workshop and was 'painted black with a new W.S.B.' before it was sold to a new client in 1824.[31] The inspection of this harp confirmed the presence of an original layer of green colour, which is visible on its neck and shoulder where the black coating has worn off.

Damaged harps that were sent back to Erard for repair were occasionally replaced by similar instruments by the firm, apparently to guarantee customer satisfaction, as evidenced by the case of Erard Nº 2245. The ledgers report that 'Lady Grey', who had purchased the harp in 1816, 'returned this Harp, the S.B. being cracked & she has instead of it Nº. 2284'.[32] Erard Nº 2245 was sold to a different customer in 1817, most likely after its cracked soundboard had been repaired. Interestingly, some repaired harps were sent to the British colonies, where customers may have been less discerning. For instance, Erard Nº 2392, a harp sold in 1817, was 'Thoroughly repaired and shipp'd for Calcutta in 1829 for Capᵗ G.R. Crawford of the Bengal Artillery.'[33]

The shipment of valuable, fragile goods, including harps, was preferred not only for distant destinations such as India, but also across Britain in order to avoid the usually slow and dangerous transportation through available road networks. This, however, did not prevent fatal accidents. Although several harps like Erard Nº 2631 were lucky enough to survive their 200ᵗʰ birthday, the fate of some other Erard harps was more dramatic. One notable example is Erard Nº 2641, a harp built in 1818, the same year as Erard Nº 2631. According to the ledgers the harp was 'sent to the house

[25] Erard London Harp Ledgers, Royal College of Music, London, Special Collections (RCM 497), vol. 2, p. 37.

[26] Erard London Harp Ledgers, vol. 2, p. 87.

[27] Erard London Harp Ledgers, vol. 2, p. 112.

[28] Erard London Harp Ledgers, vol. 2, p. 162.

[29] Erard London Harp Ledgers, vol. 2, p. 181.

[30] Erard London Harp Ledgers, vol. 2, p. 152.

[31] Erard London Harp Ledgers, vol. 2, p. 27.

[32] Erard London Harp Ledgers, vol. 2, p. 88.

[33] Erard London Harp Ledgers, vol. 2, p. 102.

for Repair by Lady D'Oley in 1830. It was afterwards shipped, and the vessel was wrecked. The Harp and Cargo were all lost.'[34]

Apart from repairs, another form of authorised intervention regarded the conversion of an Erard harp using a different pedal mechanism. For instance, Erard Nº 1377, the first ever double-action harp to be sold by Erard in 1811, was altered into a single-action instrument with a different serial number, Nº 2117, probably in the late 1810s; this is the only known specimen of such a conversion. The most common conversion involved the opposite procedure: single-action harps could be 'upgraded' with the addition of the double-action mechanism, rendered possible by the fact that, apart from the mechanism, the same model was used for both harp types, as mentioned in Chapter Five. This must have been a clever and profitable service offered by the Erard firm, because in a product catalogue from the late 1810s Erard listed single-action harps 'To which instruments the Double Movement can be introduced for £31. 10s'.[35]

As shown in the Erard ledgers, numerous harps which started life as single-action instruments were modified into double-action harps, usually a few years after their manufacture. One of the earliest examples is Erard Nº 1697, built as a single-action harp c.1813 and modified into a double-action probably around 1822, when it was sold to another customer, with the relative entry reading, 'The Double action has been introduced in the room of the Single movement'.[36] The same applied to two single-action harps built c.1814. On Erard Nº 1859 the workshop 'Introduced the D. M.' in 1816, while Erard Nº 1862 was 'altered to a DM harp of the same nº & the machine put on a new harp' around 1823.[37] Similar modifications are reported in the Erard ledgers for Erard Nº 1891, built c.1814 and converted in 1817,[38] and Erard Nº 2346, built in 1817 and converted in 1821.[39] These modifications reflect the technical obsolescence in the design of early pedal harps, which led to the gradual transition from the single- to the double-action harp in the late 1810s.

Erard Grecian Harps and Issues of Functionality: To Play or to Display?

The operation of functional historical objects is a complex, and often controversial, issue within the museum community. In the case of historical instruments,

---

34 Erard London Harp Ledgers, vol. 2, p. 127. Interestingly, the remains of a shipwrecked Erard Gothic harp, Erard Nº 5331, were used to establish the identity of the ship, together with the context of the cargo, on which this instrument was transported. For more details see Seerna Cant, 'The tale of a harp', https://thewreckoftheweek.wordpress. com/2018/10/23/musical-instruments-in-the-sea/, published 23 October 2018, accessed 3 June 2022.

35 Erard Harp Catalogue (London: Erard, c.1819–1821), University of Glasgow Archives & Special Collections, A.x.24.

36 Erard London Harp Ledgers, vol. 2, p. 33.

37 Erard London Harp Ledgers, vol. 2, p. 49.

38 Erard London Harp Ledgers, vol. 2, p. 52.

39 Erard London Harp Ledgers, vol. 2, p. 98.

including pedal harps, the most common question is whether to play them or not, often creating conflicts between professionals in the music and museum sectors. In the last decades it has been increasingly accepted that in order to protect historical evidence, any treatments regarding the conservation and playability of musical instruments need to take into account various criteria which may differ from one instrument to the other. This approach has already been adopted for a wide range of functional objects in museums of diverse profiles and missions. As has been recently argued: 'Music museums are clearly far from alone in facing the challenges, expectations and opportunities posed by the combination of preserving, interpreting and documenting functional objects. The policies and practices that ensue are a result of a cultural choice that reflects the balance between the focus on the material and many intangible values of the object',[40] which include, apart from its musical value, its value as a source in understanding historical instrument-making techniques or composing and performing practices.

A decision-making protocol resulting from the investigation of numerous case studies has been based on the consideration of three factors concerning a musical instrument. These include its rarity (e.g. how many specimens of an instrument of a particular model or by a particular maker survive worldwide?), its fragility (e.g. what is the condition of preservation of the instrument and is it structurally and operationally stable?) and its state (e.g. how original and intact is the instrument, or to what extent has it been transformed?).[41] The use of this protocol for Erard Grecian harps can help to evaluate the arguments for and against the playability of these instruments.

On the one hand, the rarity of Erard Grecian harps is low, since there is a relatively large number of extant specimens, some with identical features of construction and decoration. Additionally, the originality of Erard Grecian harps is medium, because many have been repaired or modified, either by Erard employees or by others during their historical usage. Moreover, the possibility of playing surviving Erard harps can provide new information on sound and performance practice, two aspects which are crucial for understanding the intangible characteristics of these instruments. These arguments could justify the preservation or restoration of these harps as functional objects.

On the other hand, the fragility of Erard Grecian harps is high, as the wooden parts on the neck and soundboard are quite sensitive, while the metal components of the pedal mechanism are delicate and difficult to repair or replace. Furthermore, only few of the extant Erard Grecian harps are housed in public collections (less than 20%), meaning that if several of these instruments are restored to playing condition, the pool of original, unaltered instruments which can be publicly accessible for future research by musicians, instrument makers and scholars will be drastically reduced. Besides, keeping the restored harps in playing condition and using them

---

[40] Gabriele Rossi Rognoni, 'Preserving Functionality: Keeping Artefacts "Alive" In Museums', in Eric de Visscher and Kathleen Wiens (eds), Special Issue 'Sonic', *Curator: The Museum Journal*, 62/3 (New York: Wiley, 2019), pp. 403–413, at p. 411.

[41] For more details see Robert Barclay, *The Preservation and Use of Historic Musical Instruments: Display Case and Concert Hall* (London: Earthscan, 2005), pp. 236–242.

for concerts, recordings and other events involves the constant maintenance, regulation and tuning of the instruments, as well as adequate performance spaces with controlled climate, not to mention skilled musicians with experience in performing on historical instruments. This in turn requires specialised personnel and facilities, which some public institutions cannot afford on a permanent basis.[42] These arguments could speak against the playability of these harps.

Bearing in mind the above-mentioned facts, a few practical guidelines can be proposed for Erard Grecian harps and similar instruments. As a rule, harps whose original features have been severely compromised by extensive restoration, and whose condition is fairly stable and predictable, could be played on certain occasions, provided they are regularly monitored to promptly detect any potential dangers. In addition, the stringing and tuning of these harps should pay attention to the strings and pitches used historically, and should be carried out carefully and progressively to prevent any mechanical shocks resulting, for instance, from sudden changes in string tension.[43] However, concerning the restoration and playability of specimens in their original, intact state, stricter policies should be imposed; the careful examination and assessment of each harp is necessary in order to avoid the risks of irreversible damage and loss. In any case, a balance between the historical and musical significance as well as between the tangible and intangible properties of these harps is required so that these artefacts can be appreciated and enjoyed by future generations.[44]

Final Observations

The Erard Grecian harp is an instrument whose significance as the predecessor of the modern concert harp is becoming increasingly acknowledged by scholars and the wider public. This is evidenced by several exhibitions,[45] restoration and conser-

---

[42] The arguments for and against the functionality of Erard Grecian harps have been discussed in Panagiotis Poulopoulos, 'Manufacture, Usage, Recycling, and the Concept of Functionality on Historical Objects', unpublished paper presented at the International Conference 'Playing and operating: functionality in museum objects and instruments', organised by ICOM, CIMCIM and CIMUSET, Cité de la Musique – Philharmonie de Paris, Paris, 4 to 6 February 2020.

[43] For an example of harp restoration accompanied with a detailed analysis of its stringing and tuning see Markus Raquet and Klaus Martius, 'Antoinettes zersplitterte Harfe', *Arbeitsblätter für Restauratoren* 32/2 (1999), pp. 169–186.

[44] The cultural value of historical harps, including Erard harps, was a key theme of the international workshop 'The Early Pedal Harp as a Museum Artefact: Research-Conservation-Presentation', organised by Panagiotis Poulopoulos at the Research Institute for the History of Science and Technology, Deutsches Museum, Munich, 29 and 30 November 2018.

[45] One example is the exhibition 'Erard and the Invention of the Modern Harp, 1811–2011', at the Musée du Palais Lascaris, Nice, 13 May to 17 October 2011. For more details see Robert Adelson, Laure Barthel, Michel Foussard, Jenny Nex and Alain Roudier (eds), *Erard and the Invention of the Modern Harp, 1811–2011* (Nice: Musée du Palais Lascaris, 2011).

vation initiatives,[46] academic dissertations,[47] research projects,[48] and recordings[49] which focus on Erard Grecian harps. Since several of these harps, especially those in private hands, can be played, they offer the unique opportunity to hear music composed during the time when Erard harps were made and used, being performed on authentic instruments. Consequently, this can bring modern audiences closer to the original soundscape of these harps, including aspects of volume, timbre, dynamics and even any noises that would be heard during their performance. For instance, the notes accompanying the recordings of Erard N° 3804, a double-action harp built in 1825, state:

> It is likely that only few people know the difference of sound between a modern harp and a historical double-action harp. The rich bass and the clear, brilliant descant of a 19th century double-action harp lead to even greater sound 'imbalances' than with a modern instrument. However, this contrasting world of sound of the old harp makes an important contribution to understanding works from this epoch, as through the original sound this repertoire sounds considerably more transparent and more richly facetted.[50]

But even when they are silent, Erard Grecian harps are spectacular objects that can be a magnet for museum visitors, both physical and virtual. Apart from their attractive visual features, many of these harps can reveal fascinating stories about their manufacture, usage and repurposing. This material can be employed in a variety of educational activities, such as lectures and demonstrations[51] and work-

---

[46] Two recent examples concern the restoration of harps Erard N° 1945 and Erard N° 2377. For more details of the first harp see 'Hospitalfield Harp Renovation', https://www.crowdfunder.co.uk/hospitalfield-harp-renovation, accessed 3 June 2022, while for the second harp see Gregory Weidman, 'Eliza Ridgely's historic Erard Harp', *American Harp Journal* 26/1 (2017), p. 52, and 'Restoration Project for Eliza Ridgely Harp', https://www.baltimoreharp.org/historic-eliza-ridgely-harp-restoration/, accessed 3 June 2022.

[47] See, for instance, Bühl, *Untersuchung einer Erard-Doppelpedalharfe* and Luise Eva-Maria Richter, *Fassungsuntersuchung der Doppelpedalharfe No. 2631 von Sébastien Erard aus dem Deutschen Museum München: Ein Beitrag zur Harfenforschung* (BA Diss., Studiengang Restaurierung, Kunsttechnologie und Konservierungswissenschaft, Munich: Technische Universität München, 2016).

[48] See, for example, Panagiotis Poulopoulos, 'Die frühe Pedalharfe als Symbol innovativer Verwandlung' ('The Early Pedal Harp as Symbol of Innovative Transformation'), https://www.deutsches-museum.de/forschung/forschungsinstitut/projekte/detailseite/die-fruehe-pedalharfe-als-symbol-innovativer-verwandlung, accessed 3 June 2022.

[49] See, for instance, Masumi Nagasawa, *Amuse: Music for single and double action harp from the Age of Enlightenment & Romanticism* (CD recording with booklet; Lummen: Etcetera Records, 2004); Floraleda Sacchi, *Sophia Giustina Corri: Works for Solo Harp* (CD recording with booklet; Bologna: Tactus, 2009); and Elisabeth Plank, *1825: Echoes of Vienna on Historical Harp* (CD recording with booklet; Vienna: Gramola, 2019). Several music pieces in these three works have been recorded on Erard Grecian harps, Erard N° 3972, N° 2219 and N° 3804, respectively.

[50] Plank, *1825: Echoes of Vienna on Historical Harp*, p. 15.

[51] For instance, aspects of multipedalling techniques on single- and double-action harps were demonstrated by harpist Maria Christina Cleary on an Erard Grecian harp during her lecture 'Harmonic Changes in Music of the Classical Era: The Example of the Pedal

shops,[52] as well as in innovative digital media, such as virtual exhibition tours, videos and podcasts,[53] facilitating discovery and knowledge about museum collections and their objects. For instance, Erard N° 2428, a Grecian harp built c.1817 that had been kept in storage for decades, was displayed for the first time after its restoration in the temporary exhibition 'Georgians: the Pride and the Prejudice' at the Worcester City Art Gallery & Museum (2020); the placement of the instrument next to a contemporary dress aimed to juxtapose the harp with other artefacts from the same era and place, enabling a broader understanding of their usage and purpose (Figure 40).

Furthermore, the implementation of new technologies and novel presentation concepts[54] can enable museums to exhibit these harps from diverse perspectives, making them more appealing to a broader audience.[55] For instance, the display and contextualisation of these harps not only as musical instruments, but as symbolic objects

---

Harp', presented at the Montagskolloquium 'Klangforschung im Museum' (Monday colloquium 'Sound Research in the Museum'), Deutsches Museum, 15 May 2017.

[52] For example, Erard N° 2631 was one of three representative study objects during the interactive workshop 'Das Exponat im Fokus: Objekt-basierte Forschung im Museum' ('The Exhibit in Focus: Object-based Research in the Museum'), co-organised by Panagiotis Poulopoulos, Rebecca Wolf and Marisa Pamplona for young museum trainees. The workshop took place at the Deutsches Museum during the 28th Bundesvolontärstagung 'Forschung an Museen und Kulturinstitutionen' ('Research at Museums and Cultural Institutions'), Museumspädagogisches Zentrum München, Munich, 1 and 2 March 2018.

[53] See, for instance, Panagiotis Poulopoulos and Ralph Würschinger, 'Die Revolution im Spiel – von der Erfindung der Doppelpedalharfe' ('The Revolution in the Game: About the Invention of the Double-action Harp'), available at http://www.deutsches-museum. de/forschung/podcast, podcast broadcasted on 30 January 2019, article published on 8 March 2019, accessed 3 June 2022. For more details on the making of this podcast see Anette Lein, Panagiotis Poulopoulos and Ralph Würschinger, 'Warum Podcasts?' ('Why Podcasts'), in 'DM Podcast: Hinter die Kulissen hören' ('DM Podcast: Listening behind the Scenes'), article in the online portal 'wissenschaftskommunikation.de', published 15 June 2019, available at https://www.wissenschaftskommunikation.de/dm-podcast-hinter-die-kulissen-hoeren-26963/, accessed 3 June 2022.

[54] One example of implementing new technologies is the reconstruction of a mould for making composition harp ornaments that was built for the new exhibition of musical instruments at the Deutsches Museum with the collaboration of the curatorial team, the digitisation department and various other workshops. The original mould, which was kindly loaned by the Royal College of Music, London (Inv. No. RCM 976), was scanned with a 3-D scanning device by Claus Henkensiefken (Deutsches Museum Digital), and its central part, showing the 'negative' ornamental motif of a palm leaf, as well as the 'positive' composition ornaments that were applied on the capital of Erard Grecian harps, were printed with a 3-D printer. The results of this project are shown at the new harp display that focuses on the manufacture of Erard harps, illustrating the various materials and methods employed by the firm.

[55] Several museological aspects concerning historical harps have been discussed in Panagiotis Poulopoulos, 'A Creative Triangle of Mechanics, Acoustics and Aesthetics: The Early Pedal Harp (1780–1830) as a Symbol of Innovative Transformation', unpublished paper presented at the international conference 'Welche Museen für welche Gesellschaft? 10 Jahre Forschung in Museen' ('Which Museums for Which Society? 10 Years Research in Museums'), end conference of the funding programme 'Research in Museums' of the Volkswagen Foundation, Schloss Herrenhausen, Hannover, 18 to 20 March 2019.

Figure 40. View of Erard Nº 2428, a double-action Grecian harp built c.1817, displayed next to a contemporary dress in the temporary exhibition 'Georgians: the Pride and the Prejudice' at the Worcester City Art Gallery & Museum (2020).

Figure 41. Detail of the harp display entitled 'Sébastien Erard and the Development of the Modern Harp' in the new permanent exhibition of musical instruments at the Deutsches Museum, opened in 2022.

and 'time capsules', can enhance awareness of history and culture among visitors of different backgrounds and interests.[56] This concept has been used in the harp display entitled 'Sébastien Erard and the Development of the Modern Harp' in the new permanent exhibition of musical instruments at the Deutsches Museum, which intends to present many of the research findings described in this book in an engaging and entertaining way, using a combination of original artefacts, facsimiles, 'hands-on' objects and demonstrations, along with texts, images and drawings (Figure 41).[57]

As a concluding remark, the long and rich history of Erard Grecian harps in public and private collections around the world has shown that whether on the concert stage or behind glass, these musical instruments are multidimensional artefacts of cultural heritage, which continue to entice and inspire, as they did when they were introduced in London two centuries ago.

[56] The educational potential of Erard harps has been highlighted in Panagiotis Poulopoulos and Hayato Sugimoto, 'Learning from Musical Instruments as Manifestations of Production and Consumption', unpublished paper presented at the ICOM General Conference 'Museums as Cultural Hubs: The Future of Tradition', CIMCIM Session 'Music Museums and Education: Current and Future Perspectives', Kyoto International Conference Center, Kyoto, 1 to 7 September 2019.

[57] Some aspects of the exhibition concept have been presented by the author in his paper 'A Time Capsule with Strings: The Chronicle of the Erard Grecian Harp', presented at the Oberseminar, Deutsches Museum, Munich, 7 June 2021.

Conclusions

'Thank you very much for your enquiry. We do indeed have an Erard harp in our collection. […] It is funny that you should email at this time – we have very recently had some restoration work done on the harp and it is currently on display in our own galleries for the first time.'[1]

The Erard Grecian Harp as a Symbol of Innovative Transformation

The Erard Grecian harp was one of the most advanced, fashionable and expensive instruments of its time. With is technically, visually and musically innovative features, it was quite distinctive when compared not only to earlier harps, but also to other instruments, representing the cutting edge in instrument making during the early nineteenth century. Developed in the competitive and stimulating environment of Regency London, Erard's Grecian model exemplified above all the transformative processes that took place in various sectors of business, industry and trade in Britain and abroad. These processes, which strongly affected the production and consumption of harps, were fuelled by drastic changes in the technological, political, economic and sociocultural landscape of Western Europe.

It is reasonable to argue that the Erard Grecian harp was the child of revolution. Its design was shaped by the transitional period commonly referred to as the Industrial Revolution, which brought about new engineering and mechanical standards as well as a new range of manufacturing materials and methods based on the concepts of specialisation, standardisation and interchangeability. Furthermore, its aesthetics were heavily influenced by the French Revolution and its consequences, which led to the decline of the *Ancien Régime* and its pompous, flamboyant Baroque style, giving way to democratic, liberal movements that were expressed in the austere elegance and symmetry of the neoclassical style. Additionally, its commercial reception and diffusion were driven by the so-called 'Consumer Revolution', which generated and sustained the manufacture and marketing of novel, trendy objects, and enabled their distribution to a large international clientele.

The modern harp, embodied in Erard's Grecian model, was thus born in a historical period in which groundbreaking events altered social order, triggered uprisings and wars, caused massive migration and urbanisation, instigated the rise of imperialism, colonialism and nationalism and initiated the unprecedented exploration

---

[1] Personal communication with a curator from Museums Worcestershire on 3 February 2020 regarding Erard N° 2428, a double-action harp of the Grecian model built c.1817. For more details see Claire Cheshire, 'Erard Harp (London, around 1817)' (available at https:// researchworcestershire.wordpress.com/2020/08/14/erard-harp-london-around-1817/, published 14 August 2020; accessed 3 June 2022).

and exploitation of natural and human resources. However, these events were also accompanied by intellectual awakening, scientific discovery and flourishing of the arts. This resulted in the growth of the music business and in the emergence of new musical styles based on expression, harmonic modulation, dynamics and virtuosity, as well as of new timbre and tonal ideals. Simultaneously, new instruments that were capable of meeting these new demands appeared, among which the double-action harp constitutes a prime example.

The Chronicle of the Erard Grecian Harp: Reflecting the History and Culture of an Era

As described in Chapter One, although the harp had been used worldwide for centuries, until the eighteenth century the instrument did not occupy a central position in European musical life, largely because of several limitations in terms of construction, range and possibilities for modulation. However, the ingenious idea of introducing pedals to the harp for shortening the strings transformed the instrument forever. From then on, it was a matter of time – and of extensive experimentation, collaboration and competition – to move from Hochbrucker's single-action harp to Erard's double-action harp. The frantic race for the improvement of the single-action harp, which began in Paris with Cousineau's 14-pedal harp from 1782, reached its peak in London with the introduction of the Grecian harp by Erard in 1811. However, this was neither a linear, nor an even procedure: from its early development in the last decades of the eighteenth century to its steady establishment in the first decades of the nineteenth century, the evolution of the double-action harp went through a series of inventions and patents of varying ingenuity and success, witnessing several cases of industrial espionage, imitation and legal conflict along the way.

Why and how did Erard succeed where others might have failed? Regardless of any lucky coincidences, which can always affect the fate of a particular inventor, maker or product, the secret of Sébastien Erard, and of the firm he founded, seems to have been, on the one hand, the willingness to adjust to new challenges and to find practical, reliable solutions, and on the other hand, the ability to embrace and absorb new influences. As discussed in Chapter Two, Erard's revolutionary contributions to harp design and engineering, which allowed the serial production of state-of-the-art instruments in great numbers, were stimulated as much from changes in contemporary lutherie as from radical developments in scientific instruments, machines and precision tools. For instance, without the transition from wood to metal for the building and mounting of the pedal mechanism, which improved the harp's overall strength, reliability and accuracy, the operation and function of Erard's double-action harp would have been quite problematic, turning into a musician's nightmare. Likewise, without the refinement and implementation of saws, lathes or screws for industrial applications, Erard's double-action harp may have remained only a costly experiment in harp history.

From this perspective, although it is legitimate to compare Sébastien Erard with famous instrument makers, such as the piano manufacturers Broadwood and Clementi, he should also be measured against prolific mechanical engineers, such

Maudslay and Holtzapffel, whose workshop methods had parallels to those of Erard. Two notable instances regard the incorporation of technical drawings, as well as of jigs, moulds and templates, in product design and construction, and the adoption of numbering and marking systems, both of which were essential for the large-scale production of objects in workshops involving rationalisation of manufacture and division of labour.

Apart from his pioneering approach to the construction of the harp, Erard also introduced innovative concepts in the decoration and branding of the instrument, epitomised by the Grecian model, as analysed in Chapter Three. By transferring and adapting various available materials, techniques and styles that were applied to other fields, Erard managed to produce harps that looked highly ornate and expensive, yet were made relatively fast and cheaply. Two representative examples of effective substitution on the Grecian harp concern the use of composition ornaments and decoupage prints, which replaced the time-consuming and pricey woodcarvings and paintings used on earlier harps. Equally inventive was the adornment of the double-action harp with figures and motives inspired from classical Greece, which helped to promote Erard's instruments among connoisseurs and enthusiasts of the neoclassical style. Sébastien Erard was aware of Neoclassicism's impact on contemporary European art, fashion and culture: as an avid art collector himself, Erard had certainly encountered samples of Greek antiquities in publications, auctions and exhibitions, or had seen their modern interpretations in the architecture, furniture, sculpture and ornamental pottery created by entrepreneurs such as Adam or Wedgwood.

A further original feature of Grecian harps concerns their conspicuous branding with permanent, consistent engravings bearing the manufacturer's name and details, which, in contrast to the small inked inscriptions, stamps or paper labels previously used on harps, rendered them easily recognisable and difficult to fake. Emphasising the firm's prominence and noble connections, these engravings acted as powerful trademarks that were useful for identification, authentication and advertising purposes. The success of Erard's above-mentioned practices is confirmed by the fact that they were widely copied by other harp makers in London and elsewhere.

It is no surprise then that during the early nineteenth century the Erard London branch was a hub for harp making, where young craftsmen could gain valuable training and experience, as evidenced by several ambitious Erard workers who later opened their own businesses. As the leading manufacturer of harps in London, Sébastien Erard, and later also his nephew Pierre, were at the head of a comprehensive firm employing diverse specialists under the same roof, an entrepreneurial scheme that was commonly adopted in the production of luxury goods in nineteenth-century Britain. Erard Grecian harps demonstrate the business organisation and administration that was indispensable for the making and selling of instruments of such great complexity and quality, as examined in Chapter Four. The building of these harps resulted from the cross-fertilisation between different crafts: internally, manufacture relied on the knowledge and expertise of numerous skilled artisans occupied in woodworking, metalworking and decorating tasks, while externally it was dependent on the firm's extensive network of suppliers and subcontractors, who provided Erard with a wide assortment of specialised materials and services.

The number and variety of Erard's business associates are indicated by the many different professionals, some of outstanding calibre, that are detected in the firm's instruments and archives, from the clock makers Kessels and Breguet to the composition makers Thorpe and Jackson. With the help of a few trustworthy employees, like Wilhelm, Horn or Bruzaud, Sébastien and Pierre were able to supervise staff, facilities and resources efficiently and to make appropriate adjustments when necessary. In addition, meticulous bookkeeping, personal interacting and lobbying with bankers, sponsors and patrons, and communication via regular correspondence allowed the firm's management to keep the business operation under control while dealing with various financial issues, from weekly expenses and fluctuating seasonal income to pending debts and prospective investments.

Erard's carefully calculated production and marketing strategies paid off. With the increased status and prestige of patent-protected, branded instruments, Erard Grecian harps were quickly endorsed by the British royalty and nobility, and their European peers. Costing between 120 and 160 guineas – a sum equivalent to the price of a grand piano or three times the annual wages of a manual labourer – these instruments were mainly aimed at affluent customers of the upper and middle classes. As presented in Chapter Five, in the emerging consumerist society of Regency Britain, Grecian harps and their accessories were highly desirable objects, with the British elite acquiring almost the entire catalogue of Erard's costliest products and with those of a lower class, who were keen to imitate their superiors, usually buying the firm's cheapest harps and only the most necessary accessories.

Regarding the profile and consuming habits of Erard's clientele, the majority of the firm's customers did not have a title, but possessed money and social standing, while in most cases, even if the recorded buyer was a man, the harp was intended for a woman, indicating the gendered identity of the instrument. Like other luxury products, Erard Grecian harps were usually purchased on credit and, although they were generally sold as quickly as they were made, their sale patterns were greatly reliant on the London season. Within only a few years from their debut in London, Erard's Grecian harps were in great demand not only in the British capital but also across the provinces, sent as far as Edinburgh and Dublin. This was achieved through Erard's shrewd promotional tactics, which involved engaging renowned composers, performers and music teachers, such as Bochsa, Horn or Meyer, in writing music, giving concerts and offering lessons for the double-action harp, as well as in persuading eminent music publishers and sellers, such as Chappell & Co, to act as Erard's agents. As a reward for their services, these professionals were usually offered attractive commissions or discounts from Erard. Additional publicity was attained through maintaining personal contacts with prominent musicians, instrument makers and dealers, as well as with esteemed members of fashionable London society.

The word-of-mouth recommendation of Erard harps by public figures and celebrities helped enormously to boost both the reputation and the profits of the Erard firm, providing a testimony to Erard's entrepreneurial acumen. Even with minimum advertising in the press, Erard managed to develop a global customer base, selling harps all over Europe and the British colonies. Erard Grecian harps travelled to distant destinations stretching from Spain to Russia, while the firm's instruments could also be found in rich homes in North America, India, Australia and New Zealand.

An icon of wealth, taste and sophistication, the harp, as envisaged by the Grecian model and its imitations, turned from a mere musical instrument into an instantly familiar object that permeated contemporary lifestyle. As shown in Chapter Six, during the early nineteenth century the harp played an essential role in education, art and fashion, especially for young women. Conduct manuals and treatises praised the beneficial aspects of playing the harp in the upbringing of girls, with the instrument often receiving favourable comments when compared with the piano, because apart from allowing expression of talent and personality, it offered maximum visibility of the performer's body and face. Female members of respectable families were expected to demonstrate both their musical skills and beauty on the harp, with the instrument acting as an important means of social interaction and courtship.

With their stunning looks and majestic sounds, Erard Grecian harps fulfilled this purpose admirably. The depiction of Erard Grecian harps in British iconography of the Regency era continued the tradition of portraits, fashion plates and prints showing elegantly dressed ladies with harps that had begun in France in the 1760s. Most of these images were extremely stylised, with the female musicians standing or sitting with their harps in a domestic setting, usually alone or in duets with pianos, and in most cases facing the viewer rather than focusing on their instrument. Additionally, the harp was included in satirical cartoons and caricatures with social or political undertones, in which the instrument was presented as a common female accessory and pastime.

The harp eventually became a cultural phenomenon that left its indelible mark on the literature of the Romantic era. As mentioned in Chapter Seven, there are countless references to the harp in novels and poems of this period, pointing to the instrument's diverse, and often contrasting, meanings, allegories and symbolisms. Used in fictional scenes ranging from the heroic and sacred to the humorous and erotic, the harp could serve at once as a faithful companion of distressed girls, a melodious weapon of rebellious warriors, a vehicle of female attraction and seduction, a sign of pride and superficiality or a metaphor for virtue and harmony.

The harp was therefore portrayed in the hands of literary characters as contrasting as the privileged but arrogant Mary Crawford in Jane Austen's *Mansfield Park* and the deprived but modest Juliet Granville in Frances Burney's *The Wanderer*, both published in the same year. Either by introducing the harp only briefly in a passage or by adopting it as a central element of storytelling, several acclaimed female and male writers, from Mary Wollstonecraft Shelley, Maria Edgeworth and Charlotte Brontë, to William Makepeace Thackeray, Charles Dickens and Leo Tolstoy, exploited the harp's theatricality and narrative potential in books that are now of classical magnitude.

Interestingly, some of these references to the harp may have been inspired by Erard harps, which the authors had frequently seen and heard at their homes or at social events, as suggested by the cases of Jane Austen, Sir Walter Scott or Lord Byron. It is indeed tempting to imagine Sir Water Scott writing the scenes of Flora singing charmingly with her harp in *Waverley* or of the Black Knight discovering a harp in *Ivanhoe*, while enjoying the sounds and looks of the Erard Grecian harps that his daughters Sophia and Anne played upon!

Epilogue: The Legacy of the Erard Grecian Harp in the Present and Future

From the middle of the nineteenth century the popularity of the Grecian harp waned and the instrument started falling into oblivion. Although the hegemony of the double-action harp was never challenged in the world of pedal harps, the Grecian model itself was superseded initially by Erard's upgraded Gothic model and later by newer double-action harps, much like it had replaced single-action harps a few decades earlier. Now, two centuries since they first appeared, Erard Grecian harps are facing new challenges and new prospects, this time not as novel, state-of-the-art musical instruments, but as important artefacts of cultural heritage.

As observed in Chapter Eight, about 300 specimens, only a small fraction of the around 3,500 Grecian harps produced by Erard in London, are known to have survived to date. All originally built in the same manufactory within a period of about 30 years, they are now dispersed across numerous locations around the world and are owned by individuals and institutions with diverse interests and missions. The majority of them, about 80%, are in private hands, typically in the possession of harpists or instrument collectors. These harps are usually maintained in playing condition and are occasionally used for concerts, lectures or recordings, allowing modern musicians and their audiences to experience their sound, performance practice and repertoire. However, some of them have been extensively restored and repurposed, often with detrimental effects concerning their material authenticity.

In contrast, a rather small percentage of Grecian harps, about 20%, had a different fate. Being entrusted to public collections mainly for display and research, and not as sounding devices, these harps have typically retained their original features intact. Nevertheless, some of them have never been exhibited or documented, consequently having fallen into neglect for decades in museum storerooms.

The time has come to offer Erard Grecian harps an alternative between deteriorating slowly as functional musical tools that are deemed to have their tangible features distorted or lost, and remaining forever unscathed as static display pieces, but devoid of their intangible properties. The growing interest in Erard Grecian harps, and in historical pedal harps in general, can provide new opportunities for the evaluation and appreciation of these instruments, and this book aims to form the basis for further initiatives.

As proven in this book, the story of the Erard Grecian harp can connect objects, people or notions that were previously unrelated, allowing for a more thorough comprehension of the past. For example, it can build bridges between musical instruments and machine tools, scientific instruments, printed media, artworks or luxury household objects, from furniture and porcelain to automata and clocks, whose production and consumption are usually studied separately, despite sharing many similarities. Furthermore, it can link the actions of celebrated personalities, such as Napoleon Bonaparte, King George IV or the Duke of Wellington, whose biographies fill endless pages in history books, with the unknown lives and oeuvres of countless craftsmen who have remained anonymous, such as most of Erard's employees, but whose toil decorates our museum galleries and concert halls. Moreover, it can provide new material for discussing seemingly modern phenomena, such as industrialisation, mass production, capitalism, globalisation, imperialism or consumerism, in their historical context.

What began with the examination and preparation of a single harp, Erard N° 2631, for a new exhibition, turned into an extensive research project, raising new questions and opening new paths of enquiry, as described in this book. Hopefully, future research, publication and dissemination activities will contribute with new information to the existing knowledge we have about Erard Grecian harps, and will help to establish more objective criteria and methods regarding their usage and conservation. For example, very little is still known about the original stringing and tuning of these harps or about the maintenance of their mechanism. In addition, the implementation of more respectful and balanced approaches resulting from the discourse between various professionals, such as musicians, scholars, museum curators and conservators, will assist the future preservation, study and presentation of these harps, either on the concert stage or behind glass.

Consequently, this will enable all stakeholders, from harp students to museum visitors, to understand and recognise the value of Erard Grecian harps both as musical instruments and as multidimensional objects of historical and cultural significance. Because which other artefacts can reveal so much about the history and culture of an era, while looking as elegant and sounding as nice as Erard Grecian harps?

Appendix: List of Surviving Grecian
Double-Action Harps Produced by Erard
in London between 1811 and c.1845

Official serial number	Secondary serial number	Present owner, location and inventory number	Country	Source of information [references]	Date of registration in Erard ledgers	First transaction (sale, hire, etc.) noted in Erard ledgers
1387		Private collection, England	UK	Information from Robert Adelson [Robert Adelson, *Erard: Empire of the Harp* (Ancenis: Les Harpes Camac, 2022), pp. 58–62]		30 November 1811
1436		Present owner and location unknown		Information from Michael Parfett		29 February 1812
1437		Present owner and location unknown		Lot 237 at Christie's 6289, London, UK, 1 November 1993		27 January 1812
1481		Present owner and location unknown		Lot 716 at Christie's 2335, New York, USA, 31 August–1 September 2010		14 July 1812
1513		Present owner and location unknown		Lot 123 at Christie's 1186, London, UK, 18–19 September 2013		26 September 1812
1536		Present owner and location unknown		Lot 29 at Bonhams 13463, London, UK, 6 November 2006		12 November 1812
1571		Present owner and location unknown		Available for sale in July 2019 by Silverman Galleries Antiques, Alexandria, VA, USA		13 March 1815
1587	1612	Museum of Fine Arts, Boston, 2012.991	USA	Information from Darcy Kuronen and Christina Storti		8 April 1813
1608		Present owner and location unknown		Available for sale on eBay in January 2022; information from Jon Hunnisett		7 April 1813

Official serial number	Secondary serial number	Present owner, location and inventory number	Country	Source of information [references]	Date of registration in Erard ledgers	First transaction (sale, hire, etc.) noted in Erard ledgers
1635		Present owner and location unknown		Information from John Hoare (Pilgrim Harps)		7 May 1813
1643		Scenkonstmuseet, Stockholm, M2281	Sweden	Information from the MIMO (Musical Instrument Museums Online) website		16 March 1814
1658		Present owner and location unknown		Information from John Hoare (Pilgrim Harps)		29 July 1813
1663		Lacock Abbey, Fox Talbot Museum and Village, Wiltshire, NT 995846.1	UK	Information from the National Trust Collections online catalogue		20 September 1813
1670		Private collection, Bedminster, Bristol	UK	Information from the internet		17 July 1813
1705		Château de Fontainebleau, Fontainebleau, F 2465 C.1	France	Information from Patricia Kalensky		4 September 1813
1708		Hamamatsu Museum of Musical Instruments, Hamamatsu, C-0043R	Japan	Information from Kazuhiko Shima and Hayato Sugimoto; personally examined on 6 September 2019 [Hamamatsu Museum of Musical Instruments (ed.), *General Guide to the Hamamatsu Museum of Musical Instruments* (Hamamatsu: Hamamatsu City, 2015), p. 179]		11 August 1813
1731		Private collection	UK	Information from Jon Hunnisett		9 November 1813

Official serial number	Secondary serial number	Present owner, location and inventory number	Country	Source of information [references]	Date of registration in Erard ledgers	First transaction (sale, hire, etc.) noted in Erard ledgers
1735		Present owner and location unknown		Information from the internet		21 December 1813
1747		Present owner and location unknown		Available for sale on eBay in April 2020, former owner in Australia; information from Jon Hunnisett		17 December 1813
1753	1795	Museu de la Música de Barcelona, Barcelona, MDMB 513	Spain	Information from Marisa Ruiz Magaldi; personally examined on 5 and 6 September 2016 [Romà Escalas i Llimona (ed.), *Museu de la Música: 1/Catàleg d'instruments* (Barcelona: Ajuntament de Barcelona, 1991), p. 29]		
1767		Present owner and location unknown		Information from John Hoare (Pilgrim Harps)		3 March 1814
1774		Parham House, Pulborough	UK	Information from Jon Hunnisett		27 April 1814
1807		Private collection of Elinor Bennett	UK	Information from the internet and from John Hoare (Pilgrim Harps)		6 July 1814
1822		Present owner and location unknown		Information from Michael Parfett		31 July 1821
1824	1856 R	Private collection, Milan	Italy	Information from Beat Wolf [Beat Wolf, *Harp Archives* (Schaffhausen: Wolf, 2016): BW 40/450/1824]		4 August 1814

Official serial number	Secondary serial number	Present owner, location and inventory number	Country	Source of information [references]	Date of registration in Erard ledgers	First transaction (sale, hire, etc.) noted in Erard ledgers
1874		Present owner and location unknown		Lot 36 at Bonhams 19022, London, UK, 18 January 2012		17 February 1814
1883		Present owner and location unknown		Lot 643 at Gardinger Houlgate, Corsham, UK, 16 June 2017		27 August 1814
1884		Present owner and location unknown		In 2009 in private collection, USA; information from Nancy Hurrell		11 September 1814
1904		Private collection of Elinor Bennett	UK	Information from the internet		15 June 1814
1933		Present owner and location unknown		Last owner in Rhos, Pontardawe, Swansea, UK; information from the internet		22 December 1814
1945	1989 K	Hospitalfield, Arbroath	UK	Information from Lucy Byatt and Laura Simpson; personally examined on 5 June 2017		14 January 1815
1954		Temple Newsam House and Estate, West Yorkshire, 294	UK	[Jane Elizabeth Troughton, *The Role of Music in the Yorkshire Country House 1770–1850* (PhD Diss., York: University of York, 2014), p. 532]		28 February 1815
1967		Kunsthistoriches Museum, Vienna, SAM 502	Austria	Information from the Kunstdatenbank website	January 1826	10 January 1827
1974		Private collection	USA	Information from Donna Youngblood		10 June 1818
1984		Present owner and location unknown		Information from John Hoare (Pilgrim Harps)		18 June 1824

Official serial number	Secondary serial number	Present owner, location and inventory number	Country	Source of information [references]	Date of registration in Erard ledgers	First transaction (sale, hire, etc.) noted in Erard ledgers
1985	1985	Museo dell'Arpa Victor Salvi, Piasco, 410	Italy	Information from Beat Wolf [Wolf, *Harp Archives*: BW 40/450/1985]		20 June 1815
2017		Present owner and location unknown		Lot 35 at Bonhams 19022, London, UK, 18 January 2012		8 April 1815
2023		Present owner and location unknown		Lot 914 at Freeman's, Philadelphia, PA, USA, 19 September 2004		April 1839
2057		Private collection, Winterhur	Switzerland	Information from Beat Wolf [Wolf, *Harp Archives*: BW 40/450/2057]		29 September 1819
2059		Present owner and location unknown		Information from Michael Parfett		20 May 1815
2092		Present owner and location unknown		Lot 29 at Bonhams 14845, London, UK, 9 July 2007		7 August 1815
2108		Private collection	Germany	Information from Klaus Horngacher (Horngacher Harps)		4 October 1815
2114		Present owner and location unknown		Information from John Hoare (Pilgrim Harps)		21 October 1815
2141		Private collection of Anne Vanschothorst	Netherlands	Information from the internet		19 July 1817
2202	2180 RB	Private collection, Basel	Switzerland	Information from Beat Wolf [Wolf, *Harp Archives*: BW 40/450/2202]		13 June 1829
2204		Present owner and location unknown		Lot 28 at Bonhams 16013, London, UK, 4 November 2008		8 May 1816

Official serial number	Secondary serial number	Present owner, location and inventory number	Country	Source of information [references]	Date of registration in Erard ledgers	First transaction (sale, hire, etc.) noted in Erard ledgers
2210		Present owner and location unknown		Information from John Hoare (Pilgrim Harps)		16 January 1818
2213		Present owner and location unknown		Information from John Hoare (Pilgrim Harps)		6 May 1816
2214		Private collection of Rosemary Margaret Hallo, Adelaide	Australia	[Rosemary Margaret Hallo, *Erard, Bochsa and their impact on harp music-making in Australia (1830–1866): An early history from documents* (PhD Diss., Adelaide: The University of Adelaide, 2014), pp. 148, 193]		8 May 1816
2217		Present owner and location unknown		Available for sale in 2016 by Michael Parfett, London, UK		25 May 1816
2219		Private collection of Floraleda Sacchi, Como	Italy	Information from Beat Wolf and Floraleda Sacchi [Wolf, *Harp Archives*: BW 40/450/2219; Floraleda Sacchi, *Sophia Giustina Corri: Works for Solo Harp* (CD recording with booklet; Bologna: Tactus, 2009), pp. 6, 17]		11 May 1816
2224		Present owner and location unknown		Lot 95 at Christie's 2465, Amsterdam, Netherlands, 20 June 2000		22 May 1816
2264	2561? R	Private collection, Bad Krozingen	Germany	Information from Heidrun Rosenzweig		23 October 1816

Official serial number	Secondary serial number	Present owner, location and inventory number	Country	Source of information [references]	Date of registration in Erard ledgers	First transaction (sale, hire, etc.) noted in Erard ledgers
2295		National Music Centre, Calgary, 2202.07.01	Canada	Information from the museum's online catalogue		18 December 1816
2301		Present owner and location unknown		Lot 922 at New Orleans Auction Galleries 1905, New Orleans, USA, 12 October 2019		14 November 1816
2324		Dudmaston, Shropshire, NT 814125	UK	Information from the National Trust Collections online catalogue		20 March 1817
2348		Attingham Park, Shropshire, NT 608942	UK	Information from the National Trust Collections online catalogue		23 April 1817
2377		Museo dell'Arpa Victor Salvi, Piasco, SC0700	Italy	Information from Beat Wolf and Roberta Scarzello [Wolf, *Harp Archives*: BW 40/450/2377]		12 July 1817
2372		Hampton National Historic Site, Towson, HAMP 2598	USA	Information from Gregory Weidman, Manu Frederickx and Jennifer Schnitker [Robert Wilson Torchia, 'Eliza Ridgely and the Ideal of American Womanhood, 1787–1820', *Maryland Historical Magazine* 90/4 (1995), pp. 405–423, at p. 406, and Gregory Weidman, 'Eliza Ridgely's historic Erard Harp', *American Harp Journal* 26/1 (2017), p. 52]		26 June 1817
2411		Present owner and location unknown		Lot 151 at Christie's 6059, London, UK, 17 March 1993		2 October 1817

Official serial number	Secondary serial number	Present owner, location and inventory number	Country	Source of information [references]	Date of registration in Erard ledgers	First transaction (sale, hire, etc.) noted in Erard ledgers
2419	2316 RB	Abbotsford, The Home of Sir Walter Scott, T. AT. 3665	UK	Information from Kirsty Archer-Thompson; personally examined on 31 May 2017		26 April 1822
2428		Worcester Museum and Art Gallery, Worcester	UK	Information from Claire Cheshire [Cheshire, Claire, 'Erard Harp (London, around 1817)' (https:// researchworcestershire.wordpress. com/2020/08/14/erard-harp-london-around-1817/, published 14 August 2020, accessed 3 June 2022)]		15 December 1817
2432		Present owner and location unknown		Lot 985 at Christie's 2857, Amsterdam, Netherlands, 27–29 April 2010		10 December 1817
2437		Private collection of Jacquie Spring, Melbourne	Australia	[Hallo, *Erard, Bochsa and their impact on harp music-making in Australia*, p. 194]		11 December 1817
2496		Present owner and location unknown		Lot 1124 at Christie's 4973, London, UK, 12 December 2006	16 February 1818	26 February 1818
2501		Present owner and location unknown		Available for sale in August 2019 by Affairs of the Harp, St. Albans, UK; previous owner at Wrexham, UK	2 March 1818	7 March 1818
2502		Present owner and location unknown		Lot 152 at Sotheby's, London, UK, 8 November 1979	2 March 1818	31 March 1818

Official serial number	Secondary serial number	Present owner, location and inventory number	Country	Source of information [references]	Date of registration in Erard ledgers	First transaction (sale, hire, etc.) noted in Erard ledgers
2504		Present owner and location unknown		Available for sale in 2016 by Michael Parfett, London, UK	9 March 1818	13 August 1825
2514		Present owner and location unknown		Available for sale on eBay in August 2020; information from Jon Hunnisett	30 March 1818	17 March 1818
2518	2497	Helsinki City Museum, Helsinki, XLII-690	Finland	Information from the museum's online catalogue	6 April 1818	6 April 1818
2527		Present owner and location unknown		Lot 852 at icollector.com, UK, 17 July 2002	27 April 1818	7 May 1818
2532		Present owner and location unknown		Available for sale in 2016 by Clive Morley Harps, Filkins, UK; information from John Hoare (Pilgrim Harps)	4 May 1818	6 May 1818
2540		Present owner and location unknown		Information from John Hoare (Pilgrim Harps)	18 May 1818	3 July 1818
2551		Present owner and location unknown		Information from John Hoare (Pilgrim Harps)	8 June 1818	3 July 1818
2554		Private collection, Augsburg	Germany	Formerly owned by WDR, Cologne; information from Beat Wolf and Christine Steinbrecher [Wolf, *Harp Archives*: BW 40/450/2554]	15 June 1818	22 June 1818
2555		Private collection	UK	Information from John Hoare (Pilgrim Harps) and Jon Hunnisett	15 June 1818	25 June 1818
2563		Holst Birthplace Museum, Cheltenham	UK	Information from the museum's website	6 July 1818	11 July 1818

Official serial number	Secondary serial number	Present owner, location and inventory number	Country	Source of information [references]	Date of registration in Erard ledgers	First transaction (sale, hire, etc.) noted in Erard ledgers
2565		Present owner and location unknown		Information from Michael Parfett	6 July 1818	11 July 1818
259?		Present owner and location unknown		Information from Jon Hunnisett		
2631	2634 RB	Deutsches Museum, Munich, 16147	Germany	Personally examined on several dates from 2014 to 2022 [Bettina Wackernagel, *Europäische Zupf- und Streichinstrumente, Hackbretter und Äolsharfen. Deutsches Museum München. Musikinstrumentensammlung Katalog* (Frankfurt am Main: Bochinsky, 1997), pp. 184–185; Panagiotis Poulopoulos and Julin Lee, 'A Synergy of Form, Function and Fashion in the Manufacture of the Erard Harp', in Marco A. Pérez and Emanuele Marconi (eds), *Wooden Musical Instruments: Different Forms of Knowledge* (Paris: Cité de la Musique - Philharmonie de Paris, 2018), pp. 367–398, at pp. 377–392; and Panagiotis Poulopoulos, Marisa Pamplona, Luise Richter and Elke Cwiertnia, 'Technological Study of the Decoration on an Erard Harp from 1818', *Studies in Conservation* 65/2 (2020), pp. 86–102.	30 November 1818	18 January 1819

Official serial number	Secondary serial number	Present owner, location and inventory number	Country	Source of information [references]	Date of registration in Erard ledgers	First transaction (sale, hire, etc.) noted in Erard ledgers
2648		Present owner and location unknown		Information from John Hoare (Pilgrim Harps)	18 January 1819	15 February 1819
2672	2656 RB	Muziekinstrumentenmuseum, Brussels, 3952	Belgium	Information from Anne-Emmanuelle Ceulemans and Joris De Valck; personally examined on 4 October 2017	15 February 1819	26 March 1819
2677		Present owner and location unknown		Information from John Hoare (Pilgrim Harps)	22 February 1819	16 June 1819
2683		Present owner and location unknown		Information from John Hoare (Pilgrim Harps)	8 March 1819	10 May 1819
2685		Present owner and location unknown		Information from John Hoare (Pilgrim Harps)	15 March 1819	1 May 1819
2690		Present owner and location unknown		Lot 37 at Bonhams 19022, London, UK, 18 January 2012	29 March 1819	8 April 1819
2704		Metropolitan Museum of Art, New York, 1978.291.1	USA	Information from Susana Caldeira [Laurence Libin, *A Checklist of European Harps* (New York: Metropolitan Museum of Art, 1979), pp. 10–11]	26 April 1819	18 June 1819
2710		Present owner and location unknown		Sold by Carter's Antiques & Collectables, Armadale, Australia	10 May 1819	8 June 1819
2727		Present owner and location unknown		Information from Michael Parfett	7 June 1819	28 July 1819

Official serial number	Secondary serial number	Present owner, location and inventory number	Country	Source of information [references]	Date of registration in Erard ledgers	First transaction (sale, hire, etc.) noted in Erard ledgers
2788		Museo Interactivo de la Música de Málaga, Malaga	Spain	[Miguel Ángel Piédrola Lluch (ed.), *Colección MIMMA / Miguel Ángel Piédrola Orta* (2nd edn; Málaga: Club de amigos del Museo Interactivo de la Música Málaga, 2017), p. 63.]	4 October 1819	3 November 1819
2814		Present owner and location unknown		Information from John Hoare (Pilgrim Harps)	22 November 1819	14 January 1820
2839		Present owner and location unknown		Information from John Hoare (Pilgrim Harps)	31 January 1820	22 April 1820
2852		Present owner and location unknown		Information from John Hoare (Pilgrim Harps)	28 February 1820	3 June 1820
2879		Present owner and location unknown		Lot 77 at Bonham's 16904, London, UK, 23 June 2009; information from John Hoare (Pilgrim Harps)	20 March 1820	13 April 1820
2887		Present owner and location unknown		Available for sale in 2019 by Clive Morley Harps, Filkins, UK	10 April 1820	28 April 1820
2904		Museum of Applied Arts & Sciences, Sydney, 93/379/1	Australia	Information from the museum's online catalogue	15 May 1820	24 May 1820
2914	2917 RB	Abbotsford, The Home of Sir Walter Scott, T. AT. 1784	UK	Information from Kirsty Archer-Thompson; personally examined on 31 May 2017	4 June 1820	10 June 1820

Official serial number	Secondary serial number	Present owner, location and inventory number	Country	Source of information [references]	Date of registration in Erard ledgers	First transaction (sale, hire, etc.) noted in Erard ledgers
2920		Present owner and location unknown		Lot 45 at A.B. Levy, West Palm Beach, Florida, USA, 4 September 2014	11 June 1820	23 June 1820
2921		Present owner and location unknown		Information from John Hoare (Pilgrim Harps)	19 June 1820	19 June 1820
2925		Present owner and location unknown		Lot 7 at Christie's 9343, London, UK, 13 March 2002	26 June 1820	20 June 1820
2936		Present owner and location unknown		Information from John Hoare (Pilgrim Harps)	10 July 1820	8 July 1820
2944		Present owner and location unknown		Available for sale in 2019 at Tunbridge Wells from Pilgrim Harps, Reference: 1448	24 July 1820	12 January 1822
2945		Present owner and location unknown		Owned c.2008–2011 by Darcy Bell-Myers; information from the internet	24 July 1820	27 July 1820
3006	2953 RB	Musée de la musique, Paris, E.991.14.1	France	Information from Thierry Maniguet; personally examined on 21 and 22 June 2016	23 October 1820	21 December 1820
3012		Present owner and location unknown		Lot 22 at Bonhams 20019, London, UK, 31 October 2012, and Lot 450 at Bonhams 20762, London, UK, 24 September 2013	6 November 1820	17 November 1820
3022		Present owner and location unknown		Information from John Hoare (Pilgrim Harps)	4 December 1820	26 December 1820

Official serial number	Secondary serial number	Present owner, location and inventory number	Country	Source of information [references]	Date of registration in Erard ledgers	First transaction (sale, hire, etc.) noted in Erard ledgers
3042		Present owner and location unknown		Information from John Hoare (Pilgrim Harps)	15 January 1821	24 January 1821
3045		Private collection	UK	Lot 478 at Byrne's, Chester, UK, 13 May 2019; information from Jon Hunnisett	22 January 1821	31 January 1821
3070	3071 RB	Musée de la musique, Paris, E.0997	France	Information from Thierry Maniguet; personally examined on 21 and 22 June 2016	5 March 1821	12 March 1821
3106		Culzean Castle, Ayrshire, UK, NT 45.2218	UK	Information from the MINIM-UK (Musical Instruments Interface for Museums and Collections) website	14 May 1821	17 May 1821
3151		Present owner and location unknown		Information from John Hoare (Pilgrim Harps)	11 August 1821	23 August 1821
3191		Present owner and location unknown		Information from John Hoare (Pilgrim Harps)	20 October 1821	8 November 1821
3201		Present owner and location unknown		Information from the internet; sold online 28 December 2016, previous owner at Eccles, UK	10 November 1821	19 November 1821
3202		Present owner and location unknown		Lot 135 at Christie's 5995, London, UK, 23 November 2010	17 November 1821	6 December 1821
3210		Present owner and location unknown		Information from John Hoare (Pilgrim Harps)	1 December 1821	5 February 1822

Official serial number	Secondary serial number	Present owner, location and inventory number	Country	Source of information [references]	Date of registration in Erard ledgers	First transaction (sale, hire, etc.) noted in Erard ledgers
3213		Monasterio de Montserrat, Barcelona	Spain	[Cristina Bordas, 'Erard Pianos and Harps in Spain and Portugal', in Rudolf Frick (ed.), *Sébastien Erard: ein europäischer Pionier des Instrumentenbaus. Internationales Erard-Symposium Michaelstein 13.–14. November 1994, Michaelsteiner Konferenzberichte* 48 (Blankenburg: Stiftung Kloster Michaelstein, 1995), pp. 30–32, at p. 32]	8 December 1821	28 January 1822
3218	3193	Fernanda Giulini Collection, Milan, 51	Italy	Lot 3 at Christie's, London, UK, 17 June 1998; personally examined on 5 July 2016 [Wolf, *Harp Archives*: BW 40/450/3218; Dagmar Droysen-Reber, 'Schedules of the harps from no. 42 to no. 52', in John Henry van der Meer (ed.), *In Search of Lost Sounds: Art and Music in the Instruments Collection of Fernanda Giulini* (Milan and Briosco: Villa Medici Giulini, 2006), pp. 432–501, at pp. 486–491]	22 December 1821	8 January 1822
3226		Present owner and location unknown		Information from John Hoare (Pilgrim Harps)	12 January 1822	30 January 1822

Official serial number	Secondary serial number	Present owner, location and inventory number	Country	Source of information [references]	Date of registration in Erard ledgers	First transaction (sale, hire, etc.) noted in Erard ledgers
3236		National Music Museum, South Dakota University, Vermillion, NMM 12636	USA	Information from Emanuele Marconi and from the museum's online catalogue	2 February 1822	25 June 1822
3242		Present owner and location unknown		Information from John Hoare (Pilgrim Harps)	16 February 1822	4 December 1824
3244		Private collection, Lucerne	Switzerland	Information from Beat Wolf [Wolf, *Harp Archives*: BW 40/450/3244]	16 February 1822	20 February 1822
3264		Present owner and location unknown		Sold online by 1stDibs, reference number: LU1944311612713; previous owner in Bedford, UK	16 March 1822	28 October 1824
3265		Present owner and location unknown		Information from John Hoare (Pilgrim Harps)	16 March 1822	18 March 1822
3277		Present owner and location unknown		Lot 3 at Thierry de Maigret, Paris, France, 14 June 2017	6 April 1822	16 May 1822
3287		Present owner and location unknown		Lot 204 at Country House Collections, Slane Castle, Meath, Ireland, 5 October 2010	4 May 1822	22 June 1822
3292		Present owner and location unknown		Information from John Hoare (Pilgrim Harps)	18 May 1822	30 May 1822
3302		Present owner and location unknown		Information from Michael Parfett	June 1822	25 July 1822

Official serial number	Secondary serial number	Present owner, location and inventory number	Country	Source of information [references]	Date of registration in Erard ledgers	First transaction (sale, hire, etc.) noted in Erard ledgers
3312		Present owner and location unknown		Information from Michael Parfett	July 1822	12 July 1822
3348		Present owner and location unknown		Information from John Hoare (Pilgrim Harps)	7 October 1822	7 November 1822
3351		Present owner and location unknown		Information from John Hoare (Pilgrim Harps)	16 October 1822	5 February 1823
3353		Present owner and location unknown		Information from a list dated 2008 of Erard harps restored by H. Bryan & Co, Lynchburg, VA, USA; list provided by Nancy Hurrell	23 October 1822	20 December 1822
3358		Present owner and location unknown		Information from John Hoare (Pilgrim Harps)	November 1822	23 December 1822
3362		Present owner and location unknown		Information from John Hoare (Pilgrim Harps)	March 1822	8 September 1823
3364		Private collection	UK	Information from Jon Hunnisett	November 1822	10 October 1835
3391		Nydahl Collection, Stockholm, IKN009	Sweden	Information from Göran Grahn and Elise Kolle	March 1823	26 March 1823
3411		Present owner and location unknown		Lot 868 at Carlo Bonte Auctions, Bruges, Belgium, 14 June 2017	April 1823	13 May 1823

Official serial number	Secondary serial number	Present owner, location and inventory number	Country	Source of information [references]	Date of registration in Erard ledgers	First transaction (sale, hire, etc.) noted in Erard ledgers
3415		Present owner and location unknown		Sold by Mealy's, Kilkenny, Ireland, December 2016; Item #:0420-0251-2016-December	May 1823	31 May 1823
3425		Present owner and location unknown		Information from John Hoare (Pilgrim Harps)	June 1823	11 June 1823
3462		Present owner and location unknown		Information from John Hoare (Pilgrim Harps)	September 1823	14 August 1824
3480		Present owner and location unknown		Information from John Hoare (Pilgrim Harps)	November 1823	8 January 1824
3489		Present owner and location unknown		Information from John Hoare (Pilgrim Harps)	December 1823	1 January 1824
3491		Present owner and location unknown		Lot 221 at Bonhams 11696, Oxford, UK, 29 November 2005	December 1823	29 December 1823
3493		Present owner and location unknown		Available for sale in July 2019 by H. Bryan & Co, Lynchburg, VA, USA; previous owner in USA; information from Donna Youngblood	December 1823	12 January 1824
3500		Present owner and location unknown		Information from John Hoare (Pilgrim Harps)	January 1824	28 January 1824

Official serial number	Secondary serial number	Present owner, location and inventory number	Country	Source of information [references]	Date of registration in Erard ledgers	First transaction (sale, hire, etc.) noted in Erard ledgers
3520		Present owner and location unknown		Lot 236 at Julien's Auctions, Culver City, CA, USA, 26–27 October 2017; previously Lot 412 at Christie's 7410, London, UK, 20 November 1996	March 1824	6 March 1824
3535		Present owner and location unknown		Lot 159 at Bentley's Auction Rooms, Cranbrook, UK, 3 August 2019	April 1824	17 April 1824
3574		Czech Museum of Music, Prague, E 1994	Czech Republic	Information from Daniela Kotašová [Daniela Kotašová, 'Erard Harps in the Collection of the Czech Museum of Music', *Musicalia: Journal of the Czech Museum of Music* 10/1–2 (2018), pp. 85–114, at pp. 87, 95, 111]	June 1824	3 July 1824
3584		Present owner and location unknown		Information from John Hoare (Pilgrim Harps)	July 1824	26 July 1824
3609		Soho House, Birmingham	UK	Information from Laura Cassidy and Nadine Lees	September 1824	22 September 1824
3629		Present owner and location unknown		Lot 476 at Christie's 8295, New York, NY, USA, 14 October 1999	October 1824	28 October 1824
3634		Private collection, Saragossa	Spain	Information from Beat Wolf [Wolf, *Harp Archives*: BW 40/450/3634]	October 1824	16 November 1824

Official serial number	Secondary serial number	Present owner, location and inventory number	Country	Source of information [references]	Date of registration in Erard ledgers	First transaction (sale, hire, etc.) noted in Erard ledgers
3639		Present owner and location unknown		Information from a list dated 2008 of Erard harps restored by H. Bryan & Co, Lynchburg, VA, USA; list provided by Nancy Hurrell	November 1824	28 December 1824
3643		Private collection, Munich	Germany	Information from Franziska Bühl [Franziska Bühl, *Untersuchung einer Erard-Doppelpedalharfe von 1820–1825* (BA Diss., Studiengang Restaurierung, Kunsttechnologie und Konservierungswissenschaft, Munich: Technische Universität München, 2014), pp. 11–20]	November 1824	10 December 1284
3655		Present owner and location unknown		Information from John Hoare (Pilgrim Harps)	December 1824	27 January 1825
3656		Present owner and location unknown		Information from John Hoare (Pilgrim Harps)	January 1825	11 September 1828
3664		Present owner and location unknown		Information from John Hoare (Pilgrim Harps)	January 1825	26 February 1825
3666		Present owner and location unknown		Information from Michael Parfett	January 1825	16 February 1825
3693		Present owner and location unknown		Sold by harp maker Tim Hampson, Devon, UK	April 1825	23 April 1825

Official serial number	Secondary serial number	Present owner, location and inventory number	Country	Source of information [references]	Date of registration in Erard ledgers	First transaction (sale, hire, etc.) noted in Erard ledgers
3704	3721	Fernanda Giulini Collection, Milan, 52	Italy	Personally examined on 5 July 2016 [Wolf, *Harp Archives*: BW 40/450/3704; Droysen-Reber, 'Schedules of the harps from no. 42 to no. 52', pp. 492–497]	May 1825	16 August 1825
3721		Present owner and location unknown		Information from John Hoare (Pilgrim Harps)	July 1825	11 February 1826
3745		Museum van Loon, Amsterdam	Netherlands	Information from Elise Kolle and Jon Hunnisett	August 1825	30 August 1825
3758		Ceredigion Museum, Aberystwyth, 2002.11.1	UK	Information from the internet	December 1825	30 December 1825
3766		Present owner and location unknown		Sold by 1stDibs; previous owner in Dallas, TX, USA	February 1826	16 February 1826
3794		Present owner and location unknown		Information from Michael Parfett	November 1825	20 December 1825
3804		Private collection of Elisabeth Plank, Vienna	Austria	Information from Elisabeth Plank; the harp was available for sale in May 2018 by Rainer Thurau [Elisabeth Plank, *1825: Echoes of Vienna on Historical Harp* (CD recording with booklet; Vienna: Gramola, 2019), p. 15]	December 1825	29 December 1825
3814		Present owner and location unknown		Information from John Hoare (Pilgrim Harps)	January 1826	30 January 1826

Official serial number	Secondary serial number	Present owner, location and inventory number	Country	Source of information [references]	Date of registration in Erard ledgers	First transaction (sale, hire, etc.) noted in Erard ledgers
3819		Private collection of Constance Allanic, Amsterdam	Netherlands	Information from the owner's website	February 1826	26 September 1829
3828		Present owner and location unknown		Information from Nancy Hurrell	March 1826	15 March 1826
3830	3837	Musée de la musique, Paris, E.2003.5.8	France	Information from Thierry Maniguet; personally examined on 21 and 22 June 2016 [Wolf, *Harp Archives*: BW 40/450/3830]	March 1826	25 August 1826
3844		Smithsonian Museum, Washington DC, MI.324705	USA	Information from Nancy Hurrell and from the museum's online catalogue	April 1826	26 April 1826
3873		Present owner and location unknown		Lot 562 at Wolley & Wallis, Salisbury, Wiltshire, UK, 7 October 2014	June 1826	29 July 1826
3905		Present owner and location unknown		Information from John Hoare (Pilgrim Harps)	October 1826	6 December 1826
3907		Present owner and location unknown		Information from John Hoare (Pilgrim Harps)	July 1826	31 August 1826
3908	3944 R	Fitzwilliam Museum, Cambridge University, Cambridge, M.9-1941	UK	Information from Nik Zolman; personally examined on 7 December 2017	August 1826	16 September 1826
3909		Palacio Real, Madrid, 10011895	Spain	[Bordas, 'Erard Pianos and Harps in Spain and Portugal', pp. 31–32]	August 1826	19 August 1826

Official serial number	Secondary serial number	Present owner, location and inventory number	Country	Source of information [references]	Date of registration in Erard ledgers	First transaction (sale, hire, etc.) noted in Erard ledgers
3914		Brady C. Jefcoat Museum, Murfreesboro, NC	USA	Information from Nancy Hurrell		1 October 1828
3916	3943	Musikinstrumentenmuseum der Universität Leipzig, Leipzig, 4801	Germany	Information from Josef Focht and Sebastian Kirsch; personally examined on 17 July 2018	October 1826	4 October 1827
3923	S. 3925	Museum für Kunst und Gewerbe, Hamburg, 1995.245	Germany	Information from Olaf Kirsch	November 1826	12 December 1826
3930	3905	Instituto Sant'Anna, Palermo	Italy	Information from Giovanni Paolo di Stefano [Giovanni Paolo di Stefano, Selima Giorgia Giuliano and Sandra Proto (eds), *Strumenti musicali in Sicilia* (Palermo: CRICD-Regione Siciliana, 2013), pp. 178–179]	January 1827	22 March 1827
3947		Present owner and location unknown		Information from John Hoare (Pilgrim Harps)	November 1826	10 February 1827
3950		Present owner and location unknown		Available for sale in 2006 by Clive Morley Harps, Filkins, UK	December 1826	4 January 1827
3955		Present owner and location unknown		Information from John Hoare (Pilgrim Harps)	March 1827	18 May 1827
3956		Present owner and location unknown		Information from John Hoare (Pilgrim Harps)	March 1827	28 August 1828

Official serial number	Secondary serial number	Present owner, location and inventory number	Country	Source of information [references]	Date of registration in Erard ledgers	First transaction (sale, hire, etc.) noted in Erard ledgers
3965		Present owner and location unknown		Available for sale in 2016 by Clive Morley Harps, Filkins, UK	January 1827	17 February 1827
3970		Present owner and location unknown		Information from John Hoare (Pilgrim Harps)	March 1827	27 April 1827
3972	4006 R	Private collection of Masumi Nagasawa, Amsterdam	Netherlands	Information from Masumi Nagasawa; personally examined on 7 September 2018 [Wolf, *Harp Achives*: BW 40/450/3972]	March 1827	7 May 1827
3984		Present owner and location unknown		Lot 561 at Roseberys, London, UK, 26 January 2022; information from Jon Hunnisett	June 1827	6 July 1827
3996		Present owner and location unknown		Information from a list dated 2008 of Erard harps restored by H. Bryan & Co, Lynchburg, VA, USA; list provided by Nancy Hurrell	August 1827	28 August 1827
4002		Present owner and location unknown		Information from John Hoare (Pilgrim Harps)	May 1827	30 May 1827
4006		Vyne Estate, Basingstoke, Hampshire, NT 719354	UK	Information from the National Trust Collections online catalogue	September 1827	21 September 1827
4023		Present owner and location unknown		Information from John Hoare (Pilgrim Harps)	June 1827	5 July 1827

Official serial number	Secondary serial number	Present owner, location and inventory number	Country	Source of information [references]	Date of registration in Erard ledgers	First transaction (sale, hire, etc.) noted in Erard ledgers
4034		Present owner and location unknown		Available for sale in July 2019 by H. Bryan & Co, Lynchburg, VA, USA	November 1827	10 November 1827
4057		Present owner and location unknown		Information from Jon Hunnisett	December 1829	31 December 1831
4062		Present owner and location unknown		Information from John Hoare (Pilgrim Harps)	December 1827	7 January 1828
4077		Present owner and location unknown		Information from John Hoare (Pilgrim Harps)	February 1828	3 December 1828
4090		Present owner and location unknown		Lot 1 at Christie's 14404, London, UK, 22 February 2017	April 1828	24 May 1828
4098		Kenwood House, Hampstead, London	UK	Information from Catalina Vicens [David Irwin, *Neoclassicism* (London: Phaidon, 2000), pp. 360–361]	March 1828	19 March 1828
4113		Present owner and location unknown		Information from John Hoare (Pilgrim Harps)	April 1828	30 April 1828
4140		Present owner and location unknown		Information from John Hoare (Pilgrim Harps)	August 1828	4 November 1828
4153	4175 R	Private collection, Fürth	Germany	Information from Heidrun Rozenzweig; personally examined on 11 May 2017	August 1828	3 December 1830
4164		Present owner and location unknown		Available for sale in 2018 at Preloved.co.uk	September 1828	3 October 1828

Official serial number	Secondary serial number	Present owner, location and inventory number	Country	Source of information [references]	Date of registration in Erard ledgers	First transaction (sale, hire, etc.) noted in Erard ledgers
4176		Present owner and location unknown		Information from John Hoare (Pilgrim Harps)	October 1828	16 December 1828
4180		Private collection, The Hague	Netherlands	Information from Beat Wolf [Wolf, *Harp Archives*: BW 40/450/4180]	November 1828	23 January 1829
4181		Present owner and location unknown		Information from Michael Parfett	November 1828	10 January 1829
4193		Private collection, Solothurn	Switzerland	Information from Beat Wolf [Wolf, *Harp Archives*: BW 40/450/4193]	December 1828	23 December 1828
4195		Museo del Conservatorio san Pietro a Majella, Naples, 2001/ arpa 8	Italy	[Luigi Sisto, Emanuele Cardi and Sergio Tassi, *Il Museo della Musica. Strumenti Antichi e Documenti del Conservatorio di S. Pietro a Majella: Guida alla mostra a cura di Luigi Sisto, Emanuele Cardi, Sergio Tassi* (Naples: Conservatorio di S. Pietro a Majella, 2002), p. 10]	December 1828	12 January 1829
4202		Present owner and location unknown		Information from John Hoare (Pilgrim Harps)	December 1828	28 January 1829
4205		Present owner and location unknown	UK	Information from Michael Parfett	January 1829	2 February 1829
4218		Museo internazionale e biblioteca della musica di Bologna, MCP39386	Italy	Information from the museum's online catalogue	March 1829	27 April 1829

Official serial number	Secondary serial number	Present owner, location and inventory number	Country	Source of information [references]	Date of registration in Erard ledgers	First transaction (sale, hire, etc.) noted in Erard ledgers
4220		Present owner and location unknown		Information from John Hoare (Pilgrim Harps)	March 1829	31 March 1829
4226		Present owner and location unknown		Information from John Hoare (Pilgrim Harps)	March 1829	1 March 1829
4229		Present owner and location unknown		Information from the internet; available for sale in September 2019 by www.charish.com	April 1829	22 May 1829
4250	R 4351	Lyme, Cheshire, NT 500496	UK	Information from the National Trust Collections online catalogue	July 1829	24 September 1829
4277		Present owner and location unknown		Lot 346 at Christie's 5589, Paris, France, 19 March 2010	August 1829	29 December 1831
4279		Present owner and location unknown		Available for sale on 14 July 2017 by Niebisch & Tree, High Wycombe, UK	August 1829	14 September 1829
4285		Present owner and location unknown		Information from John Hoare (Pilgrim Harps)	October 1829	11 November 1829
4287		Present owner and location unknown		Lot 4 at Christie's 4720, London, UK, 18 March 1992	September 1829	26 September 1829
4296		Present owner and location unknown		Lot 207 at Christie's 2646, Amsterdam, Netherlands, 14–15 December 2004	November 1829	18 November 1829
4382		Present owner and location unknown		Information from John Hoare (Pilgrim Harps)	August 1830	9 August 1832

Official serial number	Secondary serial number	Present owner, location and inventory number	Country	Source of information [references]	Date of registration in Erard ledgers	First transaction (sale, hire, etc.) noted in Erard ledgers
4408		Present owner and location unknown		Available for sale in July 2019 from Pilgrim Harps, Reference: 1462	November 1830	23 March 1831
4432		Present owner and location unknown		Lot 10 at Bonhams 20510, Edinburgh, UK, 24 October 2012	January 1831	25 March 1831
4449		Present owner and location unknown		Lot 209 at Veritas Arts Auctioneers 104, Lisbon, Portugal, 14 April 2021; information from Jon Hunnisett	April 1831	28 April 1831
4458	R 4551 R	National Music Museum, South Dakota University, Vermillion, NMM 1218	USA	Information from Nancy Hurrell and Emanuele Marconi, and from the museum's online catalogue	April 1831	28 October 1831
4462		Present owner and location unknown		Information from John Hoare (Pilgrim Harps)	May 1831	14 June 1831
4463		Present owner and location unknown		Information from John Hoare (Pilgrim Harps)	May 1831	4 June 1831
4474		Present owner and location unknown		Lot 5 at Christie's 9671, London, UK, 16 July 2013	May 1831	1 June 1832
4490		Present owner and location unknown		Information from the internet	May 1831	29 June 1831
4493		Stearns Collection, University of Michigan, Ann Arbor, 1620	USA	Information from Nancy Hurrell and from the collection's online catalogue	June 1831	8 August 1831
4504		Present owner and location unknown		Information from John Hoare (Pilgrim Harps)	September 1831	6 September 1834

Official serial number	Secondary serial number	Present owner, location and inventory number	Country	Source of information [references]	Date of registration in Erard ledgers	First transaction (sale, hire, etc.) noted in Erard ledgers
4512		Ceredigion Museum, Aberystwyth, 2002.11.2	UK	Information from the internet	September 1831	21 December 1831
4520		Present owner and location unknown		Information from John Hoare (Pilgrim Harps)	September 1831	4 October 1831
4531		Present owner and location unknown		Information from John Hoare (Pilgrim Harps)	December 1831	26 March 1832
4534	4455	Private collection of Nancy Thym (Museum und Archiv für Harfengeschichte), Freising	Germany	Information from Nancy Thym; personally examined on 13 July 2017	January 1832	30 April 1832
4543		Present owner and location unknown		Information from John Hoare (Pilgrim Harps)	April 1832	8 October 1835
4561		Private collection	UK	Information from Jon Hunnisett	February 1832	9 May 1832
4567		Present owner and location unknown		Available for sale in May 2018 by https://www.harfe.de/boerse	March 1832	11 April 1832
4568	C 4622	Musical Instruments Museum Edinburgh, Edinburgh, 176	UK	Information from Jenny Nex and Jonathan Santa Maria Bouquet; personally examined on 6 June 2017	March 1832	27 April 1832
4587		Present owner and location unknown		Information from Michael Parfett	July 1832	12 July 1833
4596		Present owner and location unknown		Information from the internet; available for sale in 2017	July 1832	30 September 1834

Official serial number	Secondary serial number	Present owner, location and inventory number	Country	Source of information [references]	Date of registration in Erard ledgers	First transaction (sale, hire, etc.) noted in Erard ledgers
4603		Present owner and location unknown		Information from John Hoare (Pilgrim Harps)	July 1832	11 August 1832
4607		Present owner and location unknown		Information from John Hoare (Pilgrim Harps)	August 1832	19 March 1834
4618		Private collection of Linky Muller, Gold Coast	Australia	[Hallo, *Erard, Bochsa and their impact on harp music-making in Australia*, p. 194]	August 1832	2 November 1832
4626		Present owner and location unknown		Information from John Hoare (Pilgrim Harps)	September 1832	15 November 1832
4633		Mount Stewart, County Down, Northern Ireland, NT 1220958	UK	Information from the National Trust Collections online catalogue	November 1832	8 December 1832
4637		Present owner and location unknown		Information from a list dated 2008 of Erard harps restored by H. Bryan & Co, Lynchburg, VA, USA; list provided by Nancy Hurrell	November 1832	18 December 1832
4667		Present owner and location unknown		Information from John Hoare (Pilgrim Harps)	March 1833	16 July 1833
4676		Present owner and location unknown		Information from John Hoare (Pilgrim Harps)	February 1833	22 March 1833

Official serial number	Secondary serial number	Present owner, location and inventory number	Country	Source of information [references]	Date of registration in Erard ledgers	First transaction (sale, hire, etc.) noted in Erard ledgers
4679		Castello Sforzesco, Milan, 300	Italy	Information from Francesca Tasso; personally examined on 4 July 2016 [Alessandro Restelli, *Museo degli Strumenti Musicali del Casello Sforzesco a Milano* (Milan: Skira, 2014), pp. 48, 55, 57]	February 1833	13 September 1834
4691		Present owner and location unknown		Lot 7 at Bonhams 17825, London, UK, 10 March 2010	May 1833	25 July 1833
4697		Present owner and location unknown		Information from John Hoare (Pilgrim Harps)	April 1833	8 August 1833
4721	4769	Present owner and location unknown		Information from the internet	July 1833	19 March 1834
4770		Present owner and location unknown		Information from John Hoare (Pilgrim Harps)	December 1833	29 January 1834
4783		Present owner and location unknown		Lot 6 at Bonhams 11253, London, UK, 6 September 2004	March 1834	17 March 1834
4785		Present owner and location unknown		Information from John Hoare (Pilgrim Harps)	March 1834	26 April 1834
4824		Ceredigion Museum, Aberystwyth, 2009.201.1	UK	Information from the internet	June 1834	22 July 1834
4842		Present owner and location unknown		Lot 262 at Christie's 6714, London, UK, 31 October 1994	September 1834	29 September 1834

Official serial number	Secondary serial number	Present owner, location and inventory number	Country	Source of information [references]	Date of registration in Erard ledgers	First transaction (sale, hire, etc.) noted in Erard ledgers
4870		Present owner and location unknown		Information from John Hoare (Pilgrim Harps)	November 1834	19 August 1835
4880		Present owner and location unknown		Information from John Hoare (Pilgrim Harps)	January 1835	10 April 1835
4911		Present owner and location unknown		Information from Michael Parfett	June 1835	30 June 1835
4945		Present owner and location unknown		Information from Michael Parfett	July 1835	13 December 1838
4962		Mildred Dilling Harp Collection, Jacobs School of Music, Indiana University, Bloomington	USA	Information from Nancy Hurrell and Ken Yeung, and from the University's website	September 1836	10 November 1835
4998		Present owner and location unknown		Information from John Hoare (Pilgrim Harps)	March 1836	3 January 1838
5017	5031 JC	Present owner and location unknown		Formerly housed at the Schola Cantorum Basiliensis, Basel, Switzerland; information from Kathrin Menzel and Beat Wolf [Wolf, *Harp Archives*: BW 40/450/5017]	June 1836	8 September 1836
5018		Present owner and location unknown		Information from John Hoare (Pilgrim Harps)	July 1836	13 December 1839

Official serial number	Secondary serial number	Present owner, location and inventory number	Country	Source of information [references]	Date of registration in Erard ledgers	First transaction (sale, hire, etc.) noted in Erard ledgers
5027		Present owner and location unknown		Information from John Hoare (Pilgrim Harps)	August 1836	3 October 1837
5051		Present owner and location unknown		Available for sale in July 2019 by Michael Parfett, London, UK	July 1836	29 February 1840
5121		Present owner and location unknown		Information from John Hoare (Pilgrim Harps)	August 1837	8 December 1838
5206	5192 WH	Scenkonstmuseet, Stockholm, X5713	Sweden	Personally examined in August 2014; information from the MIMO website	April 1838	21 May 1838
5369		Present owner and location unknown		Lot 183 at Kodner Galleries, Dania Beach, Florida, USA, 11 October 2010	March 1840	18 September 1844
5389		Present owner and location unknown		Lot 2193 at Dargate Auction Galleries, Pittsburgh, PA, USA, 27 January 2008	April 1840	24 August 1841
5429		Present owner and location unknown		Information from John Hoare (Pilgrim Harps)	October 1840	24 January 1843
5466	WH 5436	Helsinki City Museum, Helsinki, XLII-1314	Finland	Information from the museum's online catalogue	March 1841	23 January 1843
5485		Present owner and location unknown		Information from John Hoare (Pilgrim Harps)	June 1841	1 November 1845

Total: 273

Extant Erard Grecian harps with unverified serial numbers housed in public and private collections

Official serial number	Secondary serial number	Present owner, location and inventory number	Country	Source of information [references]	Date of registration in Erard ledgers	First transaction (sale, hire, etc.) noted in Erard ledgers
?		National Museums Wales, Cardiff, F83.25	UK	Information from the MINIM-UK website		
?		Kirklees Museums and Galleries, Huddersfield, KL 3563	UK	Information from the MINIM-UK website		
?		Cliffe Castle Museum, Keighley, 154:1956	UK	Information from the MINIM-UK website		
?		Westwood Manor, Wiltshire, NT 222417	UK	Information from the National Trust Collections online catalogue		
?		Royal Welsh College of Music & Drama, Cardiff	UK	Information from the College's website		
?		Château de Cheverny, Cheverny	France	Information from the internet		
?		Laurel Hill Mansion, Philadelphia	USA	Information from the Mansion's website		
?		Private collection of Stephen Dunstone	UK	Information from the owner's website		
?		Private collection of Aimée van Delden	Netherlands	Information from the owner's website		

Official serial number	Secondary serial number	Present owner, location and inventory number	Country	Source of information [references]	Date of registration in Erard ledgers	First transaction (sale, hire, etc.) noted in Erard ledgers
?		Private collection of Mechteld Karlien de Jongh	Netherlands	Information from the owner's website		1818
?		Present owner and location unknown		Sold by David Wolfenden Antiques, Northern Ireland, UK		1825
?		Present owner and location unknown		Information from the internet		1825
?		Private collection of Robert Pacey	UK	Information from the owner's website		1828
?		Private collection of Tom Monger	UK	Information from the owner's website		1829
?		Present owner and location unknown		Information from the internet; according to the source, the harp was 'restored to playing condition in 1990 by New Zealand harpmaker Kim Webby'		1830
?		Present owner and location unknown		Information from the internet (YouTube video); according to the source, the harp was owned in 2011 by Vanessa Wood-Davies		1838
?		Present owner and location unknown		Lot 3294 at Bonhams 16119, San Francisco, CA, USA, 27 October 2008		
?		Present owner and location unknown		Lot 447 at Art La Rosa, Catania, Italy, 26 January 2019		

Official serial number	Secondary serial number	Present owner, location and inventory number	Country	Source of information [references]	Date of registration in Erard ledgers	First transaction (sale, hire, etc.) noted in Erard ledgers
?		Present owner and location unknown		Lot 35 at Bonhams 16004, London, UK, 24 June 2008		
?		Present owner and location unknown		Lot 1336 at Reeman Dansie, Colchester, UK, 16 February 2010		
?		Present owner and location unknown		Lot 49 at Sotheby's, London, UK, 27 November 1975		
?		Present owner and location unknown		Sold by Carter's Antiques & Collectables, Armadale, Australia		
?		Present owner and location unknown		Available for sale in August 2019 by Niebisch & Tree, High Wycombe, UK		
?		Present owner and location unknown		Available for sale in August 2019 by Affairs of the Harp, St Albans, UK; previous owner in St Albans, UK		
?		Present owner and location unknown		Information from the internet (Facebook page)		
?		Present owner and location unknown		Information from the internet (www.worthpoint.com)		
?		Present owner and location unknown		Information from the internet (online catalogue of the Bibliothèque national de France, reference: ark:/12148/cb39897950k)		

Total: 27

Bibliography

Manuscript and Archival Collections

Archives Érard (1788–1983), Musée de la Musique, Paris (E.2009.5.40–E.2009.5.177).

Erard Harp Bill, 27 May 1818. Attingham Park Collection, Shropshire Archives, Shrewsbury, 112/6/54/381.

Erard Harp Catalogue (London: Erard, c.1819–1821). University of Glasgow Archives & Special Collections, A.x.24.

Erard London Harp Ledgers, vols 1–3. Royal College of Music, London, Special Collections (RCM 497).

Holtzapffel and Company, London Metropolitan Archives, CLC/B/121/MS09475.

Jackson, George and Sons Ledger. V&A Archive of Art and Design, London, AD/2012/1/2/1.

Records of Charles Holtzapffel and Company, University of Edinburgh Centre for Research Collections, Gen. 879F–882F (4 vols; F H and K between 1811 and 1822 and customers' journal 1892–1897).

Printed Primary Sources

Contemporary Books and Articles

These titles include works written or published up to c.1850; works written or published after 1850 have been included in secondary sources.

Adam, Robert and James, *Works in Architecture of Robert and James Adam* (London: Adam, 1773–1779).

Adams, Samuel and Sarah, *The Complete Servant: Being a Practical Guide to the Peculiar Duties and Business of All Descriptions of Servants* (London: Knight and Lacey, 1825).

Appleton, Elizabeth, *Private Education; or a Practical Plan for the Studies of Young Ladies. With an Address to Parents, Private Governesses, and Young Ladies* (London: Henry Colburn, 1815).

Austen, Jane, *Sense and Sensibility: A Novel* (3 vols; London: Thomas Egerton, 1811).

——, *Pride and Prejudice: A Novel* (3 vols; London: Thomas Egerton, 1813).

——, *Mansfield Park: A Novel* (3 vols; London: Egerton, 1814).

——, *Emma: A Novel* (3 vols; London: John Murray, 1816).

——, *Sanditon* (New York: Simon and Schuster, 1998).

——, *Northanger Abbey: and Persuasion* (4 vols; London: John Murray, 1818).

 Bibliography

Bochsa, Robert Nicolas-Charles, *Forty Studies Expressly Composed for Sebastian Erard's Double Movement Harp* (London: Chappell & Co, 1818). Pendlebury Library of Music, University of Cambridge, XRa.850.18A.X22.

——, *A New and Improved Method of Instruction for the Harp* (London: Chappell & Co, c.1819).

Brontë, Charlotte, *Jane Eyre: An Autobiography* (3 vols; London: Smith, Elder & Co., 1847).

Burney, Frances, *The Wanderer; or, Female Difficulties* (5 vols; London: Longman, Hurst, Rees, Orme and Brown, 1814).

Cignani, Pietro A. (ed.), *Manuel Du Voyageur, Or, the Traveller's Pocket Companion: Consisting of Familiar Conversations in English, French, and Italian; With Models of Letters, Notes etc. Also a Table of French and Italian Coins, and the Various Terms Used in Music. By Madame de Genlis* (12th edn, London: Samuel Leigh, 1819).

Cobbet, William, *Cobbett's Political Register* (London: Cox and Baylis, 1811).

Colburn and Company, *A New System of Practical Domestic Economy* (London: H. Colburn and Company, 1823).

D' Harcanville, Baron (Pierre François Hugues), *Collection of Etruscan, Greek and Roman antiquities from the cabinet of the Honourable William Hamilton* (4 vols; Naples: Morelli, 1766–1767).

Desilver, Robert, *Memoirs of the late Princess Charlotte Augusta, of Wales and Saxe Cobourg* (Philadelphia: Robert Desilver, 1818).

Dickens, Charles, *The posthumous papers of the Pickwick Club* (London: Chapman & Hall, 1837).

——, *A Christmas Carol. In Prose. Being a Ghost Story of Christmas* (London: Chapman & Hall, 1843).

——, *Dombey and Son* (London: Bradbury & Evans, 1848).

——, *The Personal History of David Copperfield* (London: Bradbury & Evans, 1850).

Dougall, John, *The Modern Preceptor; Or, a General Course of Education*, vol. 1 (London: Vernon, Hood and Sharpe, 1810).

Edgeworth, Maria, *Helen, a Tale* (3 vols; London: Richard Bentley, 1834).

Erard, Pierre, *The Harp: In its present improved State Compared with The Original Pedal Harp* (London: Erard, 1821).

Hall, John E., 'Choice of Musical Instruments for Females', in John E. Hall (ed.), *The Port Folio* 10, No.1 (Philadelphia: Harrison Hall, 1820), pp. 91–93.

Halleck, Fitz-Greene (ed.), *The Works of Lord Byron, in Verse and Prose, Including his Letters, Journals, etc. with a Sketch of his Life* (New York: G. Dearborn, 1833).

Hoffmann, Ernst Theodor Amadeus, *Hoffmann's Strange Stories* (trans. from German by Burnham Brothers; Boston: Burnham Brothers, 1855).

Holtzapffel, Charles, *Turning and mechanical manipulation intended as a work of general reference and practical instruction on the lathe, and the various mechanical pursuits followed by amateurs* (3 vols; London: Holtzapffel & Co; vol. 1 1843; vol. 2 1846; vol. 3 published posthumously 1850).

Lamb, Caroline, *Glenarvon* (3 vols; London: Henry Colburn, 1816).

Le Roy, David, *Les ruines des plus beaux monuments de la Grèce* (Paris, 1758).

Light, Edward, *New and Compleat Instructions for playing on the Harp-Lute* (London: Light, c.1813).

Rehberg, Friedrich, *Drawings Faithfully copied from Nature at Naples* (Naples, 1794).

Reichardt, Johann Friedrich, *Johann Friedrich Reichardt's vertraute Briefe aus Paris geschrieben in den Jahren 1802–1803* (Hamburg: B. G. Hoffmann, 1805).

Sainsbury, John, *A Dictionary of Musicians, from the Earliest Ages to the Present Time, Vol.1* (2nd edn; London: Sainsbury, 1827).

Scott, Walter, *The Lady of the Lake: A Poem* (Edinburgh: John Ballantyne & Co, 1810).

——, *Ivanhoe: A Romance* (3 vols; Edinburgh: Archibald Constable, 1820).

——, *Waverley; or, 'Tis Sixty Years Since* (3 vols; Edinburgh: John Ballantyne & Co, 1814).

Stuart, James, and Nicholas Revett, *The antiquities of Athens* (London: Haberkorn, 1762).

Thackeray, William Makepeace, *Vanity Fair: A Novel without a Hero* (London: Bradbury & Evans, 1848).

Wollstonecraft Shelley, Mary, *Frankenstein; or, The Modern Prometheus* (3 vols; London: Lackington, Hughes, Harding, Mavor & Jones, 1818).

——, *Valperga: or, The life and adventures of Castruccio, prince of Lucca* (3 vols; London: G. and W. B. Whittaker, 1823).

——, *The Last Man* (3 vols; London: Henry Colburn, 1826).

——, *The Fortunes of Perkin Warbeck, a Romance* (3 vols; London: H. Colburn and R. Bentley, 1830).

——, *Lodore* (3 vols; London: R. Bentley, 1835).

——, *Mathilda* (Auckland: The Floating Press, 2010).

Contemporary Newspapers, Periodicals and Directories

Anonymous sources have been arranged in alphabetical order according to their title.

Ackermann, Rudolph, *The Repository of arts, literature, fashions, commerce, manufactures, &c.* (London: Rudolph Ackermann, 1819).

'A Second Series of Twelve Fantasias, or Exercises for the Harp', *The Quarterly Musical Magazine and Review* 5 (1823), pp. 101–104.

'Fourth letter from a young married lady, to her sister in the country', *Belle Assemblée; being Bell's Court and Fashionable Magazine* (London: John Bell, 1818), pp. 39–40.

'Grecian Triumph; Or, the Harp of Victory', *The Mirror of Literature, Amusement, and Instruction* 4 (London: J. Limbird, 1824), p. 339.

'Hymenea in search of a husband', *La Belle Assemblée: being Bell's Court and Fashionable Magazine, Addressed Particularly to the Ladies* 4 (London: John Bell, 1811), pp. 7–11.

Johnstone, Andrew, *Johnstone's London Commercial Guide and Street Directory* (London: Barnard & Farley, 1818).

'London full dress', *The Lady's Magazine, Or, Entertaining Companion for the Fair Sex* 36 (London: G. and J. Robinson, 1805), p. 321.

New Guide. An historical and descriptive account of Leamington and Warwick; to which are added, short notices of the towns, villages, etc. within the circuit of ten miles (Warwick, 1825).

'On the management of the person in dancing, and in the exercise of other female accomplishments', *The Mirror of the Graces; Or, The English Lady's Costume* (Edinburgh: A. Black, 1830), pp. 136–160.

'On the Preservation of the Independence of the Female Character', *Belle Assemblée; being Bell's Court and Fashionable Magazine* (London: John Bell, 1818), pp. 164–165.

'Records of the Beau-Monde. Fashions for April 1826', *La Belle Assemblée, or Court and Fashionable Magazine* 3 (London: George Whitaker, 1826).

Scheidler, Johann David, 'Ueber Harfen und die besten Verfertiger dieses Instruments', *Jounal des Luxus und der Moden* 17 (1802), pp. 85–86.

The Musical World 19 (London: G. Purkess, 1844).

Urban, Sylvanus, *The Gentleman's Magazine: and Historical Chronicle. From January to June 1816. Vol. 86* (London: Nichols, Son and Bentley, 1816).

Wakefield, Roger, *Wakefield's Merchant and Tradesman's General Directory* (London: T. Davison, 1794).

Wycliffe, Bernard, 'Missolonghi', *The Oriental Herald, and Journal of General Literature* 10 (London: J. M. Richardson, 1826), p. 304.

Secondary Sources

Adelson, Robert, 'The Viscountess de Beaumont's Harp and Music Album (1780)', *The Galpin Society Journal* 62 (2009), pp. 159–166.

——, 'Inside an Eighteenth-Century Instrument Builder's Workshop: Erard's Letter Copy Book (1791–1797)', *Journal of the American Musical Instrument Society* 47 (2017), pp. 5–57.

——, *The Harp, from Marie-Antoinette to the Present* (Ancenis: Editions Camac, 2017).

——, 'Originality and Influence: Charles Gröll's Role in the Invention of the Double-action Harp', *Muzyka* 64/1 (2019), pp. 3–21.

——, *Erard: A Passion for the Piano* (Oxford and New York: Oxford University Press, 2021).

——, *Erard: Empire of the Harp* (Ancenis: Les Harpes Camac, 2022).

Adelson, Robert, and Jacqueline Letzter, '"For a woman when she is young and beautiful": The Harp in Eighteenth-Century France', in Annette Kreutziger-Herr and Katrin Losleben, *History/Herstory: Alternative Musikgeschichten* (Cologne, Weimar, Vienna: Böhlau, 2009), pp. 314–335.

Adelson, Robert, Alan Roudier and Francis Duvernay, 'Rediscovering Cousineau's Fourteen-Pedal Harp', *The Galpin Society Journal* 63 (2010), pp. 159–178.

Adelson, Robert, Laure Barthel, Michel Foussard, Jenny Nex and Alain Roudier (eds), *Erard and the Invention of the Modern Harp, 1811–2011* (Nice: Musée du Palais Lascaris, 2011).

Adelson, Robert, Alain Roudier, Jenny Nex, Laure Barthel and Michel Foussard, (eds), *The History of the Erard Piano and Harp in Letters and Documents, 1785–1959* (Cambridge: Cambridge University Press, 2015).

Alder, Ken, 'Innovation and Amnesia: Engineering Rationality and the Fate of Interchangeable Parts Manufacturing in France', *Technology and Culture* 38/2 (1997), pp. 273–311.

Anderson, Benjamin, '"An alternative discourse": Local interpreters of antiquities in the Ottoman Empire', *Journal of Field Archaeology* 40/4 (2015), pp. 450–460.

Anderson, Mark J. and Sally Malenka, 'The characterization and treatment of gilded surfaces on an early nineteenth-century harp', in Deborah Bigelow (ed.), *Gilded Wood: Conservation and History* (Madison, Connecticut: Sound View Press, 1991), pp. 319–330.

Anderson, William Eric Kinloch (ed.), *The Journal of Sir Walter Scott* (Edinburgh: Canongate, 1998).

Andrew, James, Jeremy Stein, Jennifer Tann and Christine MacLeod, 'The Transition from Timber to Cast Iron Working Beams for Steam Engines: A Technological Innovation', *Transactions of the Newcomen Society* 70/1 (1998), pp. 197–220.

Ashworth, William J., '"System of Terror": Samuel Bentham, Accountability and Dockyard Reform during the Napoleonic Wars', *Social History* 23/1 (1998), pp. 63–79.

Bailey, Candace, *Charleston Belles Abroad: The Music Collections of Harriet Lowndes, Henrietta Aiken, and Louisa Rebecca McCord* (Columbia: University of South Carolina Press, 2019).

Baldwin, Mike, 'The Erat Harp Manufactory: Painted and Gilded Decoration 1821–1826', *The Galpin Society Journal* 66 (2013), pp. 149–164.

——, *Harp Making in Late-Georgian London* (London: Baldwin & Bright Light, 2020).

Barbieri, Patrizio, 'Harps Versus Pianos: Parisian *querelles* on Tuning 1770–1830', *The Galpin Society Journal* 77 (2017), pp. 149–164.

Barclay, Robert, *The Art of the Trumpet-maker: The Materials, Tools, and Techniques of the Seventeenth and Eighteenth Centuries in Nuremberg* (Oxford: Clarendon Press, 1992).

——, *The Preservation and Use of Historic Musical Instruments: Display Case and Concert Hall* (London: Earthscan, 2005).

Barthel, Laure, *Au cœur de la harpe au XVIIIème siècle* (Paris: Garnier-François, 2005).

Beall, Karen F., 'The Interdependence of Printer & Printmaker in Early 19th-Century Lithography', *Art Journal* 39/3 (1980), pp. 195–201.

Berg, Maxine, 'Markets, Trade and European Manufacture', in Maxine Berg (ed.), *Markets and Manufacture in Early Industrial Europe* (London and New York: Routledge, 1991), pp. 3–27.

——, 'From Imitation to Invention: Creating Commodities in Eighteenth-Century Britain', *The Economic History Review* 55/1 (2002), pp. 1–30.

Bernasconi, Gianenrico, *Objets portatifs au Siècle des lumières* (Paris: CTHS, 2015).

Bonnington, Moira, 'The Oldest Harp Maker in the World', *The Galpin Society Journal* 54 (2001), pp. 45–55.

Bordas, Cristina, 'Erard Pianos and Harps in Spain and Portugal', in Rudolf Frick (ed.), *Sébastien Erard: ein europäischer Pionier des Instrumentenbaus. Internationales Erard-Symposium Michaelstein 13.–14. November 1994, Michaelsteiner Konferenzberichte 48* (Blankenburg: Stiftung Kloster Michaelstein, 1995), pp. 30–32.

Bowles, Edmund A., 'Nineteenth-century innovations in the use and construction of the timpani', *Journal of the American Musical Instrument Society* 5–6 (1980), pp. 74–143.

Brake, Laurel, Bill Bell and David Finkelstein, (eds), *Nineteenth-Century Media and the Construction of Identities* (Basingstoke and New York: Palgrave, 2000).

Breguet, Emmanuel, 'Das Gewicht der Welt: Breguets Internationales Vertriebsnetz', in Emmanuel Breguet, Nicole Minder and Rodolphe De Pierri (eds), *Abraham-Lousis Breguet: Die Uhrmacherkunst erobert die Welt* (Paris: Somogy, 2011), pp. 78–137.

——, 'Breguet Makes the First Wristwatch fit for a Queen', *Le Quai de l'Horloge* 1 (2011), pp. 33–39.

Brenner, Klaus-Peter, *Die Naderman-Harfe in der Musikinstrumentensammlung der Universität Göttingen. Ein französisches Instrument des 18. Jahrhunderts als Maschine, Skulptur, Möbel, Prestigefetisch, Ware und Klangwerkzeug. Orbis Musicarum 14* (Göttingen: Edition Re, 1998).

Britten, Frederick James, *Old Clocks and Watches & Their Makers* (5th edn; London: E. & F. N. Spon, 1922).

Brooks, Randall Chapman, 'Origins, Usage and Production of Screws: An Historical Perspective', *History and Technology* 8/1 (1990), pp. 51–76.

Bryans, Dennis, 'The Double Invention of Printing', *Journal of Design History* 13/4 (2000), pp. 287–300.

Butlin, Martin R. F., 'Lawrence's Portrait of Mrs Francis Robertson: Some New Letters', *The Burlington Magazine* 99/646 (1957), pp. 27–29.

Cantrell, John, 'Henry Maudslay', in John Cantrell and Gillian Cookson (eds), *Henry Maudslay and the Pioneers of the Machine Age* (Stroud: Tempus, 2002), pp. 18–38.

Carnevali, Francesca and Lucy Newton, 'Pianos for the People: From Producer to Consumer in Britain, 1851–1914', *Enterprise & Society* 14/1 (2013), pp. 37–70.

Carpenter, Kirsty, *Refugees of the French Revolution: Émigrés in London, 1789–1802* (Basingstoke: MacMillan, 1999).

——, 'London: Capital of the Emigration', in Kirsty Carpenter and Philip Mansel (eds), *The French Emigres in Europe and the Struggle against Revolution, 1789–1814* (London: MacMillan, 1999), pp. 43–67.

Clarke, Linda, *Building Capitalism: Historical Change and the Labour Process in the Production of Built Environment* (London and New York: Routledge, 2011).

Cleary, Maria Christina, 'The Invention of the 18th Century: the Harpe Organisée and Pedals', *American Harp Journal* 26/2 (2018), pp. 22–38.

Clifford, Timothy, 'The Plaster Shops of the Rococo and Neo-Classical Era in Britain', *Journal of the History of Collections* 4/1 (1992), pp. 39–65.

Cole, Michael, *The Pianoforte in the Classical Era* (Oxford: Clarendon Press, 1998).

Coltman, Viccy, 'Sir William Hamilton's Vase Publications (1766–1776): A Case Study in the Reproduction and Dissemination of Antiquity', *Journal of Design History* 14/1 (2001), pp. 1–16.

Cookson, Gillian, 'Introduction', in John Cantrell and Gillian Cookson (eds), *Henry Maudslay and the Pioneers of the Machine Age* (Stroud: Tempus, 2002), pp. 12–17.

Cooper, Carolyn C., 'The Portsmouth System of Manufacture', *Technology and Culture* 25/2 (1984), pp. 182–225.

Coquery, Natacha, 'The Language of Success: Marketing and Distributing Semi-Luxury Goods in Eighteenth-Century Paris', *Journal of Design History* 17/1 (2004), pp. 71–89.

Craske, Matthew, 'Plan and Control: Design and the Competitive Spirit in Early and Mid-Eighteenth Century England', *Journal of Design History* 12/3 (1999), pp. 187–216.

D'Arcy Wood, Gillen, *Romanticism and Music Culture in Britain, 1770–1840: Virtue and Virtuosity* (Cambridge: Cambridge University Press, 2010).

Darmstädter, Beatrix, Rudolf Hopfner and Alfons Huber (eds), *Die Sammlung alter Musikinstrumente/The Collection of Historic Musical Instruments - Die ersten 100 Jahre/The First 100 Years* (Vienna: Praesens, 2018).

Deutsches Museum Jahresbericht 2016 (Munich: Deutsches Museum, 2016).

Deutsches Museum Jahresbericht 2017 (Munich: Deutsches Museum, 2017).

Deutsches Museum Jahresbericht 2018 (Munich: Deutsches Museum, 2018).

Devale, Sue Carol, 'Harp: V7.III: The double-action pedal harp', in Laurence Libin (ed.), *The Grove Dictionary of Musical Instruments* (2nd edn, New York: Oxford University Press, 2014), vol. 2, pp. 574–576.

Devale, Sue Carol, and Nancy Thym-Hochrein, 'Harp: V7.I. Hook harps and single-action pedal harps', in Laurence Libin (ed.), *The Grove Dictionary of Musical Instruments* (2nd edn, New York: Oxford University Press 2014), vol. 2, pp. 572–573.

Di Stefano, Giovanni Paolo, Selima Giorgia Giuliano and Sandra Proto (eds), *Strumenti musicali in Sicilia* (Palermo: CRICD-Regione Siciliana, 2013).

Donovan, Julie, *Sydney Owenson, Lady Morgan and the Politics of Style. Irish Research Series* 55 (Bethesda, Dublin and Palo Alto: Academica Press, 2009).

Droysen-Reber, Dagmar, *Harfen des Berliner Musikinstrumenten-Museums* (Berlin: Staatliches Institut für Musikforschung Preußischer Kulturbesitz, 1999).

——, 'Die Cousineau-Harfe mit den "chevilles tournantes"', *Musica instrumentalis* 3 (2001), pp. 129–137.

——, 'Schedules of the harps from no. 42 to no. 52', in John Henry van der Meer (ed.), *In Search of Lost Sounds: Art and Music in the Instruments Collection of Fernanda Giulini* (Milan and Briosco: Villa Medici Giulini, 2006), pp. 432–501.

Dubois, Pierre, *Music in the Georgian Novel* (Cambridge: Cambridge University Press, 2015).

Dugot, Joël, 'Sonorités inouïes: la nouvelle harpe de Messieurs Krumpholtz et Naderman', *Music, Images, Instruments* 7 (2005), pp. 86–109.

Edwards, Clive, *Encyclopedia of Furniture Materials, Trades and Techniques* (Aldershot: Ashgate, 2000).

Escalas i Llimona, Romà (ed.), *Museu de la Música: 1/Catàleg d'instruments* (Barcelona: Ajuntament de Barcelona, 1991).

Falkus, Malcolm E., 'The Early Development of the British Gas Industry, 1790–1815', *The Economic History Review* 35/2 (1982), pp. 217–234.

Faxon, Alicia Craig, 'Preserving the Classical Past: Sir William and Lady Emma Hamilton', *Visual Resources* 20/4 (2004), pp. 259–273.

Fisher, Megan, 'Women and Harps in the Home in Early Nineteenth-century London: Part 1', *Harp* 2016/1 (2016), pp. 18–19.

——, 'Women and Harps in the Home in Early Nineteenth-century London: Notes on Harp and Piano Duets', *Harp* 2016/2 (2016), pp. 12–13.

Fox, Celina, *The Arts of Industry in the Age of Enlightenment* (New Haven, Conn.: Yale University Press for The Paul Mellon Centre for Studies in British Art, 2009).

Frick, Rudolf (ed.), *Sébastien Erard: ein europäischer Pionier des Instrumentenbaus. Internationales Erard-Symposium Michaelstein 13.–14. November 1994, Michaelsteiner Konferenzberichte 48* (Blankenburg: Stiftung Kloster Michaelstein, 1995).

Gash, Norman, 'After Waterloo: British Society and the Legacy of the Napoleonic Wars', *Transactions of the Royal Historical Society* 28 (1978), pp. 145–157.

Gétreau, Florence, 'Erard', in Ludwig Finscher (ed.) *Die Musik in Geschichte und Gegenwart. Personenteil 6 E-Frau* (2nd edn; Stuttgart: Bärenreiter/Metzler, 2001), p. 394.

Goebl-Streicher, Uta, *Das Reisetagebuch des Klavierbauers Johann Baptist Streicher 1821–1822: Text und Kommentar* (Tutzing: Schneider, 2009).

Grattan Flood, William Henry, *The Story of the Harp* (London: Scott & New York: Scribner, 1905).

Grego, Joseph, *Rowlandson the Caricaturist: A Selection from His Works* (2 vols; London: Chatto and Windus, 1880).

Greig, Hannah, *The Beau Monde: Fashionable Society in Georgian London* (Oxford: Oxford University Press, 2013).

Griffiths, Ann, Robert Adelson and Jenny Nex, 'Erard', in Laurence Libin (ed.), *The Grove Dictionary of Musical Instruments* (2nd edn, New York: Oxford University Press 2014), vol. 2, pp. 234–237.

Haag, Volker, Valentina Zemke, Swati Tamantini and Panagiotis Poulopoulos, 'Das Barberini-Harfen-Projekt: Untersuchungen an einem Meisterwerk aus dem Jahr 1630', *Holz-Zentralblatt* 147/49 (2021), pp. 881–882.

Haimes, Geoffrey, 'New Zealand, an Erard island', in Rudolf Frick (ed.), *Sébastien Erard: ein europäischer Pionier des Instrumentenbaus. Internationales Erard-Symposium Michaelstein 13.–14. November 1994, Michaelsteiner Konferenzberichte 48* (Blackenburg: Stiftung Kloster Michaelstein, 1995), pp. 34–36.

Hamamatsu Museum of Musical Instruments (ed.), *General Guide to the Hamamatsu Museum of Musical Instruments* (Hamamatsu: Hamamatsu City, 2015).

Hellman, Jesse M., 'Lady Hamilton, Nelson's Enchantress, and the Creation of Pygmalion', *Shaw* 35/2 (2015), pp. 213–237.

Henderson, John P. with John B. Davis [Warren J. Samuels and Gilbert B. Davis, (eds)], *The Life and Economics of David Ricardo* (Boston: Kluwer Academic, 1997).

Henkel, Hubert, *Besaitete Tasteninstrumente. Deutsches Museum. Kataloge der Sammlungen. Musikinstrumenten-Sammlung* (Frankfurt am Main: Bochinsky, 1994).

Highfill, Philip H. Jr., Kalman A. Burnim and Edward A. Langhans, *A biographical dictionary of actors, actresses, musicians, dancers, managers & other stage personnel in London, 1660–1800* (Carbondale: Southern Illinois University Press, 1993).

Hills, Richard L., 'Richard Roberts', in John Cantrell and Gillian Cookson (eds), *Henry Maudslay and the Pioneers of the Machine Age* (Stroud: Tempus, 2002), pp. 54–73.

Hoffmann, Freia, *Instrument und Körper: die musizierende Frau in der bürgerlichen Kultur* (Frankfurt am Main: Insel, 1991).

Hoffmann, Freia, and Jannis Wichmann, 'Karrieren mit Hindernissen. Professionelle Harfen- und Gitarrenspielerinnen im 19. Jahrhundert', *Phoibos: Zeitschrift für Zupfmusik* 5/2 (2012), pp. 93–110.

Hurrell, Nancy, *The Egan Irish Harps: Tradition, Patrons and Players* (Dublin: Four Courts Press, 2019).

Irwin, David, *Neoclassicism* (London: Phaidon, 2000).

Joppig, Gunther, 'Die Stumpffharfe im Kunstgewerbemsueum Dresden', in Wolfram Steude und Hans-Günter Ottenberg (eds), *Theatrum instrumentorum Dresdense – Bericht über die Tagungen zu Historischen Musikinstrumenten, Dresden, 1996, 1998 und 1999* (Schneverdingen: Verlag der Musikalienhandlung Wagner, 2003), pp. 99–107.

Jost, Kilian, '"Daß Harmonie in der Natur tief gegründet (…) zeigt uns ganz besonders auch die Aeolsharfe". Eine vergessene akustische Ausstattung des frühen Landschaftsgartens', *Die Gartenkunst* 26/2 (2014), pp. 201–208.

Kastner, Alfred, 'The Harp', *Proceedings of the Musical Association* 35/1 (1908), pp. 1–14.

Kassler, Michael, 'Vollweiler's Introduction of Music Lithography to England', in Michael Kassler (ed.), *The Music Trade in Georgian England* (Farnham and Burlington: Ashgate, 2011), pp. 451–506.

Kellermann, Rudolf and Wilhelm Treue, *Die Kulturgeschichte der Schraube* (Munich: Bruckmann, 1962).

Kirkham, Pat, 'The London Furniture Trade, 1700–1870', *Furniture History* 24 (1988), pp. 1–219.

Kisluk-Grosheide, Daniëlle O., '"Cutting up Berchems, Watteaus, and Audrans": A *Lacca Povera* Secretary at The Metropolitan Museum of Art', *Metropolitan Museum Journal* 31 (1996), pp. 81–97.

Koschatzky, Walter, *Die Kunst der Graphik. Technik, Geschichte, Meisterwerke* (11th edn; Munich: Deutscher Taschenbuch Verlag, 1993).

Kotašová, Daniela, 'Erard Harps in the Collection of the Czech Museum of Music', *Musicalia: Journal of the Czech Museum of Music* 10/1–2 (2018), pp. 85–114.

Lakwete, Angela, *Inventing the Cotton Gin: Machine and Myth in Antebellum America* (Baltimore and London: Johns Hopkins University Press, 2003).

Langley, Leanne, 'Sainsbury's *Dictionary*, the Royal Academy of Music, and the Rhetoric of Patriotism', in Christina Bashford and Leanne Langley (eds), *Music and British Culture, 1785–1914: Essays in Honor of Cyril Ehrlich* (Oxford: Oxford University Press, 2000), pp. 65–97.

Lane, Hannah, 'L'orage des passions: Expressing Emotion on the Eighteenth-Century French Single-action Harp', *Ceræ: An Australasian Journal of Medieval and Early Modern Studies* 1 (2014), pp. 75–89.

Le Carrou, Jean-Loic, Sandie Le Conte and Joel Dugot, '18th and 19th [century] French Harp classification using vibration analysis', *Journal of Cultural Heritage* 27 (2017), pp. 112–119.

Le Faye, Deirdre, *A Chronology of Jane Austen and Her Family: 1700–2000* (Cambridge: Cambridge University Press, 2006).

Le Faye, Deidre (ed.), *Jane Austen's Letters* (4th edn; Oxford and New York: Oxford University Press, 2011).

Leppert, Richard, *Music and Image: Domesticity, Ideology and Socio-cultural formation in Eighteenth-century England* (Cambridge: Cambridge University Press, 1988).

——, *The Sight of Sound: Music, Representation, and the History of the Body* (Berkeley and Los Angeles: University of California Press, 1993).

Libin, Kathryn L., 'Daily Practice, Musical Accomplishment, and the Example of Jane Austen', in Natasha Duquette and Elisabeth Lenckos (eds), *Jane Austen and the Arts: Elegance, Propriety, and Harmony* (Bethlehem: Lehigh University Press, 2013), pp. 3–20.

Libin, Laurence, *A Checklist of European Harps* (New York: Metropolitan Museum of Art, 1979).

——, 'Robert Adam's Instruments for Catherine the Great', *Early Music* 29/3 (2001), pp. 355–367.

'Liste wünschenswerter Sammlungsgegenstände aus dem Gebiete des Musikinstrumentenbaues für das Deutsche Museum in München', *Zeitschrift für Instrumentenbau* 26/15 (1906), pp. 441–475.

Lluch, Miguel Ángel Piédrola (ed.), *Colección MIMMA / Miguel Ángel Piédrola Orta* (2nd edn; Málaga: Club de amigos del Museo Interactivo de la Música Málaga, 2017).

Louw, Hentie L., 'The Rise of the Metal Window during the Early Industrial Period in Britain, c.1750–1830', *Construction History* 3 (1987), pp. 31–54.

MacLeod, Christine, *Inventing the Industrial Revolution: The English Patent System, 1660-1800* (Cambridge: Cambridge University Press, 1988).

Manning, Hiram, *Manning on Decoupage* (2nd edn; New York: Dover Publications, 1980).

Marsden, Ben, *Watt's Perfect Engine: Steam and the Age of Invention* (New York: Columbia University Press, 2002).

Marshall, Julian, *The Life & Letters of Mary Wollstonecraft Shelley* (2 vols; London: Richard Bentley & Son, 1889).

Mattioli, Giuliano Marco, *La famiglia Érard: Un percorso storico fra documenti e strumenti musicali* (Varese: Zechini Editore, 2022).

Maurice, Klaus, *Der drechselnde Souverän: Materialien zu einer fürstlichen Maschinenkunst* (Zurich: Ineichen, 1985).

May, Marion R., *The ornamental Jacksons: a brief history of George Jackson & Sons Limited, ornamental composition manufacturers* (London: May, 2001).

McKendrick, Neil, 'Josiah Wedgwood: An Eighteenth-Century Entrepreneur in Salesmanship and Marketing Techniques', *The Economic History Review* 12/3 (1960), pp. 408–433.

——, 'Josiah Wedgwood and Cost Accounting in the Industrial Revolution', *The Economic History Review* 23/1 (1970), pp. 45–67.

Millward, James A., 'The Silk Road and the Sitar: Finding Centuries of Sociocultural Exchange in the History of an Instrument', *Journal of Social History* 52/2 (2018), pp. 206–233.

Mori, Jennifer, *Britain in the Age of the French Revolution: 1785–1820* (Harlow: Longman, 2000).

Morrissey, Joseph, *Women's Domestic Activity in the Romantic-Period Novel, 1770–1820: Dangerous Occupations* (Basingstoke: Pallgrave Macmillan, 2018).

Morrison-Low, Alison D., *Making Scientific Instruments in the Industrial Revolution* (Aldershot: Ashgate, 2007).

——, 'The Gentle Art of Persuasion: Advertising Instruments during Britain's Industrial Revolution', in Alison D. Morrison-Low, Sara J. Schechner, and Paolo Brenni (eds), *How Scientific Instruments Have Changed Hands. History of Science and Medicine Library 56: Scientific Instruments and Collections* (Leiden and Boston: Brill, 2017), pp. 43–56.

Myers, Arnold, 'Use of Serial Numbers in Dating Musical Instruments', in Stéphane Vaiedelich and Anne Houssay (eds), *'Dater l'instrument de musique': Actes de la journée d'étude du 6 juin 2009* (Paris: Cité de la musique, 2009), pp. 36–47.

Nagasawa, Masumi, *Amuse: Music for single and double action harp from the Age of Enlightenment & Romanticism* (CD recording with booklet; Lummen: Etcetera Records, 2004).

Nex, Jenny, 'Gut String Makers in nineteenth-century London', *The Galpin Society Journal* 65 (2012), pp. 131–160.

O'Donnell, Mary Louise, *Ireland's Harp: The Shaping of Irish Identity c.1770–1880* (Dublin: University College Dublin Press, 2014).

Oestmann, Günther, *Heinrich Johann Kessels: Ein bedeutender Verfertiger von Chronometern und Präzisionspendeluhren. Biographische Skizze und Werkverzeichnis* [Acta Historicae Astronomomiae 44] (Frankfurt am Main: Harri Deutsch, 2011).

O'Keeffe, Stephen, 'The Art of Ornamental Turning', *Studies in Design Education Craft & Technology* 12/1 (1979), pp. 46–52.

Page, Christopher, *The Guitar in Georgian England: A Social and Musical History* (New Haven and London: Yale University Press, 2020).

Parker, Michael, *Child of Pure Harmony: A Source Book for the Single-Action Harp* (London: Parker, 2005).

Plank, Elisabeth, *1825: Echoes of Vienna on Historical Harp* (CD recording with booklet; Vienna: Gramola, 2019).

Plantinga, Leon, *Clementi: his life and music* (London and New York: Oxford University Press, 1977).

Poulopoulos, Panagiotis, 'Musik im Freien in der Zeit des Biedermeier: Die Beispiele der Orphica, der Gitarre und des Csakans', *Phoibos: Zeitschrift für Zupfmusik* 15 (2015), pp. 43–68.

——, 'The Guitar as an "Open-air" Instrument in the Early Romantic Era', *Soundboard Scholar: Journal of the Guitar Foundation of America* 1 (2015), pp. 4–15.

——, *New Voices in Old Bodies: A Study of 'Recycled' Musical Instruments with a Focus on the Hahn Collection in the Deutsches Museum. Deutsches Museum Studies* 2 (Munich: Deutsches Museum, 2016).

——, 'The Impact of François Chanot's Experimental Violins on the Development of the Earliest Guitar with an Arched Soundboard by Francesco Molino in the 1820s', *Early Music* 46/1 (2018), pp. 67–86.

——, '"So wenig kultivirt, so ganz vernachlässigt": Die Pedalharfe in Deutschland um 1800', *Phoibos: Zeitschrift für Zupfmusik* 19 (2021), pp. 131–158.

——, 'Aspects of Technology in Populuxe Musical Instruments of the Late Eighteenth and Early Nineteenth Centuries', in Artemis Yagou (ed.), *Novelty, Technology and Luxury. Deutsches Museum Studies* 12 (Munich: Deutsches Museum, 2022), pp. 15–43.

——, 'Serial Numbers as Information Source and Tool for Building Virtual Instrument Collections', in *Proceedings of the CIMCIM Conference 'Global Crises and Music Museums: representing music after the pandemic', London (Royal College of Music-Horniman Museum and Gardens), 6 to 8 September 2021* (forthcoming).

Poulopoulos, Panagiotis and Rachael Durkin, '"A very mistaken identification": The "Sultana" or "Cither viol", and its Links to the Bowed Psaltery, Viola d'Amore and Guittar', *Early Music* 44/2 (2016), pp. 307–333.

Poulopoulos, Panagiotis and Julin Lee, 'A Synergy of Form, Function and Fashion in the Manufacture of the Erard Harp', in Marco A. Pérez and Emanuele Marconi (eds), *Wooden Musical Instruments: Different Forms of Knowledge* (Paris: Cité de la Musique – Philharmonie de Paris, 2018), pp. 367–398.

Poulopoulos, Panagiotis, Marisa Pamplona, Luise Richter and Elke Cwiertnia, 'Technological Study of the Decoration on an Erard Harp from 1818', *Studies in Conservation* 65/2 (2020), pp. 86–102.

Poulopoulos, Panagiotis, Marisa Pamplona and Luise Richter, 'The Industrialisation of the Early Pedal Harp: Detecting Evidence on Wood and Metal', in Marco A. Pérez and Sandie Le Conte (eds), *Making Wooden Musical Instruments: An Integration of Different Forms of Knowledge. Proceedings of the 3rd Annual Conference of the COST Action FP1302 WoodMusICK* (Barcelona: Museu de la Música, 2016), pp. 185–190.

Poulopoulos, Panagiotis, Marisa Pamplona, Luise Richter and Niko Plath, 'Conservation Issues on Historical Pedal Harps: Preserving Tangible and Intangible Properties', in Pascale Vandervellen (ed.), *Preservation of Wooden Musical Instruments: Ethics, Practice and Assessment. Proceedings of 4th Annual Conference of the COST Action FP1302 WoodMusICK* (Brussels: Muziekinstrumentenmuseum, 2017), pp. 69–72.

Ramage, Nancy Hirschland, 'Sir William Hamilton as Collector, Exporter, and Dealer: The Acquisition and Dispersal of His Collections', *American Journal of Archaeology* 94/3 (1990), pp. 469–480.

——, 'The English Etruria: Wedgwood and the Etruscans', *Etruscan Studies* 14 (2011), pp. 187–199.

Raquet, Markus and Klaus Martius, 'Antoinettes zersplitterte Harfe', *Arbeitsblätter für Restauratoren* 32/2 (1999), pp. 169–186.

Rensch, Roslyn, *The Harp: Its History, Technique and Repertoire* (London: Duckworth, 1969).

——, *Harps and Harpists* (Bloomington and Indianapolis: Indiana University Press, 1989).

——, *Three Centuries of Harp Making* (Chicago: Western Central, 2002).

Restelli, Alessandro, *Museo degli Strumenti Musicali del Casello Sforzesco a Milano* (Milan: Skira, 2014).

Richter, Luise Eva-Maria, *Fassungsuntersuchung der Doppelpedalharfe No. 2631 von Sébastien Erard aus dem Deutschen Museum München: Ein Beitrag zur Harfenforschung* (BA Diss., Studiengang Restaurierung, Kunsttechnologie und Konservierungswissenschaft, Munich: Technische Universität München, 2016).

——, *Ergänzende Untersuchung an der Doppelpedalharfe No. 2631 von Sébastien Erard aus dem Deutschen Museum München* (Project Diss., Studiengang Restaurierung, Kunsttechnologie und Konservierungswissenschaft, Technische Universität München, Munich, 2017).

Riello, Giorgio, 'Strategies and Boundaries: Subcontracting and the London Trades in the Long Eighteenth Century', *Enterprise & Society* 9/2 (2008), pp. 243–280.

Rossi Rognoni, Gabriele, 'Preserving Functionality: Keeping Artefacts "Alive" in Museums', in Eric de Visscher and Kathleen Wiens (eds), Special Issue 'Sonic', *Curator: The Museum Journal*, 62/3 (New York: Wiley, 2019), pp. 403–413.

Rule, John, *Albion's People: English Society 1714–1815* (London: Longman, 1992).

Russell, Ben, 'The British Machine Tool Industry (1790–1825)', *Ferrum: Nachrichten aus der Eisenbibliothek der Stiftung der Georg Fischer AG* 81 (2009), pp. 37–44.

——, *James Watt: Making the World Anew* (London: Reaktion Books, 2014).

Rybczynski, Witold, *One Good Turn: A Natural History of the Screwdriver and the Screw* (New York: Scribner, 2000).

Sacchi, Floraleda, *Sophia Giustina Corri: Works for Solo Harp* (CD recording with booklet; Bologna: Tactus, 2009).

Selwyn, David, *Jane Austen and Leisure* (The Hambledon Press: London and Rio Grande, 1999).

Sève, Michel, 'La colonnade des Incantadas à Thessalonique', *Revue archéologique* 1 (2013), pp. 125–133.

Sheldon, Julie (ed.), *The Letters of Elizabeth Rigby* (Liverpool: Liverpool University Press, 2009).

Sisto, Luigi, Emanuele Cardi and Sergio Tassi, *Il Museo della Musica. Strumenti Antichi e Documenti del Conservatorio di S. Pietro a Majella: Guida alla mostra a cura di Luigi Sisto, Emanuele Cardi, Sergio Tassi* (Naples: Conservatorio di S. Pietro a Majella, 2002).

Snodin, Michael and John Styles, *Design & the Decorative Arts. Georgian Britain 1714–1837* (London: V&A Publications, 2004).

Steiger, Adrian von, 'Sax figures: can we deduce details of Adolphe Sax's instrument production from the sources?', *Revue belge de Musicologie / Belgisch Tijdschrift voor Muziekwetenschap* 70, Issue 'Adolphe Sax, his influence and legacy: a bicentenary conference' (2016), pp. 129–148.

Stuart, Susan, 'A Survey of Marks, Labels, and Stamps used on Gillow and Waring & Gillow Furniture 1770–1960', *Regional Furniture* 12 (1998), pp. 58–93.

Styles, John, 'Design for Large-Scale Production in Eighteenth-Century Britain', *Oxford Art Journal* 11 (1988), pp. 10–16.

——, 'Product Innovation in Early Modern London', *Past & Present* 168 (2000), pp. 124–169.

Sugimoto, Hayato, 'Mordaunt Levien and his Instruments', *The Galpin Society Journal* 71 (2018), pp. 57–72.

Sumner, Ann, 'Gainsborough's "Portrait of Lady Clarges"', *The Burlington Magazine* 130/1027 (1988), pp. 761–763.

Tames, Richard, *Josiah Wedgwood: An illustrated life of Josiah Wedgwood, 1730–1795* (2nd edn; Aylesbury: Shire Publications Ltd, 1984).

Thom, Colin, 'Fine Veneers, Army Boots and Tinfoil: New Light on Marc Isambard Brunel's Activities in Battersea', *Construction History* 25 (2010), pp. 53–67.

Thornton, Jonathan and William Adair, 'Applied Decoration for Historic Interiors: Preserving Composition Ornament', *Preservation Briefs* 34 (1994), pp. 1–16.

Thurau, Rainer, 'Die Harfenmechanik Erards – ihre Funktion und Restaurierung', in Rudolf Frick (ed.), *Sébastien Erard: ein europäischer Pionier des Instrumentenbaus. Internationales Erard-Symposium Michaelstein 13.–14. November 1994, Michaelsteiner Konferenzberichte 48* (Blankenburg: Stiftung Kloster Michaelstein, 1995), pp. 28–29.

Tolstoy, Leo, *War and Peace* (first published 1869; trans. from Russian by Louise and Aylmer Maude; Chicago, London and Toronto: Encyclopædia Britannica Inc., 1952).

Torchia, Robert Wilson, 'Eliza Ridgely and the Ideal of American Womanhood, 1787–1820', *Maryland Historical Magazine* 90/4 (1995), pp. 405–423.

Torchia, Robert Wilson, Deborah Chotner and Ellen G. Miles, *American Paintings of the Nineteenth Century, Part II* (Washington: National Gallery of Art, 1998).

Wackernagel, Bettina, *Europäische Zupf- und Streichinstrumente, Hackbretter und Äolsharfen. Deutsches Museum München. Musikinstrumentensammlung Katalog* (Frankfurt am Main: Bochinsky, 1997).

Wainwright, David, *Broadwood, by Appointment: A History* (London: Quiller Press, 1982).

Waller, David, *Iron Men: How One London Factory Powered the Industrial Revolution and Shaped the Modern World* (London and New York: Anthem Press, 2016).

Walter, Sandra, *Die Einfachpedalharfe 512 der Brüder Erard aus dem Couven-Museum Aachen: Untersuchungen zu Bestand, Zustand, historischer Kontextualisierung, sowie Durchführung der Konservierung, Restaurierung und Neubesaitung* (Diplomarbeit, Fachrichtung Konservierung und Restaurierung, Erfurt: Fachhochschule Erfurt, 2011).

Wayne, Neil, 'The Wheatstone English Concertina,' *The Galpin Society Journal* 44 (1991), pp. 117–149.

Weber, William, 'London: A City of Unrivalled Riches', in Neal Zaslaw (ed.), *The Classical Era: from the 1740s to the end of the 18th century* (London: Macmillan, 1989), pp. 293–326.

Weidman, Gregory, 'Eliza Ridgely's historic Erard Harp', *American Harp Journal* 26/1 (2017), p. 52.

Werrett, Simon, *Thrifty Science: Making the Most of Materials in the History of Experiment* (Chicago: University of Chicago Press, 2019).

Westbrook, James, 'General Thompson's Enharmonic Guitar', *Soundboard, Quarterly Magazine of the Guitar Foundation of America* 38/4 (2012), pp. 45–52.

——, 'Louis Panormo: "The only Maker of Guitars in the Spanish style"', *Early Music* 41/4 (2013), pp. 571–584.

Wetherall, Judith, 'History and Techniques of Composition', in Sophie Budden (ed.), *Gilding and Surface Decoration* (London: United Kingdom Institute for Conservation, 1991), pp. 26–29.

White, Ian, *English Clocks for the Eastern Markets: English Clockmakers Trading in China and the Ottoman Empire 1580–1815* (Ticehurst: Antiquarian Horological Society, 2012).

Willetts, Pamela J., 'Johann Andreas Stumpff, 1769–1846', *The Musical Times* 118/1607 (1977), pp. 29, 31 and 32.

Wiltshire, John, 'Exploring Mansfield Park: In the Footsteps of Fanny Price', *Persuasions* 28 (2006), pp. 81–100.

Wilson, Harriette, *The Memoirs of Harriette Wilson: Written by Herself* (2 volumes; London: Eveleigh Nash, 1909).

Wilson, Margaret, *Almost another Sister: The Family and Life of Fanny Knight, Jane Austen's Favourite Niece* (Canterbury: Kent Arts and Libraries, 1990).

Wilton-Ely, John, 'Pompeian and Etruscan Tastes in the Neo-Classical Country-House Interior', *Studies in the History of Art 25; Symposium Papers X: The Fashioning and Functioning of the British Country House* (1989), pp. 51–73.

Woodcroft, Bennet, *Patents for Inventions, Abridgements of Specifications relating to Music and Musical Instruments, AD. 1694–1866* (facsimile edn of the original 1871 edn; London: Bingham, 1984).

Woodfield, Ian, *Music of the Raj: A Social and Economic History of Music in Late Eighteenth-Century Anglo-Indian Society* (Oxford: Oxford University Press, 2000).

Woolrich, Anthony P., 'The London Engineering Industry at the time of Henry Maudslay', in John Cantrell and Gillian Cookson (eds), *Henry Maudslay and the Pioneers of the Machine Age* (Stroud: Tempus, 2002), pp. 39–53.

——, 'Joseph Clement', in John Cantrell and Gillian Cookson (eds), *Henry Maudslay and the Pioneers of the Machine Age* (Stroud: Tempus, 2002), pp. 94–108.

Wordsworth, Christopher, *Memoirs of William Wordsworth. Volume 2* (Cambridge: Cambridge University Press, 2014).

Yagou, Artemis, 'Novel and Desirable Technology: Pocket Watches for the Ottoman Market (late18[th] c.–mid 19th c.)', *ICON: Journal of the International Committee for the History of Technology* 24 (2018/2019), pp. 78–107.

Young, Hilary (ed.), *The Genius of Wedgwood* (London: Victoria and Albert Museum, 1995).

Zaunbrecher, Eve, *An Enlightened Instrument: The Design, Education, and Sociability of the Single Action Pedal Harp in* Ancien Régime *Paris, 1760–1789* (MA Diss., London: Royal College of Art, 2016).

Web-Based Sources

Author's note: The titles have been arranged in alphabetical order, either according to the author's name or, when the author could not be verified, according to the title of the article. All entries were last accessed on 3 June 2022.

'Ange Laurent de La Live de Jully', https://www.nga.gov/collection/art-object-page.32686.html, accessed 3 June 2022.

'A Young Lady Playing the Harp', https://www.tate.org.uk/art/artworks/northcote-a-young-lady-playing-the-harp-n04376, accessed 3 June 2022.

'Automaton', http://www.nationaltrustcollections.org.uk/object/608416, accessed 3 June 2022.

Brooks, Jeanice, 'The Austen Family Music Books', available at https://archive.org/details/austenfamilymusicbooks, published 2015, accessed 3 June 2022.

Cant, Serena, 'The tale of a harp', https://thewreckoftheweek.wordpress.com/2018/10/23/musical-instruments-in-the-sea/, published 23 October 2018, accessed 3 June 2022.

'Caroline, Princess of Wales, and Princess Charlotte', https://www.rct.uk/collection/407292/caroline-princess-of-wales-and-princess-charlotte, accessed 3 June 2022.

'Centre Sébastien Erard', https://www.sebastienerard.org/en/, accessed 3 June 2022.

Cheshire, Claire, 'Erard Harp (London, around 1817)', available at https://researchworcestershire.wordpress.com/2020/08/14/erard-harp-london-around-1817/, published 14 August 2020, accessed 3 June 2022.

Clarke, Christopher, 'The Locksmith's Tale: How Harp-making Practice Shaped the Érard Firm's Pianos', available at https://earlypedalharp.wordpress.com/abstracts/#clarkeabs, accessed 3 June 2022.

'Correspondance diverse (1816–1842)', available at https://www.sebastienerard.org/fr/?m=cdiverse, accessed 3 June 2022.

'Currency, Coinage and the Cost of Living', https://www.oldbaileyonline.org/static/Coinage.jsp, accessed 3 June 2022.

'Dissolution of the association', https://www.britishmuseum.org/collection/object/P_1868-0808-8920, accessed 3 June 2022.

'Dissolution of the association', https://www.npg.org.uk/collections/search/portrait/mw297448, accessed 3 June 2022.

'Duet stand', http://www.nationaltrustcollections.org.uk/object/608181.2, accessed 3 June 2022.

'Elizabeth Rigby (Lady Eastlake)', https://www.tate.org.uk/art/artworks/rigby-title-not-known-t09803, accessed 3 June 2022.

'French watercolour of a seated lady with a harp', https://www.oldmusicalinstruments.co.uk/iconography/icon_detail.php?id=37&cat=PS, accessed 3 June 2022.

'Great Marlborough Street Area', available at https://www.british-history.ac.uk/survey-london/vols31-2/pt2/pp250-267#h3-0013, accessed 3 June 2022.

'Grecian harp', https://collection.beta.fitz.ms/id/object/77348, accessed 3 June 2022.

Griffiths, Ann, 'A Dynasty of Harp Makers', available at http://www.adlaismusicpublishers.co.uk/pages/harpists/erard.htm, first published in World Harp Congress Review 2002, accessed 3 June 2022.

'Harmony before matrimony', https://www.britishmuseum.org/collection/object/P_1935-0522-4-132, accessed 3 June 2022.

'Harpe à double mouvement', https://collectionsdumusee.philharmoniedeparis.fr/doc/MUSEE/0156103/harpe-a-double-mouvement, accessed 3 June 2022.

'Hospitalfield Harp Renovation', https://www.crowdfunder.co.uk/hospitalfield-harp-renovation, accessed 3 June 2022.

Kolle, Elise, 'Portraits of Harpists: A database for portraits of people with their harps, from 1500 to 1900', available at https://historicalharpportraits.wordpress.com/, accessed 3 June 2022.

'Lady Caroline Spencer, later Viscountess Clifden, and her sister, Lady Elizabeth Spencer', at http://emuseum.huntington.org/objects/197/lady-caroline-spencer-later-viscountess-clifden-and-her-si?ctx=ab108333-9f30-4e8f-9b4e-e1e51307d9af&idx=0, accessed 3 June 2022.

'Lady with a Harp: Eliza Ridgely', https://www.nga.gov/collection/art-object-page.32577.html, accessed 3 June 2022.

Lein, Anette, Panagiotis Poulopoulos and Ralph Würschinger, 'Warum Podcasts?' ('Why Podcasts'), in 'DM Podcast: Hinter die Kulissen hören' ('DM Podcast: Listening behind the Scenes'), article in the online portal 'wissenschaftskommunikation.de', published 15 June 2019, available at https://www.wissenschaftskommunikation.de/dm-podcast-hinter-die-kulissen-hoeren-26963/, accessed 3 June 2022.

'London fashionable full dress', https://www.npg.org.uk/collections/search/portrait/mw279959/London-fashionable-full-dress-June-1805?LinkID=mp64662&role=art&rNo=12, accessed 3 June 2022.

'Louisa Skrine, Lady Clarges', http://collections.holburne.org/object-l1988-1, accessed 3 June 2022.

'March of Intellect', https://www.britishmuseum.org/collection/object/P_1988-1001-17, accessed 3 June 2022.

'Miss Laura Dorothea Ross (Mrs Francis Robertson)', https://www.tate.org.uk/art/artworks/lawrence-miss-laura-dorothea-ross-mrs-francis-robertson-n00136, accessed 3 June 2022.

'MIMO: Musical Instrument Museums Online', https://mimo-international.com/MIMO/, accessed 3 June 2022.

'MIMNIM-UK: Musical Instruments Interface for Museums and Collections', https://minim.ac.uk/, accessed 3 June 2022.

'Musical Instruments at Attingham – The Harp', available at https://attinghamparkmansion.wordpress.com/tag/harp/, accessed 3 June 2022.

'Music stool', http://www.nationaltrustcollections.org.uk/object/608181.1, accessed 3 June 2022.

'National Trust Collections', https://www.nationaltrustcollections.org.uk/, accessed 3 June 2022.

'Nicador's Nightmare', https://www.bonhams.com/auctions/20945/lot/86/, accessed 3 June 2022.

Nigro, Jeffrey A., '"Favourable to Tenderness and Sentiment": The Many Meanings of Mary Crawford's Harp', *Persuasions On-Line* 35/1, available at http://www.jasna.org/persuasions/on-line/vol35no1/nigro.html, published 2014, accessed 3 June 2022.

'O Ruin'd Harp, Unique', https://www.doeandhope.com/products/o-ruin-d-harp-unique, accessed 3 June 2022.

Parker, Mike, 'The Eighth Pedal, Fact or Fiction?', published 2008; available at http://www.harpspectrum.org/historical/the_eighth_pedal.shtml, accessed 3 June 2022.

'Portrait of a lady in a white dress', http://www.artnet.com/artists/sir-martin-archer-shee/portrait-of-a-lady-in-a-white-dress-with-a-yellow-h5wo-a9T-FYUwHTekJrfaA2, accessed 3 June 2022.

'Portrait of Miss Emily de Visme', https://www.britishmuseum.org/collection/object/P_1953-0214-41, accessed 3 June 2022.

'Portrait of Miss Jane Reade', https://spencerartapps.ku.edu/collection-search#/object/10023, accessed 3 June 2022.

Poulopoulos, Panagiotis, 'Die frühe Pedalharfe als Symbol innovativer Verwandlung' ('The Early Pedal Harp as Symbol of Innovative Transformation'), https://www.deutsches-museum.de/forschung/forschungsinstitut/projekte/detailseite/die-fruehe-pedalharfe-als-symbol-innovativer-verwandlung, accessed 3 June 2022.

Poulopoulos, Panagiotis and Ralph Würschinger, 'Die Revolution im Spiel - von der Erfindung der Doppelpedalharfe' ('The Revolution in the Game: About the Invention of the Double-action Harp'), available at https://blog.deutsches-museum.de/2019/03/08/die-revolution-im-spiel, podcast broadcasted on 30 January 2019, article published on 8 March 2019, accessed 3 June 2022.

'Restoration Project for Eliza Ridgely Harp', https://www.baltimoreharp.org/historic-eliza-ridgely-harp-restoration/, accessed 3 June 2022.

Sahlqvist, Leif, 'Clementi & Co. 1798–1830: Piano Manufacture in London', available at http://www.friendsofsquarepianos.co.uk/the-clementi-page/, published 26 May 2013, updated 4 February 2014, accessed 3 June 2022, pp. 1–34.

'The Harp Lesson', https://collections.dma.org/artwork/5340929, accessed 3 June 2022.

'The journal of Amélina Petit de Billier', http://amelina.dmu.ac.uk/diary_1827_ talbot_finds_magna_carta_transcript.html, published 2012; accessed 3 June 2022.

'The mad music master', https://www.britishmuseum.org/collection/object/P_ 1868-0808-6918, accessed 3 June 2022.

'Trade Card for Adolpho, Seal Engraver', available at https://www.metmuseum. org/art/collection/search/820838, accessed 3 June 2022.

Trey, Juliette, 'Jean-Baptiste-André Gautier-Dagoty portraiturant la Reine dans sa chambre', http://collections.chateauversailles.fr/#7ca71495-248a-4386-88bc-8acae1ef7991, accessed 3 June 2022.

'Two women sitting on stools and playing music', https://www.britishmuseum. org/collection/object/P_1887-0722-177, accessed 3 June 2022.

'Two young girls, one sitting at a piano and the other a harp', https://www. britishmuseum.org/collection/object/P_1878-0511-1150, accessed 3 June 2022.

Wolf, Beat, 'The Louis XVI–Harp', available at https://www.harpspectrum.org/ historical/wolf_long_updated.shtml, published 2009, accessed 3 June 2022.

——, 'Timeline: The development of the single action harp', available at https://www.harpspectrum.org/historical/Beat%20Wolf%20Timeline_ pedalharps_2014.pdf, published 2014, accessed 3 June 2022.

Unpublished Theses, Essays, Conference Papers and Reports

Baldwin, Mike, *The Harp in Early Nineteenth-century Britain: Innovation, Business, and Making in Jacob Erat's Manufactory* (PhD Diss., London: London Metropolitan University, 2017).

Barnett, David Colin, *The Structure of Industry in London, 1775–1825* (PhD Diss., Nottingham: University of Nottingham, 1996).

Brooks, Randall Chapman, *The Precision Screw in Scientific Instruments of the 17th–19th Centuries: with Particular Reference to Astronomical, Nautical and Surveying Instruments* (PhD Diss., Leicester: University of Leicester, 1989).

Bühl, Franziska, *Untersuchung einer Erard-Doppelpedalharfe von 1820–1825* (BA Diss., Studiengang Restaurierung, Kunsttechnologie und Konservierungswissenschaft, Munich: Technische Universität München, 2014).

Cleary, Maria Christina, *The 'harpe organisée', 1720–1840: Rediscovering the lost pedal techniques on harps with a single-action pedal mechanism* (PhD Diss., Leiden: Leiden University, 2016).

Cranmer, John Leonard, *Concert Life and the Music Trade in Edinburgh c.1780–c.1830* (PhD Diss., Edinburgh: University of Edinburgh, 1991).

Deval, Dorothy Jean, *Gradus ad Parnassum: The Pianoforte in London, 1770–1820* (PhD Diss., London: University of London, 1991).

Guillaume-Castel, Fanny, *Erard: study of a firm based in Paris and London between the 1790s and 1810s through the manufacturing and sales of the harps* (Masters Diss., Paris: Université Paris 1 Panthéon-Sorbonne, 2017).

Haag, Volker, 'KO/1385/18: Holzartenbestimmung Erard Harfe (London 1818, Inventarnummer DM 16147), Deutsches Museum München' (unpublished report; Hamburg: Thünen-Institut für Holzforschung, 2019).

Hallo, Rosemary Margaret, *Erard, Bochsa and their impact on harp music-making in Australia (1830–1866): An early history from documents* (PhD Diss., Adelaide: The University of Adelaide, 2014).

Kolle, Elise, *Feminine Portraits: Lady Harpists and Their Music in the Age of Enlightenment* (Masters Diss., Glasgow: University of Glasgow, 2020).

Nex, Jenny, *The Business of Musical-Instrument Making in Early Industrial London* (PhD Diss., London: Goldsmiths College, 2013).

Phatak, Neeti, 'Analysis of Erard Harp N⁰ 2631 with XRF' (unpublished report; Munich: Deutsches Museum, 2018).

Plath, Niko, 'Vibroacoustic Examination of Erard Harp N° 2631' (unpublished report; Hamburg: Institut für Systematische Musikwissenschaft, Universität Hamburg, 2017).

Poulopoulos, Panagiotis, *The Guittar in the British Isles, 1750–1810* (PhD Diss., Edinburgh: The University of Edinburgh, 2011).

——, 'The Harp, Lyre, Lute, Cittern, and Guitar around 1800', unpublished paper presented at the 4th Colloquium of the Consortium for Guitar Research, Sidney Sussex College, University of Cambridge, 9 to 12 April 2016.

——, 'The Pedal Harp in Europe between 1780 and 1830', unpublished paper presented at the Forschungskolloquium of the Institut für Musikwissenschaft, Ludwig-Maximilians-Universität, Munich, 15 June 2016.

——, 'Composition Ornaments on Historic Harps: From Research to Exhibition', unpublished paper presented at the annual conference of CIMCIM 'Presentation, Preservation, Interpretation – The Challenges of Musical Instrument Collections in the 21st Century', Basel and Bern, 22 to 25 February 2017.

——, 'Shedding New Light on the Production Strategies of Erard', unpublished paper presented at the joint conference of the Galpin Society and the American Musical Instrument Society (AMIS), Musical Instrument Museums Edinburgh (MIMEd), Edinburgh, 1 to 4 June 2017.

——, 'Serial Production and Trademarking on Historic Musical Instruments from Ruckers to Erard', unpublished paper presented at the Oberseminar, Deutsches Museum, Munich, 3 July 2017.

——, 'Engineering the Harp: The Erard London Firm 1800–1830', unpublished paper presented at the 37th Symposium of the Scientific Instrument Society (SIC), 'Instruments and the "Empire of Man over Things"', Session 'Sound', Leiden and Haarlem, 3 to 7 September 2018.

——, 'Das neue Holz: Bruch mit der Tradition am Beispiel der Pedalharfe', unpublished paper presented at the conference 'Knock on Wood: Holz, Handwerk und Wissen im Instrumentenbau', organised by the research group 'Materiality of Musical Instruments: New Approaches to a Cultural History of Organology', Deutsches Museum, Munich, 17 and 18 January 2019.

——, 'A Creative Triangle of Mechanics, Acoustics and Aesthetics: The Early Pedal Harp (1780–1830) as a Symbol of Innovative Transformation', unpublished paper presented at the international conference 'Welche Museen für welche Gesellschaft? 10 Jahre Forschung in Museen' ('Which Museums for Which Society? 10 Years Research in Museums'), end conference of the funding programme 'Research in Museums' of the Volkswagen Foundation, Schloss Herrenhausen, Hannover, 18 to 20 March 2019.

——, 'Technological substitution and innovation in the production of musical instruments at the turn of the 19th century', unpublished paper presented at the Annual Conference of the Society of the History of Technology (SHOT) 'Exploring the Interface between Technology, Art, and Design', Session 'Technology and Luxury', Museo Nazionale della Scienza e della Tecnologia 'Leonardo Da Vinci', Milan, 24 to 27 October 2019.

——, 'Manufacture, Usage, Recycling, and the Concept of Functionality on Historical Objects', unpublished paper presented at the International Conference 'Playing and operating: functionality in museum objects and instruments', organised by ICOM, CIMCIM and CIMUSET, Cité de la Musique – Philharmonie de Paris, Paris, 4 to 6 February 2020.

——, 'A Time Capsule with Strings: The Chronicle of the Erard Grecian Harp', unpublished presented at the Oberseminar, Deutsches Museum, Munich 7 June 2021.

——, 'Serial Numbers as Information Source and Tool for Building Virtual Instrument Collections' unpublished paper presented at the Annual Conference of CIMCIM 'Global Crises and Music Museums: representing music after the pandemic', Royal College of Music and Horniman Museum and Gardens, London, 6 to 8 September 2021.

——, 'The Role of Technical Drawings and Models in the Promotion of the Steam Engine', unpublished paper presented at the 41st Symposium of the Scientific Instrument Society (SIC), 'The Past, Present, and Future of Scientific Instrument Studies', Session '18th and 19th Century Instruments', National Hellenic Research Foundation, Athens, 19 to 23 September 2022.

Panagiotis Poulopoulos, Marisa Pamplona and Luise Richter, 'The Industrialisation of the Early Pedal Harp: Detecting Evidence on Wood and Metal', unpublished paper presented at the 3rd Annual Conference of the COST Action FP1302 WoodMusICK (Wooden Musical Instrument Conservation and Knowledge), 'Making Wooden Musical Instruments: An Integration of Different Forms of Knowledge', Museu de la Música, Barcelona, 7 to 9 September 2016.

Panagiotis Poulopoulos, Marisa Pamplona, Luise Richter and Niko Plath, 'Conservation Issues on Historical Pedal Harps: Preserving Tangible and Intangible Properties', unpublished paper presented at the 4th annual conference of the COST Action FP1302 WoodMusICK (Wooden Musical Instrument Conservation and Knowledge), 'Preservation of Wooden Musical Instruments: Ethics, Practice and Assessment', Muziekinstrumentenmuseum, Brussels, 5 to 7 October 2017.

Panagiotis Poulopoulos and Hayato Sugimoto, 'Learning from Musical Instruments as Manifestations of Production and Consumption', unpublished paper presented at the ICOM General Conference 'Museums as Cultural Hubs: The Future of Tradition', CIMCIM Session 'Music Museums and Education: Current and Future Perspectives', Kyoto International Conference Center, Kyoto, 1 to 7 September 2019.

Riello, Giorgio, *The Boot and Shoe Trades in London and Paris in the Long Eighteenth Century* (PhD Diss., London: University College London, 2002).

Sugimoto, Hayato, *Harp Lutes in Britain, 1800–1830: A Study of the Inventor, Edward Light and His Instruments* (PhD Diss., Edinburgh: University of Edinburgh, 2015).

Troughton, Jane Elizabeth, *The Role of Music in the Yorkshire Country House 1770–1850* (PhD Diss., York: University of York, 2014).

Verberkmoes, Geerten, *Boussu Inside Out: A multifaceted organological study of the life, instruments and methods of the violin maker Benoit Joseph Boussu (1703–1773)* (PhD Diss., Ghent: Ghent University, 2020).

Wolf, Beat, *Harp Archives* (Schaffhausen: Wolf, 2016). [The archives include unpublished restoration reports and other information concerning about 380 historical harps.]

Index of Names

Author's note: Page numbers in **bold type** refer to illustrations and their captions.

Index of Places

Author's note: Page numbers in **bold type** refer to illustrations and their captions.

Abbotsford   **80**, 194, **195**
Altona   120
America (United States of America; North
        America)   115, 122, 140, 153, 176, 205,
        226
Amiens   131
Arbroath   **59**
Athens   75
Augsburg   1
Australia   153, 205, 226
Austria   205

Baltimore   140, 176
Bath   152–153, 161, 175 n.31
Bekesbourne   187
Belgium   205
Berlin   4, 17, 203
Bordeaux   131
Boston   **78**, 177
Brazil   122
Bristol   152
Britain (Great Britain, United
        Kingdom)   2–4, 11–12, 15 n.2, 17, 23,
        34, 37, 41, 48–49, 51, 56, 60 n.90, 61,
        64–66, 81, 84, 86, 88, 90, 107–108, 132–
        133, 136–137, 148, 150, 152–153, 168–169,
        175–176, 184–186, 188, 190–191, 202,
        205, 214, 223, 225–226

Calcutta   153, 214
Canada   205
Charleston   115, 153
Czech Republic   205
Cheltenham   153
Copenhagen   196

Derby   153
Donauwörth   1, 16
Dublin   156, 161, 196, 226

Edinburgh   **59**, **118**, 152–153, 226
Egypt   26
England   57, 120, 131, 136, 184, 200

Etobon   11

Finland   205
Fontainebleau   **79**, 88 n.89, **147**, 148
France   1, 2 n.4, 11, 17, 20, 26, 37, 44, 67, 70,
        76, 88–89, 96, 112, 114, 136, 148–149, 169
        n.2, 170, 175–176, 205, 227

Geneva   139
Germany   16–17, 70, 120, 203, 205, **209**
Greece   26, 74, 81, 85, 94, 225

Hamburg   17
Hannover   16

India   58, 153, 162, 211, 214, 226
Ireland   153, 156, 159, 161, 184–185, 199
Italy   70, 81, 139, 153, 198, 205

Japan   205

Leipzig   17, 47, 67, **68**, 210
Liverpool   153
London   2–3, 5, 8–11, 15, 17, 22–23, 26, 33–34,
        37, 42, 51–52, 55–59, 61–64, 69–70, 73,
        76, 87, 91–92, 95–96, 98 n.10, 101–108,
        111, 115–116, 119–121, 124, 126, 131, 136,
        138–140, 144, 151–152, 154–156, 158, 161,
        165–166, 168, 174, 180, 187–188, 192, 199,
        207, 210, 222–226, 228

Madrid   92, 131
Maynooth   153
Meissen   92
Missolonghi (Messolonghi)   86
Moscow   196, 201
Munich   5, 8, 16–17, **30**, **35**, 71, **97**, **204**, 205,
        206

Naples   81, 113, 196
Netherlands   205
New Zealand   153, 226
Nuremberg   17

Index of Themes

Printed and bound by CPI Group (UK) Ltd, Croydon, CR0 4YY

07/07/2026

14916225-0001